Sybase® SQL Server™

Performance and Tuning Guide

Sybase SQL Server Release 11.0.x

Karen Paulsell

International Thomson Computer Press
I(T)P® An International Thomson Publishing Company

London • Bonn • Boston • Johannesburg • Madrid • Melbourne • Mexico City • New York • Paris
Singapore • Tokyo • Toronto • Albany, NY • Belmont, CA • Cincinnati, OH • Detroit, MI

For more information, contact:

International Thomson Computer Press
20 Park Plaza, 13th Floor
Boston, MA 02116
USA

International Thomson Publishing GmbH
Königswinterer Strasse 418
53227 Bonn
Germany

International Thomson Publishing Europe
Berkshire House
168–173 High Holborn
London WCIV 7AA
England

International Thomson Publishing Asia
221 Henderson Road #05-10
Henderson Building
Singapore 0315

Thomas Nelson Australia
102 Dodds Street
South Melbourne, 3205
Victoria
Australia

International Thomson Publishing Japan
Hirakawacho Kyowa Building, 3F
2-2-1 Hirakawacho
Chiyoda-ku, 102 Tokyo
Japan

Nelson Canada
1120 Birchmount Road
Scarborough, Ontario
Canada M1K 5G4

International Thomson Editores
Campos Eliseos 385, Piso 7
Col. Polanco
11560 Mexico D.F. Mexico

International Thomson Publishing Southern Africa
Bldg. 19, Constantia Park
239 Old Pretoria Road, P.O. Box 2459
Halfway House, 1685 South Africa

International Thomson Publishing France
1, rue st. Georges
75 009 Paris France

QEBFF 16 15 14 13 12 11 10 9 8 7 6 5 4 3 2
Library of Congress Cataloging-in-Publication Data available upon request)

ISBN: 1-85032-883-8

Publisher/Vice President: Jim DeWolf, ITCP/Boston
Manufacturing Manager: Sandra Sabathy Carr, ITCP/Boston
Marketing Manager: Kathleen Raftery, ITCP/Boston

Table of Contents

Introduction

Section A: Basics of Performance Tuning: Essential Tools

Chapter 1. Performance Analysis

Chapter 2. Database Design and Denormalizing for Performance

Chapter 3. Data Storage

Chapter 4. How Indexes Work

Section B: Tuning the Performance of Queries

Chapter 6. Indexing for Performance

Chapter 7. The SQL Server Query Optimizer

Chapter 8. Understanding Query Plans

Chapter 9. Advanced Optimizing Techniques

Chapter 12. Cursors and Performance

Section C: Hardware Tuning Issues and Application Maintenance

Chapter 13. Controlling Physical Data Placement

Foreword

The Sybase SQL Server Performance and Tuning Guide is the best document we've ever produced. And it's something that we should have done years ago! Right or wrong, for years Sybase held on to performance and tuning information as if it were proprietary.

Working with the experts at Sybase who really know the code, Karen Paulsell has now pulled together in a single reference all the information that database administrators need to know to optimize SQL Server. Administrators must understand how SQL Server works in order really to understand the nuances of system performance tuning; this book is an indispensable resource in that regard.

Tuning is still a black art: but the Performance and Tuning Guide is a very, very big step towards making it less black and more art. This book answers most of the questions I am asked at seminars and presentations. I always refer people to it. If customers read this book instead of proceeding by trial and error, it can save them a lot of time.

Speaking for myself, you only have so much hair you can lose! Even if you can find the time to prototype and test, and immerse yourself in client/server and performance (as I did early in my career as a system and database architect), reading this book can prevent wasting time on wrong approaches. When I was learning Sybase SQL Server performance tuning, I literally beat my head against the wall time and again, going down avenues that seemed to be correct at first, but turned out to be completely wrong.

A book like this provides a way to jump past Go, collect your $200, and get to a point of understanding that might otherwise take years to reach.

Karen Paulsell, already well qualified to write this book because of her years of experience with SQL Server, also had the benefit of having all of the experts at her disposal. She was able to call on people who really understand how the code works. Moreover, she was able to make a coherent presentation of all the different performance tuning topics: she put it all together, and made it make sense.

The new performance monitoring tool, sp_sysmon, is a good complement to this book. With sp_sysmon, Sybase for the first time provides a tool that lets developers get at the internals of the product. Karen and I collaborated on the development of sp_sysmon: originally for internal use by Sybase Engineering, sp_sysmon became a public tool because our customers really need its capabilities. People have been dying for real performance monitoring information that they can use to understand their systems. The combination of this book and the sp_sysmon tool should really strike a responsive chord with our customers.

Peter Thawley

Architect Director

Sybase Enterprise Performance Group

Peter Thawley, a Sybase Architect Director specializing in performance tuning, has authored numerous technical articles and is in high demand as a speaker for technical presentations and seminars. Peter began using Sybase products in 1989 when he led a team developing a back office securities trading systems using both SQL Server and PowerBuilder.

Introduction

About This Book

The Sybase Press edition of the *Sybase SQL Server Performance and Tuning Guide* is a modest revision of the technical manual of the same name. The standard-edition technical manual is part of the SyBooks CD and the Sybase SQL Server documentation set. (For your reference, the SyBooks CD is also included with this book). The order of chapters and general presentation of material in this book are the same as in the technical manual. You may notice some maintenance and formatting changes.

This edition has new front matter, and Chapter 1 incorporates parts of the original preface. In addition to its already substantial glossary and index, the book now includes a bibliography of recommended sources for further information. You should also check the International Thomson Computer Press Web site (**www.itcpmedia.com**) for updates, additional resources, reviews, and correspondence.

Why the New Edition?

The *Sybase SQL Server Performance and Tuning Guide* appears in a commercial edition to make Sybase performance and tuning information widely available. Both experienced SQL Server users and developers just beginning to explore SQL Server can take advantage of this book's explanation of performance and tuning principles and features.

This book should be especially useful to Sybase system administrators, database designers, and application developers. Database performance and tuning is an ongoing journey that begins with database design, gains focus by its use with applications, and determines how easily system administrators can keep the enterprise up and running.

How to Use This Book

Busy computer professionals rarely read a reference book cover to cover. And it's not likely that readers of this book will read all of each chapter; nor will they read chapters in any particular sequence.

However, each chapter in this book does build on information that a previous chapter supplies. Your chances of performance and tuning success will increase if you take the time to learn the basics before launching into random query and system tuning experiments.

Essential Chapters

The heart of this book—its most crucial information—lies in Chapters 3, 4, 6, 7, and 8. These five chapters are essential to your understanding.

The core chapters cover:

- How SQL Server stores data and runs queries on unindexed data (Chapter 3,"Data Storage");

- How proper index selection can speed performance (Chapter 4, "How Indexes Work" and Chapter 6, "Indexing for Performance");

- How SQL Server builds an optimized query processing plan (Chapter 7, "The SQl Server Query Optimizer"); and

- How you can use the **showplan** tool to analyze the performance of your queries (Chapter 8, "Understanding Query Plans").

Road Map

After reading Chapters 3, 4, 6, 7, and 8, you can use the rest of the book as a reference, selecting topics as appropriate. It's worth mentioning that Chapter 19, "Using **sp_sysmon**" contains valuable information about SQL Server's comprehensive performance monitoring tool. As you tune SQL Server you will be running **sp_sysmon** frequently.

This book has three sections:

Section A (Chapters 1-5): Basics of Performance Tuning: Essential Tools

Chapter 1, "Performance Analysis," describes the major components to be analyzed when addressing performance.

Chapter 2, "Database Design and Denormalizing for Performance," provides a brief description of relational databases and good database design.

Chapter 3, "Data Storage," describes Sybase SQL Server™ page types, how data is stored on pages, and how queries on heap tables are executed.

Chapter 4, "How Indexes Work," provides information on how indexes are used to resolve queries.

Chapter 5, "Estimating the Size of Tables and Indexes," describes different methods for determining the current size of database objects, and for estimating their future size.

Section B (Chapters 6–12): Tuning the Performance of Queries

Chapter 6, "Indexing for Performance," provides guidelines and examples for choosing indexes.

Chapter 7, "The SQL Server Query Optimizer," describes the operation of the SQL Server query optimizer.

Chapter 8, "Understanding Query Plans," provides examples of **showplan** messages.

Chapter 9, "Advanced Optimizing Techniques," describes advanced tools for tuning query performance.

Chapter 10, "Transact-SQL Performance Tips," contains tips and workarounds for specific types of queries.

Chapter 11, "Locking on SQL Server," describes locking on SQL Server and techniques for reducing lock contention.

Chapter 12, "Cursors and Performance," details some issues with cursors and performance.

Section C (Chapters 13–19): Server and System Tuning

Chapter 13, "Controlling Physical Data Placement," describes the uses of segments and partitions for controlling the physical placement of data on storage devices.

Chapter 14, "tempdb Performance Issues," stresses the importance of the temporary database, *tempdb*, and provides suggestions for improving its performance.

Chapter 15, "Memory Use and Performance," describes how SQL Server uses memory for the procedure and data caches.

Chapter 16, "Networks and Performance," describes network issues.

Chapter 17, "Using CPU Resources Effectively," provides information for tuning servers with multiple CPUs.

Chapter 18, "Maintenance Activities and Performance," describes the performance impact of maintenance activities.

Chapter 19, "Monitoring SQL Server Performance with sp_sysmon," describes how to use a system procedure that monitors SQL Server performance.

SQL Server Release Levels

The Sybase Press edition of the *Sybase SQL Server Performance and Tuning Guide* was prepared after the shipment of SQL Server 11.0.1 and before the release of SQL Server 11.1. Since a number of performance-related features made their first appearance with SQL Server 10.0, you could use the information in this guide with both System 10 and System 11 Server products. See "Notes for Users of SQL Server 10.0 and Earlier," below.

Focus on SQL Server 11.0

SQL Server users who care about performance should upgrade to Release 11.0. High performance and flexible tuning tools were major goals of the SQL Server 11.0 release. These features are discussed throughout this book, which was planned and developed especially for Release 11.0.

Notes for Users of SQL Server 10.0.X and Earlier

Much of the material describing SQL Server internals and tuning techniques is still accurate for System 10. However, if you are still using Release 10.0, the following 11.0 features do not exist, or exist in a different form:

- Named caches, large I/O and cache replacement —in previous releases, there is a single named data cache, with only 2K I/O size. All cache replacement in earlier releases is by LRU strategy.

- Partitioning—you cannot partition tables in releases before 11.0

- Update methods—in earlier releases, all updates were either performed "direct in place" or "deferred". Starting in Release 11.0, there are several types of direct updates, and SQL Server is more likely to perform direct updates.

- New subquery processing in 11.0 differs from subquery processing in earlier releases.

- **showplan** messages were improved in content and formatting in Release 11.0.

- There are other small changes to query processing and query optimization, so you may see slightly different **showplan** output in different releases.

- Level 0 locking is not available in earlier releases. Also, Release 11.0 introduced configurable lock escalation levels.

- Most of the advanced optimizing tools discussed in Chapter 9 are new in Release 11.0.

- The housekeeper task is new in Release 11.0

- **sp_sysmon** is new in Release 11.0.1.

- Some of the **sp_configure** parameters mentioned in this book were introduced in the 11.0 Release.

Related Documents

A complete picture of the context of SQL Server operation will necessarily lead you to other manuals in the SQL Server documentation set. With the exception of installation and configuration documents and certain platform-specific information, you can find all of these manuals on the SyBooks CD in the back of this book.

In particular, the *SQL Server System Administration Guide* is a useful complement to the *Performance and Tuning Guide*, and it contains syntax and examples for many of the operations described in this book. The *System Administration Guide* provides in-depth information about administering servers and databases. The manual includes instructions and guidelines for managing physical resources and user and system databases, and specifying character conversion, international language, and sort order settings.

Other manuals you may find useful are:

- *SQL Server Monitor User's Guide*, which describes how to use a separate Sybase product that monitors SQL Server performance and graphically displays the results.

- *SQL Server Reference Manual*, which contains detailed information on all of the commands and system procedures discussed in this manual.

- *SQL Server Reference Supplement*, which contains a list of the Transact-SQL® reserved words, definitions of system tables, a description of the *pubs2* sample database, a list of SQL Server error messages, and other reference information that is common to all the manuals.

- The *SQL Server* utility programs manual, which documents the Sybase utility programs such as **isql** and **bcp**, that are executed at the operating system level.

- The SQL Server installation and configuration guides, which describes the installation procedures for SQL Server and the operating system-specific system administration, security administration, and tuning tasks.

Example Database

Many of the examples in this manual are based on a database called *pubtune*. The database schema is the same as the *pubs2* database, but the tables used in the examples have more rows: *titles* has 5000, *authors* has 5000, and *titleauthor* has 6250. Different indexes are generated to show different features for many examples, and these indexes are described in the text.

The *pubtune* database is not provided. Since most of the examples show the results of commands such as **set showplan** or **set statistics io**, running the queries in this manual on *pubs2* tables will not produce the same I/O results, and in many cases, will not produce the same query plans.

Diagram of the Pubs2 Database

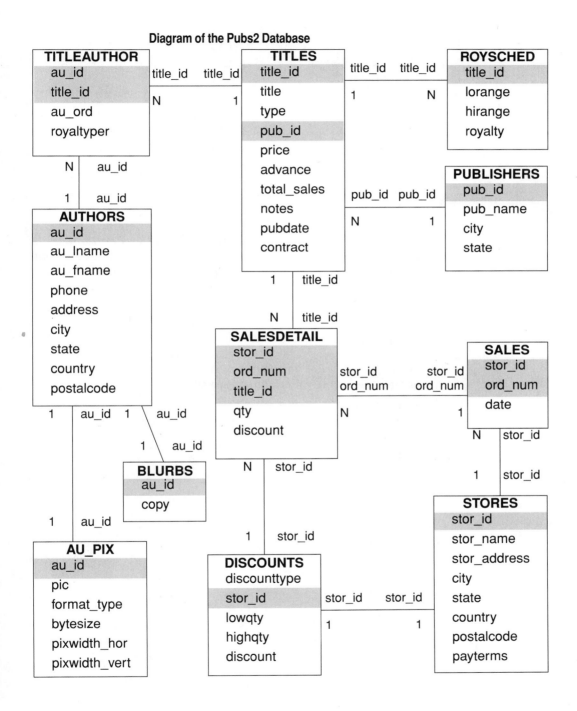

If You Need Help

Help with your Sybase software is available in the form of documentation and Sybase Technical Support.

Each Sybase installation that has purchased a support contract has one or more designated people who are authorized to contact Sybase Technical Support. If you cannot resolve your problem using the manuals, ask a designated person at your site to contact Sybase Technical Support.

Acknowledgments

This book assembles the knowledge and experience of a great many people at Sybase, and it was a great pleasure to work with many of them personally in the effort. I can't possibly name all of the people who provided answers to my many questions, just some of the main sources and assistants along the way.

Special thanks to Peter Thawley, whose sessions on performance and tuning at Sybase User Conferences are always standing room only, and with good reason. He knows it all, and loves to tell it, and provided an excellent resource for some of the thornier questions. Peter reviewed many of the chapters, and had his brain picked for many hours—especially on **sp_sysmon** and buffer cache tuning.

The Learning Products Group's Performance and Tuning course provided a good foundation for the early development of this book.

Rachael Fish's persistence and questioning and arranging of meetings led to great improvements in buffer cache tuning recommendations, and in the **sp_sysmon** documentation.

My managers, Frances Thomas and Dee Elling provided support and encouragement throughout the project. Other members of the Server Publications group contributed to this guide, notably Anneli Meyer's work on the 11.0 update modes and subquery processing and David Yozie's work on partitions. Tanya Knoop did extensive work on the **sp_sysmon** chapter.

And thanks to the many reviewers in Engineering and Technical Support who read sections of the book, and especially to Jerry Brenner and Sandra Dellafiora for reading the whole thing. Jim Pantajja of Pantajja Consulting provided an excellent and thorough review from an "outside" perspective.

Special thanks to Sandy Emerson for her valuable help in preparing this International Thomson Computer Press version of the book.

And thanks also to those programmers at Sybase who comment their code, who tell the whole truth in their functional specifications, and who are sympathetic to the customer perspective when we pesky pubs-types ask them to explain the nuances and details.

About the Author

Karen Paulsell is a Staff Technical Writer in the Server Publications Group at Sybase, where she has worked for 9 years. She holds a Master's degree in Interactive Telecommunication from New York University and a Bachelor in Broadcast Communication Arts from San Francisco State University.

She lives a seven-minute bicycle commute away from work, with one dog, three cats, twenty goldfish and a garden filled with 400 plants. Which she keeps track of with a Sybase database, of course.

Basics of Performance Tuning:
Essential Tools

Chapter 1, "Performance Analysis," describes the major components to be analyzed when addressing performance.

Chapter 2, "Database Design and Denormalizing for Performance," provides a brief description of relational databases and goofqd database design.

Chapter 3, "Data Storage," describes Sybase SQL Server™ page types, how data is stored on pages, and how queries on heap tables are executed.

Chapter 4, "How Indexes Work," provides information on how indexes are used to resolve queries.

Chapter 5, "Estimating the Size of Tables and Indexes," describes different methods for determining the current size of database objects, and for estimating their future size.

1 Performance Analysis

What Is "Good Performance"?

Performance is the measure of efficiency of an application or multiple applications running in the same environment. Performance is usually measured in **response time** and **throughput**.

Response time is the time that a single task takes to complete. You can shorten response time by:

- Reducing contention and wait times, particularly disk I/O wait times
- Using faster components
- Reducing the amount of time the resources are needed

In some cases, SQL Server is also optimized to reduce **initial response time**, that is, the time it takes to return the first row to the user. This is especially useful in applications where a user may retrieve several rows with a query, but then browse through them slowly with a front-end tool.

Throughput refers to the volume of work completed in a fixed time period. There are two ways of thinking about throughput:

- For a single transaction: for example, "5 UpdateTitle transactions per minute"
- For the entire SQL Server: for example, "50 or 500 Server-wide transactions per minute"

Throughput is commonly measured in transactions per second (tps), but it can also be measured per minute (tpm), per hour, per day, and so on.

Designing for Performance

Most of the gains in performance derive from good database design, thorough query analysis, and appropriate indexing. The largest performance gains can be realized by establishing a good database design, and by learning to work with the SQL Server query optimizer as you develop your applications.

Other considerations, such as hardware and network analysis, can locate performance bottlenecks in your installation.

What Is Tuning?

Tuning is optimizing performance. A system model of SQL Server and its environment can be used to identify performance problems at each layer.

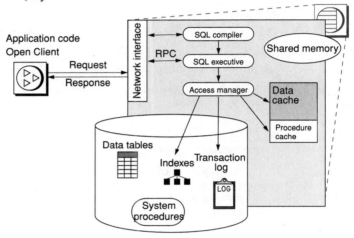

Figure 1-1: The SQL Server system model

A major part of tuning is reducing contention for system resources. As the number of users increases, applications contend for resources such as the data and procedure caches, spinlocks on system resources, and the CPU or CPUs. The probability of lock contention on data pages also increases.

Tuning Layers

SQL Server and its environment and applications can be broken into components, or tuning layers, in order to isolate certain components of the system for analysis. In many cases, two or more layers must be tuned to work optimally together.

In some cases, removing a resource bottleneck at one layer can reveal another problem area. On a more optimistic note, resolving one problem can sometimes alleviate other problems. For example, if physical I/O rates are high for queries, and you add more memory to speed response time and increase your cache hit ratio, you may ease problems with disk contention.

The tuning layers in SQL Server are:

- **Applications layer** – most of your performance gains come from tuning the queries in your SQL application, which in turn is based on good database design. Most of this guide is devoted to an explanation of SQL Server internals and query processing techniques and tools.

- **Database layer** – applications share resources at the database layer, including disks, the transaction log, data cache,

- **Server layer** – at the server layer, there are many shared resources, including the data and procedure caches, locks, CPUs

- **Devices layer** – the disk and controllers that store your data. At this level you concern yourself with disk I/O, in particular

- **Network layer** – the network or networks that connect users to SQL Server

- **Hardware layer** – the CPU or CPUs available

- **Operating system layer** – ideally, SQL Server is the only major application on a machine, and must only share CPU, memory, and other resources with the operating system, and other Sybase software such as the Backup Server™ or SQL Server Monitor™.

For your reference, here's a brief definition of each layer and its associated performance issues.

Application Layer

The application layer is of great interest to application developers, since tuning the performance of the application is an easily accessible function with results that are observable and testable. The performance of queries is also one major axis of overall SQL application performance.

Consequently, the majority of this guide describes how to tune SQL-based applications. Although queries do not bear sole responsibility for performance, maintaining high SQL Server performance *always* involves tuning the queries on your server.

Issues at the application layer include the following:

- Decision support vs. online transaction processing (OLTP) require different performance strategies

- Transaction design can reduce concurrency, since long transactions hold locks, and reduce the access of other users to the data
- Referential integrity requires joins for data modification
- Indexing to support selects increases time to modify data
- Auditing for security purposes can limit performance

Options at the application layer include:

- Remote processing or replicated processing can move decision support off the OLTP machine
- Using stored procedures to reduce compilation time and network usage
- Use the minimum locking level that meets your application needs

Database Layer

Issues at the database layer include:

- Developing a backup and recovery scheme
- Distribution of data across devices
- Auditing affects performance; audit only what you need
- Scheduling maintenance activities that can slow performance and lock users out of tables

Options include:

- Transaction log thresholds to automate logs dumps and avoid running out of space
- Use of thresholds for space monitoring in data segments
- Use of partitions to speed loading of data
- Object placement to avoid disk contention
- Caching for high availability of critical tables and indexes

SQL Server Layer

Issues at the SQL Server layer are:

- Application types—is the server supporting OLTP or DSS (Decision Support) or a mix?

- Number of users to be supported can affect tuning decisions–as the number of users increases, contention for resources can shift.
- Network loads.
- Replication Server® or other distributed processing can be an option when the number of users and transaction rate reach high levels.

Options include:

- Tuning memory, the most critical configuration parameter and other parameters
- Deciding on client vs. server processing—can some processing take place at the client side?
- Configuring cache sizes and I/O sizes
- Adding multiple CPUs
- Scheduling batch jobs and reporting for off-hours
- Reconfiguring certain parameters for shifting workload patterns
- Determine whether it is possible to move DSS to another SQL Server

Devices Layer

Issues at the devices layer include:

- Will the master device, the devices that hold the user database, or database logs be mirrored?
- How do you distribute system databases, user databases, and database logs across the devices?
- Are partitions needed for high insert performance on heap tables?

Options include:

- Using more medium-sized devices and more controllers may provide better I/O throughput than a few large devices
- Distributing databases, tables, and indexes to create even I/O load across devices

Network Layer

Virtually all users of SQL Server access their data via the network. Major issues with the network layer are:

- The amount of network traffic
- Network bottlenecks
- Network speed

Options include:

- Configuring packet sizes to match application needs
- Configuring subnets
- Isolating heavy network uses
- Moving to higher-capacity network
- Configuring for multiple network engines
- Designing applications to limit the amount of network traffic required

Hardware Layer

Issues at the hardware layer include:

- CPU throughput
- Disk access: controllers as well as disks
- Disk backup
- Memory usage

Some options are:

- Adding CPUs to match workload
- Configuring the housekeeper task to improve CPU utilization
- Following multiprocessor application design guidelines to reduce contention
- Configuring multiple data caches

Operating System Layer

At the operating system layer, the major issues are:

- File systems—are they available only to SQL Server?
- Memory management—accurately estimating operating system overhead and other program memory use
- CPU utilization—how many CPUs are available overall, and how many are allocated to SQL Server?

Options include:

- Network interface
- Choosing between files and raw partitions
- Increasing the memory size
- Moving client operations and batch processing to other machines
- Multiple CPU utilization for SQL Server

When to Stop Tuning

You should stop tuning performance when you have reached the system limits, or when you have achieved pre-determined performance goals. Despite your best efforts, sooner or later your system's performance will stabilize within some range. If you understand your system's limitations and have determined what level of performance is acceptable, you can tailor your tuning efforts accordingly.

Certainly, the number of performance options and variables available to SQL Server administrators and developers could make performance tuning a career-long occupation. There are, however, limits to maximum performance. The physical limits of the CPU, disk subsystems and networks impose limits. Some of these can be overcome by purchasing more memory and faster components. Examples are adding memory, using faster disk drives, switching to higher bandwidth networks, and adding CPUs.

Given a set of components, any individual query has a minimum response time. Given a set of system limitations, the physical subsystems impose saturation points.

For many systems, a performance specification developed early in the application life cycle sets out the expected response time for specific types of queries and the expected throughput for the system as a whole.

Steps in Performance Analysis

When there are performance problems, you need to determine the sources of the problems and your goals in resolving them. The steps for analyzing performance problems are:

1. Collect performance data to get baseline measurements. For example, you might use one or more of the following tools:

   - Benchmark tests developed in house or industry standard third-party tests.

- **sp_sysmon**, a system procedure that monitors SQL Server performance and provides statistical output describing the behavior of your SQL Server system. See Chapter 19, "Monitoring SQL Server Performance with sp_sysmon" for information about how to use **sp_sysmon**.

- SQL Server Monitor, a separate Sybase product that provides graphical performance and tuning tools and object-level information on I/O and locks.

- Any other appropriate tools.

2. Analyze the data to understand the system and any performance problems. Create and answer a list of questions to analyze your SQL Server environment. The list might include questions such as the following:

   - What are the symptoms of the problem?

   - What components of the system model affect the problem?

   - Does the problem affect all users, or only users of certain applications?

   - Is the problem intermittent or constant?

3. Define system requirements and performance goals:

   - How often is this query executed?

   - What response time is required?

4. Define the SQL Server environment—know the configuration and limitations at all layers.

5. Analyze application design—examine tables, indexes, and transactions.

6. Formulate a hypothesis about possible causes of the performance problem and possible solutions based on performance data.

7. Test the hypothesis by implementing the solutions from the last step:

   - Adjust configuration parameters

   - Redesign tables

   - Add or redistribute memory resources

8. Use the same tests used to collect baseline data in step 1 to determine the effects of tuning. Performance tuning is usually an iterative process.

- If actions taken based on step 7 do not meet the performance requirements and goals set in step 3, or if adjustments made in one area cause new performance problems, repeat this analysis starting with step 2. You might need to reevaluate system requirements and performance goals.

9. If testing shows that the hypothesis was correct, implement the solution in your development environment.

Using *sp_sysmon* to Monitor Performance

Use the system procedure **sp_sysmon** while tuning to monitor the effects of adjustments you make.

Performance tuning is usually an iterative process. While specific tuning might enhance performance in one area, it can simultaneously diminish performance in another area. Check the entire **sp_sysmon** output and make adjustments as necessary to achieve your tuning goals.

For more information about using **sp_sysmon** see Chapter 19, "Monitoring SQL Server Performance with sp_sysmon."

SQL Server Monitor, a separate Sybase product, can pinpoint where problems are at the object level.

2 Database Design and Denormalizing for Performance

How Design Is Related to Performance

Performance and tuning begins with a good database design. If your database is poorly designed, the information in the other chapters of this book may help you speed up your queries a little, but you may never attain optimum overall performance.

This chapter doesn't attempt to discuss all of the material presented in database design courses. It cannot teach you nearly as much as the many excellent books available on relational database design (refer to the Bibliography at the end of the book). This chapter presents some of the major design concepts and a few additional tips to help you move from a logical database design to a physical design on SQL Server.

Database Design

Database design is the process of moving from real-world business models and requirements to a database model that meets these requirements. For relational databases such as SQL Server, the standard design seeks to create tables in Third Normal Form. The rules of Third Normal Form stipulate that each table has one "key" identifier, and that all other "non-key" columns provide additional information only about the key. No non-key column can describe another non-key column.

Database design begins with a conceptual model that specifies the relationships among the entities or subjects of the database. When you translate a conceptual Entity-Relationship model, in Third Normal Form (3NF), to a relational model:

- Relations become tables.
- Attributes become columns.
- Relationships become data references (primary and foreign key references).

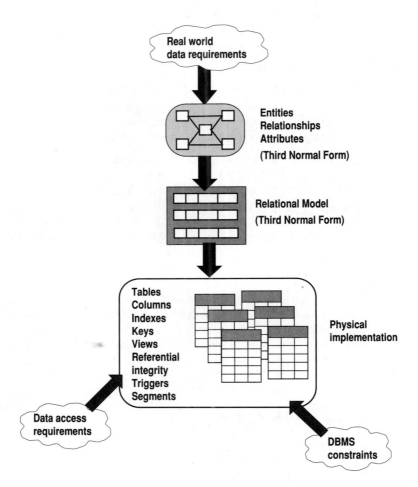

Figure 2-1: Database design

Physical Database Design for SQL Server

Having achieved Third Normal Form is no guarantee that your
particular application will perform well. On the contrary, selective
moves away from strict normal form may be necessary to maximize
performance. Once your database design reflects Third Normal
Form, you can judiciously manipulate the design to meet your
application's requirements. The final design will reflect the real-
world access requirements and constraints that may dictate
divergence from the Third Normal Form abstraction.

Based on your experience with the application, you can refine your physical database design as follows:

- Denormalize where appropriate
- Partition tables where appropriate
- Group tables into databases where appropriate
- Determine use of segments
- Determine use of devices
- Implement referential integrity constraints

Before discussing these design strategies, this chapter elaborates on the definition and use of normal forms in database design.

Normalization

When a table is normalized, the non-key columns depend on the key, the whole key, and nothing but the key.

From a relational model point of view, it is standard to have tables that are in Third Normal Form. Normalized physical design provides the greatest ease of maintenance, and databases in this form are clearly understood by teams of developers.

However, a fully normalized design may not always yield the best performance. It is recommended that you design for Third Normal Form, and then, as performance issues arise, denormalize to solve them.

Levels of Normalization

Each level of normalization relies on the previous level, as shown in Figure 2-2. For example, to conform to 2NF, entities must be in 1NF.

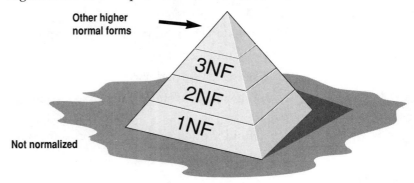

Figure 2-2: Levels of normalization

When determining if a database is in a normal form, start with the assumption that the relation (or table) is not normalized. Then apply the rigor of each normal form level to it.

Benefits of Normalization

Normalization produces smaller tables with smaller rows:

- More rows per page (less logical I/O)
- More rows per I/O (more efficient)
- More rows fit in cache (less physical I/O)

The benefits of normalization include:

- Searching, sorting, and creating indexes are faster, since tables are narrower, and more rows fit on a data page.
- You usually wind up with more tables. You can have more clustered indexes (you get only one per table) so you get more flexibility in tuning queries.
- Index searching is often faster, since indexes tend to be narrower and shorter.
- More tables allow better use of segments to control physical placement of data.
- You usually wind up with fewer indexes per table, so data modification commands are faster.

- You wind up with fewer null values and less redundant data, making your database more compact.

- Triggers execute more quickly if you are not maintaining redundant data.

- Data modification anomalies are reduced.

- Normalization is conceptually cleaner and easier to maintain and change as your needs change.

While fully normalized databases require more joins, joins are generally very fast if indexes are available on the join columns. (See Chapter 4 for a thorough discussion of the benefits of indexes). SQL Server is optimized to keep higher levels of the index in cache, so each join performs only one or two physical I/Os for each matching row. The cost of finding rows already in the data cache is extremely low.

First Normal Form

The rules for First Normal Form are:

- Every column must be atomic. It cannot be decomposed into two or more subcolumns.

- You cannot have multivalued columns or repeating groups.

- Every row and column position can have only one value.

The table in Figure 2-3 violates first normal form, since the *dept_no* column contains a repeating group:

Employee (emp_num, emp_lname, dept__no)

Employee

emp_num	emp_lname	dept_no	
10052	Jones	A10 C66	Repeating group
10101	Sims	D60	

Figure 2-3: A table that violates first normal form

Normalization creates two tables and moves *dept_no* to the second table:

Employee (emp_num, emp_lname)   **Emp_dept (emp_num, dept_no)**

Employee

emp_num	emp_lname
10052	Jones
10101	Sims

Emp_dept

emp_num	dept_no
10052	A10
10052	C66
10101	D60

Figure 2-4:   Correcting first normal form violations by creating two tables

Second Normal Form

For a table to be in Second Normal Form, every non-key field must depend on the entire primary key, not on part of a composite primary key. If a database has only single-field primary keys, it is automatically in Second Normal Form.

In the table in Figure 2-5, the primary key is a composite key on *emp_num* and *dept_no*. But the value of *dept_name* depends only on *dept_no*, not on the entire primary key.

Emp_dept (emp_num, dept_no, dept_name)

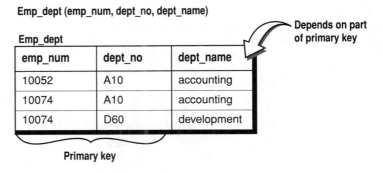

Emp_dept

emp_num	dept_no	dept_name
10052	A10	accounting
10074	A10	accounting
10074	D60	development

Depends on part of primary key

Primary key

Figure 2-5:   A table that violates second normal form

To normalize this table, move *dept_name* to a second table as shown in Figure 2-6.

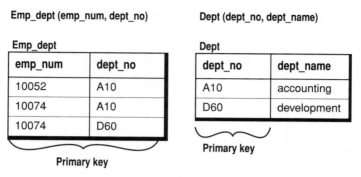

Figure 2-6:   Correcting second normal form violations by creating two tables

Third Normal Form

For a table to be in Third Normal Form, a non-key field cannot depend on another non-key field. The table in Figure 2-7 violates Third Normal Form because the *mgr_lname* field depends on the *mgr_emp_num* field, which is not a key field.

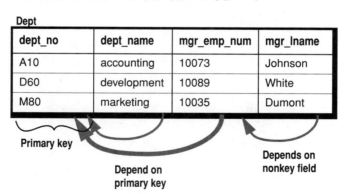

Figure 2-7:   A table that violates Third Normal Form

The solution is to split the *Dept* table into two tables, as shown in Figure 2-8. In this case, the *Employees* table, shown in Figure 2-4 already stores the information about last names and employees numbers, including those employees who are managers. Removing the *mgr_lname* field from *Dept* brings the table into Third Normal Form.

Dept (dept_no, dept_name, mgr_emp_num)

Dept

dept_no	dept_name	mgr_emp_num
A10	accounting	10073
D60	development	10089
M80	marketing	10035

Primary key

Employee (emp_num, emp_lname)

Employee

emp_num	emp_lname
10073	Johnson
10089	White
10035	Dumont

Primary key

Figure 2-8: Correcting Third Normal Form violations by creating two tables

Denormalizing for Performance

Once you have created your database in normalized form, you have can perform baseline performance benchmarks and begin your performance analysis. Based on how your application is using your database, you may decide to "denormalize," to back away from normalization to improve performance for specific queries or applications.

The process of denormalizing:

• Can be done with tables or columns

• Assumes prior normalization

• Requires a thorough knowledge of how the data is being used

Good reasons for denormalizing are:

• All or nearly all of the most frequent queries require access to the full set of joined data

- A majority of applications perform table scans when joining tables

- Computational complexity of derived columns requires temporary tables or excessively complex queries

Risks of Denormalization

Denormalization should be based on a thorough knowledge of the application, and it should be performed only if performance issues indicate that it is needed. For example, the *ytd_sales* column in the *titles* table of the *pubs2* database is a denormalized column that is maintained by a trigger on the *salesdetail* table. The same values can be obtained using this query:

```
select title_id, sum(qty)
    from salesdetail
    group by title_id
```

To obtain the summary values and the document title requires a join with the *titles* table:

```
select title, sum(qty)
    from titles t, salesdetail sd
    where t.title_id = sd.title_id
    group by title
```

It makes sense to denormalize this table if the query is run frequently. But there is a price to pay: you must create an insert/update/delete trigger on the *salesdetail* table to maintain the aggregate values in the *titles* table. Executing the trigger and performing the changes to *titles* adds processing cost to each data modification of the *qty* column value.

This situation is a good example of the tension between decision support applications, which frequently need summaries of large amounts of data, and transaction processing applications, which perform discrete data modifications. Denormalization usually favors one form of processing at a cost to others.

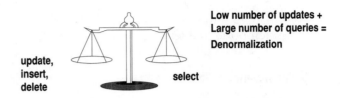

update,
insert,
delete

select

Low number of updates +
Large number of queries =
Denormalization

Figure 2-9:   Balancing denormalization issues

Whatever form of denormalization you choose, it has the potential for causing data integrity problems: such potential issues must be carefully documented and addressed in application design.

Database redesign should be undertaken with caution. Create and maintain SQL scripts (runnable batches of SQL "create" statements for your databases, tables, and other database objects) so that you can restore the design to an earlier stage if needed. Scripts make it possible for you easily to re-create and re-populate a database.

Disadvantages of Denormalization

Denormalization has these disadvantages:

- It usually speeds retrieval but can slow data modification.
- It is always application-specific and needs to be re-evaluated if the application changes.
- It can increase the size of tables.
- In some instances, it simplifies coding; in others, it makes coding more complex.

Performance Advantages of Denormalization

Denormalization can improve performance by:

- Minimizing the need for joins
- Reducing the number of foreign keys on tables
- Reducing the number of indexes, saving storage space and reducing data modification time
- Precomputing aggregate values, that is, computing them at data modification time rather than at select time
- Reducing the number of tables (in some cases)

Denormalization Decision Tree

When deciding whether to denormalize, you need to analyze the data access requirements of the applications in your environment, and their actual performance characteristics. Often, good indexing and other solutions solve many performance problems.

Some of the issues to examine when considering denormalization include:

- What are the critical transactions, and what is the expected response time?
- How often are the transactions executed?
- What tables or columns do the critical transactions use? How many rows do they access each time?
- What is the mix of transaction types: select, insert, update, and delete?
- What is the usual sort order?
- What are the concurrency expectations?
- How big are the most frequently accessed tables?
- Do any processes compute summaries?
- Where is the data physically located?

Denormalization Techniques

The most prevalent denormalization techniques are:

- Adding redundant columns
- Adding derived columns
- Collapsing tables

In addition, you can duplicate or split tables to improve performance. While these are not denormalization techniques, they achieve the same purposes and require the same safeguards.

Adding Redundant Columns

You can add redundant columns to eliminate frequent joins. For example, if frequent joins are performed on the *titleauthor* and *authors* tables in order to retrieve the author's last name, you can add the *au_lname* column to *titleauthor*.

select ta.title_id, a.au_id, a.au_lname
from titleauthor ta, authors a
where ta.au_id = a.au_id

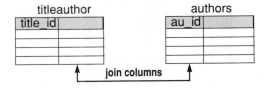

select title_id, au_id, au_lname
from titleauthor

Figure 2-10: Denormalizing by adding redundant columns

Adding redundant columns eliminates joins for many queries. The problems with this solution are that it:

- Requires maintenance of new column. All changes must be made to two tables, and possibly to many rows in one of the tables.

- Requires more disk space, since *au_lname* is duplicated.

Adding Derived Columns

Adding derived columns can help eliminate joins and reduce the time needed to produce aggregate values. The *total_sales* column in the *titles* table of the *pubs2* database provides one example of a derived column used to reduce aggregate value processing time.

The example in Figure 2-11 shows both benefits. Frequent joins are needed between the *titleauthor* and *titles* tables to provide the total advance for a particular book title.

```
select title, sum(advance)
from titleauthor ta, titles t
where ta.title_id = t.title_id
group by title_id
```

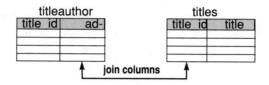

```
select title, sum_adv
from titles
```

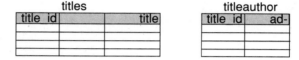

Figure 2-11: Denormalizing by adding derived columns

You can create and maintain a derived data column in the *titles* table, eliminating both the join and the aggregate at run time. This increases storage needs, and requires maintenance of the derived column whenever changes are made to the *titles* table.

Collapsing Tables

If most users need to see the full set of joined data from two tables, collapsing the two tables into one can improve performance by eliminating the join.

For example, users frequently need to see the author name, author ID, and the *blurbs* copy data at the same time. The solution is to collapse the two tables into one. The data from the two tables must be in a one-to-one relationship to collapse tables.

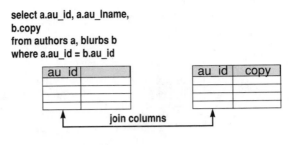

```
select a.au_id, a.au_lname,
b.copy
from authors a, blurbs b
where a.au_id = b.au_id
```

```
select * from newauthors
```

Figure 2-12: Denormalizing by collapsing tables

Collapsing the tables eliminates the join, but loses the conceptual separation of the data. If some users still need access to just the pairs of data from the two tables, this access can be restored by queries that select only the needed columns or by using views.

Duplicating Tables

If a group of users regularly needs only a subset of data, you can duplicate the critical table subset for that group.

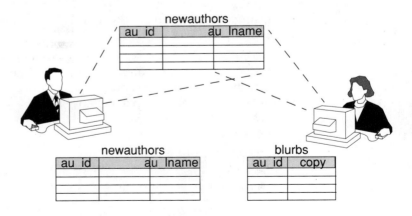

Figure 2-13: Denormalizing by duplicating tables

The kind of split shown in Figure 2-13 minimizes contention, but requires that you manage redundancy and possible latency.

Splitting Tables

Sometimes, splitting normalized tables can improve performance. You can split tables in two ways:

- Horizontally, by placing rows in two separate tables, depending on data values in one or more columns.

- Vertically, by placing the primary key and some columns in one table, and placing other columns and the primary key in another table.

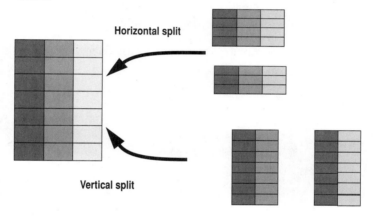

Figure 2-14: Horizontal and vertical partitioning of tables

Splitting tables—either horizontally or vertically—adds complexity to your applications. There usually needs to be a very good performance reason.

Horizontal Splitting

Use horizontal splitting in the following circumstances:

- A table is large, and reducing its size reduces the number of index pages read in a query. B-tree indexes, however, are generally very flat, and you can add large numbers of rows to a table with small index keys before the B-tree requires more levels. An excessive number of index levels may be an issue with tables that have very large keys.

- The table split corresponds to a natural separation of the rows, such as different geographical sites or historical vs. current data. You might choose horizontal splitting if you have a table that stores huge amounts of rarely used historical data, and your applications have high performance needs for current data in the same table.

- Table splitting distributes data over the physical media (there are other ways to accomplish this goal, too).

Generally, horizontal splitting adds a high degree of complication to applications. It usually requires different table names in queries, depending on values in the tables. This complexity alone usually far outweighs the advantages of table splitting in most database applications. As long as the index keys are short, and the indexes are used for queries on the table (rather than table scans being used), doubling or tripling the number of rows in the table may increase the number of disk reads required for a query by only one index level.

Figure 2-15 shows how the *authors* table might be split to separate active and inactive authors:

Problem: Usually only active records are accessed

Authors		
active		
active		
inactive		
active		
inactive		
inactive		

Solution: Partition horizontally into active and inactive data

Inactive_Authors		

Active_Authors		

Figure 2-15: Horizontal partitioning of active and inactive data

Vertical Splitting

Use vertical splitting in the following circumstances:

- Some columns are accessed more frequently than other columns.

- The table has wide rows, and splitting the table reduces the number of pages that need to be read.

Vertical table splitting makes even more sense when both of the above conditions are true. When a table contains very long columns that are not accessed frequently, placing them in a separate table can greatly speed the retrieval of the more frequently used columns. With shorter rows, more data rows fit on a data page, so fewer pages can be accessed for many queries.

Figure 2-16 shows how the *authors* table can be partitioned.

Problem:
Frequently access lname and fname,
infrequently access phone and city

Solution: Partition data vertically

Authors				
au_id	lname	fname	phone	city

Authors_Frequent		
au_id	lname	fname

Authors_Infrequent		
au_id	phone	city

Figure 2-16: Vertically partitioning a table

Managing Denormalized Data

Whatever denormalization techniques you use, you need to develop management techniques to ensure data integrity. Choices include:

- Triggers, which can update derived or duplicated data anytime the base data changes

- Application logic, using transactions in each application that updates denormalized data to be sure that changes are atomic

- Batch reconciliation, run at appropriate intervals to bring the denormalized data back into agreement

From an integrity point of view, triggers provide the best solution, although they can be costly in terms of performance.

Using Triggers to Manage Denormalized Data

In Figure 2-17, the *sum_adv* column in the *titles* table stores denormalized data. A trigger updates the *sum_adv* column whenever the *advance* column in *titleauthor* changes.

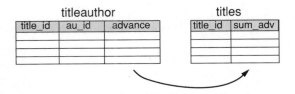

Figure 2-17: Using triggers to maintain normalized data

Using Application Logic to Manage Denormalized Data

If your application has to ensure data integrity, it will have to ensure that the inserts, deletes, or updates to both tables occur in a single transaction.

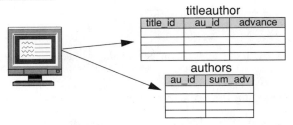

Figure 2-18: Maintaining denormalized data via application logic

If you use application logic, be very sure that the data integrity requirements are well documented and well known to all application developers and to those who must maintain applications.

➤ **Note**

Using application logic to manage denormalized data is risky. The same logic must be used and maintained in all applications that modify the data.

Batch Reconciliation

If 100-percent consistency is not required at all times, you can run a batch job or stored procedure during off hours to reconcile duplicate or derived data.

You can run short, frequent batches or longer, less frequent batches.

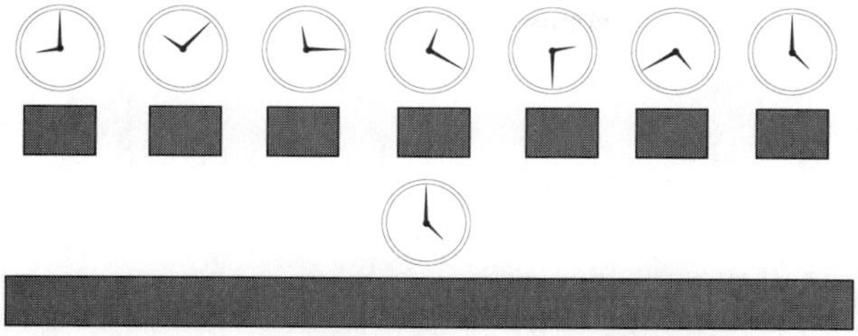

Figure 2-19: Using batch reconciliation to maintain data

Next Steps: Understanding Data Storage and Indexing

Before concluding that denormalization is necessary, you must test your database design in the context of your application. So that you can predict where bottlenecks might occur that would make denormalization necessary, you need an understanding of how SQL Server stores data objects and how your application uses indexes to the stored data. Although database design and normalization influence overall performance, data storage and access via indexes are much more important.

To provide a basis for assessing the impact of indexes on performance, the next chapter covers the fundamentals of SQL Server data storage. Once you understand how SQL Server stores data on data pages, you can better assess the relative merits of your database design and how to apply and evaluate indexes.

3

Data Storage

Performance and Object Storage

This chapter explains how SQL Server stores data rows on pages, and how these pages are used by select and data modification statements *when there are no indexes*. Since the discussion assumes that no indexes are present, it should give you insight into how SQL Server behaves when no indexes are *used*—which is the worst-case effect of poorly tuned queries.

By explaining the native storage facilities SQL Server provides, this chapter lays the foundation for understanding how to improve your SQL Server's performance by creating indexes, by tuning your queries, and by addressing object storage issues. The chapter covers:

- The types of pages in SQL Server
- How tables are stored in SQL Server
- How tables without indexes are accessed
- How SQL Server uses the data cache when reading tables

Performance Tuning Goal: Reducing Disk Reads

Most of a query's execution time is spent reading data pages from disk. Therefore, most of your performance improvement—over 80 percent, according to many performance and tuning experts—comes from reducing the number of disk reads that SQL Server needs to perform for each query.

A table scan is the worst case: if a query performs a table scan, SQL Server reads every page in the table because no useful indexes are available to help it retrieve the data you need. The individual query has very poor response time, because disk reads take time.

Queries that incur table scans also affect the performance of other queries on your server. Table scans can increase the time other users have to wait for a response, since they consume system resources such as CPU time, disk I/O, and network capacity.

Clearly, table scans maximize the number of disk reads (I/Os) for a given query. How can you predict disk reads? When you have become thoroughly familiar with the tools, the indexes on your tables, and the size and structure of the objects in your applications, you should be able to estimate the number of I/O operations a given join or select operation will perform. If you know the indexed columns on your tables and the table and index sizes, you can often look at a query and predict its behavior. For different queries on the same table, you might make these kinds of statements (ordered from best to worst in performance):

- "This point query returns a single row or a small number of rows that match the **where** clause condition. The condition in the **where** clause is indexed; it should perform two to four I/Os on the index and one more to read the correct data page."

- "All of the columns in the select list and **where** clause for this query are included in a nonclustered index. This query will probably perform a scan on the leaf level of the index, about 600 pages. If I add an unindexed column to the select list, it has to scan the table, and that would require 5000 disk reads."

- "No useful indexes are available for this query; it is going to do a table scan, requiring at least 5000 disk reads."

Later chapters explain how to determine which access method is being used for a query, the size of the tables and indexes, and the amount of I/O a query performs.

Query Processing and Page Reads

Each time you submit a Transact-SQL query, the SQL Server optimizer determines the optimal access path to find the needed data. In most database applications, you have many tables in the database, and each table has one or more indexes. The optimizer attempts to find the most efficient access path to your data for each table in the query. Depending on whether you have created indexes, and what kind of indexes you have created, the optimizer's access method options include:

- A table scan – reading all of the table's data pages, sometimes hundreds or thousands of pages

- Index access – using the index to find only the data pages needed, sometimes only a half-dozen page reads in all

- Index covering – using only a nonclustered index to return data, without reading the actual data rows, requiring only a fraction of the page reads required for a table scan

Having the right set of indexes on your tables should allow most of your queries to access the data they need with a minimum number of page reads.

SQL Server Data Pages

The basic unit of storage for SQL Server is a **page**. On most systems, a page is 2K, 2048 bytes. A page contains 32 bytes of header information. The rest of the page is available to store data rows and row pointers (the row offset table).

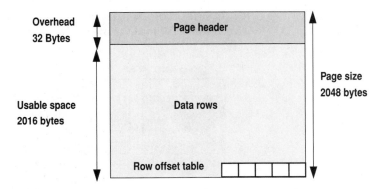

Figure 3-1:   A SQL Server data page

Page headers use 32 bytes, leaving 2016 bytes for data storage on each page.[1] Information in the page header includes pointers to the next page and the previous page used by the object, and the object ID of the table or index using that page.

Each row is stored contiguously on the page. The information stored for each row consists of the actual column data plus information such as the row number (one byte) and the number of variable-length and null columns in the row (one byte).

Rows cannot cross page boundaries, except for text and image columns. Each data row has at least 4 bytes of overhead; rows that contain variable-length data have additional overhead. Chapter 5, "Estimating the Size of Tables and Indexes," explains overhead in detail.

The row offset table stores pointers to the starting location for each data row on the page. Each pointer requires 2 bytes.

---

1. The maximum number of bytes for a data row is 1960 (plus two bytes of overhead) due to overhead for logging: the row, plus the overhead about the transaction, must fit on a single page in the transaction log.

Row Density on Data Pages

The usable space on a page, divided by the row size, tells us how many rows can be stored on a page. This figure gives us the row density. The size of rows can affect your performance dramatically: the smaller the data rows, the more rows you can store per page. When rows are small, you'll need to read fewer pages to answer your select queries, so your performance will be better for queries that perform frequent table scans.

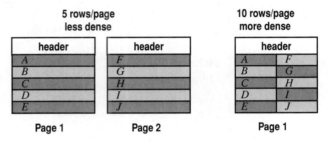

Figure 3-2: Row density

Row density can sometimes have a negative impact on throughput when data is being modified. If one user changes data in a row, the page is locked until the transaction commits. Other users cannot access the changed row or any other data on the page until the lock is released. SQL Server allows you to specify the maximum number of rows on a page for tables where such lock contention is a problem. See "Reducing Lock Contention with max_rows_per_page" on page 324 for more information.

If your table contains variable-length fields, the row size depends on the actual length of the data, so row density can vary from page to page.

Extents

SQL Server pages are always allocated to a database object, such as a table or index, in blocks of 8 pages at a time. This block of 8 pages is called an **extent**. The smallest amount of space that a table or index can occupy is one extent, or 8 data pages. Extents are deallocated only when all the pages in an extent are empty.

See Figure 3-4 on page 42 for an illustration of extents and object storage.

In most cases, the use of extents in SQL Server is transparent to the user. One place where information about extents is visible is in the output from **dbcc** commands that check allocation. These commands report information about objects and the extents used by the objects.

Reports from **sp_spaceused** display the space allocated (the *reserved* column) and the space used by data and indexes. The *unused* column displays the amount of space in extents that are allocated to an object, but not yet used to store data.

```
sp_spaceused titles

name    rowtotal  reserved  data     index_size  unused
------  --------  --------  -------  ----------  ------
titles  5000       1392 KB   1250 KB  94 KB        48 KB
```

In this report, the *titles* table and its indexes have 1392K reserved on various extents, including 48K (24 data pages) unallocated in those extents.

Linked Data Pages

Each table and each level of each index forms a doubly-linked list of pages. Each page in the object stores a pointer to the next page in the chain and to the previous page in the chain. When new pages need to be inserted, the pointers on the two adjacent pages change to point to the new page. When SQL Server scans a table, it reads the pages in order, following these page pointers.

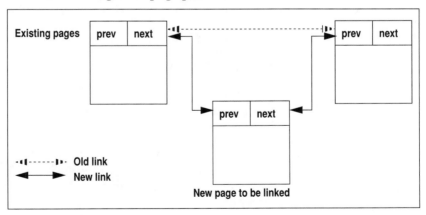

Figure 3-3:   Page linkage

SQL Server tries to keep the page allocations close together for objects, as follows:

- If there is an unallocated page in the current extent, that page is assigned to the object.

- If there is no free page in the current extent, but there is an unallocated page on another of the object's extents, that extent is used.

- If all of the object's extents are full, but there are free extents on the allocation unit, the new extent is allocated on a unit already used by the object.

For information on how page allocation is performed for partitioned tables, see "Partitioning Tables" on page 369.

Text and Image Pages

Text and image columns for a table are stored as a separate page chain, consisting of a set of text or image pages. If a table has multiple text or image columns, it still has only one of these separate data structures. Each table with a text or image column has one of these structures. The table itself stores a 16-byte pointer to the first page of the text value for the row. Additional pages for the value are linked by next and previous pointers, just like the data pages. Each text or image value is a separate page chain. The first page stores the number of bytes in the text value. The last page in the chain for a value is terminated with a null next-page pointer.

Figure shows a table with text values. Each of the three rows stores a pointer to the starting location of its text value in the text/image structure.

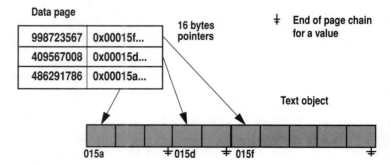

Text and image data storage

Reading or writing a text or image value requires at least two page reads or writes:

- One for the pointer

- One for the actual location of the text in the text object

Each text or image page stores up to 1800 bytes. Every non-null value uses at least one full data page.

Text objects are listed separately in *sysindexes*. The index ID column, *indid*, is always 255, and the *name* is the table name, prefixed with the letter "t".

Additional Page Types

In addition to the page types discussed above for table storage, SQL Server uses index pages and several other page types. Indexes are discussed in detail in the next chapter, and distribution pages are discussed in "How the Optimizer Uses the Statistics" on page 152.

For completeness, this section describes other types of pages that SQL Server uses to track space allocation and the location of database objects. These page types are mainly used to expedite the process of allocating and deallocating space for objects. They provide a way for SQL Server to allocate additional space for objects near space that is already used by the object. This strategy also helps performance by reducing disk-head travel.

These pages track disk space use by database objects:

- Global Allocation Map (GAM) pages, which contain allocation bitmaps for an entire database.

- Allocation pages, which track space usage and objects within groups of 256 database pages, 1/2 megabyte.

- Object Allocation Map (OAM) pages, which contain information about the extents used for an object. Each table and index has at least one OAM page to track where pages for the object are stored in the database.

- Control pages, which exist only for tables that are partitioned. There is one control page for each partition. For more information on control pages, see "Effects on System Tables" on page 371.

Global Allocation Map (GAM) Pages

Each database has a GAM page. It stores a bitmap for all allocation units of a database, with one bit per allocation unit. When an allocation unit has no free extents available to store objects, its corresponding bit in the GAM is set to 1. This mechanism expedites allocating new space for objects. Users cannot view the GAM; it appears in the system catalogs as the table *sysgams*.

Allocation Pages

When you create a database or add space to a database, the space is divided into allocation units of 256 data pages. The first page in each **allocation unit** is the allocation page. The allocation page tracks space usage by objects on all of the extents in the unit by recording the object IDs and tracking what pages are in use and what pages are free in each extent. For each extent, it also stores the page ID for the OAM page of the object stored on that extent.

dbcc allocation-checking commands report space usage by allocation unit. Page 0 and all pages that are multiples of 256 are allocation pages.

Object Allocation Map (OAM) Pages

Each table, index and text chain has one or more OAM pages stored on pages allocated to the table or index. If a table has more than one OAM page, the pages are linked in a chain. These OAM pages store pointers to each allocation unit that contains pages for the object. The first page in the chain stores allocation hints, indicating which OAM page in the chain has information about allocation units with free space. This provides a fast way to allocate additional space for objects, keeping the new space close to pages already used by the object.

Each OAM page holds allocation mappings (OAM entries) for 250 allocation units. A single OAM page stores information for 2000 to 63,750 data or index pages.

Why the Range?

Each entry in the OAM page stores the page ID of the allocation page and the number of free and used pages for the object within that allocation page. If a table is widely spread out across the storage space for a database so that each allocation unit stores only one extent (8 pages) for the table, the 250 rows on the OAM page can only point to $250 * 8 = 2000$ database pages. If the table is very compactly stored, so that it uses all 255 pages available in each of its allocation units, one OAM page stores allocation information for $250 * 255 = 63,750$ pages.

Relationships Between Objects, OAM Pages, and Allocation Pages

Figure 3-4 shows how allocation units, extents, and objects are managed by OAM pages and allocation pages.

- There are two allocation units shown, one starting at page 0 and one at page 256. The first page of each is the allocation page.

- A table is stored on four extents, starting at pages 1 and 24 on the first allocation unit and pages 272 and 504 on the second unit.

- The first page of the table is the table's OAM page. It points to the allocation page for each allocation unit where the object uses pages, so it points to pages 0 and 256.

- Allocation pages 0 and 256 store object IDs and information about the extents and pages used on the extent. So, allocation page 0 points to page 1 and 24 for the table, and allocation page 256 points to pages 272 and 504. Of course, these allocation pages also point to other objects stored in the allocation unit, but these pointers are not shown here.

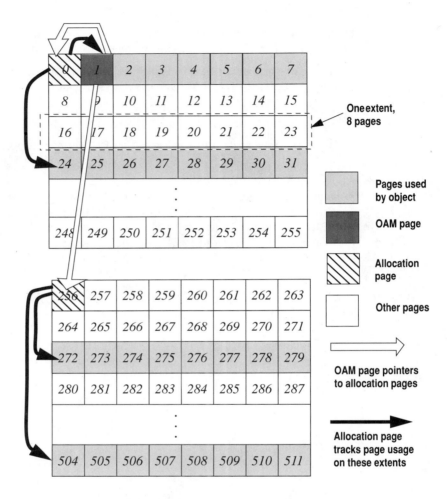

Figure 3-4: OAM page and allocation page pointers

The *sysindexes* Table and Data Access.

The *sysindexes* table stores information about indexed and unindexed tables. *sysindexes* has one row:

- For each table. If the table has a clustered index, the *indid* column is 1; if there is no clustered index, the indid column is 0.

- For each nonclustered index. The index IDs are between 2 and 250.

- Each text/image column. The index ID is always 255.

For each row in *sysindexes*, there are three columns that help optimize access to objects:

root	Stores the page number of the root pages of the index. If the row describes a table without a clustered index, this row stores a pointer to the last page of the heap.
first	Stores the page number of the first page of the data page chain for a table, or the first page of the leaf level for a nonclustered index.
distribution	Stores the page number of the page where statistics about index keys are stored.

When SQL Server needs to access a table, it uses these columns in *sysindexes* as a starting point.

Heaps of Data: Tables Without Clustered Indexes

If you create a table on SQL Server, but do not create a clustered index, the table is stored as a heap. The data rows are not stored in any particular order, and new data is always inserted on the last page of the table.

This section describes how select, insert, delete, and update operations perform on heaps when there is no nonclustered index to aid in retrieving data.

Select Operations on Heaps

When you issue a select operation on a heap and there is no useful nonclustered index, SQL Server must scan every data page in the table to find every row that satisfies the conditions in the query. There may be one row, many rows, or no rows that match. SQL Server must examine every row on every page in the table. SQL Server reads the *first* column in *sysindexes* for the table, reads the first page into cache, and then follows the next page pointers until it finds the last page of the table.

select * from employee
where emp_id = 12854

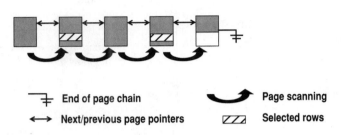

─┼─ End of page chain	Page scanning
←→ Next/previous page pointers	⟋⟋ Selected rows

Figure 3-5: Selecting from a heap

The phrase "no useful index" is important in describing the optimizer's decision to perform a table scan. Sometimes, an index exists on the columns you name in your **where** clause, but the optimizer determines that it would be more costly to use the index than to scan the table. Later chapters describe how the optimizer costs queries using indexes and how you can get more information about why the optimizer makes these choices.

Table scans are also used when you issue a **select** without a **where** clause so that you select all of the rows in a table.

The only exception is when the query includes only columns that are keys in a nonclustered index. For more information, see "Index Covering" on page 77.

Inserting Data into a Heap

When you insert data into a heap, the data row is always added to the last page of the table. If the last page is full, a new page is allocated in the current extent. If the extent is full, SQL Server looks for empty pages on other extents in use by the table. If there are no available pages, a new extent is allocated to the table.

insert employee
values (17823, "White", "Snow", ...)

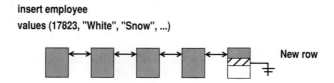

Figure 3-6:   Inserting a row into a heap table

SQL Server allows you to specify the maximum number of rows on a page. If you use this option, a heap page is "full" when you have inserted that many rows on the page, and a new page is allocated. See "Reducing Lock Contention with max_rows_per_page" on page 324 for more information.

If there is no clustered index on a table, and the table is not partitioned, the *sysindexes.root* entry for the heap table stores a pointer to the last page of the heap to locate the page where the data needs to be inserted. In addition, a special bit in the page header enables SQL Server to track whether row inserts are taking place continuously at the end of the page, and disables the normal page-split mechanism (explained on "Page Splitting on Full Data Pages" on page 63).

One of the severe performance limits on heap tables is that the page must be locked when the row is added. If many users are trying to add rows to a heap table at the same time, they will block each other's access to the page. These characteristics of heaps are true for:

- Single row inserts using **insert**

- Multiple row inserts using **select into** or **insert...select** (an insert statement that selects rows from another table, or from the same table)

- Bulk copy into the table

In many cases, creating a clustered index for the table solves these performance problems for heaps and provides real performance gains for user queries. Another workaround for the last-page problem in heaps is to use partitions to create many "last pages" for the heap table. See "Improving Insert Performance with Partitions" on page 364.

Deleting Data from a Heap

When you delete rows from a heap, and there is no useful index, SQL Server scans all of the data rows in the table to find the rows to delete. It has no way of knowing how many rows match the conditions in the query without examining every row.

When a data row is deleted from the page, the rows that follow it on the page move up so that the data on the page remains contiguous.

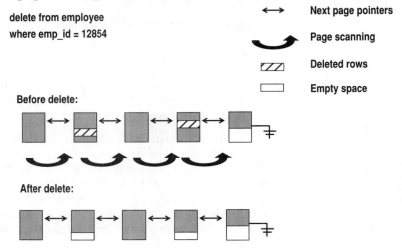

delete from employee
where emp_id = 12854

←→   Next page pointers

      Page scanning

///   Deleted rows

      Empty space

Before delete:

After delete:

Figure 3-7: Deleting rows from a heap table

If you delete the last row on a page, the page is deallocated. If there are other pages on the extent still in use by the table, the page can be used again by the table when a page is needed. If all other pages on the extent are empty, the whole extent is deallocated. It can be allocated to other objects in the database. The first data page for a table or index is never deallocated.

Update Operations on Heaps

Like other operations on heaps, an **update** that has no useful index on the columns in the **where** clause performs a table scan to locate the rows that need to be changed.

Updates on heaps can be performed in several ways:

- If the length of the row does not change, the updated row replaces the existing row, and no data moves on the page.

- If the length of the row changes, and there is enough free space on the page, the row remains in the same place on the page, but other rows move up or down to keep the rows contiguous on the page. The row offset pointers at the end of the page are adjusted to point to the changed row locations.

- If the row does not fit on the page, the row is deleted from its current page, and the "new" row is inserted on the last page of the table. This type of update can cause contention on the last page of the heap, just as inserts do.

For more information on how updates are performed, see "Update Operations" on page 195.

How SQL Server Performs I/O for Heap Operations

When a query needs a data page, SQL Server first checks to see if the page is available in a data cache. If the page is not available, then it must be read from disk.

A newly installed SQL Server has a single data cache configured for 2K I/O. Each I/O operation reads or writes a single SQL Server data page. A System Administrator can:

- Configure multiple caches

- Bind tables and other objects to the caches

- Configure data caches to perform I/O in page-sized multiples, up to eight data pages (one extent)

To use these caches most efficiently, and to reduce I/O operations, the SQL Server optimizer can:

- Choose to prefetch up to eight data pages at a time

- Choose between different caching strategies

Sequential Prefetch, or Large I/O

SQL Server's data caches can be configured by a System Administrator to allow large I/Os. When a cache is configured to allow large I/Os, SQL Server can choose to prefetch data pages.

Caches can contain pools of 2K, 4K, 8K, and 16K buffers, allowing SQL Server to read up to an entire extent (eight data pages) in a single I/O operation. When several pages are read into cache with a single I/O, they are treated as a unit: they age in cache together, and if any page in the unit has been changed, all pages are written to disk as a unit. Since much of the time required to perform I/O operations is taken up in seeking and positioning, reading 8 pages in a 16K I/O performs nearly eight times as fast as a single-page 2K I/O. If your queries are performing table scans, as described in this chapter, you will often see great performance gains using large I/O.

See Chapter 15, "Memory Use and Performance," for more information on configuring memory caches for large I/O.

Caches and Object Bindings

A table can be bound to a specific cache. If a table is not bound to a specific cache, but its database is bound to a cache, all of its I/O takes place in that cache. Otherwise, its I/O takes place in the default cache. The default cache can also have buffer pools configured for large I/O. If your applications include some heap tables, they will probably perform better when bound to a cache that allows large I/O, or when the default cache is configured for large I/O.

Heaps, I/O, and Cache Strategies

Each SQL Server data cache is managed as an MRU/LRU (most recently used/least recently used) chain of buffers. As buffers age in the cache, they move from the MRU end toward the LRU end. When pages in the cache that have been changed pass a point on the MRU/LRU chain called the **wash marker**, SQL Server initiates an asynchronous write on the page. This ensures that when the pages reach the LRU end of the cache, they are clean, and can be reused.

Overview of Cache Strategies

SQL Server has two major strategies for using its data cache efficiently:

- LRU Replacement Strategy reads the data pages sequentially into the cache, replacing a "least recently used" buffer. The buffer is placed on the MRU end of the data buffer chain. It moves down the cache toward the LRU end as more pages are read into the cache.

  SQL Server uses this strategy for:

  - Statements that modify data on pages

  - Pages that are needed more than once by a single query

  - OAM pages

- Many index pages
- Queries where LRU strategy is specified in the query

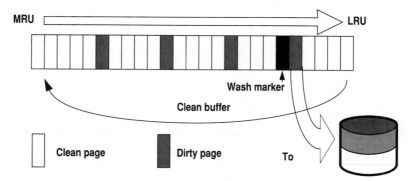

Figure 3-8: LRU strategy takes a clean page from the LRU end of the cache

- "Fetch-and-discard" or MRU replacement strategy is often used for table scanning on heaps. This strategy reads a page into the cache just before the wash marker.

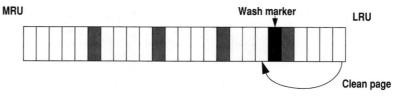

Figure 3-9: MRU strategy places pages just before the wash marker

Fetch-and-discard is most often used for queries where a page is needed only once by the query. This includes:

- Most table scans of large heaps in queries that do not use joins
- One or more tables in certain joins
- The fetch-and-discard strategy is used only on pages actually read from the disk for the query. If a page is already in cache due to earlier activity on the table, the page is placed at the MRU end of the cache.

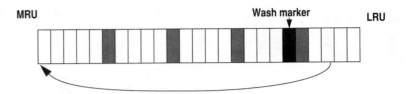

Figure 3-10: Finding a needed page in cache

SQL Server usually uses the fetch-and-discard strategy when it scans a large heap table and the table is not the inner table of a join. Each page for the table is needed only once. If the LRU strategy were used, the pages would move to the top of the MRU chain and force other pages out of cache.

Select Operations and Caching

Under most conditions, single-table select operations on a heap use:

- The largest I/O available to the table
- Fetch-and-discard (MRU) replacement strategy

For heaps, select operations performing extent-sized I/O can be very effective. SQL Server can read sequentially through all the extents in a table.

Unless the heap is being scanned as the inner table of a join, the data pages are needed only once for the query, so MRU replacement strategy reads and discards the pages from cache.

➤ *Note*

Large I/O on heaps is effective as long as the page chains are not fragmented. See "Maintaining Heaps" on page 52 for information on maintaining heaps.

Data Modification and Caching

SQL Server tries to minimize disk writes by keeping changed pages in cache. Many users can make changes to a data page while it resides in the cache. Their changes are logged in the transaction log, but the changed pages are not written to disk immediately.

Caching and Inserts on Heaps

Inserts on heaps take place on the last page of the heap table. If an insert is the first row on a new page for the table, a clean data buffer is allocated to store the data page, as shown in Figure 3-11. This page starts to move down the MRU/LRU chain in the data cache as other processes read pages into memory.

If a second insert to the page takes place while the page is still in memory, the page is located in cache, and moves back to the top of the MRU/LRU chain.

**First insert on a page takes a clean page
from the LRU and puts it on the MRU**

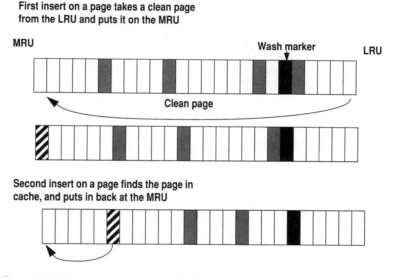

**Second insert on a page finds the page in
cache, and puts in back at the MRU**

Figure 3-11: Inserts to a heap page in the data cache

The changed data page remains in cache until it moves past the wash marker or until a checkpoint or the housekeeper task writes it to disk. "The Data Cache" on page 395 explains more about these processes.

Caching and Update and Delete Operations on Heaps

When you update or delete a row from a heap table, the effects on the data cache are similar to the process for inserts. If a page is already in the cache, the whole buffer (a single page, or up to eight pages, depending on the I/O size) is placed on the MRU end of the chain, and the row is changed. If the page is not in cache, it is read from the disk into a clean buffer from the LRU end of the cache. Its placement on the MRU/LRU chain depends on whether a row on the page needs to be changed:

- If the page needs to be changed, the buffer is placed on the MRU end. It remains in cache, where it can be updated repeatedly or be read by other users before being flushed to disk.

- If the page does not need to be changed, the buffer is placed just before the wash marker in the cache.

Heaps: Pros and Cons

Sequential disk access is efficient, however, the entire table must always be scanned to find any value.

Batch inserts can do efficient sequential I/O. However, there is a potential bottleneck on the last page if multiple processes try to insert data concurrently, unless the heap table is partitioned.

Heaps work well for small tables and for tables where changes are infrequent, but do not work well for large tables.

Guidelines for Using Heaps

Heaps can be useful for tables that:

- Are fairly small and use only a few pages
- Do not require direct access to a single random row
- Do not require ordering of result sets
- Have nonunique rows and the above characteristics
- Do not have large numbers of inserts and updates

Partitioned heaps are useful for tables with frequent, large volumes of batch inserts where the overhead of dropping and creating clustered indexes is unacceptable. With this exception, there are very few justifications for heap tables. *Most applications perform better with clustered indexes on the tables.*

Maintaining Heaps

Over time, I/O on heaps can become inefficient. Deletes and updates:

- Can result in many partially filled pages

- Can lead to inefficient large I/O, since page chains will not be contiguous on the extents

Methods for Maintaining Heaps

There are two methods to reclaim space in heaps after deletes and updates have created empty space on pages or have caused fragmentation:

- Create and then drop a clustered index
- Use **bcp** (the bulk copy utility) and **truncate table**

Reclaiming Space by Creating a Clustered Index

You can create and drop a clustered index on a heap table in order to reclaim space if updates and deletes have created many partially full pages in a heap table. To create a clustered index, you must have free space in the database of at least 120 percent of the table size. Since the leaf level of the clustered index consists of the actual data rows of the table, the process of creating the index makes a complete copy of the table before it deallocates the old pages. The additional 20 percent provides room for the root and intermediate index levels. If you use long keys for the index, it will take more space.

Reclaiming Space Using *bcp*

The steps to reclaim space with **bcp** are:

1. Copy the table out to a file using **bcp**.
2. Truncate the table with the **truncate table** command.
3. Copy the table back in again with **bcp**.

For more information on **bcp**, see the *SQL Server* utility programs manual for your platform.

The Transaction Log: A Special Heap Table

SQL Server's transaction log is a special heap table that stores information about data modifications in the database. The transaction log is always a heap table; each new transaction record is appended to the end of the log.

Later chapters in this book describe ways to enhance the performance of the transaction log. The most important technique is to use the **log on** clause to **create database** to place your transaction log on a separate device from your data. See Chapter 14, "Creating User Databases," in the *System Administration Guide* for more information on creating databases.

Transaction log writes occur frequently. Do not let them contend with other I/O in the database, which usually happens at scattered locations on the data pages. Place logs on separate physical devices from the data and index pages. Since the log is sequential, the disk head on the log device will rarely need to perform seeks, and you can maintain a high I/O rate to the log.

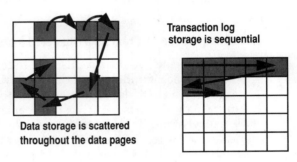

Data storage is scattered
throughout the data pages

Transaction log
storage is sequential

Figure 3-12: Data vs. log I/O

Besides recovery, these kinds of operations require reading the transaction log:

- Any data modification that is performed in deferred mode.
- Triggers that contain references to the inserted and deleted tables. These tables are built from transaction log records when the tables are queried.
- Transaction rollbacks.

In most cases, the transaction log pages for these kinds of queries are still available in the data cache when SQL Server needs to read them, and disk I/O is not required.

From Heaps to Indexes

This chapter discussed SQL Server's behavior when your data has no indexes. Except in certain instances, it is always better to index data and to provide SQL Server with a clustered index on every table.

Installing indexes must be done with an understanding of how they function. Since indexes are only useful if they are used in query processing, you need to understand their structure and function. This is fundamental information for applying and tuning indexes intelligently.

Chapter 4 describes how SQL Server stores indexes and how it uses indexes to speed data retrieval for select, update, delete, and insert operations.

After Chapter 4 covers how indexes work, Chapter 5 gives you some formulas for determining the size of your database objects. Without a fairly clear picture of how large database objects are, you will not be able to estimate the I/O load that queries entail.

4 How Indexes Work

Performance and Indexes

Indexes are the most important element of a physical design that leads to high performance:

- Indexes help prevent table scans. Instead of reading hundreds of data pages, a few index pages and data pages can satisfy many queries.

- For some queries, data can be retrieved from a nonclustered index without ever accessing the data rows.

- Clustered indexes can randomize data inserts, avoiding insert "hot spots" on the last page of a table.

- Indexes can help avoid sorts, if the index order matches the order of columns in an **order by** clause.

In addition to their performance benefits, indexes can enforce the uniqueness of data.

Indexing requires trade-offs. While indexes speed retrieval of data, they can slow down data modifications, since most changes to the data also require updating indexes. That is, proper indexing can produce the most marked performance improvements on read-intensive applications.

Optimal indexing demands:

- An understanding of the behavior of queries that access unindexed heap tables, tables with clustered indexes, and tables with nonclustered indexes

- An understanding of the mix of queries that run on your server

- An understanding of the SQL Server optimizer

What Are Indexes?

Indexes are database objects that can be created for a table to speed direct access to specific data rows. Indexes store the values of the key

or keys that were named when the index was created and logical
pointers to the data pages or to other index pages.

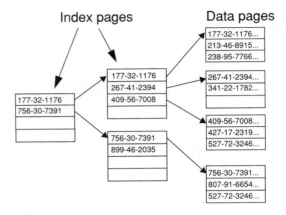

Figure 4-1: A simplified index schematic

Types of Indexes

SQL Server provides two types of indexes:

- Clustered indexes, where the table data is physically stored in the
  order of the keys on the index.

- Nonclustered indexes, where the storage order of data in the table
  is not related to index keys.

You can create only one clustered index on a table because there is
only one possible physical ordering of the data rows. You can create
up to 249 nonclustered indexes per table.

A table that has no clustered index is called a heap. The rows in the
table are in no particular order, and all new rows are added to the
end of the table. Chapter 3, "Data Storage," discusses heaps and SQL
operations on heaps.

Index Pages

Index entries are stored as rows on index pages in a format similar to
that for data rows on data pages. Index entries store the key values
and pointers to lower levels of the index, to the data pages (for
clustered indexes) or to the data rows (for the leaf level of
nonclustered indexes).

SQL Server uses **B-tree indexing**, in which all leaf pages are the same distance from the root page of the index, so each node in the index structure can have multiple children.

Index entries are usually much smaller than a data row in a data page, and index pages are much more densely populated. A data row might have 200 bytes (including row overhead), so there would be 10 rows per page. An index on a 15-byte field would have about 100 rows per index page (the pointers require 4–9 bytes per row, depending on the type of index and the index level).

Indexes can have multiple levels:

- Root level
- Leaf level
- Intermediate level

Root Level

The root level is the highest level of the index. There is only one root page. If the table is very small, so that the entire index fits on a single page, there are no intermediate levels, and the root page stores pointers to the data pages. For larger tables, the root page stores pointers to the intermediate level index pages or the leaf pages.

Leaf Level

The lowest level of the index is the leaf level. At the leaf level, the index contains a key value for each row in the table, and the rows are stored in sorted order by the index key:

- For clustered indexes, the leaf level is the data. No other level of the index contains one index row for each data row.

- For nonclustered indexes, the leaf level contains the index key values, a pointer to the page where the rows are stored, and a pointer to the rows on the data page. The leaf level is the level just above the data, and contains one index row for each data row, in order by the key values.

Intermediate Level

All levels between root and leaf are intermediate levels. An index on a large table or an index using long keys may have many intermediate levels. A very small table may not have an intermediate level; the root pages point directly to the leaf level.

Each level (except the root level) of the index is a page chain: The page headers contain next page and previous page pointers to other pages at the same index level.

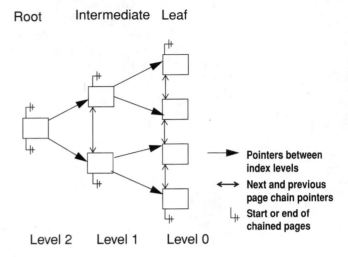

Figure 4-2: Index levels and page chains

For nonclustered indexes, the leaf level is always level 0. In clustered indexes, the level just above the data level is level 0. Each higher level is numbered sequentially, with the root page having the highest value.

B-trees are self-maintaining structures, obtaining additional space as needed without having to reorganize pages.

Clustered Indexes

In clustered indexes, leaf-level pages are also the data pages. The data rows are physically ordered by the index key. Physical ordering means that:

- All entries on a page are in index key order.
- By following the "next page" pointers at the data level, you read the entire table in index key order.

On the root and intermediate pages, each entry points to a page on the next level.

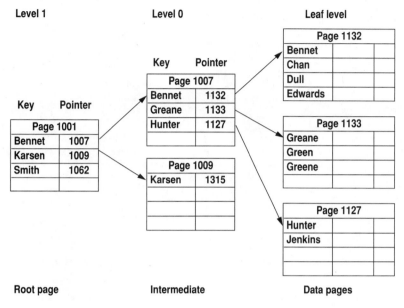

Figure 4-3: Clustered index on last name

Clustered Indexes and Select Operations

To select a particular last name using a clustered index, SQL Server first uses *sysindexes* to find the root page. It examines the values on the root page and then follows page pointers, performing a binary search on each page it accesses as it traverses the index. In this example, there is a clustered index on the "last name" column.

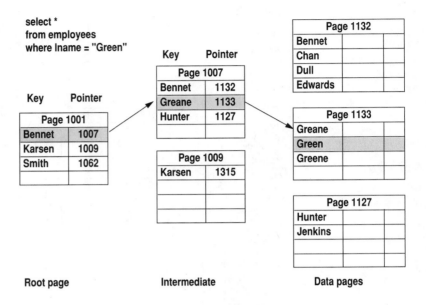

Figure 4-4: Selecting a row using a clustered index

On the root level page, "Green" is greater than "Bennet," but less than Karsten, so the pointer for "Bennet" is followed to page 1007. On page 1007, "Green" is greater than "Greane," but less than "Hunter," so the pointer to page 1133 is followed to the leaf level page, where the row is located and returned to the user.

This retrieval via the clustered index requires:

- One read for the root level of the index

- One read for the intermediate level

- One read for the data page

These reads may come either from cache (called a **logical read**) or from disk (called a **physical read**). "Indexes and I/O Statistics" on page 122 provides more information on physical and logical I/O and SQL Server tools for reporting it. On tables that are frequently used, the higher levels of the indexes are often found in cache, with lower levels and data pages being read from disk. See "Indexes and Caching" on page 79 for more details on how indexes use the cache.

This description covers point queries, queries that use the index key in the **where** clause to find a single row or a small set of rows. Chapter

7, "The SQL Server Query Optimizer," describes processing more complex types of queries.

Clustered Indexes and Insert Operations

When you insert a row into a table with a clustered index, the data row must be placed in physical order according to the key value on the table. Other rows on the data page move down on the page, as needed, to make room for the new value. As long as there is room for the new row on the page, the insert does not affect any other pages in the database. The clustered index is used to find the location for the new row. Figure 4-5 shows a simple case where there is room on an existing data page for the new row. In this case, the key values in the index do not need to change.

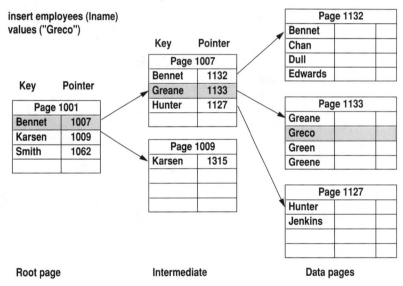

Figure 4-5: Inserting a row into a table with a clustered index

Page Splitting on Full Data Pages

If there is not enough room on the data page for the new row, a page split must be performed:

- A new data page is allocated on an extent already in use by the table. If there is no free page, a new extent is allocated.

- The next and previous page pointers on adjacent pages are changed to incorporate the new page in the page chain. This requires reading those pages into memory and locking them.

- Approximately one-half of the rows are moved to the new page, with the new row inserted in order.

- The higher levels of the clustered index change to point to the new page.

- If the table also has nonclustered indexes, all of their pointers to the affected data rows must be changed to point to the new page and row locations. See "Nonclustered Indexes" on page 69.

There are some cases where page splitting is handled slightly differently See "Exceptions to Page Splitting" on page 65.

In Figure 4-6, a page split occurs, which requires adding a new row to an existing index page, page 1007.

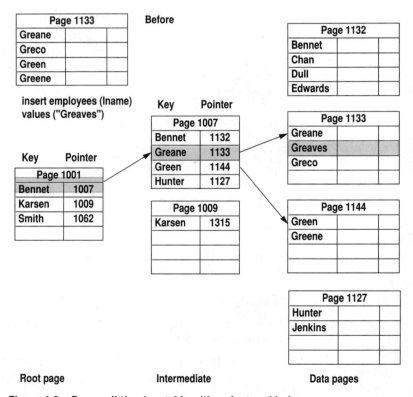

Figure 4-6: Page splitting in a table with a clustered index

How Indexes Work

Exceptions to Page Splitting

There are exceptions to the 50-50 page split:

- If you insert a huge row that cannot fit on either page before or after a page split, two new pages are allocated, one for the huge row and one for the rows that follow it.

- If possible, SQL Server keeps duplicate values together when it splits pages.

- If SQL Server detects that all inserts are taking place at the end of the page, due to a increasing key value, the page is not split when it is time to insert a new row that does not fit at the bottom of the page. Instead, a new page is allocated, and the row is placed on the new page.

- SQL Server also detects when inserts are taking place in order at other locations on the page also and the page is split at the insertion point.

Page Splitting on Index Pages

If a new row needs to be added to a full index page, the page split process on the index page is similar to the data page split. A new page is allocated, and half the index rows are moved to the new page. A new row is inserted at the next highest level of the index to point to the new index page.

Performance Impacts of Page Splitting

Page splits are expensive operations. In addition to the actual work of moving rows, allocating pages, and logging the operations, the cost is increased by:

- Updating the clustered index itself

- Updating all nonclustered indexes entries that point to the rows that are affected by the split

When you create a clustered index for a table that will grow over time, you may want to use **fillfactor** to leave room on data pages and index pages. This reduces the number of page splits for a time. See "Choosing Fillfactors for Indexes" on page 158.

Overflow Pages

Special overflow pages are created for non-unique clustered indexes when a newly inserted row has the same key as the last row on a full data page. A new data page is allocated and linked into the page chain, and the newly inserted row is placed on the new page.

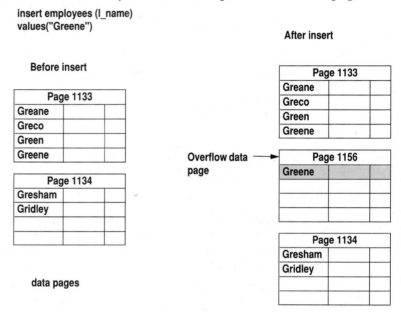

**insert employees (l_name)
values("Greene")**

Figure 4-7: Adding an overflow page to a nonunique clustered index

The only rows that will be placed on this overflow page are additional rows with the same key value. In a non-unique clustered index with many duplicate key values, there can be numerous overflow pages for the same value.

The clustered index does not contain pointers directly to overflow pages. Instead, the next page pointers are used to follow the chain of overflow pages until a value is found that does not match the search value.

Clustered Indexes and Delete Operations

When you delete a row from a table that has a clustered index, other rows on the page move up to fill the empty space so that data remains contiguous on the page. Figure 4-8 shows a page with four rows before a delete removes the second row on the page. The following two rows move up.

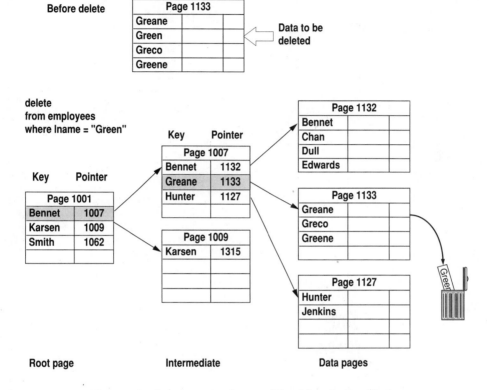

Figure 4-8: Deleting a row from a table with a clustered index

Deleting the Last Row on a Page

If you delete the last row on a data page:

- The page is deallocated.

- The next and previous page pointers on the adjacent pages are changed.

- The row that points to that page in the intermediate levels of the index is removed.

If the deallocated data page is on the same extent as other pages belonging to the table, it is used again when that table needs an additional page. If the deallocated data page is the last page on the extent that belongs to the table, the extent is also deallocated, and it becomes available for the expansion of other objects in the database.

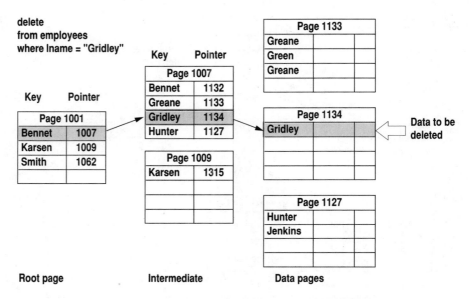

Figure 4-9: Deleting the last row on a page (before the delete)

In Figure 4-10, which shows the table after the delete, the pointer to the deleted page has been removed from index page 1007 and the following index rows on the page have been moved up to keep the space used contiguous.

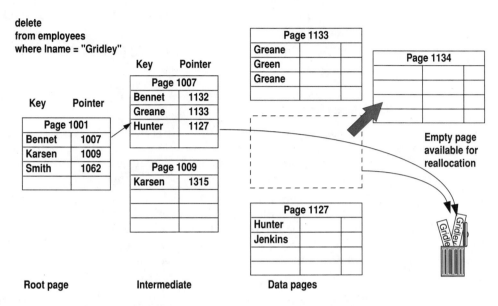

Figure 4-10: Deleting the last row on a page (after the delete)

Index Page Merges

If you delete a pointer from an index page, leaving only one row on that page, the row is moved onto an adjacent page, and the empty page is deallocated. The pointers on the parent page are updated to reflect the changes.

Nonclustered Indexes

The B-tree works much the same for nonclustered indexes as it does for clustered indexes, but there are some differences. In nonclustered indexes:

- The leaf pages are not the same as the data pages.
- The leaf level stores one key-pointer pair for **each row** in the table.
- The leaf level pages store the index keys and page pointers, plus a pointer to the row offset table on the data page. This combination of page pointer plus the row offset number is called the **row ID**, or RID.

- The root and intermediate levels store index keys and page pointers to other index pages. They also store the row ID of the key's data row.

With keys of the same size, nonclustered indexes require more space than clustered indexes.

Leaf Pages Revisited

To clearly understand the difference between clustered and nonclustered indexes, it is important to recall the definition of the leaf page of an index: It is the lowest level of the index where all of the keys for the index appear in sorted order.

In clustered indexes, the data rows are stored in order by the index keys, so by definition, the data level is the leaf level. There is no other level of a clustered index that contains one index row for each data row. Clustered indexes are sparse indexes. The level above the data contains one pointer for every data page.

In nonclustered indexes, the row just "above" the data is the leaf level: it contains a key-pointer pair for each data row. Nonclustered indexes are dense. At the level above the data, they contain one row for each data row.

Row IDs and the Offset Table

Row IDs are managed by an offset table on each data page. The offset table starts at the last byte on the page. There is a 2-byte offset table entry for each row on the page. As rows are added, the offset table grows from the end of the page upward as the rows fill from the top of the page. The offset table stores the byte at which its corresponding row on the page starts.

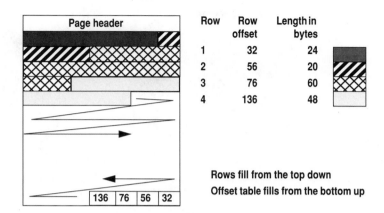

Row	Row offset	Length in bytes
1	32	24
2	56	20
3	76	60
4	136	48

Rows fill from the top down
Offset table fills from the bottom up

Figure 4-11: Data page with the offset table

When additional rows are inserted between existing rows on the page, an additional value is added to the row offset table, and the offsets for each row are adjusted. The row ID points to the offset table, and the offset table points to the start of the data on the page. When rows are added or deleted, changes are made to the offset table, but the row IDs the index pointers for existing rows do not change. If you delete a row from the page, its row offset is set to 0.

Figure 4-12 shows the same page as Figure 4-11 after a new row 20-byte row has been inserted as the second row on the page. The existing rows have moved down and their offset values have increased. A row offset entry for the new row has been added. Note that the row offset values are not sequential.

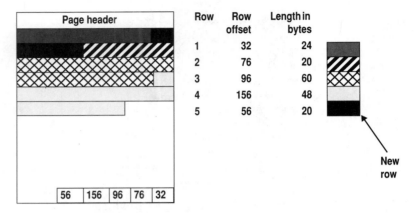

Row	Row offset	Length in bytes
1	32	24
2	76	20
3	96	60
4	156	48
5	56	20

New row

Figure 4-12: Row offset table after an insert

Nonclustered Index Structure

The table illustrated in Figure 4-13 shows a nonclustered index on *lname*. The data rows at the far right show pages in ascending order by *employee_id* (10, 11, 12, and so on), due to a clustered index on that column.

The root and intermediate pages store:

- The key value
- The row ID
- The pointer to the next level of the index

The leaf level stores:

- The key value
- The row ID

The row ID in higher levels of the index is essential for indexes that allow duplicate keys. If a data modification changes the index key or deletes a row, the row ID positively identifies all occurrences of the key at all index levels.

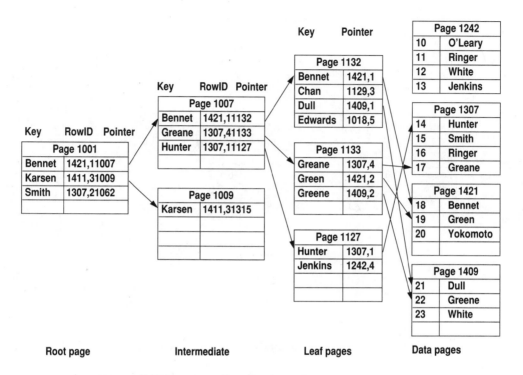

Figure 4-13: Nonclustered index structure

Nonclustered Indexes and Select Operations

When you select a row using a nonclustered index, the search starts at the root level. Just as with clustered indexes, the *sysindexes* table stores the page number for the root page of the nonclustered index.

In the example in Figure 4-14, "Green" is greater than "Bennet," but less than "Karsen," so the pointer to page 1007 is followed. "Green" is greater than "Greane," but less than "Hunter," so the pointer to page 1133 is followed. Page 1133 is the leaf page, showing that the row for "Green" is the second position on page 1421. This page is fetched, the "2" byte in the offset table is checked, and the row is returned from the byte position on the data page.

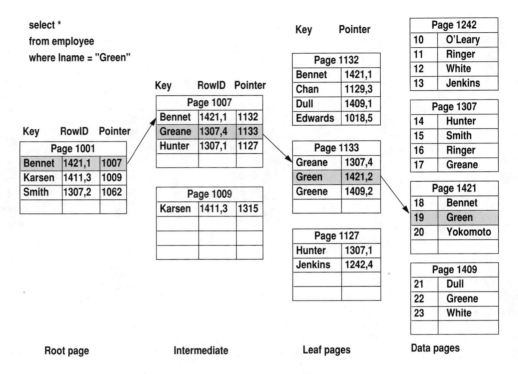

Figure 4-14: Selecting rows using a nonclustered index

Nonclustered Index Performance

The query in Figure 4-14 has the following I/O:

- One read for the root level page
- One read for the intermediate level page
- One read for the leaf level page
- One read for the data page

If your applications use a particular nonclustered index frequently, the root and intermediate pages will probably be in cache, so only one or two actual disk I/Os need to be performed. When SQL Server finds a page it needs in the cache, it is called a logical read. When SQL Server must perform disk I/O, this is called a physical read. When a physical read is performed, a logical read is required too.

Nonclustered Indexes and Insert Operations

When you insert rows into a heap that has a nonclustered index, the insert goes to the last page of the table. If the heap is partitioned, the insert goes to the last page on one of the partitions. Then the nonclustered index is updated to include the new row. If the table has a clustered index, it is used to find the location for the row. The clustered index is updated, if necessary, and then each nonclustered index is updated to include the new row.

Figure 4-15 shows an insert into a table with a clustered index. Since the ID value is 24, the row is placed at the end of the table. A row is also inserted into the leaf level of the nonclustered index, containing the row ID of the new values.

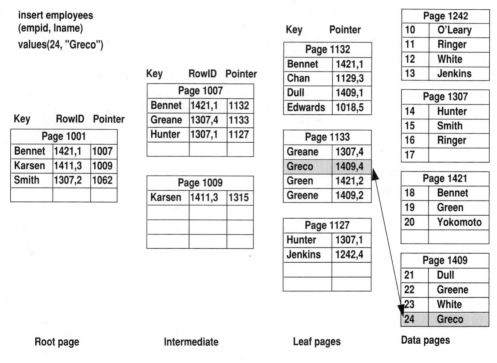

| Root page | Intermediate | Leaf pages | Data pages |

Figure 4-15: An insert with a nonclustered index

Nonclustered Indexes and Delete Operations

When you delete a row from a table, the query can use a nonclustered index on the column or columns in the **where** clause to locate the data row to delete. The row in the leaf level of the nonclustered index that points to the data row is also removed. If there are other nonclustered indexes on the table, the rows on the leaf level of those indexes are also deleted.

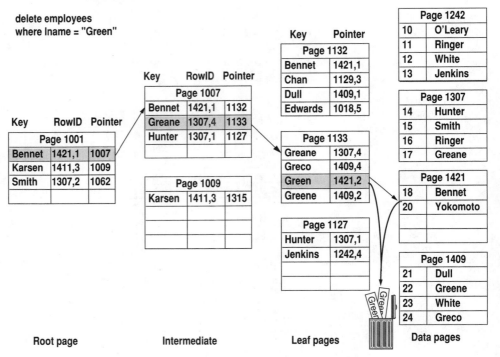

Figure 4-16: Deleting a row from a table with a nonclustered index

If the delete operation removes the last row on the data page, the page is deallocated and the adjacent page pointers are adjusted. References to the page are also deleted in higher levels of the index.

If the delete operation leaves only a single row on an index intermediate page, index pages may be merged, as with clustered indexes. See "Index Page Merges" on page 69.

There is no automatic page merging on data pages, so if your applications make many random deletes, you can end up with data pages that have only a single row, or a few rows, on a page.

Index Covering

Index covering is a nonclustered indexing tactic that can produce dramatic performance improvements. If you create a composite nonclustered index on each column referenced in the query's select list and in any **where, having, group by,** and **order by** clauses, the query can be satisfied by accessing only the index. Since the leaf level of nonclustered indexes contains the key values for each row in a table, queries that access only the key values can retrieve the information by using the leaf level of the nonclustered index as if it were the actual data. This is index covering.

You can create indexes on more than one key, called composite indexes. Composite indexes can have up to 16 columns adding up to a maximum 256 bytes.

A nonclustered index that covers the query is usually faster than a clustered index, because it reads fewer pages: index rows are smaller, more rows fit on the page, so fewer pages need to be read.

A clustered index, by definition, is covered. Its leaf level contains the complete data rows. This also means that scanning at that level (that is, the entire table) is the same as performing a table scan.

There are two forms of optimization using indexes that cover the query:

- The matching index scan
- The non-matching index scan

For both types of covered queries, the nonclustered index keys must contain all of the columns named in the select list and any clauses of your query: **where, having, group by,** and **order by.** Matching scans have additional requirements. "Choosing Composite Indexes" on page 142 describes query types that make good use of covering indexes.

Matching Index Scans

This type of index covering lets you skip the last read for each row returned by the query, the read that fetches the data page. For point queries that return only a single row, the performance gain is slight—just one page. For range queries, the performance gain is larger, since the covering index saves one read for each row returned by the query.

In addition to having all columns named in the query included in the index, the columns in the **where** clauses of the query must include the leading column of the columns in the index. For example, for an index on columns A, B, C, D, the following sets can perform matching scans: A, AB, ABC, AC, ACD, ABD, AD, and ABCD. The columns B, BC, BCD, BD, C, CD, or D do not include the leading column and cannot be used in matching scans.

When doing a matching index scan, SQL Server uses standard index access methods to move from the root of the index to the nonclustered leaf page that contains the first row. It can use information from the statistics page to estimate the number of pages that need to be read.

In Figure 4-17, the nonclustered index on *lname, fname* covers the query. The **where** clause includes the leading column, and all columns in the select list are included in the index.

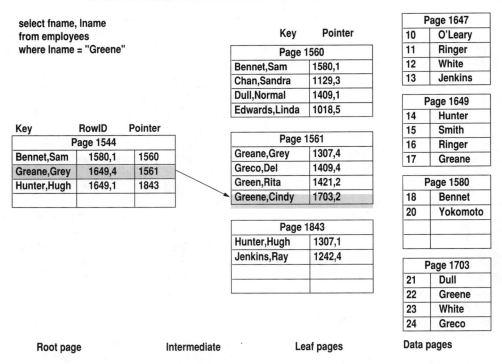

Figure 4-17: Matching index access does not have to read the data row

Nonmatching Index Scans

When the columns specified in the **where** clause do not name the leading column in the index, but all of the columns named in the select list and other query clauses (such as **group by** or **having**) are included in the index, SQL Server saves I/O by scanning the leaf level of the nonclustered index, rather than scanning the table. It cannot perform a matching scan because the first column of the index is not specified.

The query in Figure 4-18 shows a nonmatching index scan. This query does not use the leading columns on the index, but all columns required in the query are in the nonclustered index on *lname, fname, emp_id*. The nonmatching scan must examine all rows on the leaf level. It scans all leaf level index pages, starting from the first page. It has no way of knowing how many rows might match the query conditions so it must examine every row in the index.

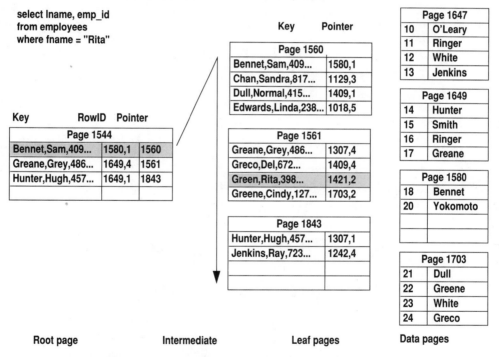

Figure 4-18: A nonmatching index scan

Indexes and Caching

"How SQL Server Performs I/O for Heap Operations" on page 47 introduces the basic concepts of the SQL Server data cache, and shows how caches are used when reading heap tables. Indexes pages get special handling in the data cache, as follows:

- Root and intermediate index pages always use LRU strategy.

- Nonclustered index scans can use fetch-and-discard strategy.

- Index pages can use one cache while the data pages use a different cache.

- Index pages can cycle through the cache many times, if **number of index trips** is configured.

When a query that uses an index is executed, the root, intermediate, leaf, and data pages are read in that order. If these pages are not in cache, they are read into the MRU end of the cache and move toward the LRU end as additional pages are read in.

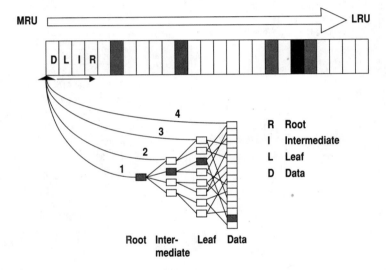

Figure 4-19: Caching used for a point query via a nonclustered index

Each time a page is found in cache, it is moved to the MRU end of the page chain, so the root page and higher levels of the index tend to stay in the cache. Figure 4-20 shows a root page moving back to the top of the cache for a second query using the same index.

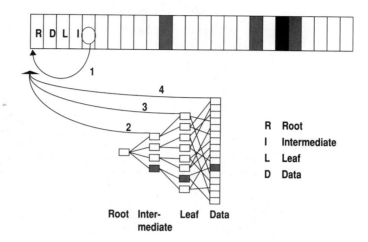

Figure 4-20: Finding the root index page in cache

Using Separate Caches for Data and Index Pages

Indexes and the tables they index can use different caches. A System Administrator or table owner can bind a clustered or nonclustered index to one cache, and its table to another.

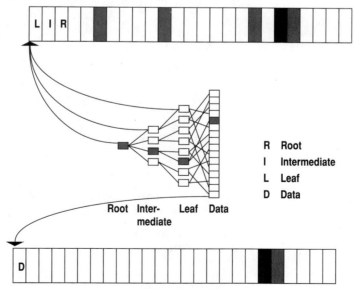

Figure 4-21: Caching with separate caches for data and log

Index Trips Through the Cache

A special strategy keeps index pages in cache. Data pages make only a single trip through the cache: They are read in at the MRU end or the cache or placed just before the wash marker, depending on the cache strategy chosen for the query. Once the pages reach the LRU end of the cache, the buffer for that page is reused when another page needs to be read into cache.

Index pages can make multiple trips through the cache, controlled by a counter. When the counter is greater than 0 for an index page and it reaches the LRU end of the page chain, the counter is decremented by one, and the page is placed at the MRU end again.

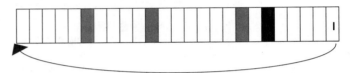

Figure 4-22: Index page recycling in the cache

By default, the number of trips that an index page makes through the cache is set to 0. A System Administrator can set the configuration parameter **number of index trips**. For more information, see "number of index trips" in Chapter 11 of the *System Administration Guide*.

Indexing and the Size of Database Objects

In order accurately to assess the effects of indexing, you should know the size of your tables and indexes, and you should be able to predict the size of your database objects as your tables grow. Knowing this information will help you:

- Decide on storage allocation, especially if you use segments
- Decide whether it is possible to improve performance for specific queries
- Determine the optimum size for named data caches for specific tables and indexes

Chapter 5, "Estimating the Size of Tables and Indexes" provides you with the formulas you need to acquire this essential information.

5 Estimating the Size of Tables and Indexes

Tools for Sizing Database Objects

SQL Server provides several tools that provide information on current object size or that can predict future size:

- The system procedure **sp_spaceused** reports on the current size of an existing table and any indexes.

- The system procedure **sp_estspace** can predict the size of a table and its indexes, given a number of rows as a parameter.

- The output of some **dbcc** commands report on page usage as well as performing database consistency checks.

You can also compute the size using formulas provided in this chapter.

Why Should You Care about the Size of Objects?

Knowing the size of your tables and indexes is key to understanding query and system behavior. Size data is essential at several stages of tuning work for:

- Understanding **statistics io** reports for a specific query plan. Chapter 6, "Indexing for Performance," describes how to use **statistics io** to examine the I/O performed.

- Understanding the optimizer's choice of query plan. SQL Server's cost-based optimizer estimates the physical and logical I/O required for each possible access method, and chooses the cheapest access method. If you feel a particular query plan is unusual, using **dbcc traceon(302)** can often show why the optimizer made the decision.

- Determining object placement, based on the size of database objects and the expected I/O patterns on that object. You can improve performance by distributing database objects across physical devices so that reads and writes to disk are evenly distributed. Object placement is described in Chapter 13, "Controlling Physical Data Placement."

- Understanding changes in performance. If objects grow, their performance characteristics can change. One example is a table that is heavily used and is usually 100% cached. If that table grows too large for its cache, queries that access the table can suddenly suffer much worse performance. This is particularly true for joins requiring multiple scans.

- Capacity planning also requires knowing object sizes. Whether you are designing a new system or planning for growth of an existing system, you will need to know the space requirements in order to plan for physical disks and memory needs.

- Understanding performance-monitor output. Output from SQL Server Monitor and from **sp_sysmon** reports on physical I/O.

Effects of Data Modifications on Object Sizes

The **sp_spaceused** and **dbcc** commands report actual space usage. The other methods presented in this chapter provide size estimates.

Over time, the effects of randomly distributed data modifications on a set of tables tends to produce data pages and index pages that average approximately 75 percent full. The major factors are:

- When you insert a row onto a full page of a table with a clustered index, the page splits, leaving two pages that are about 50 percent full.

- When you delete rows from heaps or from tables with clustered indexes, the space used on the page decreases. You can have pages that contain very few rows or even a single row.

- After some deletes and page splits have occurred, inserting rows into tables with a clustered index tends to fill up pages that have been split or pages where rows have been deleted.

Page splits also take place when rows need to be inserted into full index pages, so index pages also tend to end up being approximately 75 percent full.

OAM Pages and Size Statistics

Information about the number of pages allocated to and used by an object is stored on the OAM pages for tables and indexes. This information is updated by most SQL Server processes when pages are allocated or deallocated. For a description of OAM pages, see "Object Allocation Map (OAM) Pages" on page 40.

The **sp_spaceused** system procedure reads these values to provide quick space estimates. Some **dbcc** commands update these values while they perform consistency checks.

sp_spaceused uses system functions to locate the size values on the
OAM pages. Here is a simple query that uses the OAM page values,
returning the number of used and reserved pages for all user tables
(those with object IDs greater than 100):

```
select
substring(object_name(id) + "." +name, 1,25) Name,
    data_pgs(id, doampg) "Data Used",
    reserved_pgs(id, doampg) "Data Res",
    data_pgs(id, ioampg) "Index Used",
    reserved_pgs(id, ioampg) "Index Res"
from sysindexes
where id > 100
```

The "Name" field in this query reports the table and index name in
the form "tablename.indexname".

Name	Data Used	Data Res	Index Used	Index Res
authors.authors	223	224	0	0
publishers.publishers	2	8	0	0
roysched.roysched	1	8	0	0
sales.sales	1	8	0	0
salesdetail.salesdetail	1	8	0	0
titleauthor.titleauthor	106	112	0	0
titles.title_id_cix	621	632	7	15
titles.title_ix	0	0	128	136
titles.type_price_ix	0	0	85	95
stores.stores	23	24	0	0
discounts.discounts	3	8	0	0
shipments.shipments	1	8	0	0
blurbs.blurbs	1	8	0	0
blurbs.tblurbs	0	0	7	8

Using *sp_spaceused* to Display Object Size

The system procedure **sp_spaceused** reads values stored on the OAM page for an object to provide a quick report on the space used by an object.

```
sp_spaceused titles
```

name	rowtotal	reserved	data	index_size	unused
titles	5000	1756 KB	1242 KB	440 KB	74 KB

The *rowtotal* value can be inaccurate at times; not all SQL Server processes update this value on the OAM page. The commands **update statistics**, **dbcc checktable**, and **dbcc checkdb** correct the *rowtotal* value on the OAM page.

Table 5-1: sp_spaceused output

Column	Meaning
rowtotal	Reports an estimate of the number of rows. The value is read from the OAM page. Though not always exact, this estimate is much quicker and leads to less contention than **select count(*)**.
reserved	Reports pages reserved for use by the table and its indexes. It includes both the used unused pages in extents allocated to the objects. It is the sum of *data*, *index_size*, and *unused*.
data	Reports the kilobytes on pages used by the table.

Table 5-1: sp_spaceused output (continued)

Column	Meaning
index_size	Reports the total kilobytes on pages in use for the indexes.
unused	Reports the kilobytes of unused pages in extents allocated to the object, including the unused pages for the object's indexes.

If you want to see the size of the indexes reported separately, use this command:

```
sp_spaceused titles, 1
index_name                 size        reserved    unused
-------------------        --------    ---------   ---------
title_id_cix               14 KB       1294 KB     38 KB
title_ix                   256 KB      272 KB      16 KB
type_price_ix              170 KB      190 KB      20 KB

name          rowtotal  reserved    data        index_size  unused
-----------   --------  ----------  ---------   ----------  --------
titles        5000        1756 KB    1242 KB       440 KB     74 KB
```

For clustered indexes, the *size* value represents the space used for the root and intermediate index pages. The *reserved* value includes the index size and the reserved and used data pages, which are, by definition, the leaf level of a clustered index.

➤ **Note**

The "1" in the **sp_spaceused** syntax indicates that detailed index information should be printed. It has no relation to index IDs or other information.

Advantages of *sp_spaceused*

The advantages of **sp_spaceused** are:

- It provides quick reports without excessive I/O and locking, since it uses only values in the table and index OAM pages to return results.

- It shows space reserved for expansion of the object, but not currently used to store data.

Disadvantages of *sp_spaceused*

The disadvantages of **sp_spaceused** are:

- It may report inaccurate counts for row total and space usage.
- It does not correct inaccuracies as **dbcc** does.
- It scans *sysindexes*, adding traffic to an already busy system table.
- Output is in kilobytes, while most query-tuning activity uses pages as a unit of measure.

Using *dbcc* to Display Object Size

Some of the **dbcc** commands that verify database consistency provide reports on space used by tables and indexes. Generally, these commands should not be used on production databases for routine space checking. They perform extensive I/O and some of them require locking of database objects. See Table 17-1 on page 17-14 of the *System Administration Guide* for a comparison of locking and performance effects.

If your System Administrator runs regular **dbcc** checks and saves results to a file, you can use this output to see the size of your objects and to track changes in table and index size.

If you want to use **dbcc** commands to report on table and index size, both the **tablealloc** and the **indexalloc** commands accept the **fast** option, which uses information in the OAM page, without performing checks of all page chains. This reduces both disk I/O and the time that locks are held on your tables.

Table 5-2: dbcc commands that report space usage

Command	Arguments	Reports
dbcc tablealloc	Table name or table ID	Pages in specified table and in each index on the table.
dbcc indexalloc	Table name or table ID and index ID	Pages in specified index.
dbcc checkalloc	Database name, or current database if no argument	Pages in all tables and indexes in the specified database. At the end of the report, prints a list of the allocation units in the database and the number of extents, used pages, and referenced pages on each allocation unit.

```
                dbcc tablealloc(titles)
The default report option of OPTIMIZED is used for this run.
The default fix option of FIX   is used for this run.
****************************************************************
TABLE: titles              OBJID = 208003772
INDID=1  FIRST=2032        ROOT=2283          SORT=1
         Data level: 1.  864 Data  Pages in 109 extents.
         Indid      : 1.  15 Index Pages in 3 extents.
INDID=2  FIRST=824         ROOT=827           SORT=1
         Indid      : 2.  47 Index Pages in 7 extents.
TOTAL # of extents = 119
Alloc page 2048 (# of extent=2 used pages=10 ref pages=10)
Alloc page 2304 (# of extent=1 used pages=7 ref pages=7)
Alloc page 1536 (# of extent=25 used pages=193 ref pages=193)
Alloc page 1792 (# of extent=27 used pages=216 ref pages=216)
Alloc page 2048 (# of extent=29 used pages=232 ref pages=232)
Alloc page 2304 (# of extent=28 used pages=224 ref pages=224)
Alloc page 256 (# of extent=1 used pages=1 ref pages=1)
Alloc page 768 (# of extent=6 used pages=47 ref pages=47)
Total (# of extent=119 used pages=930 ref pages=930) in this
database
DBCC execution completed. If DBCC printed error messages,
contact a user with System Administrator (SA) role.
```

The **dbcc** report shows output for *titles* with a clustered index (the information starting with "INDID=1") and a nonclustered index.

For the clustered index, **dbcc** reports both the amount of space taken by the data pages themselves, 864 pages in 109 extents, and by the root and intermediate levels of the clustered index, 15 pages in 3 extents.

For the nonclustered index, it reports the number of pages and extents used by the index.

Notice that some of the allocation pages are reported more than once in this output, since the output reports on three objects: the table, its clustered index, and its nonclustered index.

At the end, it reports the total number of extents used by the table and its indexes. The OAM pages and distribution pages are included.

You can use **dbcc indexalloc** to display the information for each index on the table. This example displays information about the nonclustered index on titles:

```
dbcc indexalloc(titles, 2)
```

```
The default report option of OPTIMIZED is used for this run.
The default fix option of FIX   is used for this run.
**********************************************************
TABLE: titles              OBJID = 208003772
INDID=2  FIRST=824         ROOT=827          SORT=1
         Indid      : 2.  47 Index Pages in 7 extents.
TOTAL # of extents = 7
Alloc page 256 (# of extent=1 used pages=1 ref pages=1)
Alloc page 768 (# of extent=6 used pages=47 ref pages=47)
Total (# of extent=7 used pages=48 ref pages=48) in this database
DBCC execution completed.  If DBCC printed error messages,
contact a user with System Administrator (SA) role.
```

The **dbcc checkalloc** command presents summary details for an entire database. Here is just the section that reports on the *titles* table:

```
TABLE: titles              OBJID = 208003772
INDID=1  FIRST=2032        ROOT=2283         SORT=1
         Data level: 1.  864 Data  Pages in 109 extents.
         Indid      : 1.  15 Index Pages in 3 extents.
INDID=2  FIRST=824         ROOT=827          SORT=1
         Indid      : 2.  47 Index Pages in 7 extents.
TOTAL # of extents = 119
```

Advantages of *dbcc*

The advantages of using **dbcc** commands for checking the size of objects are:

- **dbcc** reports the space used for each index, and for the non-leaf portion of a clustered index.

- **dbcc** reports are in pages, which is convenient for most tuning work.

- **dbcc** reports the number of extents for each object, which is useful when estimating I/O using a 16K memory pool.

- **dbcc** reports are accurate. When **dbcc** completes, it updates the information on which **sp_spaceused** bases its reports.

- Using **dbcc tablealloc** or **indexalloc**, you can see how tables or indexes are spread across allocation units.

- You should run regular **dbcc** consistency checks of your databases. If you save the output to files, using this information to track space usage does not impact server performance.

Disadvantages of *dbcc*

The disadvantages of using **dbcc** commands for size checking are:

- **dbcc** can cause disk, data cache, and lock contention with other activities on the server.

- **dbcc** does not include space used by text or image columns.

- **dbcc** does not report reserved pages, that is, pages that are in extents that are allocated to the object, but which do not contain data. These pages cannot be used for other objects. It is possible to determine the number of reserved pages by multiplying the number of extents used by eight and comparing the result to the total number of used pages that **dbcc** reports.

Using *sp_estspace* to Estimate Object Size

sp_spaceused and **dbcc** commands report on actual space use. The system procedure **sp_estspace** can help you plan for future growth of your tables and indexes. This procedure uses information in the system tables (*sysobjects*, *syscolumns*, and *sysindexes*) to determine the length of data and index rows. It estimates the size for the table and for any indexes that exist. It does not look at the actual size of the data in the tables. You provide an estimate of the number of rows.

To use **sp_estspace**:

- Create the table, if it does not exist

- Create any indexes on the table

- Execute the procedure, estimating the number of rows that the table will hold

The output reports the number of pages and bytes for the table and for each level of the index.

The following example estimates the size of the *titles* table with 500,000 rows, a clustered index, and two nonclustered indexes:

```
sp_estspace titles, 500000
```

name	type	idx_level	Pages	Kbytes
titles	data	0	50002	100004
title_id_cix	clustered	0	302	604
title_id_cix	clustered	1	3	6
title_id_cix	clustered	2	1	2
title_ix	nonclustered	0	13890	27780
title_ix	nonclustered	1	410	819
title_ix	nonclustered	2	13	26
title_ix	nonclustered	3	1	2
type_price_ix	nonclustered	0	6099	12197
type_price_ix	nonclustered	1	88	176
type_price_ix	nonclustered	2	2	5
type_price_ix	nonclustered	3	1	2

Total_Mbytes
138.30

name	type	total_pages	time_mins
title_id_cix	clustered	50308	250
title_ix	nonclustered	14314	91
type_price_ix	nonclustered	6190	55

sp_estspace has additional features to allow you to specify a fillfactor, average size of variable length fields and text fields, and I/O speed. For more information, see the *SQL Server Reference Manual*.

Advantages of *sp_estspace*

The advantages of using **sp_estspace** to estimate the size of objects are:

- **sp_estspace** provides a quick, easy way to plan for table and index growth.

- **sp_estspace** provides a page count at each index level and helps you estimate the number of index levels.

- **sp_estspace** estimates the amount of time needed to create the index.

- **sp_estspace** can be used to estimate future disk space, cache space, and memory requirements.

Disadvantages of *sp_estspace*

The disadvantages of using **sp_estspace** to estimate the size of objects are:

- Returned sizes are only estimates and may differ from actual sizes due to fillfactors, page splitting, actual size of variable length fields, and other factors.

- Index creation times can vary widely depending on disk speed, the use of extent I/O buffers, and system load.

Using Formulas to Estimate Object Size

The following formulas help you estimate the size of tables and indexes in your database. The amount of overhead in tables and indexes that contain variable-length fields is greater than tables that contain only fixed-length fields, so two sets of formulas are required.

The basic process involves calculating the number of bytes of data, plus overhead, and dividing that number into the number of bytes available on a data page. Due to page overhead, on a 2K data page, 2016 bytes are available for data.

➤ **Note**

Do not confuse this figure with the maximum row size, which is 1960 bytes, due to overhead in other places in SQL Server.

For the most accurate estimate, **round down** divisions that calculate the number of rows per page (rows are never split across pages) and **round up** divisions that calculate the number of pages.

Factors That Can Change Storage Size

Using **fillfactor** or **max_rows_per_page** in your **create index** statement changes some of the equations. See "Effects of Setting fillfactor to 100 Percent" on page 107, and "max_rows_per_page Value" on page 109.

These formulas use the maximum size for variable length character and binary data. See "Using Average Sizes for Variable Fields" on page 107 for instructions if you want to use the average size instead of the maximum size.

If your table includes *text* or *image* datatypes, use 16 (the size of the text pointer that is stored in the row) in the calculations below. Then see "text and image Data Pages" on page 109.

If the configuration parameter **page utilization percent** is set to less than 100, SQL Server may allocate new extents before filling all pages on the allocated extents. This does not change the number of pages that an object uses, but leaves empty pages in extents allocated to the object. See "page utilization percent" on page 11-29 in the *System Administration Guide*.

Storage Sizes for Datatypes

The storage sizes for SQL Server datatypes are shown in the following table:

Table 5-3: Storage sizes for SQL Server datatypes

Datatype	Size
char	Defined size
nchar	Defined size * @@ncharsize
varchar	Actual number of characters
nvarchar	Actual number of characters * @@ncharsize
binary	Defined size
varbinary	Data size
int	4
smallint	2
tinyint	1
float	4 or 8, depending on precision
double precision	8
real	4
numeric	2–17, depending on precision and scale
decimal	2–17, depending on precision and scale
money	8
smallmoney	4
datetime	8
smalldatetime	4
bit	1
text	16 bytes + 2K * number of pages used
image	16 bytes + 2K * number of pages used

Table 5-3:   Storage sizes for SQL Server datatypes (continued)

Datatype	Size
timestamp	8

The storage size for a *numeric* or *decimal* column depends on its precision. The minimum storage requirement is 2 bytes for a 1- or 2-digit column. Storage size increases by 1 byte for each additional 2 digits of precision, up to a maximum of 17 bytes.

Any columns defined as NULL are considered variable length columns, since they involve the overhead associated with the variable length columns.

All of the calculations in the examples below are based on the maximum size for *varchar, nvarchar,* and *varbinary* data—the defined size of the columns. They also assume that the columns were defined as NOT NULL. If you want to use average values instead, see "Using Average Sizes for Variable Fields" on page 107.

The formulas and examples are divided into two sections:

- Steps 1–6 outline the calculations for a table with a clustered index, giving the table size and the size of the index tree. The example that follows Step 6 illustrates the computations on a 9,000,000-row table. (Yes, 9 *million* rows).

- Steps 7–12 outline the calculations for computing the space required by nonclustered indexes, followed by another example on the 9,000,000-row table.

Calculating the Size of Tables and Clustered Indexes

The formulas that follow show how to calculate the size of tables and clustered indexes. If your table does not have clustered indexes, skip Steps 3, 4, and 5. Once you compute the number of data pages in Step 2, go to Step 6 to add the number of OAM pages.

Step 1: Calculate the Data Row Size

Rows that store variable-length data require more overhead than rows that contain only fixed-length data, so there are two separate formulas for computing the size of a data row.

Use the first formula if all of the columns are fixed length, and defined as NOT NULL. Use the second formula if the row contains variable-length columns or columns defined as NULL.

Only Fixed-Length Columns

Use this formula if the table contains only fixed-length columns:

	4	(Overhead)
+		Sum of bytes in all fixed-length columns
		= Data row size

Some Variable-Length Columns

Use this formula if the table contains variable-length columns, or columns that allow null values:

	4	(Overhead)
+		Sum of bytes in all fixed-length columns
+		Sum of bytes in all variable-length columns
		= Subtotal

+		(Subtotal / 256) + 1 (Overhead)
+		Number of variable-length columns + 1
+	2	(Overhead)
		= Data row size

Step 2: Compute the Number of Data Pages

2016/Data row size = Number of data rows per page

Number of rows/Rows per page = Number of data pages required

Step 3: Compute the Size of Clustered Index Rows

Index rows containing variable-length columns require more overhead than index rows containing only fixed-length values. Use the first formula if all the keys are fixed length. Use the second formula if the keys include variable-length columns or allow null values.

Only Fixed-Length Columns

5	(Overhead)
+	Sum of bytes in the fixed-length index keys
	= Clustered row size

Some Variable-Length Columns

5	(Overhead)
+	Sum of bytes in the fixed-length index keys
+	Sum of bytes in variable-length index keys
	= Subtotal

+	(Subtotal / 256) + 1 (Overhead)
+ 2	(Overhead)
	= Clustered index row size

Note that the results of the division (Subtotal/256) are rounded down.

Step 4: Compute the Number of Clustered Index Pages

(2016 / Clustered row size) - 2 =   No. of clustered index rows per page

No. of rows / No. of CI rows per page =   No. of index pages at next level

If the result for the number of index pages at the next level is greater than 1, repeat the following division Step, using the quotient as the next dividend, until the quotient equals 1, which means that you have reached the root level of the index:

No. of index pages at last level	/	No. of clustered index rows per page	=	No. of index pages at next level

Step 5: Compute the Total Number of Index Pages

Add the number of pages at each level to determine the total number of pages in the index:

Index Levels	Pages
2	
1	+
0	+
	Total number of index pages

Step 6: Calculate Allocation Overhead and Total Pages

Each table and each index on a table has an object allocation map (OAM). The OAM is stored on pages allocated to the table or index. A single OAM page holds allocation mapping for between 2,000 and 63,750 data or index pages.

In the clustered index example that follows, there are 750,000 data pages, requiring between 12 and 376 OAM pages. The clustered index has 3411 pages and require 1 or 2 OAM pages. In the nonclustered index example, the index has 164,137 pages and requires between 3 and 83 OAM pages. In most cases, the number of OAM pages required is closer to the minimum value. See "Why the Range?" on page 40 for more information.

To calculate the number of OAM pages for the table, use:

Number of reserved data pages / 63,750 = Minimum OAM pages

Number of reserved data pages / 2000 = Maximum OAM pages

To calculate the number of OAM pages for the index, use:

Number of reserved index pages/ 63,750 = Minimum OAM pages

Number of reserved index pages/ 2000 = Maximum OAM pages

Total Pages Needed

Finally, add the number of OAM pages to the earlier totals to determine the total number of pages required:

	Minimum	Maximum
Clustered index pages		
OAM pages	+	+
Data pages	+	+
OAM pages	+	+
Total		

Example: Calculating the Size of a 9,000,000-Row Table

The following example computes the size of the data and clustered index for a table containing:

- 9,000,000 rows
- Sum of fixed-length columns = 100 bytes
- Sum of 2 variable-length columns = 50 bytes
- Clustered index key, fixed length, 4 bytes

Calculating the Data Row Size (Step 1)

The table contains variable-length columns.

	4	(Overhead)
+	100	Sum of bytes in all fixed-length columns
+	50	Sum of bytes in all variable-length columns
	154	= Subtotal
+	1	(Subtotal / 256) + 1 (overhead)
+	3	Number of variable-length columns + 1
+	2	(Overhead)
	160	= Data row size

Calculating the Number of Data Pages (Step 2)

In the first part of this Step, the number of rows per page is rounded down:

2016/160 = 12 Data rows per page

9,000,000/12 = 750,000 Data pages

Calculating the Clustered Index Row Size (Step 3)

	5	(Overhead)
+	4	Sum of bytes in the fixed-length index keys
	9	= Clustered Row Size

Calculating the Number of Clustered Index Pages (Step 4)

(2016/9) - 2 = 222 Clustered Index Rows Per Page

750,000/222 = 3379 Index Pages (Level 0)

3379/222 = 16 Index Pages (Level 1)

16/222 = 1 Index Page (Level 2)

Calculating the Total Number of Index Pages (Step 5)

Index Levels		Pages	Rows
2		1	16
1	+	16	3379
0	+	3379	750000
Index total:		3396	
Data total:		750000	9000000

Calculating the Number of OAM Pages and Total Pages (Step 6)

Both the table and the clustered index require one or more OAM Pages.

For Data Pages:

750,000/63,750 = 12 (minimum)

750,000/2000 = 376 (maximum)

For Index Pages:

3379/63,750 = 1 (minimum)

3379/2000 = 2 (maximum)

Total Pages Needed:

	Minimum	Maximum
Clustered index pages	3379	3379
OAM pages	1	2
Data pages	750000	750000
OAM pages	12	376
Total	753392	753757

Calculating the Size of Nonclustered Indexes

Step 7: Calculate the Size of the Leaf Index Row

Index rows containing variable-length columns require more overhead than index rows containing only fixed-length values. Use the first formula if all the keys are fixed length. Use the second formula if the keys include variable-length columns or allow null values.

Fixed-Length Keys Only

Use this formula if the index contains only fixed-length keys:

    7   (Overhead)

+ _____   Sum of Fixed-Length Keys

         = Size of Leaf Index Row

Some Variable-Length Keys

Use this formula if the index contains any variable-length keys:

	9	(Overhead)
+		Sum of length of fixed-length keys
+		Sum of length of variable-length keys
+		Number of variable-length keys + 1
		= Subtotal

+	(Subtotal / 256) + 1 (overhead)
	= Size of leaf index row

Step 8: Calculate the Number of Leaf Pages in the Index

2016/ Size of leaf index row = No. of leaf rows per page

No. of rows in table / No. of leaf rows per page =   No. of leaf pages

Step 9: Calculate the Size of the Non-Leaf Rows

		Size of leaf index row
+	4	Overhead
		= Size of non-leaf row

Step 10: Calculate the Number of Non-Leaf Pages

(2016 / Size of non-leaf row) - 2 = No. of non-leaf index rows per page

No. of leaf pages at last level	/	No. of non-leaf index rows per page	=	No. of index pages at next level

If the number of index pages at the next level above is greater than 1, repeat the following division step, using the quotient as the next dividend, until the quotient equals 1, which means that you have reached the root level of the index:

No. of Index Pages At Last Level	/	No. of Non-Leaf Index Rows per Page	=	No. of Index Pages at Next Level

Step 11: Calculate the Total Number of Non-Leaf Index Pages

Add the number of pages at each level to determine the total number of pages in the index:

Index Levels	Pages
4	
3	+
2	+
1	+
0	+
	Total number of 2K data pages used

Step 12: Calculate Allocation Overhead and Total Pages

Number of index pages / 63,750 = Minimum OAM pages

Number of index pages / 2000 = Maximum OAM pages

Total Pages Needed

Add the number of OAM pages to the total from Step 11 to determine the total number of index pages:

	Minimum	Maximum
Nonclustered index pages		
OAM pages	+	+
Total		

Example: Calculating the Size of a Nonclustered Index

The following example computes the size of a nonclustered index on the 9,000,000-row table used in the preceding example. There are two keys, one fixed length and one variable length.

- 9,000,000 rows
- Sum of fixed-length columns = 100 bytes
- Sum of 2 variable-length columns = 50 bytes
- Composite nonclustered index key:
    - Fixed length column, 4 bytes
    - Variable length column, 20 bytes

Calculate the Size of the Leaf Index Row (Step 7)

The index contains variable-length keys:

	9	(Overhead)
+	4	Sum of length of fixed-length keys
+	20	Sum of length of variable-length keys
+	2	Number of variable-length keys + 1
	35	= Subtotal

	1	(Subtotal / 256) + 1 (overhead)
	36	= Size of Leaf Index Row

Calculate the Number of Leaf Pages (Step 8)

2016/36 = 56 Nonclustered leaf rows per page

9,000,000/56 = 160,715 Leaf pages

Calculate the Size of the Non-Leaf Rows (Step 9)

	36	Size of leaf index row (from Step 7)
+	4	Overhead
	40	= Size of non-leaf index row

Calculate the Number of Non-Leaf Pages (Step 10)

(2016/40) - 2 = 48	Non-leaf index rows per page
160715/48 = 3349	Index pages, level 1
3348 /48 = 70	Index pages, level 2
70/48 = 2	Index pages, level 3
2/48 = 1	Index page, level 4

Totals (Step 11)

Index Levels	Pages	Rows
4	1	2
3	2	70
2	70	3348
1	3349	160715
0	160715	9000000
	164137	

OAM Pages Needed (Step 12)

164137 /63,750 = 3 (minimum)

164137 /2000 = 83 (maximum)

Total Pages Needed

	Minimum	Maximum
Index pages	164137	164137
OAM pages	3	83
Total pages	164140	164220

Other Factors Affecting Object Size

In addition to the effects of data modifications over time, other factors can affect object size and size estimates:

- The **fillfactor** value used when an index is created
- Whether computations used average row size or maximum row size
- Very small text rows
- **max_rows_per_page** value
- Use of *text* and *image* data

Effects of Setting *fillfactor* to 100 Percent

With the default fillfactor of 0, the index management process leaves room for two additional rows on each index page when you first create a new index. When you set **fillfactor** to 100 percent, it no longer leaves room for these rows. The only effect on these calculations is on calculating the number of clustered index pages (Step 4) and calculating the number of non-leaf pages (Step 9). Both of these calculations subtract 2 from the number of rows per page. Eliminate the -2 from these calculations.

➤ *Note*

Fillfactor affects size at index creation time. Fillfactors are not maintained as tables are updated. Use these adjustments for read-only tables.

Other *fillfactor* Values

Other values for **fillfactor** reduce the number of rows per page on data pages and leaf index pages. To compute the correct values when using **fillfactor**, multiply the size of the available data page (2016) by the **fillfactor**. For example, if your **fillfactor** is 75 percent, your data page would hold 1471 bytes. Use this value in place of 2016 when you calculate the number of rows per page. See "Step 2: Compute the Number of Data Pages" on page 96 and "Step 8: Calculate the Number of Leaf Pages in the Index" on page 102.

Distribution Pages

Distribution pages are created when you create an index on existing data and when you run **update statistics**. A distribution page occupies one full data page. Distribution pages are essential for proper functioning of the optimizer.

Using Average Sizes for Variable Fields

The formulas use the maximum size of the variable-length fields.

One way to determine the average size of fields on an existing table is:

```
select avg(datalength(column_name))
    from table_name
```

This query performs a table scan, which may not be acceptable in a production system or for a very large table. You can limit the number of rows it searches by placing the column value in a temporary table with **set rowcount**, and running the query on the temporary table.

You can use the average value in Steps 1 and 4 in calculating table size, and in Step 6 in calculating the nonclustered index size. You will need slightly different formulas:

In Step 1

Use the sum of the **average** length of the variable length columns instead of the sum of defined length of the variable length columns to determine the average data row size.

In Step 2

Use the average data row size in the first formula.

In Step 3

You must perform the addition twice. The first time, calculate the maximum index row size, using the given formula. The second time, calculate the average index row size, substituting the sum of the **average** number of bytes in the variable-length index keys for the sum of the defined number of bytes in the variable-length index keys.

In Step 4

Substitute this formula for the first formula in Step 4, using the two length values:

$$(2016 - 2 * \text{maximum\_length}) / \text{average\_length} = \quad \text{No. of clustered index rows per page}$$

In Step 6

You must perform the addition twice. The first time, calculate the maximum leaf index row size, using the given formula. The second time, calculate the average leaf index row size, substituting the **average** number of bytes in the variable-length index keys for the **sum** of byte in the variable-length index keys.

In Step 7

Use the average leaf index row size in the first division procedure.

In Step 8

Use the average leaf index row size.

In Step 9

Substitute this formula for the first formula in Step 9, using the maximum and averages calculated in Step 6:

(2016 - 2 * Maximum_length) / Average_length=   No. of non-leaf index rows
                                                 per page

Very Small Rows

SQL Server cannot store more than 256 data or index rows on.a page. Even if your rows are extremely short, the minimum number of data pages will be:

Number of Rows / 256 =   Number of Data Pages Required

max_rows_per_page Value

The **max_rows_per_page** value (specified by **create index**, **create table**, **alter table**, or **sp_chgattrribute**) limits the number of rows on a data page.

To compute the correct values when using **max_rows_per_page**, use the **max_rows_per_page** value or the computed number of data rows per page, whichever is smaller, in the first formula in Steps 2 and 8.

text and *image* Data Pages

Each *text* or *image* column stores a 16-byte pointer in the data row with the datatype *varbinary(16)*. Each *text* or *image* column that is initialized requires at least 2K (one data page) of storage space.

text and *image* columns are designed to store "implicit" null values, meaning that the text pointer in the data row remains null, and there is no text page initialized for the value, saving 2K of storage space.

If a *text* or *image* column is defined to allow null values, and the row is created with an **insert** statement that includes NULL for the *text* or *image* column, the column is not initialized, and the storage is not allocated.

If a *text* or *image* column is changed in any way with **update**, then the text page is allocated. Of course, inserts or updates that place actual data in a column initialize the page. If the *text* or *image* column is subsequently set to NULL, a single page remains allocated.

Each text or image page stores 1800 bytes of data. To calculate the number of text chain pages that a particular entry will use, use this formula:

Data length / 1800 = Number of 2K pages

The result should be rounded up in all cases; that is, a data length of 1801 bytes requires two 2K pages.

Advantages of Using Formulas to Estimate Object Size

The advantages of using the formulas are:

- You learn more details of the internals of data and index storage.

- The formulas provide flexibility for specifying averages sizes for character or binary columns.

- While computing the index size, you see how many levels each index has, which helps estimate performance. The number of index levels indicates how many disk reads will be required to traverse the index.

Disadvantages of Using Formulas to Estimate Object Size

The disadvantages of using the formulas are:

- The estimates are only as good as your estimates of average size for variable length columns.

- The multistep calculations can be prone to error.

- Actual size may be different, based on use.

Moving Beyond the Basics

With the conclusion of Section A, you now know how SQL Server stores data, how indexes function, and how to estimate the size of database objects.

Section B, "Tuning the Performance of Queries," gives you insight into query analysis tools and methodology. Once you've designed your database and installed indexes, how can you tell what SQL Server is doing in the context of your application's queries?

Chapters 6, 7, and 8 are required reading for the serious student of performance tuning. Chapter 6, "Indexing for Performance," introduces the basic query analysis tools that can help you choose appropriate indexes, and discusses index selection criteria for point queries, range queries, and joins.

Topics in Chapter 6 include: techniques and limitations of using indexing to address performance issues; index tuning tools such as **set io statistics**; and the all-important topics of how to estimate I/O, and how to choose and maintain indexes.

section *B*

Tuning the Performance of Queries

Chapter 6 introduces some basic query analysis tools that can help you choose appropriate indexes, and discusses index selection criteria for point queries, range queries, and joins.

Chapter 7 covers the SQL Server query optimizer and the optimization strategies it uses for various types of queries. The chapter also introduces the query-analysis tools you'll need to investigate possible optimization problems.

Chapter 8 begins the discussion of how to tune and refine queries to overcome optimization problems, using query-analysis tools for diagnosis and treatment.

Chapter 9 discusses advanced optimizing techniques, which you can use to directly influence how the optimizer chooses join order, indexes, I/O size, and cache strategy.

Chapter 10, "Transact-SQL Performance Tips", is a collection of hints for simple changes to queries that could improve their performance. While in most cases these suggestions are not related to the inner workings of the query optimizer, you use the standard query-analysis tools to find out whether performance has improved.

Chapter 11 covers SQL Server's locking strategies, used to assure the consistency and integrity of data being accessed by multiple users or multiple transactions. A thorough understanding of locking is essential to monitoring the performance of your application in real-world, multi-user use.

Chapter 12's investigation of "Cursors and Performance" covers how cursors interact with SQL Server's locking mechanisms and query optimization paths.

When you reach the end of Section B, you will have mastered the software side of performance optimization. Section C delves into how to manipulate the physical performance environment, and so necessarily concerns itself with hardware and network issues.

6

Indexing for Performance

How Indexes Can Affect Performance

Carefully considered indexes, built on top of a good database design, are the foundation of a high performance SQL Server installation. However, adding indexes without proper analysis can reduce the overall performance of your system. Insert, update, and delete operations can take longer when a large number of indexes need to be updated. In general, if there is not a good reason to have an index, it should not be there.

Once you have analyzed your application workload using the techniques you learned in Section A, you can create indexes as necessary to improve the performance of the application's most critical processes.

The SQL Server query optimizer uses a probabilistic costing model. It analyzes the cost of different possible query plans and chooses the plan that has the least cost. Since much of the cost of executing a query consists of disk I/O, creating the correct set of indexes for your applications means that the optimizer can use indexes to:

- Avoid table scans when accessing data

- Target specific data pages that contain specific values in a **point query**

- Establish upper and lower bounds for reading data in a **range query**

- Avoid table access completely, when an index covers a query

- Use ordered data to avoid sorts

In addition, you can create indexes to enforce the uniqueness of data and to randomize the storage location of inserts.

Symptoms of Poor Indexing

A primary goal of improving performance with indexes is avoiding table scans. In a table scan, every page of a table must be read from disk. Since the optimizer cannot know if you have one row, or several, that match the search arguments, it can't stop when it finds a matching row; it must read every row of the table.

If a query is searching for a unique value in a table that has 600 data pages, this requires 600 disk reads. If an index points to the data value, the query could be satisfied with two or three reads, a performance improvement of 200 percent to 300 percent. On a system with a 12-ms. disk, this is a difference of several seconds compared to less than a second. Even if this response time is acceptable for the query in question, heavy disk I/O by one query has a negative impact on overall throughput.

Table scans may occur:

- When there is no index on the search arguments for a query
- When there is an index, but the optimizer determines that the index is not useful
- When there are no search arguments

Detecting Indexing Problems

Incorrect indexing results in poor query performance, as does lack of indexing. Some of the major indicators of poor indexing are:

- A select statement takes too long.
- A join between two or more tables takes an extremely long time.
- Select operations perform well, but data modification processes perform poorly.
- Point queries (for example, "where colvalue = 3") perform well, but range queries (for example, "where colvalue > 3 and colvalue < 30") perform poorly.

Among the possible problems underlying these performance problems are lack of indexes; imprecise indexes; too many indexes or an index with too large a key; or lack of index support for a particular range query. Each of these situations is described in greater detail in the following sections.

Lack of Indexes Is Causing Table Scans

If select operations and joins take too long, it is likely that an appropriate index does not exist or is not being used by the optimizer. Analyzing the query can help determine if another index is needed, if an existing index can be modified, or if the query can be modified to use an existing index. If an index exists, but is not being used, careful analysis of the query and the values used is required to determine the source of the problem.

Index Is Not Selective Enough

An index is selective if it helps the optimizer find a particular row or a set of rows. An index on a unique identifier such as a social security number is highly selective, since it lets the optimizer pinpoint a single row. An index on a non-unique entry such as sex (M, F) is not very selective, and the optimizer would use such an index only in very special cases.

Index Does Not Support Range Queries

Generally, clustered indexes and covering indexes help optimize range queries. Range queries that reference the keys of noncovering nonclustered indexes use the index for ranges that return a limited number of rows. As the range and the number of rows the query returns increases, however, using a nonclustered index to return the rows can cost more than a table scan.

As a rule of thumb, if access via a nonclustered index returns more rows than there are pages in the table, the index is more costly than the table scan (using 2K I/O on the table pages). If the table scan can use 16K I/O, the optimizer is likely to choose the table scan when the number of rows to be returned exceeds the number of I/Os (pages divided by 8).

➤ **Note**

The optimizer costs both physical and logical I/O for the query, as well as other costs. The rule of thumb above does not describe how the optimizer determines query costs.

Too Many Indexes Slow Data Modification

If data modification performance is poor, you may have too many indexes.While indexes favor select operations, they slow down data modifications. Each time an insert, update, or delete operation affects an index key, the leaf level, and sometimes higher levels, of a nonclustered index need to be updated. Analyze the requirements for each index and try to eliminate those that are unnecessary or rarely used.

Index Entries Are Too Large

Large index entries cause large indexes, so try to keep them as small as possible. You can create indexes with keys up to 256 bytes, but these indexes can store very few rows per index page, which increases the amount of disk I/O needed during queries. The index has more levels, and each level has more pages. Nonmatching index scans can be very expensive.

The following example uses **sp_estspace** to demonstrate how the number of index pages and leaf levels required increases with key size. It creates a nonclustered indexes using 10-, 20-, and 40-character keys.

```
create table demotable (c1 char(10),
                        c2 char(20),
                        c4 char(40))

create index t1 on demotable(c1)

create index t2 on demotable(c2)

create index t4 on demotable(c4)

sp_estspace demotable, 500000
```

name	type	idx_level	Pages	Kbytes
demotable	data	0	15204	37040
t1	nonclustered	0	4311	8623
t1	nonclustered	1	47	94
t1	nonclustered	2	1	2
t2	nonclustered	0	6946	13891
t2	nonclustered	1	111	222
t2	nonclustered	2	3	6
t2	nonclustered	3	1	2
t4	nonclustered	0	12501	25002
t4	nonclustered	1	339	678
t4	nonclustered	2	10	20
t4	nonclustered	3	1	2

```
Total_Mbytes
----------------
       83.58
```

name	type	total_pages	time_mins
t1	nonclustered	4359	25
t2	nonclustered	7061	34
t4	nonclustered	12851	53

The output shows that the indexes for the 10-column and 20-column keys each have three levels, while the 40-column key requires a fourth level.

The number of pages required is over 50 percent higher at each level. A nonmatching index scan on the leaf level of *t2* would require 6946 disk reads, compared to 4311 for the index on *t1*.

Index Limits and Requirements

The following limits apply to indexes on SQL Server:

- You can create only one clustered index per table, since the data for a clustered index is stored in order by the index key.

- You can create a maximum of 249 nonclustered indexes per table.

- A key can be made up of multiple columns. The maximum is 16 columns. The maximum number of bytes per index key is 256.

- When you create a clustered index, SQL Server requires an additional 120 percent of the table size in the database. It must create a copy of the table and allocate space for the root and intermediate pages for the index. Note that 120 percent is a rule of thumb; if you have very long keys, you may need even more space.

- The referential integrity constraints **unique** and **primary key** create unique indexes to enforce their restrictions on the keys. By default, **unique** constraints create nonclustered indexes and **primary key** constraints create clustered indexes.

Tools for Query Analysis and Tuning

The query analysis tools that you use most often while tuning queries and indexes are listed in Table 6-1.

Table 6-1:   Tools for managing index performance

Tool	Function
set showplan on	Shows the query plan for a query, including the indexes selected, join order, and worktables. See Chapter 8, "Understanding Query Plans."
set statistics io on	Shows how many logical and physical reads and writes are performed to process the query. See "Indexes and I/O Statistics" on page 122.
set statistics time on	Shows how long it takes to execute the query.

Table 6-1: Tools for managing index performance

Tool	Function
set noexec on	Usually used with **set showplan on**, this command suppresses execution of the query. You see the plan the optimizer would choose, but the query is not executed. **noexec** is useful when the query would return very long results or could cause performance problems on a production system. Note that output from **statistics io** is not shown when **noexec** is in effect (since the query does not perform I/O).
dbcc traceon (302)	This special trace flag lets you see the calculations the optimizer uses to determine whether indexes should be used. See "Tuning with dbcc traceon 302" on page 272.

Tools that provide information on indexes or help in tuning indexes are listed in Table 6-2.

Table 6-2: Additional tools for managing index performance

Tool	Function
sp_configure fillfactor	Sets or displays the default fillfactor for index pages.
sp_help, sp_helpindex	Provides information on indexes that exist for a table.
sp_estspace	Provides estimates of table and index size, the number of pages at each level of an index, and the time needed to create each index.
sp_spaceused	Provides information about the size of tables and its indexes.
update statistics	Updates the statistics kept about distribution and density of keys in an index.

The commands that provide information on space usage are described in Chapter 5, "Estimating the Size of Tables and Indexes."

Table 6-3 lists additional tools.

Table 6-3: Advanced tools for query tuning

Tool	Function
set forceplan	Forces the query to use the tables in the order specified in the **from** clause.

Table 6-3:   Advanced tools for query tuning

Tool	Function
set table count	Increases the number of tables optimized at once.
select, delete, update clauses: **(index...prefetch...mru_lru)**	Specifies the index, I/O size, or cache strategy to use for the query.
set prefetch	Toggles prefetch for query tuning experimentation.
sp_cachestrategy	Sets status bits to enable or disable prefetch and fetch-and-discard cache strategy.

The tools listed in Table 6-3 are described in Chapter 9, "Advanced Optimizing Techniques."

Figure 6-1 on page 121 shows how many of these tools relate to the process of running queries on SQL Server.

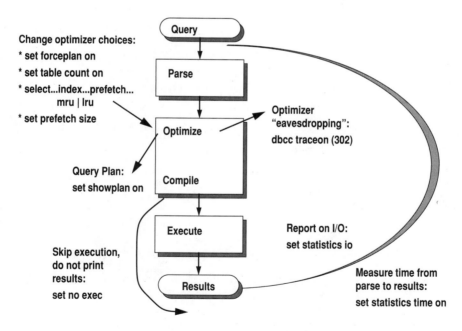

Figure 6-1:   Query processing analysis tools and query processing

Monitoring the Effects of Index Tuning

Use monitoring tools such as the system procedure **sp_sysmon** (or the separate product, SQL Server Monitor) as you work on index tuning. Look at the output for improved cache hit ratios, a reduction in the number of physical reads, and fewer context switches for physical reads.

For more information about using **sp_sysmon** see Chapter 19, "Monitoring SQL Server Performance with sp_sysmon," especially the section "Index Management" on page 496.

Indexes and I/O Statistics

The **statistics io** option of the **set** command reports information about physical and logical I/O and the number of times a table was accessed.

Reports from **set statistics io** follow the query results and provide actual I/O performed by the query.

set statistics io provides the following information for queries:

Table 6-4:   Values reported by set statistics io

Output	Meaning
scan count	Number of times an index or table was searched
logical reads	Number of times a page is referenced in cache
physical reads	Number of reads performed from disk
Total writes	Number of writes to disk

Here is a sample query:

```
select title
from titles
where title_id = "T5652"
```

If there is no index on *title_id*, the output for the table scan reports these values, using 2K I/O:

```
Table: titles scan count 1, logical reads: 624, physical reads: 624
Total writes for this command: 0
```

With a clustered index on *title_id*, the output shows:

```
Table: titles  scan count 1, logical reads: 3, physical reads: 2
Total writes for this command: 0
```

Adding the index improves performance by a factor of 200.

Scan Count

The scan count shows the number of times a table or index was used in the query. It does not necessarily mean that a table scan was performed. A scan can represent any of these access methods:

- A table scan.

- An access via a clustered index. Each time the query starts at the root page of the index, and follows pointers to the data pages, it is counted.

- An access via a nonclustered index. Each time the query starts at the root page of the index, and follows pointers to the leaf level of the index (for a covered query) or to the data pages, it is counted.

You need to use **showplan**, as described in Chapter 8, "Understanding Query Plans," to determine which access method is used.

Queries Reporting Scan Count of 1

Examples of queries that return a scan count of 1 are:

- A point query:

```
select title_id
from titles
    where title_id = "T55522"
```

- A range query:

```
select au_lname, au_fname
    from authors
    where au_lname > "Smith"
    and au_lname < "Smythe"
```

If the columns in the **where** clauses of these queries are indexed, they use the indexes to probe the tables; otherwise, they perform table scans. But in either case, they require only a single probe of the table to return the required rows.

Queries Reporting Scan Count Greater Than 1

Examples of queries that return larger scan count values are:

- Queries that have indexed **where** clauses connected by **or** report a scan for each **or** clause; for example, with an index on *title_id*, and another on *pub_id*:

```
select title_id
from titles
    where title_id = "T55522"
    or pub_id   = "P302"
```

Table: titles scan count 2, logical reads: 8, physical reads: 1

Note that if any **or** clause is not indexed, the query performs a single table scan.

- In joins, inner tables are scanned once for each qualifying row in the outer table. In the following example, the outer table, *publishers*, has three *publishers* with the state "NY", so the inner table, *titles*, reports a scan count of 3:

```
select title_id
from titles t, publishers p
where t.pub_id = p.pub_id
    and p.state = "NY"
```

Table: titles scan count 3, logical reads: 1872, physical reads: 624
Table: publishers scan count 1, logical reads: 2, physical reads: 2
Total writes for this command: 0

This query performs table scans on both tables. *publishers* occupies only 2 data pages, so 2 physical I/Os are reported. There are 3 matching rows, so the query scans *titles* 3 times, reporting 1,872 logical reads (624 pages * 3).

Queries Reporting Scan Count of 0

Queries that report a scan count of 0:

- Those that perform deferred updates

- **select...into** queries

- Some queries that create worktables

Deferred Updates and Scan Count = 0

Deferred updates perform the changes to the data in two steps:

- Finding the rows using appropriate indexes if any. This step has a scan count of 1 or more. Log records are written to the transaction log during this step.

- Changing the data pages. This step is labeled "scan count 0".

If there is no index on *title_id*, this query is done in deferred mode:

```
update titles set title_id = "T47166"
    where title_id = "T33040"
```

```
Table: titles   scan count 0,  logical reads: 34,  physical reads: 12
Table: titles   scan count 1,  logical reads: 624,  physical reads: 624
Total writes for this command: 2
```

This command which inserts data that is selected from the same table is also performed in deferred mode, and reports a scan count of 0:

```
insert pub_table
     select * from pub_table
```

```
Table: pub_table   scan count 0,  logical reads: 34,  physical reads: 0
Table: pub_table   scan count 1,  logical reads: 1,  physical reads: 0
Total writes for this command: 3
```

insert...select and select...into Commands

The **insert...select** and **select into** commands that work in direct mode report I/O for scan count 0 on the target table:

```
select *
     into pub_table
     from publishers
```

```
Table: publishers   scan count 1,  logical reads: 2,  physical reads: 2
Table: pub_table   scan count 0,  logical reads: 31,  physical reads: 0
Total writes for this command: 7
```

Worktables and Scan Count of 0

Queries that include **order by** and **distinct** sometimes create worktables and sort the results. The I/O on these worktables is reported with a scan count equal to 0:

```
select distinct state
     from authors
```

```
Table: authors   scan count 1,  logical reads: 223,  physical reads: 223
Table: Worktable1 scan count 0,  logical reads: 5120,  physical reads: 0
Total writes for this command: 3
```

Reads and Writes

In addition to reporting how many times a table is accessed, **statistics io** reports the actual physical I/O required and the number of times the query needed to access pages in memory. It reports the I/O in three values:

- Physical reads, the number of times a page (or a group of pages, if using large I/O) must be read from disk.

- Logical reads, the number of times that a page in the cache is referenced during query execution. Logical reads always counts those pages brought in by a physical read as well as pages already in the cache.

- The number of writes to disk, "Total writes".

If a page needs to be read from disk, it is counted as a physical read and a logical read. Logical I/O is always greater than or equal to physical I/O.

Logical I/O always reports 2K data pages. Physical reads and writes are reported in buffer-sized units. Multiple pages that are read in a single I/O operation are treated as a unit: They are read, written, and move through the cache as a single buffer.

Logical Reads, Physical Reads, and 2K I/O

With 2K I/O, the number of times that a page is found in cache for a query is logical reads minus physical reads. When you see output like this:

```
logical reads: 624, physical reads: 624
```

it means that all of the pages for a table had to be read from disk.

Often, when indexes are used to access a table, or when you are rerunning queries during testing, **statistics io** reports a combination of logical and physical reads, like this output from a point query:

```
logical reads: 3, physical reads: 2
```

In this case, one of the pages was already in memory, probably the root page of the index. Two pages, usually the intermediate or leaf page plus the data page, needed to be read from disk.

Physical Reads and Large I/O

Physical reads are not reported in pages, but are reported as the actual number of times SQL Server needs to access the disk. If the query uses 16K I/O (as reported by **showplan**), a single physical read brings 8 data pages into cache. If a query reports 100 16K physical reads, it has read 800 data pages. If the query needs to scan each of those data pages, it reports 800 logical reads. If a query, such as a join query, must read the page multiple times because other I/O has flushed the page from the cache, each physical read is counted.

Reads and Writes on Worktables

Reads and writes are also reported for any worktable that needs to be created for the query. When a query creates more than one worktable, the worktables are numbered in **statistics io** output to correspond to the worktable numbers used in **showplan** output.

Effects of Caching on Writes

The number of writes reported for a query may be misleading. Sometimes, when you are just selecting data, **statistics io** may report writes for the command. SQL Server writes modified pages to disk only at checkpoints, when the housekeeper task writes dirty pages, or when data cache space is needed for new data pages, and the pages near the end of the buffer were changed while they were in the cache. **statistics io** does not report on checkpoint or housekeeper I/O, but does report writes when your query causes pages at the end of the cache to be written to disk.

Effects of Caching on Reads

If you are testing a query and checking its I/O, and you execute the same query a second time, you may get surprising physical reads results if the query uses LRU replacement strategy. The first execution reports a high number of physical reads, while the second attempt reports 0 physical reads. However, this does not mean that your tuning efforts have been instantly successful.

The first time you execute the query, all the data pages are read into cache and remain there until some other server processes flushes them from the cache. Depending on the cache strategy used for the query, the pages may remain in cache for a longer or shorter time.

- If the query performs fetch-and-discard (MRU) caching, the pages are read into the cache at the wash marker. In small or very active caches, pages read into the cache at the wash marker are flushed fairly quickly.

- If the query reads the pages in at the top of the MRU/LRU chain, the pages remain in cache for much longer periods of time. This is especially likely to happen if you have a large data cache and the activity on your server is low.

For more information on testing and cache performance, see "Testing Data Cache Performance" on page 398.

Estimating I/O

Checking the output from **set statistics io** provides information when you actually execute a query. However, if you know the approximate size of your tables and indexes, you can make I/O estimates without running queries. Once you develop this knowledge of the size of your tables and indexes, and the number of index levels in each index, you can quickly determine whether I/O performance for a query is reasonable, or whether a particular query needs tuning efforts.

Following are some guidelines and formulas for making these estimates.

Table Scans

When a query requires a table scan, SQL Server:

- Reads each page of the table from disk into the data cache

- Checks the data values (if there is a **where** clause) and returns matching rows

If the table is larger than your data cache, SQL Server keeps flushing pages out of cache so that it can read in additional pages until it processes the entire query. It may use one of two strategies:

- Fetch-and-discard (MRU) replacement strategy: If the optimizer estimates that the pages will not be needed again for a query, it reads the page into the cache just before the wash marker. Pages remain in cache for a short time, and do not tend to flush other more heavily used pages out of cache.

- LRU replacement strategy: Pages replace a least-recently-used buffer and are placed on the most-recently-used end of the chain. They remain in cache until other disk I/O flushes them from the cache.

Table scans are performed:

- When no index exists on the columns used in the query.

- When the optimizer chooses not to use an index. It makes this choice when it determines that using the index is more expensive than a table scan. This is more likely with nonclustered indexes. The optimizer may determine that it is faster to read the table pages directly than it is to go through several levels of indexes for each row that is to be returned.

  As a rule, table scans are chosen over nonclustered index access when the query returns more rows than there are pages in the table when using 2K I/O. For larger I/O sizes, the calculation is pages returned divided by pages per I/O.

Evaluating the Cost of a Table Scan

Performance of a table scan depends on:

- Table size, in pages
- Speed of I/O
- Data cache sizes and bindings
- I/O size available for the cache

The larger the cache available to the table, the more likely it is that all or some of the table pages will be in memory because of a previous read. But the optimizer makes the pessimistic assumption. It cannot know what pages are in cache, so it assumes that the query must perform all of the physical I/O required.

To estimate the cost of a table scan:

1. Determine the number of pages that need to be read. Use **sp_spaceused, dbcc tablealloc**, or **sp_estspace** to check the number of pages in the table, or use **set statistics io on** and execute a query that scans the table using 2K I/O.

2. Determine the I/O size available in your data cache. Execute **sp_help** *tablename* to see if the table is bound to a cache and **sp_cacheconfig** to see the I/O sizes available for that cache.

   Divide the number of pages in the table by the number of pages that can be read in one I/O.

   Determine the number of disk I/Os that your system can perform per second; divide total reads by that number.

$$\text{I/O time} = \frac{\text{Pages in the table/pages per IO}}{\text{Disk reads per second}}$$

Figure 6-2: Formula for computing table scan time

For example, if **sp_estspace** gives table size of 76,923 pages and your system reads 50 pages per second into 2K buffers, the time to execute a table scan on the table is:

76923 pages/50 reads per second = 1538 seconds, about 25 minutes

If your cache can use 16K buffers, the value is:

76,923 pages/8 pages per read = 9615 reads
9615 reads/50 reads per second = 192 seconds, about 3 minutes

The speed could improve if some of the data were in cache.

Evaluating the Cost of Index Access

If you are selecting a specific value, the index can be used to go directly to the row containing that value, making fewer comparisons than it takes to scan the entire table. In range queries, the index can point to the beginning and end of a range. This is particularly true if the data is ordered by a clustered index or if the query uses a covering index.

When SQL Server estimates that the number of index and data page I/Os is less than the number required to scan the entire table, it uses the index.

To determine the number of index levels, use one of these methods:

* Use **sp_estspace**, giving the current number of rows in the table, or perform space estimates using the formulas.

* Use **set statistics io** and run a point query that returns a single row. The number of levels is the number of reads minus 1.

Evaluating the Cost of a Point Query

A point query that uses an index performs one I/O for each index level plus one read for the data page. In a frequently used table, the root page and intermediate pages of indexes are often found in cache, so that physical I/O is lower by one or two reads.

Evaluating the Cost of a Range Query

Range queries perform very differently, depending on the type of index. Range queries on clustered indexes and on covering nonclustered indexes are very efficient. They use the index to find the first row, and then scan forward on the leaf level.

Range queries using nonclustered indexes (those that do not cover the query) are more expensive, since the rows may be scattered across many data pages. The optimizer always estimates that access via a nonclustered index requires a physical I/O for each row that needs to be returned.

Range Queries Using Clustered Indexes

To estimate the number of page reads required for a range query that uses the clustered index to resolve a range query, you can use this formula:

$$\text{Reads required} = \text{Number of index levels} + \frac{\text{\# of rows returned/\# of rows per page}}{\text{Pages per IO}}$$

Figure 6-3: Computing reads for a clustered index range query

If a query returns 150 rows, and the table has 10 rows per page, the query needs to read 15 data pages, plus the needed index pages. If the query uses 2K I/O, it requires 15 or 16 I/Os for the data pages, depending on whether the range starts in the middle of a page. If your query uses 16K I/O, these 15 data pages require a minimum of 2 or 3 I/Os for the database. 16K I/O reads entire extents in a single I/O, so 15 pages might occupy 2 or 3 extents if the page chains are contiguous in the extents. If the page chains are not contiguous, because the table has been frequently updated, the query could require as many as 15 or 16 16K I/Os to read the entire range. See "Maintaining Data Cache Performance for Large I/O" on page 418 for more information on large I/O and fragmentation.

Figure 6-4 shows how a range query using a clustered index uses the index to find the first matching row on the data pages. The next-page pointers are used to scan forward until a non-matching row is encountered.

select fname, lname, id
from employees
where lname between "Greaves"
and "Highland"

Clustered index on lname

Root page   Intermediate   Data pages

Figure 6-4: Range query on a clustered index

Range Queries with Covering Nonclustered Indexes

Range queries via covering nonclustered indexes can perform very well:

- The index can be used to position the search at the first qualifying row in the index.

- Each index page contains more rows than corresponding data rows, so fewer pages need to be read.

- Index pages tend to remain in cache longer than data pages, so fewer physical I/Os are needed.

- If the cache used by the nonclustered index allows large I/O, up to 8 pages can be read per I/O.

- The data pages do not have to be accessed.

Figure 6-5 shows a range query on a covering nonclustered index.

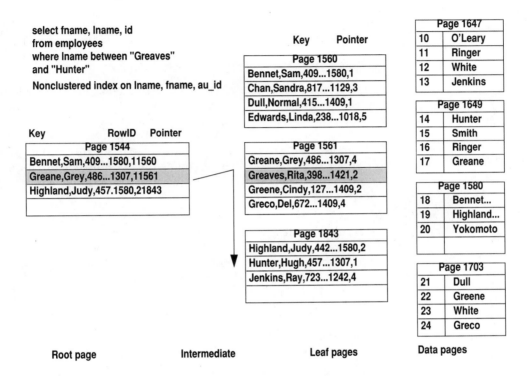

Figure 6-5: Range query with a covering nonclustered index

To estimate the cost of using a covering nonclustered index, you need to know:

- The number of index levels

- The number of rows per page on the leaf level of the index

- The number of rows that the query returns

- The number of leaf pages read per I/O:

$$\text{Reads required} = \text{Number of index levels} + \frac{\text{\# of rows returned/\# of rows per page}}{\text{Pages per IO}}$$

Figure 6-6: Computing reads for a covering nonclustered index range query

Range Queries with Noncovering Nonclustered Indexes

Clustered indexes and covering nonclustered indexes generally perform extremely well for range queries on the leading index key, because they scan leaf pages that are in order by the index key. However, range queries on the key of noncovering nonclustered indexes are much more sensitive to the size of the range in the query. For small ranges, a nonclustered index may be efficient, but for larger ranges, using a nonclustered index can require more reads than a table scan.

At the leaf level of a nonclustered index, the keys are stored sequentially, but at the data level, rows can be randomly placed throughout the data pages. The keys on a single leaf page in a nonclustered index can point to a large number of data rows. When SQL Server returns rows from a table using a nonclustered index, it performs these steps:

- It locates the first qualifying row at the leaf level of the nonclustered index.

- It follows the pointers to the data page for that index.

- It finds the next row on the index page, and locates its data page. The page may already be in cache, or it may have to be read from disk.

When you run this query on the *authors* table in the *pubtune* database, with an index on *au_lname*, it selects 265 rows, performing a table scan of the table's 223 data pages:

```
select au_fname, au_lname, au_id
from authors
where au_lname between "Greaves"
      and "Highland"
```

Especially with short keys, a single leaf-level page in a nonclustered index can point to 100 or more data pages. Using a clustered index, SQL Server follows the index pointers to the first data page with the correct value, and then follows the page chain to read subsequent rows. However, with a nonclustered index, the data pages for a given range can be scattered throughout the database, so it may be necessary to read each page several times. The formula for estimating I/O for range queries accessing the data through a nonclustered index is:

$$\text{Reads required} = \text{Number of index levels} + \frac{\text{\# of rows returned}}{\text{\# of rows per leaf level index page}} + \text{\# of rows returned}$$

Figure 6-7: Computing reads for a nonclustered index range query

The optimizer estimates that a range query that returns 500 rows, with an index structure of 3 levels and 100 rows per page on the leaf level of the nonclustered index, requires 507 or 508 I/Os:

- 1 read for the root level and 1 read for the intermediate level

- 5 or 6 reads for the leaf level of the index

- 500 reads for the data pages

Although it is possible that some of the rows in the result set will be found on the same data pages, or that they will be found on data pages already in cache, this is not predictable. The optimizer costs a physical I/O for each row to be returned, and if this estimate exceeds the cost of a table scan, it chooses the table scan. If the table in this example has less than 508 pages, the optimizer chooses a table scan.

Indexes and Sorts

When there are no indexes and an **order by** clause is included in a query, the query must perform a table scan and sort the results. Sorts and worktables are also required when the index used for the **where** clause does not match the **order by** clause. The use of **desc** in an **order by** clause, to get results in descending order, always requires a sort.

When SQL Server optimizes queries that require sorts, it computes the physical and logical I/O cost of creating a work table and performing the sort for every index where the index order does not match the sort order. This favors the use of an index that supports the **order by** clause.

For composite indexes, the order of the keys in the index must match the order of the columns named in the **order by** clause.

Sorts and Clustered Indexes

If the data is clustered in the order required by the sort, the sort is not needed and is not performed.

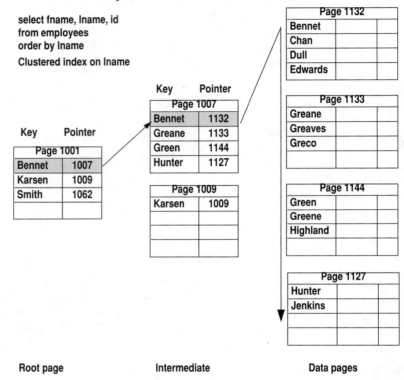

Figure 6-8: An order by query using a clustered index

The following range query returns about 2000 rows. It can use a clustered index on *title_id* to reduce I/O:

```
select * from titles
where title_id between 'T43' and 'T791'
order by title_id
```

```
Table: titles scan count 1, logical reads: 246, physical reads: 246
Total writes for this command: 0
```

Since the data is stored in ascending order, a query requiring descending sort order (for example, **order by title_id desc**) cannot use any indexes, but must sort the data.

Sorts and Nonclustered Indexes

With a nonclustered index, SQL Server determines whether using the nonclustered index is faster than performing a table scan, inserting rows into a worktable, and then sorting the data.

To use the index, SQL Server needs to retrieve the index pages and use them to access the proper data pages in the proper order. If the number of rows to be returned is small, nonclustered index access is cheaper than a table scan. But if the number of rows to be returned is greater than the number of I/Os required to perform the table scan, perform the sort, and to construct and read the worktable, a table scan and sort is performed.

If there is a nonclustered index on *title_id*, this query requires a worktable to sort the results:

```
select * from titles
where title_id between 'T43' and 'T791'
order by title_id
```

It produces this report from **statistics io**:

```
Table: titles scan count 1, logical reads: 621,  physical reads: 621
Table: Worktable scan count 0, logical reads: 2136, physical reads: 0
Total writes for this command: 0
```

This is the same query that produces only 246 physical reads and no worktable when it uses a clustered index to return the 2000 rows— but for a nonclustered index, the I/O estimate would be 2000 physical I/Os to use the index and avoid the sort.

Sorts When the Index Covers the Query

When all the columns named in the select list, the search arguments, and **group by** and **order by** clauses are included in a nonclustered index, SQL Server uses the leaf level of the nonclustered index to retrieve the data and does not have to read the data pages.

If the sort is in ascending order, and the **order by** columns form a **prefix subset** of the index keys, the rows are returned directly from the nonclustered index leaf pages.

If the sort is in descending order, or the columns do not form a prefix subset of the index keys, a worktable is created and sorted.

With an index on *au_lname, au_fname, au_id* of the *authors* table, this query can return the data directly from the leaf pages:

```
select au_id, au_lname
from authors
order by au_lname, au_fname
```
```
Table: authors    scan count 1,  logical reads: 91,  physical reads: 81
Total writes for this command: 0
```

Choosing Indexes

Questions to ask when working with index selection are:

- What indexes are associated currently with a given table?
- What are the most important processes that make use of the table?
- What is the overall ratio of select operations to data modifications performed on the table?
- Has a clustered index been assigned to the table?
- Can the clustered index be replaced by a nonclustered index?
- Do any of the indexes cover one or more of the critical queries?
- Is a composite index required to enforce the uniqueness of a compound primary key?
- What indexes can be defined as unique?
- What are the major sorting requirements?
- Do the indexes support your joins and referential integrity checks?
- Does indexing affect update types (direct vs. deferred)?
- What indexes are needed for cursor positioning?
- If dirty reads are required, are there unique indexes to support the scan?
- Should IDENTITY columns be added to tables and indexes to generate unique indexes? (Unique indexes are required for updatable cursors and dirty reads.)

When deciding how many indexes to use, consider:

- Space constraints
- Access paths to table
- Percentage of data modifications vs. select operations
- Performance requirements of reports vs. OLTP
- Performance impacts of index changes

- How often you can **update statistics**

Index Keys and Logical Keys

Index keys need to be differentiated from logical keys. Logical keys are part of the database design, defining the relationships between tables: primary keys, foreign keys, and common keys. When you optimize your queries by creating indexes, these logical keys may or may not be used as the physical keys for creating indexes. You can create indexes on columns that are not logical keys, and you may have logical keys that are not used as index keys.

Guidelines for Clustered Indexes

These are general guidelines for clustered indexes:

- Most tables should have clustered indexes or use partitions to reduce contention on last page of heaps. In a high-transaction environment, the locking on the last page severely limits throughput.

- If your environment requires a lot of inserts, the clustered index key should not be placed on a monotonically increasing value such as an IDENTITY column. Choose a key that places inserts on "random" pages to minimize lock contention while remaining useful in many queries. Often, the primary key does not meet this guideline.

- Clustered indexes provide very good performance when the key matches the search argument in range queries, such as:

```
where colvalue >= 5 and colvalue < 10
```

- Other good candidates for clustered index keys are columns used in **order by** and **group by** clauses and in joins.

Choosing Clustered Indexes

Choose indexes based on the kinds of **where** clauses or joins you perform. Candidates for clustered indexes are:

- The primary key, if it is used for **where** clauses and if it randomizes inserts

➤ *Note*

If the primary key is a monotonically increasing value, placing a clustered index on this key can cause contention for the data page where the inserts take place. This severely limits concurrency. Be sure that your clustered index key randomizes the location of inserts.

- Columns that are accessed by range, such as:

  `col1 between "X" and "Y" or col12 > "X" and < "Y"`
- Columns used by **order by** or **group by**
- Columns that are not frequently changed
- Columns used in joins

If there are multiple candidates, choose the most commonly needed physical order as a first choice. As a second choice, look for range queries. During performance testing, check for "hot spots," places where data modification activity encounters blocking due to locks on data or index pages.

Candidates for Nonclustered Indexes

When choosing columns for nonclustered indexes, consider all the uses that were not satisfied by your clustered index choice. In addition, look at columns that can provide performance gains through index covering.

The one exception is noncovered range queries, which work well with clustered indexes, but may or may not be supported by nonclustered indexes, depending on the size of the range.

Consider composite indexes to cover critical queries and support less frequent queries:

- The most critical queries should be able to perform point queries and matching scans.
- Other queries should be able to perform nonmatching scans using the index, avoiding table scans.

Other Indexing Guidelines

Here are some other considerations for choosing indexes:

- If an index key is unique, be sure to define the index as unique. Then, the optimizer knows immediately that only one row will be returned for a search argument or a join on the key.

- If your database design uses referential integrity (the **references** or **foreign key...references** keywords in the **create table** statement), the referenced columns **must** have a unique index. However, SQL Server does not automatically create an index on the referencing column. If your application updates and deletes primary keys, you may want to create an index on the referencing column so that these lookups do not perform a table scan.

- If your applications use cursors, see "Index Use and Requirements for Cursors" on page 340.

- If you are creating an index on a table where there will be a lot of insert activity, use **fillfactor** to temporarily:

  - Minimize page splits

  - Improve concurrency and minimize deadlocking

- If you are creating an index on a read-only table, use a **fillfactor** of 100 to make the table or index as compact as possible.

- Keep the size of the key as small as possible. Your index trees remain flatter, accelerating tree traversals. More rows fit on a page, speeding up leaf-level scans of nonclustered index pages. Also, more data fits on the distribution page for your index, increasing the accuracy of index statistics.

- Use small datatypes whenever it fits your design.

  - Numerics compare faster than strings internally.

  - Variable-length character and binary types require more row overhead than fixed-length types, so if there is little difference between the average length of a column and the defined length, use fixed length. Character and binary types that accept null values are by definition variable length.

  - Whenever possible, use fixed-length, non-null types for short columns that will be used as index keys.

- Keep datatypes of the join columns in different tables compatible. If SQL Server has to convert a datatype on one side of a join, it may not use an index for that table. See "Datatype Mismatches and Joins" on page 181 for more information.

Choosing Nonclustered Indexes

When you consider nonclustered indexes, you must weigh the improvement in retrieval time against the increase in data modification time.

In addition, you need to consider these questions:

- How much space will the indexes use?
- How volatile is the candidate column?
- How selective are the index keys? Would a scan be better?
- Is there a lot of duplication?

Because of overhead, add nonclustered indexes only when your testing shows that they are helpful.

Candidates include:

- Columns used for aggregates
- Columns used for joins, **order by, group by**

Performance Price for Data Modification

With each insert, all nonclustered indexes have to be updated, so there is a performance price to pay each time you index column. The leaf level has one entry per row, so you will have to change that the leaf page with every insert or delete.

All nonclustered indexes need to be updated:

- For each insert into the table.
- For each delete from the table.
- For any update to the table that changes any part of an index's key, or that deletes a row from one page and inserts it on another page.
- For almost every update to the clustered index key. Usually, such an update means that the row moves to a different page.
- For every data page split.

Choosing Composite Indexes

If your needs analysis shows that more than one column would make a good candidate for a clustered index key, you may be able to provide clustered-like access with a composite index that covers a particular query or set of queries. These include:

- Range queries
- Vector (grouped) aggregates, if both the grouped and grouping columns are included
- Queries that return a high number of duplicates
- Queries that include **order by**
- Queries that table scan, but use a small subset of the columns on the table

Tables that are read-only or read-mostly can be heavily indexed, as long as your database has enough space available. If there is little update activity, and high select activity, you should provide indexes for all of your frequent queries. Be sure to test the performance benefits of index covering.

User Perceptions and Covered Queries

Covered queries can provide excellent response time for specific queries, while sometimes confusing users by providing much slower response time for very similar-looking queries. With the composite nonclustered index on *au_lname, au_fname, au_id*, this query runs very fast:

```
select au_id
    from authors
where au_fname = "Eliot" and au_lname = "Wilk"
```

This covered point query needs to perform only three reads to find the value on the leaf level row in the nonclustered index of a 5000-row table.

Users might not understand why this similar-looking query (using the same index) does not perform quite as well:

```
select au_fname, au_lname
    from authors
where au_id = "A1714224678"
```

However, this query does not include the leading column of the index, so it has to scan the entire leaf level of the index, about 95 reads.

Adding a column to the select list, which may seem like a minor change to users, makes the performance even worse:

```
select au_fname, au_lname, phone
    from authors
where au_id = "A1714224678"
```

This query performs a table scan, reading 222 pages. In this case, the performance is noticeably worse. But the optimizer has no way of knowing the number of duplicates in the third column (*au_id*) of a nonclustered index: it could match a single row, or it could match one-half of the rows in a table. A composite index can be used only when it covers the query or when the first column appears in the **where** clause.

Adding an unindexed column to a query that includes the leading column of the composite index adds only a single page read to this query, when it must read the data page to find the phone number:

```
select au_id, phone
    from authors
where au_fname = "Eliot" and au_lname = "Wilk"
```

The Importance of Order in Composite Indexes

The examples above highlight the importance of the ordering of columns in composite indexes. Table 6-5 shows the performance characteristics of different **where** clauses with a nonclustered index on *au_lname, au_fname, au_id* and no other indexes on the table. The performance described in this table is for **where** clauses in the form:

```
where column_name = value
```

Table 6-5:   Composite nonclustered index ordering and performance

Columns Named in the where Clause	With Only *au_lname*, *au_fname* and/or *au_id* in the Select List	With Other Columns in the Select List
au_lname or *au_lname, au_fname* or *au_lname, au_fname, au_id*	Good; index used to descend tree; data level is not accessed	Good; index used to descend tree; data is accessed (one more page read per row)
au_fname or *au_id* or *au_fname, au_id*	Moderate, index is scanned to return values	Poor, index not used, table scan

Choose the right ordering of the composite index so that most queries form a prefix subset.

Advantages of Composite Indexes

Composite indexes have these advantages:

- A dense composite index provides many opportunities for index covering.

- A composite index with qualifications on each of the keys will probably return fewer records than a query on any single attribute.

- A composite index is a good way to enforce uniqueness of multiple attributes.

Good choices for composite indexes are:

- Lookup tables

- Columns frequently accessed together

Disadvantages of Composite Indexes

The disadvantages of composite indexes are:

- Composite indexes tend to have large entries. This means fewer index entries per index page and more index pages to read.

- An update to any attribute of a composite index causes the index to be modified. The columns you choose should not be those that are updated often.

Poor choices are:

- Indexes that are too wide because of long keys

- Composite indexes where only the second or third portion, or an even later portion, is used in the **where** clause

Key Size and Index Size

Small index entries yield small indexes, producing less index I/O to execute queries. Longer keys produce fewer entries per page, so an index requires more pages at each level, and in some cases, additional index levels.

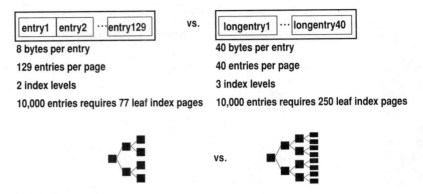

Figure 6-9: Sample rows for small and large index entries

The disadvantage of a covering, nonclustered index, particularly if the index entry is wide, is that there is a larger index to traverse, and updates are more costly.

Techniques for Choosing Indexes

This section presents a study of two queries that must access a single table, and the indexing choices that these queries present as standalone queries, and when index choices need to be made between the two queries.

Examining a Single Query

Assume that you need to improve performance of the following query:

```
select title
from   titles
where  price between $20.00 and $30.00
```

You know the size of the table in rows and pages, the number of rows per page, and the number of rows that the query returns:

- 1,000,000 rows (books)

- 190,000 (19 percent) are priced between $20 and $30

- 10 rows per page; pages 75 percent full; approximately 135,000 pages

With no index, the query would scan all 140,000 pages.

With a clustered index on *price*, the query would find the first $20 book and begin reading sequentially until it gets to the last $30 book. With pages about 75% full, there are an average of 7.5 rows per page. To read 190,000 matching rows, the query would read approximately 25,300 pages plus 3 or 4 index pages.

With a nonclustered index on *price* and random distribution of *price* values, using the index to find the rows for this query would require 190,000 page reads plus about 19 percent of the leaf level of index, adding about 1500 pages. Since a table scan requires only 135,000 pages, the nonclustered index would probably not be used.

Another choice is a nonclustered index on *price, title*. The query can perform a matching index scan, finding the first page with a price of $20 via index pointers, and then scanning forward on the leaf level until it finds a price more than $30. This index requires about 35,700 leaf pages, so to scan the matching leaf pages requires about 6,800 reads.

For this query, the nonclustered index on *price, title* is best.

Examining Two Queries with Different Indexing Requirements

This query also needs to run against the same table:

```
select price
from   titles
where  title = "Looking at Leeks"
```

You know that there are very few duplicate titles, so this query returns only one or two rows.

Here are four possible indexing strategies, identified by the numbers used in subsequent discussion:

1. Nonclustered index on *titles(title)*; clustered index on *titles(price)*

2. Clustered index on *titles(title)*; nonclustered index on *titles(price)*

3. Nonclustered index on *titles(title, price)*

4. Nonclustered index on *titles(price,title)*

Table 6-6 shows some estimates of index sizes and I/O for the range query on *price* and the point query on *title*. The estimates for the numbers of index and data pages were generated using a fillfactor of 75 percent with **sp_estspace**:

```
sp_estspace titles, 1000000, 75
```

The values were rounded for easier comparison.

Table 6-6:   Comparing index strategies for two queries

Index Choices	Index Pages	Range Query on *price*	Point Query on *title*
1 Nonclustered on *title* Clustered on *price*	36,800 650	Clustered index, about 26,600 pages (135,000 * .19) With 16K I/O: 3,125 I/Os	Nonclustered index, 6 I/Os
2 Clustered on *title* Nonclustered on *price*	3,770 6,076	Table scan, 135,000 pages With 16K I/O: 17,500 I/Os	Clustered index, 6 I/Os
3 Nonclustered on *title, price*	36,835	Nonmatching index scan, about 35,700 pages With 16K I/O: 4,500 I/Os	Nonclustered index, 5 I/Os
4 Nonclustered on *price, title*	36,835	Matching index scan, about 6,800 pages (35,700 * .19) With 16K I/O: 850 I/Os	Nonmatching index scan, about 35,700 pages With 16K I/O: 4,500 I/Os

Examining these figures shows that:

- For the range query on *price*, indexing choice 4 is best, and choices 1 and 3 are acceptable with 16K I/O.

- For the point query on *titles*, indexing choices 1, 2, and 3 are excellent.

The best indexing strategy for the combination of these two queries is to use two indexes:

- The nonclustered index in *price, title*, for range queries on *price*

- The clustered index on *title*, since it requires relatively little space

Other information could help determine which indexing strategy to use to support multiple queries:

- What is the frequency of each query? How many times per day or per hour is the query run?

- What are the response time requirements? Is one of them especially time critical?

- What are the response time requirements for updates? Does creating more than one index slow updates?

- Is the range of values typical? Is a wider or narrower range of prices, such as $20 to $50 often used? How do these ranges affect index choice?

- Is there a large data cache? Are these queries critical enough to provide a 35,000-page cache for the nonclustered composite indexes in index choice 3 or 4? Binding this index to its own cache would provide very fast performance.

Index Statistics

When you create an index on a table that contains data, SQL Server creates a distribution page containing two kinds of statistics about index values:

- A distribution table

- A density table

An index's distribution page is created when you create an index on a table that contains data. If you create an index on an empty table, no distribution page is created. If you truncate the table (removing all of its rows) the distribution page is dropped.

The data on the distribution page is not automatically maintained by SQL Server. You must run the **update statistics** command to update the data. You should run this command:

- When you feel that the distribution of the keys in an index has changed

- If you truncate a table and reload the data

- When you determine that query plans may be less optimal due to incorrect statistics

The Distribution Table

The distribution table stores information about the distribution of key values in the index. If the index is a composite index, it only stores distribution information about the first key.

The distribution table is a list of key values called steps. The number of steps on the distribution page depends on the key size and whether the column stores variable-length data.

The statistics page looks very much like a data page or index page. One major difference is that it does not contain a row offset table. The density table occupies this space on the page; for each key in the index, the density uses 2 bytes of storage. The rest of the page is available to store the steps. Figure 6-10 shows how to compute the number of steps that will be stored on the distribution page. Fixed-length columns have 2bytes of overhead per step; variable-length columns have 7 bytes of overhead per step.

Fixed-Length Key

$$\text{Number of keys} = \frac{2016 - (\text{Number of keys} * 2)}{\text{Bytes per key} + 2}$$

Variable-Length Key

$$\text{Number of keys} = \frac{2016 - (\text{Number of keys} * 2)}{\text{Bytes per key} + 7}$$

Figure 6-10: Formulas for computing number of distribution page values

For variable-length columns, the defined (maximum) length is always used.

Once the number of steps is determined, SQL Server divides the number of rows in the table by the number of steps, and then stores the data value for every Nth row in the distribution table. Figure 6-11 shows this process for a small part of an index.

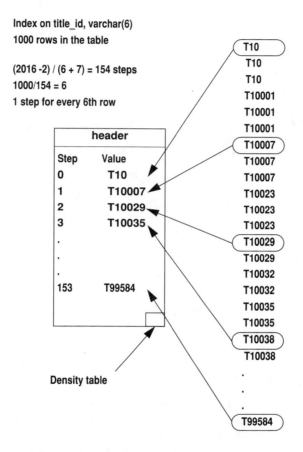

Index on title_id, varchar(6)
1000 rows in the table

(2016 -2) / (6 + 7) = 154 steps
1000/154 = 6
1 step for every 6th row

Figure 6-11: Building the distribution page

The Density Table

The query optimizer uses statistics to estimate the cost of using an index. One of these statistics is called the **density**. The density is the average proportion of duplicate keys in the index. It varies between 0 and 100 percent. An index with N rows whose keys are unique will have a density of $1/N$, while an index whose keys are all duplicates of each other will have a density of 100 percent.

Figure 6-11 shows a single-entry density table, since the index is built on a single key. For indexes with multiple keys, there will be a value for each prefix of keys in the index. SQL Server maintains a density for each prefix of columns in composite indexes. That is, for an index on columns A, B, C, D, it stores the density for:

- A
- A, B
- A, B, C
- A, B, C, D

If density statistics are not available, the optimizer uses default percentages, as shown in Table 6-7.

Table 6-7: Default density percentages

Condition	Examples	Default
Equality	col = x	10%
Closed interval	col > x and col < y	25%
	or	
	col between x and y	
Open end range	col > x	33%
	col >= x	
	col < x	
	col <= x	

For example, if there is no statistics page for an index on *authors(city)*, the optimizer estimates that 10 percent of the rows would be returned for this query:

```
select au_fname, au_lname, pub_name
    from authors a, publishers p
    where a.city = p.city
```

How the Optimizer Uses the Statistics

The optimizer uses index statistics to estimate the usefulness of an index and to decide join order. For example, this query finds a large number of titles between $20 and $30:

```
select title from titles
where price between $20.00 and $30.00
```

However, this query finds only a few rows between $1000 and $1010:

```
select titles from titles
where price between $1000.00 and $1010.00
```

The number of rows returned may be different, and this affects the usefulness of nonclustered indexes.

The statistics the optimizer uses include:

- The number of rows in the table
- The number of pages for the table or on the leaf level of the nonclustered index
- The density value
- The distribution table

How the Optimizer Uses the Distribution Table

When the optimizer checks for a value in the distribution table, it will find that one of these conditions holds:

- The value falls between two consecutive rows in the table.
- The value equals one row in the middle of the table.
- The value equals the first row or the last row in the table.
- The value equals more than one row in the middle of the table.
- The value equals more than one row, including the first or last row in the table.
- The value is less than the first row, or greater than the last row in the table. (In this case, you should run **update statistics**.)

Depending on which cases match the query, the optimizer uses formulas involving the step location (beginning, end, or middle of the page), the number of steps, the number of rows in the table, and the density to compute an estimated number of rows.

How the Optimizer Uses the Density Table

The optimizer uses the density table to help compute the number of rows that a query will return. Even if the value of a search argument is not known when the query is optimized, SQL Server can use the density values in an index, as long as the leading column or columns are specified for composite indexes.

Index Maintenance

Indexes should evolve as your system evolves.

- Over time, indexes should be based on the transactions and processes that are being run, not on the original database design.
- Drop and rebuild indexes only if they are hurting performance.
- Keep index statistics up to date.

Monitoring Index Usage Over Time

Periodically check the query plans, as described in Chapter 8, "Understanding Query Plans," and the I/O statistics for your most frequent user queries. Pay special attention to nonclustered indexes that support range queries. They are most likely to switch to table scans if the data changes.

Dropping Indexes That Hurt Performance

Drop indexes when they hurt performance. If an application performs data modifications during the day and generates reports at night, you may want to drop some of the indexes in the morning and re-create them at night.

Many system designers create numerous indexes that are rarely, if ever, actually used by the query optimizer. Use query plans to determine whether your indexes are being used.

Index Statistics Maintenance

When you create an index after a table is loaded, a data distribution table is created for that index. The distribution page is not automatically maintained. The database owner must issue an **update statistics** command to ensure that statistics are current. The syntax is:

```
update statistics table_name [index_name]
```

For example, this command updates all the indexes on the *authors* table:

```
update statistics authors
```

To update a single index, give the table name and index name:

```
update statistics titles titles_idx
```

Run **update statistics**:

- After deleting or inserting rows which change the skew of data
- After adding rows to a table whose rows had previously been deleted with **truncate table**

- After updating values in index columns
- As often as needed

Run **update statistics** after inserts to any index that includes IDENTITY columns or an increasing key value. Date columns, such as those in a sales entry application, often have regularly increasing keys. Running **update statistics** on these types of indexes is especially important if the IDENTITY column or other increasing key is the leading column in the index. After a number of inserts past the last key that was included in the index, all that the optimizer can tell is that the search value lies beyond the last row in the distribution page but it cannot accurately determine how many rows are represented.

➤ *Note*

Failure to update statistics can severely hurt performance.

SQL Server is a very efficient transaction processing engine. However, it relies heavily on distribution page data to perform well. If statistics are not up to date, a query that should take only a few seconds could take much longer.

Rebuilding Indexes

Rebuilding indexes reclaims space in the B-trees. As pages split and as rows are deleted, indexes can contain many pages that are only half full or that only contain a few rows. Also, if your application performs scans on covering nonclustered indexes and large I/O, rebuilding the nonclustered index maintains the effectiveness of large I/O by reducing fragmentation.

Rebuild indexes under the following conditions:

- Data and usage patterns have changed significantly.
- A period of heavy inserts is expected, or has just been completed.
- The sort order has changed.
- Queries that use large I/O require more disk reads than expected.
- Space usage exceeds estimates because heavy data modification has left many data and index pages partially full.
- **dbcc** has identified errors in the index.

If you rebuild a clustered index, all nonclustered indexes are re-created, since data pages and rows will be in a new clustered order and will have their pages copied to a new location. Nonclustered indexes must be re-created to point to the correct pages.

Rebuilding indexes takes time. Use the **sp_estspace** procedure to estimate the time needed to generate indexes. See the sample output in "Index Entries Are Too Large" on page 117.

In most database systems, there are well-defined peak periods and off-hours. You can use off-hours to your advantage, for example:

- To delete all indexes to allow more efficient bulk inserts

- To create a new group of indexes to help generate a set of reports.

See "Creating Indexes" on page 456 for information about configuration parameters to increase the speed of creating indexes.

Speeding Index Creation with *sorted data*

If data is already sorted, use **sorted_data** option to **create index.** This option:

- Checks to see that the rows in the table are in order by the index keys

- Makes a copy of the data at a new location, if the index is a clustered index

- Builds the index tree

Using this option saves the time that would otherwise be required for the sort step. For large tables that require numerous passes to build the index, the time saved is considerable.

➤ *Note*

The sorted data option copies the entire data level of a clustered index. It does not delete the old data pages until the command completes. This means that you need approximately 120 percent of the space required for the table available in your database.

Displaying Information About Indexes

The *sysindexes* table in each database contains one row for each:

- Index

- Heap table

- Table that contains text or image columns.

The contents are maintained by SQL Server. To display index information, use **sp_helpindex**.

Table 6-8:   Page pointers for unpartitioned tables in the sysindexes table

Object Type	*indid*	*root*	*first*
Heap table	0	Last data page in the table's data chain	First data page in the table's data chain
Clustered index	1	Root page of the index	First data page in the table's data chain
Nonclustered index	2–250	Root page of the index	First leaf page of the nonclustered index
Text/image object	255	First page of the object	First page of the object

The *sysindexes.distribution* column displays 0 if no statistics exist for an index because the index was created on an empty table. If *distribution* is not equal to zero, the value points to the distribution page.

The *doampg* and *ioampg* columns in *sysindexes* store pointers to the first OAM page for the data pages (*doampg*) or index pages (*ioampg*). The system functions **data_pgs, reserved_pgs** and **used_pgs** use these pointers and the object ID to quickly provide information about space usage. See "OAM Pages and Size Statistics" on page 84 for a sample query.

Tips and Tricks for Indexes

Here are some additional suggestions that can lead to improved performance when you are creating and using indexes:

- Modify the logical design to make use of an artificial column and a lookup table for tables that require a large index entry.

- Reduce the size of an index entry for a frequently used index.

- Drop indexes during periods when frequent updates occur and rebuild them before periods when frequent selects occur.

- If you do frequent index maintenance, configure your server to speed sorting. See "Configuring SQL Server to Speed Sorting" on page 457 for information about configuration parameters that enable faster sorting.

Creating Artificial Columns

When indexes become too large, especially composite indexes, it is beneficial to create an artificial column that is assigned to a row, with a secondary lookup table that is used to translate between the internal ID and the original columns. This may increase response time for certain queries, but the overall performance gain due to a more compact index is usually worth the effort.

Keeping Index Entries Short and Avoiding Overhead

Avoid storing purely numeric IDs as character data (*varchar*, *char*, or *nvarchar*). Use integer or numeric IDs whenever possible to:

- Save storage space on the data pages

- Make index entries more compact

- Allow more rows on the distribution page, if the ID is used as an index key

- Compare faster internally

Indexes entries on *varchar* columns require more overhead than entries on *char* columns. For short index keys, especially those with little variation in length in the column data, use *char* for more compact index entries, and to increase the number of distribution page entries.

Dropping and Rebuilding Indexes

You might drop nonclustered indexes prior to a major set of inserts, and then rebuild them afterwards. In that way, the inserts and bulk copies go faster, since the nonclustered indexes do not have to be updated with every insert. See "Rebuilding Indexes" on page 155.

Choosing Fillfactors for Indexes

By default, SQL Server creates indexes that are completely full at the leaf level and leaves room for two rows on the intermediate pages for growth. The **fillfactor** option for the **create index** command allows you to specify how full to create index pages and the data pages of clustered indexes. Figure 6-12 illustrates a table with a fillfactor of 50 percent.

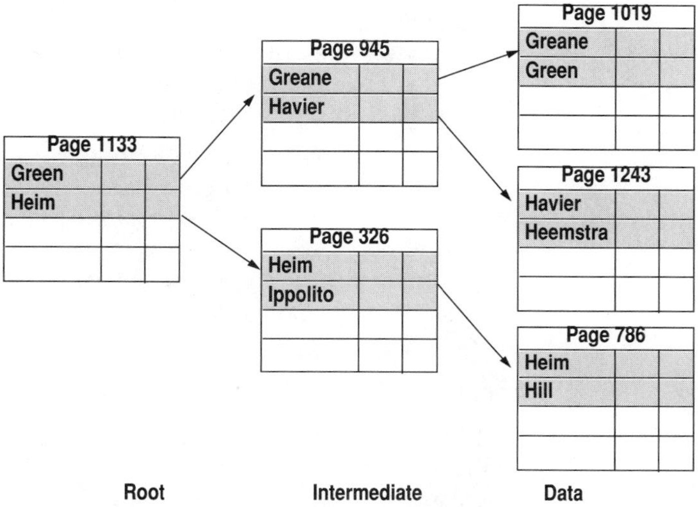

Figure 6-12: Table and clustered index with fillfactor set to 50 percent

If you are creating indexes for tables that will grow in size, you can reduce the impact of page splitting on your tables and indexes by using the **fillfactor** option for **create index**. Note that the fillfactor is used only when you create the index; it is not maintained over time. The purpose of **fillfactor** is to provide a performance boost for tables that will experience growth; maintaining that fillfactor by continuing to split partially full pages would defeat the purpose.

When you use **fillfactor**, except for a fillfactor value of 100 percent, data and index rows are spread out across the disk space for the database farther than they are by default.

Disadvantages of Using *fillfactor*

If you use **fillfactor**, especially a very low **fillfactor**, you may notice these effects on queries and maintenance activities:

- More pages must be read for each query that does a table scan or leaf-level scan on a nonclustered index. In some cases, it may also add a level to an index's B-tree structure, since there will be more pages at the data level and possibly more pages at each index level.

- The number of pages that must be checked by your **dbcc** commands increases, so these commands will take more time.

- The number of pages dumped with **dump database** increases. **dump database** copies all pages that store data, but does not dump pages that are not yet in use. Your dumps and loads will take longer to complete and possibly use more tapes.

- Fillfactors fade away over time. If you use **fillfactor** only to help reduce the performance impact of lock contention on index rows, you may wish to use **max_rows_per_page** instead. If you use **fillfactor** to reduce the performance impact of page splits, you need to monitor your system and re-create indexes when page splitting begins to hurt performance.

Advantages of Using *fillfactor*

Setting **fillfactor** to a low value provides a temporary performance enhancement. Its benefits fade away as inserts to the database increase the amount of space used on data pages. The benefits are that a lower fillfactor:

- Reduces page splits.

- Can reduce lock contention, since it reduces the likelihood that two processes will need the same data or index page simultaneously.

- Can help maintain large I/O efficiency for the data pages and for the leaf levels of nonclustered indexes, since page splits occur less frequently. This means that a set of eight pages on an extent are likely to be read sequentially.

Using *sp_sysmon* to Observe the Effects of Changing *fillfactor*

sp_sysmon generates output that allows you to observe how different **fillfactor** values affect system performance. Pay particular attention to the performance categories in the output that are most likely to be affected by changes in **fillfactor**: page splits and lock contention.

See Chapter 19, "Monitoring SQL Server Performance with sp_sysmon" and the topics "Lock Management" on page 503 and "Page Splits" on page 499 in that chapter.

SQL Server Monitor, a separate Sybase product, can pinpoint where problems are at the object level.

Armed to Face the Optimizer

With the tools discussed in this chapter, you are now prepared to scrutinize the query optimizer and its query plans.

Even the most carefully chosen indexes can sometimes fail to have the desired effect on performance. The next level of insight comes with a view into SQL Server's cost-based query optimizer. This view is provided in Chapter 7, "The SQL Server Query Optimizer."

7 The SQL Server Query Optimizer

What Is Query Optimization?

Query optimization is the process of analyzing individual queries to determine what resources they use and whether the use of resources can be reduced. For any query, you need to understand how it accesses database objects, the size of the objects, and indexing on the tables in order to determine whether it is possible to improve the query's performance. This material was covered in Chapters 2–6.

The final component for query optimization is understanding the query optimizer itself and learning to use the query-analysis reporting tools.

SQL Server's Cost-Based Optimizer

The optimizer is the part of SQL Server's code that examines parsed and normalized queries and information about database objects. The input to the optimizer is a parsed SQL query; the output from the optimizer is a **query plan**. The query plan is the ordered set of steps required to carry out the query, including the methods (table scan, index choice, and so on) to access each table. A query plan is compiled code that is ready to run.

The SQL Server optimizer finds the best query plan—the plan that is least costly in terms of time. For many Transact-SQL queries, there are many possible query plans. The optimizer reviews all possible plans and estimates the cost of each plan. SQL Server selects the least costly plan, and compiles and executes it.

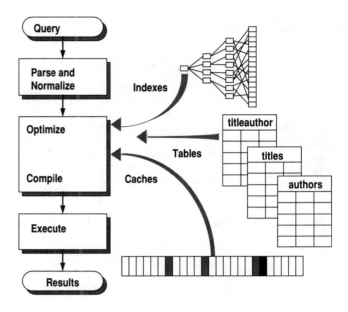

Figure 7-1: Query execution steps

Steps in Query Processing

When you execute a Transact-SQL query, SQL Server processes it in these steps:

1. The query is parsed and normalized. The parser ensures that the SQL syntax is correct and that all the objects referenced in the query exist.

2. The query is optimized. It is analyzed, and the best query plan is chosen:

   - Each table is analyzed

   - Cost of each index is estimated

   - Join order is chosen

   - Final access method is determined

3. The chosen query plan is compiled.

4. The query is executed, and the results are returned to the user.

Optimization Problems and their Roots

Some symptoms of optimization problems are:

- A query runs more slowly than you expect, based on indexes and table size.

- A query runs more slowly than similar queries.

- A query suddenly starts running more slowly than usual.

- A query processed within a stored procedure takes longer than when it is processed as an ad hoc statement.

- The query plan shows the use of a table scan when you expect it to use an index.

Problems such as these indicate that although SQL Server is using the best information at its disposal to select the query processing plan with the least cost, it is either lacking up-to-date information or arriving at the wrong conclusion. Either of these inaccuracies result in the optimizer choosing the wrong plan.

The root causes of optimization problems include:

- Index statistics have not been updated recently, so that actual data distribution does not match the values that SQL Server uses to optimize queries.

- A **where** clause is causing the optimizer to select an inappropriate strategy.

- The rows that will be referenced by a given transaction do not fit the pattern reflected by the index statistics.

- An index is being used to access a large portion of the table.

- No appropriate index exists for a critical query.

- A stored procedure was compiled before significant changes to the underlying tables were performed.

Working with the Optimizer

The goal of the optimizer is to select the access method that reduces the total time needed to process a query. The optimizer bases its choice on the contents of the tables being queried and other factors such as cache strategies, cache size, and I/O size. Since disk access is generally the most expensive operation, the most important task in optimizing queries is to provide the optimizer with appropriate index choices, based on the transactions to be performed.

SQL Server's cost-based query optimizer has evolved over many years, taking into account many different issues. However, because of its general-purpose nature, the optimizer may select a query plan that is different from the one you expect. In certain situations, it may make the incorrect choice of access methods. In some cases, this may be the result of inaccurate or incomplete information. In other cases, additional analysis and the use of special query processing options can determine the source of the problem and provide solutions or workarounds. Chapter 9, "Advanced Optimizing Techniques" describes additional tools for debugging problems like this.

How Is "Fast" Determined?

Knowing what the optimizer considers to be fast and slow can significantly improve your understanding of the query plan chosen by the optimizer. The significant costs in query processing are:

- Physical I/Os, when pages must be read from disk

- Logical I/Os, when pages in cache must be read repeatedly for a query

For queries with **order by** clauses or **distinct**, the optimizer adds the physical and logical I/O cost for performing sorts to the cost of the physical and logical I/O to read data and index pages.

The optimizer assigns 18 as the cost of a physical I/O and 2 as the cost of a logical I/O. Some operations using worktables use 5 as the cost of writing to the worktable. These are relative units of cost and do not represent time units such as milliseconds or ticks.

Query Optimization and Plans

Query plans consist of retrieval tactics and an ordered set of execution steps to retrieve the data needed by the query. In developing query plans, the optimizer examines:

- The size of each table in the query, both in rows and data pages.

- The size of the available data cache, the size of I/O supported by the cache, and the cache strategy to be used.

- The indexes, and the types of indexes, that exist on the tables and columns used in the query.

- Whether the index covers the query, that is, whether the query can be satisfied by retrieving data from index keys without having to access the data pages. SQL Server can use indexes that cover queries even if no **where** clauses are included in the query.

- The density and distribution of keys in the indexes. SQL Server maintains statistics for index keys. See "Index Statistics" on page 149 for more information on index statistics.

- The estimated cost of physical and logical reads and cost of caching.

- Optimizable join clauses and the best join order, considering the costs and number of table scans required for each join and the usefulness of indexes in limiting the scans.

- Where there are no useful indexes, whether building a worktable (an internal, temporary table) with an index on the join columns would be faster than repeated table scans.

- Whether the query contains a **max** or **min** aggregate that can use an index to find the value without scanning the table.

- Whether the pages will be needed repeatedly to satisfy a query such as a join or whether a fetch-and-discard strategy can be employed because the pages need to be scanned only once.

For each plan, the optimizer determines the total cost in milliseconds. SQL Server then uses the best plan.

Stored procedures and triggers are optimized when the object is first executed, and the query plan is stored in cache. If other users execute the same procedure while an unused copy of the plan resides in cache, the compiled query plan is copied in cache rather than being recompiled.

Diagnostic Tools for Query Optimization

SQL Server provides the following diagnostic tools for query optimization:

- **set showplan on** displays the steps performed for each query in a batch. It is often used with **set noexec on**, especially for queries that return large numbers of rows.

- **set statistics io on** displays the number of logical and physical reads and writes required by the query. This tool is described in Chapter 6, "Indexing for Performance."

- **set statistics subquerycache on** displays the number of cache hits and misses and the number of rows in the cache for each subquery.

See "Displaying Subquery Cache Information" on page 194 for examples.

- **set statistics time on** displays the time it takes to parse and compile each command. It displays the time it takes to execute each step of the query. The "parse and compile" and "execution" times are given in timeticks, the exact value of which is machine-dependent. The "elapsed time" and "cpu time" are given in milliseconds. See "Using set statistics time" on page 169 for more information.

- **dbcc traceon(302)** provides additional information about why particular plans were chosen, and is often used in cases when the optimizer chooses plans that seem incorrect.

You can use many of these options at the same time, but some of them suppress others, as described below.

showplan, statistics io, and other commands produce their output while stored procedures are run. The system procedures that you might use for checking table structure or indexes as you test optimization strategies can produce voluminous output. You may want to have hard copies of your table schemas and index information or you can use separate windows for running system procedures such as **sp_helpindex**.

For longer queries and batches, you may want to save **showplan** and **statistics io** output in files. The "echo input" flag to **isql** echoes the input into the output file, with line numbers included. The syntax is:

UNIX, Windows NT, and OS/2

```
isql -P password -e -i input_file -o outputfile
```

Novell NetWare

```
load isql -P password -e -i input_file
        -o outputfile
```

VMS

```
isql /password = password
        /echo
        /input = inputfile
        /output = outputfile
```

Using *showplan* and *noexec* Together

showplan is often used in conjunction with **set noexec on**, which prevents the SQL statements from being executed. Be sure to issue the **showplan** command, or any other **set** commands, before the **noexec** command. Once you issue **set noexec on**, the only command that SQL Server executes is **set noexec off**. This example shows the correct order:

```
set showplan on
set noexec on
go
select au_lname, au_fname
    from    authors
    where   au_id = "A137406537"
go
```

noexec and *statistics io*

While **showplan** and **noexec** make useful companions, **noexec** stops all the output of **statistics io**. The **statistics io** command reports actual disk I/O; while **noexec** is in effect, no I/O takes place, so the reports are not printed.

Using *set statistics time*

set statistics time displays information about the time it takes to execute SQL Server commands. It prints these statistics:

- Parse and compile time – the number of CPU ticks taken to parse, optimize, and compile the query.

- Execution time – the number of CPU ticks taken to execute the query.

- SQL Server CPU time – the number of CPU ticks taken to execute the query, converted to milliseconds.

  To see the *clock_rate* for your system, execute:

  ```
  sp_configure "sql server clock tick length"
  ```

  See "sql server clock tick length" on page 11-93 of the *System Administration Guide* for more information.

- SQL Server elapsed time – the elapsed time is the difference between the time the command started and the current time, as taken from the operating system clock, in milliseconds.

The following formula converts ticks to milliseconds:

$$\text{Milliseconds} = \frac{CPU\_ticks * clock\_rate}{1000}$$

Figure 7-2: Formula for converting ticks to milliseconds

```
select type, sum(advance)
from titles t, titleauthor ta, authors a, publishers
p
where t.title_id = ta.title_id
      and ta.au_id = a.au_id
      and p.pub_id = t.pub_id
      and (a.state = "NY" or a.state ="CA")
      and p.state != "NY"
group by type
having max(total_sales) > 100000
```

The following output shows that the query was parsed and compiled in one clock tick, or 100 ms. It took 120 ticks, or 12,000 ms., to execute. Total elapsed time was 17,843 ms., indicating that SQL Server spent some time processing other tasks or waiting for disk or network I/O to complete.

```
Parse and Compile Time 1.
SQL Server cpu time: 100 ms.
 type
 ----------- ------------------------
 UNDECIDED                210,500.00
 business                 256,000.00
 cooking                  286,500.00
 news                     266,000.00

Execution Time 120.
SQL Server cpu time: 12000 ms. SQL Server elapsed time: 17843 ms.
```

Optimizer Strategies

The following sections explain how the optimizer analyzes these specific types of queries:

- Search arguments in the **where** clause
- Joins
- Queries using **or** clauses and the **in (*values_list*)** predicate
- Aggregates

- Subqueries
- Updates

Search Arguments and Using Indexes

It is important to distinguish between **where** clause specifications that are used as search arguments to find query results via indexes and those that are used later in query processing. This distinction creates a finer definition for search argument:

- Search arguments, or SARGs, can be used to determine an access path to the data rows. They match index keys and determine which indexes are used to locate and retrieve the matching data rows.
- Other selection criteria are additional qualifications that are applied to the rows after they have been located.

Consider this query, with an index on *au_lname, au_fname*:

```
select au_lname, au_fname, phone
    from authors
    where au_lname = "Gerland"
        and city = "San Francisco"
```

The clause:

```
au_lname = "Gerland"
```

qualifies as a SARG because:

- There is an index on *au_lname.*
- There are no functions or other operations on the column name.
- The operator is a valid SARG operator.
- The datatype of the constant matches the datatype of the column.

The clause:

```
city = "San Francisco"
```

matches all the criteria above except the first. There is no index on the *city* column. In this case, the index on *au_lname* would probably be used as the search argument for the query. All pages with a matching author name are brought into cache, and each matching row is examined to see if the city also matches.

One of the first steps the optimizer performs is to separate the SARGs from other qualifications on the query so that it can cost the access methods for each SARG.

SARGs in *where* Clauses

The optimizer looks for SARGs in the **where** clauses of a query and for indexes that match the columns. If your query uses one or more of these clauses to scan an index, you will see the **showplan** output "Keys are: *<keylist>*" immediately after the index name information. If you think your query should be using an index, and it causes table scans instead, look carefully at the search clauses and operators.

Indexable Search Argument Syntax

Indexable search arguments are expressions one of these forms:

```
<column> <operator> <expression>

<expression> <operator> <column>

<column> is null
```

The *column* must be only a column name. Functions, expressions, or concatenation added to the column name always require a table scan.

The *operator* must be one of the following:

```
=, >, <, >=, <=, !>, !<, <>, !=, is null.
```

The *expression* can be a constant or an expression that evaluates to a constant. The optimizer uses the index statistics differently, depending on whether the value of the expression is a constant or an expression:

- If the expression is a constant, its value is known when the query is optimized. It can be used by the optimizer to look up distribution values in the index statistics.

- If the value of the expression is not known at compile time, the optimizer uses the density from the distribution page to estimate the number of rows that the query returns. The value of variables, mathematical expressions, concatenation and functions cannot be known until the query is executed.

The non-equality operators **< >** and **!=** are special cases. The optimizer can check for covering nonclustered indexes on the column name, and perform a nonmatching index scan if the index covers the query, but these queries cannot use indexes to limit the number of rows that must be examined or to position a search.

Search Argument Equivalents

The optimizer looks for equivalents that it can convert to SARGs. These are listed in Table 7-1.

Table 7-1: SARG equivalents

Clause	Conversion
between	Converted to **>=** and **<=** clauses.
like	If the first character in the pattern is a constant, **like** clauses can be converted to greater than or less than queries. For example, **like "sm%"** becomes **>= "sm" and < "sn"**. The expression **like "%x"** is not optimizable.
expressions	If the expression portion of the **where** clause contains arithmetic expressions that can be converted to a constant, the optimizer can use the density values, and may use the index, but cannot use the distribution table on the index.

The following are some examples of optimizable search arguments:

```
au_lname = "Bennett"
price >= $12.00
advance > 10000 and advance < 20000
au_lname like "Ben%" and price > $12.00
```

These search arguments are optimizable, but use only the density, not the distribution values from the index statistics:

```
salary = 12 * 3000
price = @value
```

The following arguments are **not** optimizable search arguments:

```
salary = commission /*both are column names*/
advance * 2 = 5000   /*expression on column side
                       not permitted */
advance = $10000
  or price = $20.00 /*see "OR strategy" */
substring(au_lname,1,3) = "Ben" /* no functions on
                                  column name */
```

Guidelines for Creating Search Arguments

Use these guidelines when you write search arguments for your queries:

- Avoid functions, arithmetic operations, and other expressions on the column side of search clauses.

- Avoid incompatible datatypes.

- Use the leading column of a composite index. The optimization of secondary keys provides less performance.

- Use all the search arguments you can to give the optimizer as much as possible to work with.

- Check **showplan** output to see which keys and indexes are used.

Figure 7-3 shows how predicates are applied by the optimizer and in query execution, and questions to ask when examining predicates and index choices.

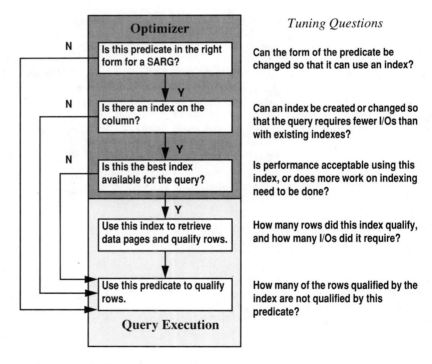

Figure 7-3: SARGs and index choices

Adding SARGs to Help the Optimizer

Providing the optimizer as with much information as possible for every table in the query gives the optimizer more choices. Consider the following three queries. The *titles* and *titleauthor* tables are in a one-to-many (1:M) relationship. *title_id* is unique in the *titles* table. The first query, with the SARG on *titles*, would probably perform better than the second query, with the SARG on *titleauthor*.

The third query, with SARGs provided for both tables, gives the optimizer more flexibility in the optimization of the join order.

```
1. select au_lname, title
   from titles t, titleauthor ta, authors a
   where t.title_id = ta.title_id
         and a.au_id = ta.au_id
         and t.title_id = "T81002"

2. select au_lname, title
   from titles t, titleauthor ta, authors a
   where t.title_id = ta.title_id
         and a.au_id = ta.au_id
         and ta.title_id = "T81002"

3. select au_lname, title
   from titles t, titleauthor ta, authors a
   where t.title_id = ta.title_id
         and a.au_id = ta.au_id
         and t.title_id = "T81002"
         and ta.title_id = "T81002"
```

Optimizing Joins

Joins pull information from two or more tables, requiring **nested iterations** on the tables involved. In a two-table join, one table is treated as the outer table; the other table becomes the inner table. SQL Server examines the outer table for rows that satisfy the query conditions. For each row that qualifies, SQL Server must then examine the inner table, looking at each row where the join columns match.

In showplan output, the order of "FROM TABLE" messages indicates the order in which SQL Server chooses to join tables. See ""FROM TABLE" Message" on page 211 for an example that joins three tables.

Optimizing the join columns in queries is extremely important. Relational databases make extremely heavy use of joins. Queries that perform joins on several tables are especially critical, as explained in the following sections.

Some subqueries are also converted to joins. These are discussed on page 189.

Join Syntax

Join clauses take the form:

```
table1.column_name <operator> table2.column_name
```

The join operators are:

```
=,  >,  >=,  <,  <=,  !>,  !<,  !=,  <>,  *=,  =*
```

How Joins Are Processed

When the optimizer creates a query plan for a join query:

- It determines which index to use for each table, by estimating the I/O required for each possible index and for a table scan.

- If there is no useful index on the inner table of a join, the optimizer may decide to build a temporary index, a process called **reformatting**. See "Saving I/O Using the Reformatting Strategy" on page 179.

- It determines the join order, basing the decision on the total cost estimates for the possible join orders.

- It determines the I/O size and caching strategy. If an unindexed table is small, it may decide to read the entire table into cache.

Factors such as indexes and density of keys, which determine costs on single-table selects, become much more critical for joins.

Basic Join Processing

The process of creating the result set for a join is to nest the tables, and to scan the inner tables repeatedly for each qualifying row in the outer table.

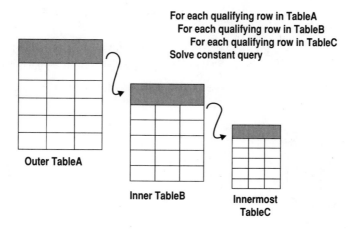

For each qualifying row in TableA
For each qualifying row in TableB
For each qualifying row in TableC
Solve constant query

Outer TableA

Inner TableB

Innermost TableC

Figure 7-4: Nesting of tables during a join

In Figure 7-4, the access to the tables to be joined is nested:

- *TableA* is accessed once.

- *TableB* is accessed once for each qualifying row in *TableA*.

- *TableC* is accessed once for each qualifying row in *TableB*, **each time** that *TableB* is accessed.

For example, if 15 rows from *TableA* match the conditions in the query, *TableB* is accessed 15 times. If 20 rows from *TableB* match for each matching row in *TableA*, then *TableC* is scanned 300 times. If *TableC* is small, or has a useful index, the I/O count stays reasonably small. If *TableC* is large and unindexed, the optimizer may choose to use the reformatting strategy to avoid performing extensive I/O.

Choice of Inner and Outer Tables

The outer table is usually the one that has:

- The smallest number of qualifying rows, and/or

- The largest numbers of reads required to locate rows.

The inner table usually has:

- The largest number of qualifying rows, and/or

- The smallest number of reads required to locate rows.

For example, when you join a large, unindexed table to a smaller table with indexes on the join key, the optimizer chooses:

- The large table as the outer table. It will only have to read this large table once.

- The indexed table as the inner table. Each time it needs to access the inner table, it will take only a few reads to find rows.

Figure 7-5 shows a large, unindexed table and a small, indexed table.

```
select TableA.colx, TableB.coly
from TableA, TableB
where TableA.col1 = TableB.col1
   and TableB.col2 = "anything"
   and TableA.col2 = "something"
```

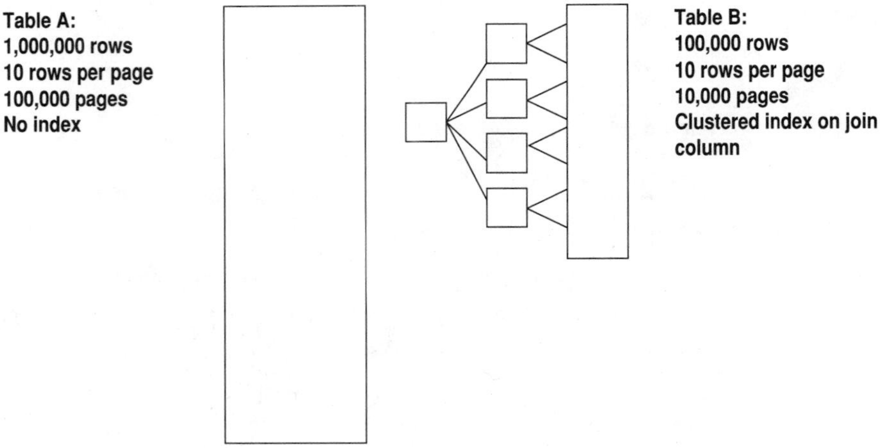

Table A:
1,000,000 rows
10 rows per page
100,000 pages
No index

Table B:
100,000 rows
10 rows per page
10,000 pages
Clustered index on join column

Figure 7-5: Alternate join orders and page reads

If *TableA* is the outer table, it is accessed via a table scan. When the first qualifying row is found, the clustered index on *TableB* is used to find the row or rows where *TableB.col1* matches the value retrieved from *TableA*. When that completes, the scan on *TableA* continues until another match is found. The clustered index is used again to retrieve the next set of matching rows from *TableB*. This continues until *TableA* has been completely scanned. If 10 rows from *TableA* match the search criteria, the number of page reads required for the query is:

	Pages Read
Table scan of *TableA*	100,000
10 clustered index accesses of *TableB* +	30
Total	100,030

If *TableB* is the outer table, the clustered index is used to find the first row that matches the search criteria. Then, *TableA* is scanned to find the rows where *TableA.col1* matches the value retrieved from *TableB*. When the table scan completes, another row is read from the data pages for *TableB*, and *TableA* is scanned again. This continues until all matching rows have been retrieved from *TableB*. If there are 10 rows in *TableB* that match, this access choice would require the following number of page reads:

	Pages Read
1 clustered index access of *TableB* +	3
10 table scans of *TableA*	1,000,000
Total	1,000,003

Saving I/O Using the Reformatting Strategy

Adding another large, unindexed table to the query in Figure 7-5 would create a huge volume of required page reads. If the new table also contained 100,000 pages, for example, and contained 20 qualifying rows, *TableA* would need to be scanned 20 times, at a cost of 100,000 reads each time. The optimizer costs this plan, but also costs a process called **reformatting**. It can create a temporary clustered index on the join column for the inner table.

The steps in the reformatting strategy are:

- Creating a worktable
- Inserting all of the needed columns from the qualifying rows
- Creating a clustered index on the join columns of the worktable
- Using the clustered index in the join to retrieve the qualifying rows from each table.

The main cost of the reformatting strategy is the time and I/O necessary to create the worktable and to build the clustered index on the worktable. SQL Server uses reformatting only when this cost is cheaper than the cost of joining the tables by repeatedly table-scanning the table.

A showplan messages indicates when SQL Server is using the reformatting strategy and includes other messages showing the steps used to build the worktables. See "Reformatting Message" on page 239.

Index Density and Joins

For any join using an index, the optimizer uses a statistic called the **density** to help optimize the query. The density is the average proportion of duplicate keys in the index. It varies between 0 percent and 100 percent. An index whose keys are all duplicates of each other will have a density of 100 percent, while an index with N rows, whose keys are all unique, will have a density of $1/N$.

The query optimizer uses the density to estimate the number of rows that will be returned for each scan of the inner table of a join for a particular index. For example, if the optimizer is considering a join with a 10,000-row table, and an index on the table has a density of 25 percent, the optimizer would estimate 2500 rows per scan for a join using that index.

SQL Server maintains a density for each prefix of columns in composite indexes. That is, it keeps a density on the first column, the first and second columns, the first, second, and third columns, and so on, up to and including the entire set of columns in the index. The optimizer uses the appropriate density for an index when estimating the cost of a join using that index. In a 10,000-row table with an index on seven columns, the entire seven-column key might have a density of $1/10,000$, while the first column might have a density of only $1/2$, indicating that it would return 5000 rows.

The densities on an index are part of the statistics that are maintained by the **create index** and **update statistics** commands.

If statistics are not available, the optimizer uses default percentages:

Table 7-2: Default density percentages

Condition	Examples	Default
Equality	col = x	10 percent
Closed interval	col > x and col < y col >= x and col <= y col between x and y	25 percent
Open end range	col > x col >= x col < x col <= x	33 percent

For example, if there is no statistics page for an index on *authors(city)*, the optimizer estimates that 10 percent of the rows must be returned for this query:

```
select au_fname, au_lname, pub_name
    from authors a, publishers p
    where a.city = p.city
```

Datatype Mismatches and Joins

One of the most common problems in optimizing joins on tables that have indexes is that the datatypes of the join columns are incompatible. When this occurs, one of the datatypes must be implicitly converted to the other using SQL Server's datatype hierarchy. Datatypes that are lower in the hierarchy are always converted to higher types.

Some examples where problems frequently arise are:

- Joins between *char not null* with *char null* or *varchar*. A *char* datatype that allows null values is stored internally as a *varchar*.

- Joins using numeric datatypes such as *int* and *float*. Allowing null values is not a problem with numeric datatypes in joins.

To avoid these problems, make sure that datatypes are exactly the same when creating tables. This includes use of nulls for *char*, and matching precision and scale for numeric types. See "Joins and Datatypes" on page 290 for more information and for workarounds for existing tables.

Join Permutations

When you are joining four or fewer tables, SQL Server considers all possible permutations of the four tables. It establishes this cutoff because the number of permutations of join orders multiplies with each additional table, requiring lengthy computation time for large joins.

The method the optimizer uses to determine join order has excellent results for most queries with much less CPU time than examining all permutations of all combinations. The **set table count** command allows you to specify the number of tables that the optimizer considers at once. See "Increasing the Number of Tables Considered by the Optimizer" on page 265.

Joins in Queries with More Than Four Tables

Changing the order of the tables in the **from** clause normally has no effect on the query plan, even on tables that join more than four tables.

When you have more than four tables in the **from** clause, SQL Server optimizes each subset of four tables. Then, it remembers the outer table from the best plan involving four tables, eliminates it from the set of tables in the **from** clause, and optimizes the best set of four tables out of the remaining tables. It continues until only four tables remain, at which point it optimizes those four tables normally.

For example, suppose you have a **select** statement with the following **from** clause:

```
from T1, T2, T3, T4, T5, T6
```

The optimizer looks at all possible sets of 4 tables taken from these 6 tables. The 15 possible combinations of all 6 tables are:

```
T1, T2, T3, T4
T1, T2, T3, T5
T1, T2, T3, T6
T1, T2, T4, T5
T1, T2, T4, T6
T1, T2, T5, T6
T1, T3, T4, T5
T1, T3, T4, T6
T1, T3, T5, T6
T1, T4, T5, T6
T2, T3, T4, T5
T2, T3, T4, T6
T2, T3, T5, T6
T2, T4, T5, T6
T3, T4, T5, T6
```

For each one of these combinations, the optimizer looks at all the join orders (permutations). For each set of 4 tables listed above, there are 24 possible join orders, for a total of 360 (24 * 15) permutations. For example, for the set of tables T2, T3, T5, T6, the optimizer looks at these 24 possible orders:

```
T2, T3, T5, T6
T2, T3, T6, T5
T2, T5, T3, T6
T2, T5, T6, T3
T2, T6, T3, T5
T2, T6, T5, T3
T3, T2, T5, T6
T3, T2, T6, T5
T3, T5, T2, T6
T3, T5, T6, T2
T3, T6, T2, T5
T3, T6, T5, T2
T5, T2, T3, T6
T5, T2, T6, T3
T5, T3, T2, T6
T5, T3, T6, T2
T5, T6, T2, T3
T5, T6, T3, T2
T6, T2, T3, T5
T6, T2, T5, T3
T6, T3, T2, T5
T6, T3, T5, T2
T6, T5, T2, T3
T6, T5, T3, T2
```

Let's say that the best join order is:

```
T5, T3, T6, T2
```

At this point, T5 is designated as the outermost table in the query.

The next step is to choose the second-outermost table. The optimizer eliminates T5 from consideration as it chooses the rest of the join order. Now, it has to determine where T1, T2, T3, T4, and T6 fit into the rest of the join order. It looks at all the combinations of four tables chosen from these five:

```
T1, T2, T3, T4
T1, T2, T3, T6
T1, T2, T4, T6
T1, T3, T4, T6
T2, T3, T4, T6
```

It looks at all the join orders for each of these combinations, remembering that T5 is the outermost table in the join. Let's say that the best order in which to join the remaining tables to T5 is T3, T6, T2, T4.

So T3 is chosen as the next table after T5 in the join order for the entire query. T3 is eliminated from consideration in choosing the rest of the join order.

The remaining tables are:

```
T1, T2, T4, T6
```

Now we're down to four tables, so it looks at all the join orders for all the remaining tables. Let's say the best join order is:

```
T6, T2, T4, T1
```

This means that the join order for the entire query is:

```
T5, T3, T6, T2, T4, T1
```

Even though SQL Server looks at the join orders for only four tables at a time, the fact that the optimizer does this for all combinations of four tables that appear in the **from** clause makes the order of tables in the **from** clause irrelevant.

The only time that the order of tables in the **from** clause can make any difference is when the optimizer comes up with the same cost estimate for two join orders. In that case, it chooses the first of the two join orders that it encounters. The order of tables in the **from** clause affects the order in which the optimizer evaluates the join orders, so in this one case, it can have an effect on the query plan. Notice that it does not have an effect on the query cost, or on the query performance.

Optimization of *or* clauses and *in (values_list)*

Optimization of queries that contain **or** clauses or an **in (*values_list*)** clause depend on the indexes that exist on the tables named in these clauses, and whether it is possible for the set of clauses to result in duplicate values.

or syntax

or clauses take the form:

```
where column_name1 = <value>
      or column_name1 = <value>
```

or:

```
where column_name1 = <value>
      or column_name2 = <value>
```

in (values_list) Converts to *or* Processing

The parser converts **in** lists to **or** clauses, so this query:

```
select title_id, price
    from titles
    where title_id in ("PS1372", "PS2091","PS2106")
```

becomes:

```
select title_id, price
    from titles
    where title_id = "PS1372"
        or title_id = "PS2091"
        or title_id = "PS2106"
```

How *or* Clauses Are Processed

A query using **or** clauses is a union of more than one query. Although some rows may match more than one of the conditions, each row must be returned only once.

If any of the columns used in an **or** clause or the column in the **in** clause are not indexed, the query must use a table scan. If indexes exist on all of the columns, the optimizer chooses one of two strategies:

- Multiple matching index scans
- A special strategy called the **OR strategy**

or Clauses and Table Scans

A query with **or** clauses or an **in (values)** lists uses a table scan if either of these conditions is true:

- The cost of all the index accesses is greater than the cost of a table scan.

- At least one of the clauses names a column that is not indexed, so the only way to resolve the clause is to perform a table scan.

If the query performs a table scan, all of the conditions are applied to each row as the pages are scanned.

Multiple Matching Index Scans

SQL Server uses multiple matching index scans when there is no possibility that the **or** clauses will return duplicate rows. The example in Figure 7-6 on page 187 shows two **or** clauses, with a row that satisfies both conditions. This query must be resolved by the OR strategy.

On the other hand, this query cannot return any duplicate rows:

```
select title
    from titles
    where title_id in ("T6650", "T95065", "T11365")
```

This query can be resolved using multiple matching index scans.

The optimizer determines which index to use for each **or** clause or value in the **in (values_list)** clause by costing each clause or value separately. If each column named in a clause is indexed, a different index can be used for each clause or value.

If the query performs a multiple matching index scan, the query uses the appropriate index for each **or** clause **or** value in the **in** list, and returns the rows to the user as data rows are accessed.

The OR Strategy

If the query must use the special OR strategy because the query could return duplicate rows, the query uses the appropriate index, but first retrieves all the **row IDs** for rows that satisfy each **or** clause and stores them in a worktable in *tempdb*. SQL Server then sorts the worktable to remove the duplicate row IDs. In **showplan** output, this worktable is called a **dynamic index**. The row IDs are used to retrieve the rows from the base tables.

Figure 7-6: Resolving or queries illustrates the process of building and sorting a dynamic index for this query:

```
select title_id, price
  from titles
  where price < $15
  or title like "Compute%"
```

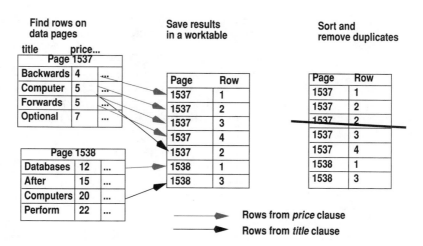

Figure 7-6:   Resolving or queries

The optimizer estimates the cost of index access for each clause in the query. For queries with **or** clauses on different columns in the same table, SQL Server can choose to use a different index for each clause. Queries in cursors cannot use the OR strategy, and must perform a table scan. However, queries in cursors can use the multiple matching index scans strategy.

Locking and the OR Strategy

During a **select** operation, the OR strategy maintains a shared lock on all of the accessed pages during the entire operation, since the row ID's cannot change until the rows are returned to the user. For extremely long sets of **or** clauses or **in (values_list)** sets, this can affect concurrency, since it limits access of other users. Be especially careful of queries that use the OR strategy if you are using isolation level 3 or the **holdlock** clause.

Optimizing Aggregates

Aggregates are processed in two steps:

- First, appropriate indexes are used to retrieve the appropriate rows, or the table is scanned. For vector (grouped) aggregates, the results are placed in a worktable. For scalar aggregates, results are computed in a variable in memory.

- Second, the worktable is scanned to return the results for vector aggregates, or the results are returned from the internal variable.

In many cases, aggregates can be optimized to use a composite nonclustered index on the aggregated column and the grouping column, if any, rather than performing table scans. For example, if the *titles* table has a nonclustered index on *type, price*, the following query retrieves its results from the leaf level of the nonclustered index:

```
select type, avg(price)
    from titles
    group by type
```

Table 7-3 shows some of other optimization methods for aggregates.

Table 7-3:   Optimization of aggregates of indexed columns

Function	Access Method
min	With no **where** or **group by** clause, uses first value on root page of index.
max	With no **where** or **group by** clause, follows last pointer on index pages to last data page.
count(*)	Counts all rows in nonclustered index with the smallest number of leaf pages if there is no **where** clause, or in covering index if there is a **where** clause. Table scans if there is only a clustered index, or no index.
count(*col_name*)	Counts non-null rows in nonclustered index with the smallest number of leaf pages containing *col_name*; table scan if only clustered index or no index.

Combining *max* and *min* Aggregates

When used separately, **max** and **min** aggregates on indexed columns use special processing if there is no **where** clause in the query:

- **min** aggregates retrieve the first value on the root page of the index, performing a single read to find the value.

- **max** aggregates follow the last entry on the last page at each index level until they reach the leaf level. For a clustered index, the number of reads required is the height of the index tree plus one read for the data page. For a nonclustered index, the number of reads required is the height of the index tree.

However, when **min** and **max** are used together, this optimization is not available. The entire leaf level of a nonclustered index is scanned to pick up the first and last values. If no nonclustered index exists, a table scan is used if no nonclustered index includes the value. For more discussion and a workaround, see "Aggregates" on page 289.

Optimizing Subqueries

➤ *Note*

This section describes SQL Server release 11.0 subquery processing. If your stored procedures, triggers, and views were created on SQL Server prior to release 11.0 and have not been dropped and re-created, they may not use the same processing. See **sp_procqmode** in the *SQL Server Reference Manual* for more information on determining the processing mode.

Subqueries use the following special optimizations to improve performance:

- Flattening – converting the subquery to a join
- Materializing – storing the subquery results in a worktable
- Short circuiting – placing the subquery last in the execution order
- Caching subquery results – recording the results of executions

The following sections explain these strategies. See "showplan Messages for Subqueries" on page 242 for an explanation of the **showplan** messages for subquery processing.

Flattening *in, any,* and *exists* Subqueries

SQL Server can flatten some quantified predicate subqueries (those introduced with **in, any,** or **exists**) to an **existence join**. Instead of the usual nested iteration through a table that returns all matching values, an existence join returns TRUE when it finds the first matching value, and then stops processing. If no matching value is found, it returns FALSE.

A subquery introduced with **in**, **any**, or **exists** is flattened to an existence join unless:

- The outer query also uses **or**

- The subquery is correlated and contains one or more aggregates

All **in**, **any**, and **exists** queries test for the existence of qualifying values and return TRUE as soon as a matching row is found.

Existence joins can be optimized as effectively as regular joins. The major difference is that existence joins stop looking as soon as they find the first match.

For example, the optimizer converts the following subquery to an existence join:

```
select title
    from titles
    where title_id in
        (select title_id
         from titleauthor)
    and title like "A Tutorial%"
```

The join query looks like the following ordinary join, although it does not return the same results:

```
select title
    from titles T, titleauthor TA
    where T.title_id = TA.title_id
        and title like "A Tutorial%"
```

In the *pubtune* database, two books match the search string on *title*. Each book has multiple authors, so it has multiple entries in *titleauthor*. A regular join returns five rows, but the subquery returns only two rows, one for each *title_id*, since it stops execution of the join at the first matching row.

Flattening Expression Subqueries

Expression subqueries are subqueries that are included in a query's select list or that are introduced by >, >=, <, <=, =, or !=. SQL Server converts, or **flattens**, expression subqueries to **equijoins** if:

- The subquery joins on unique columns or returns unique columns, and

- There is a unique index on the columns.

Materializing Subquery Results

In some cases, the subquery is processed in two steps: the results from the inner query are materialized, or stored in a temporary worktable, before the outer query is executed. The subquery is executed in one step, and the results of this execution are stored and then used in a second step. SQL Server materializes these types of subqueries:

- Noncorrelated expression subqueries

- Quantified predicate subqueries containing aggregates where the **having** clause includes the correlation condition

Noncorrelated Expression Subqueries

Noncorrelated expression subqueries must return a single value.

When the subquery is not correlated, it returns the same value, regardless of the row being processed in the outer query. The execution steps are:

- SQL Server executes the subquery and stores the result in an internal variable.

- SQL Server substitutes the result value for the subquery in the outer query.

The following query contains a noncorrelated expression subquery:

```
select title_id
from titles
where total_sales = (select max(total_sales)
                     from ts_temp)
```

SQL Server transforms the query to:

```
select <internal_variable> = max(total_sales)
    from ts_temp

select title_id
    from titles
    where total_sales = <internal_variable>
```

The search clause in the second step of this transformation can be optimized. If there is an index on *total_sales*, the query can use it.

Quantified Predicate Subqueries Containing Aggregates

Some subqueries that contain vector (grouped) aggregates can be materialized. These are:

- Noncorrelated quantified predicate subqueries

- Correlated quantified predicate subqueries correlated only in the **having** clause

The materialization of the subquery results in these two steps:

- SQL Server executes the subquery first and stores the results in a worktable.

- SQL Server joins the outer table to the worktable as an existence join. In most cases, this join cannot be optimized because statistics for the worktable are not available.

Materialization saves the cost of evaluating the aggregates once for each row in the table. For example, this query:

```
select title_id
from titles
where total_sales in (select max(total_sales)
                        from titles
                        group by type)
```

Executes in these steps:

```
select maxsales = max(total_sales)
    into #work
    from titles
    group by type

select title_id
    from titles, #work
    where total_sales = maxsales
```

Short Circuiting

When there are **where** clauses in addition to a subquery, SQL Server executes the subquery or subqueries last to avoid unnecessary executions of the subqueries. Depending on the clauses in the query, it is often possible to avoid executing the subquery because other clauses have already determined whether the row is to be returned:

- If any **and** clauses are false, the row will not be returned.

- If any **or** clauses are true, the row will be returned.

In both of these cases, as soon as the status of the row is determined by the evaluation of one clause, no other clauses need to be applied to that row.

Subquery Introduced with an *and* Clause

When **and** joins the clauses, the evaluation of the list stops as soon as any clause evaluates to FALSE.

This query contains two **and** clauses in addition to the subquery:

```
select au_fname, au_lname, title, royaltyper
from titles t, authors a, titleauthor ta
where t.title_id = ta.title_id
and a.au_id = ta.au_id
and advance >= (select avg(advance)
                        from titles t2
                        where t2.type = t.type)
and price > 100
and au_ord = 1
```

SQL Server orders the execution steps to evaluate the subquery last. If a row does not meet an **and** condition, SQL Server discards the row without checking any more **and** conditions and begins to evaluate the next row, so the subquery is not processed unless the row meets all of the **and** conditions.

Subquery Introduced with an *or* Clause

If the query's **where** conditions are connected by **or**, evaluation stops early if any clause is true, and the row is returned to the user without evaluating the subquery.

This query contains two **and** clauses in addition to the subquery:

```
select au_fname, au_lname, title
from titles t, authors a, titleauthor ta
where t.title_id = ta.title_id
and a.au_id = ta.au_id
and (advance > (select avg(advance)
                        from titles t2
                        where t.type = t2.type)
        or title = "Best laid plans"
        or price > $100)
```

Again, SQL Server reorders the query to evaluate the subquery last. If a row meets the condition of the **or** clause, SQL Server does not process the subquery and proceeds to evaluate the next row.

Subquery Results Caching

When it cannot flatten or materialize a subquery, SQL Server uses an in-memory cache to store the results of each evaluation of the subquery. The lookup key for the subquery cache is:

- The values in the correlation columns, plus

- The join column for quantified subqueries

While the query runs, SQL Server tracks the number of times a needed subquery result is found in cache, called a **cache hit**. If the cache hit ratio is high, it means that the cache is reducing the number of times that the subquery executes. If the cache hit ratio is low, the cache is not useful and it is reduced in size as the query runs.

Caching the subquery results improves performance when there are duplicate values in the join columns or the correlation columns. It is even more effective when the values are ordered, as in a query that uses an index. Caching does not help performance when there are no duplicate correlation values.

Displaying Subquery Cache Information

The **set statistics subquerycache on** command displays the number of cache hits and misses and the number of rows in the cache for each subquery.

```
select type, title_id
from titles
where price > all
    (select price
        from titles
        where advance < 15000)
```

Statement: 1   Subquery: 1   cache size: 75   hits: 4925   misses: 75

If the statement includes subqueries on either side of a union, the subqueries are numbered sequentially through both sides of the union. For example:

```
select id from sysobjects a
where id = 1 and id =
    (select max(id)
        from sysobjects b where a.id = b.id)
union
select id from sysobjects a
where id = 1 and id =
    (select max(id)
    from sysobjects b where a.id = b.id)
```

```
Statement: 1  Subquery:1  cache size: 1  hits:  0  misses:1
Statement: 1  Subquery:2  cache size: 1  hits:  0  misses:1
```

Optimizing Subqueries

When queries containing subqueries are not flattened or materialized:

- The outer query and each of the unflattened subqueries is optimized one at time.

- The innermost subqueries (the most deeply nested) are optimized first.

- The estimated buffer cache usage for each subquery is propagated outward to help evaluate the I/O cost and strategy of the outer queries.

In many queries that contain subqueries, a subquery is "attached" to one of the outer table scans by a two-step process. First, the optimizer finds the point in the join order where all the correlation columns are available. Then, the optimizer searches from that point to find the table access that qualifies the fewest rows and attaches the subquery to that table. The subquery is then executed for each qualifying row from the table it is attached to.

Update Operations

SQL Server handles updates in different ways, depending on the changes being made to the data and the indexes used to locate the rows. The two major types of updates are **deferred updates** and **direct updates**. SQL Server performs direct updates whenever possible.

Direct Updates

SQL Server performs direct updates in a single pass, as follows:

- Locates the affected index and data rows

- Writes the log records for the changes to the transaction log

- Makes the changes to the data pages and any affected index pages

There are three techniques for performing direct updates: in-place updates, cheap direct updates, and expensive direct updates.

Direct updates require less overhead than deferred updates and are generally faster, as they limit the number of log scans, reduce logging, save traversal of index B-trees (reducing lock contention), and save I/O because SQL Server does not have to refetch pages to perform modifications based on log records.

In-Place Updates

SQL Server performs in-place updates whenever possible.

When SQL Server performs an in-place update, subsequent rows on the page do not move; the row IDs remain the same and the pointers in the row offset table do not change.

For an in-place update, all the following requirements must be met:

- The row being changed must not change its length.

- The column being updated cannot be the key, or part of the key, of a clustered index. Because the rows in a clustered index are stored in key order, a change to the key almost always means that the row changes location.

- The update statement does not include a join.

- The affected columns are not used for referential integrity.

- There cannot be a trigger on the column.

- The table cannot be replicated (via Replication Server).

Figure 7-7 shows an in-place update. The *pubdate* column is fixed length, so the length of the data row does not change. The access method in this example could be a table scan or a clustered or nonclustered index on *title_id*.

```
update titles set pubdate = "Jun 30 1988"
where title_id = "BU1032"
```

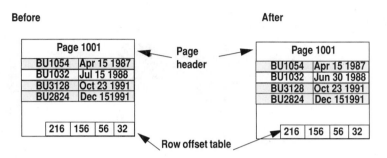

Figure 7-7: In-place update

An in-place update is the fastest type of update because a single change is made to the data page, and all affected index entries are updated by deleting the old index rows and inserting the new index row. In place updates affect only indexes whose keys are changed by the update, since the page and row locations do not change.

Cheap Direct Updates

If SQL Server cannot perform the update in place, it tries to perform a cheap direct update—changing the row and rewriting it at the same offset on the page. Subsequent rows on the page move up or down so that the data remains contiguous on the page, but the row IDs remain the same. The pointers in the row offset table change to reflect the new locations.

For a cheap direct update, all the following requirements must be met:

- The length of the data in the row changes, but the row still fits on the same data page, or the row length does not change, but there is a trigger on the table or the table is replicated.

- The column being updated cannot be the key, or part of the key, of a clustered index. Because SQL Server stores the rows of a clustered index in key order, a change to the key almost always means that the row changes location.

- The update statement does not include a join.

- The affected columns are not used for referential integrity.

**update titles set title = "Coping with Computer Stress in
the Modern Electronic Work Environment"
where title_id = "BU1032"**

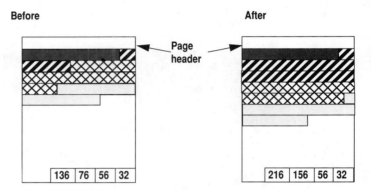

Figure 7-8:   Cheap direct update

The update in Figure 7-8 changes the length of the second row from 20 to 100 bytes, so the row offsets change for the rows that follow it on the page.

Cheap direct updates are almost as fast as in-place updates. They require the same amount of I/O, but slightly more processing. Two changes are made to the data page (the row and the offset table). Any changed index keys are updated by deleting old values and inserting new values. Cheap direct updates affect only indexes whose keys are changed by the update, since the page and row ID do not change.

Expensive Direct Updates

If the data does not fit on the same page, SQL Server performs an expensive direct update, if possible. An expensive direct update deletes the data row, including all index entries, and then inserts the modified row and index entries.

SQL Server uses a table scan or index to find the row in its original location and then deletes the row. If the table has a clustered index, SQL Server uses the index to determine the new location for the row; otherwise, SQL Server inserts the new row at the end of the heap.

For an expensive direct update, all the following requirements must be met:

- The length of a data row changes so that the row no longer fits on the same data page and the row needs to move to a different page, or the update affects key columns for the clustered index.

- The index used to find the row is not changed by the update.

- The update statement does not include a join.

- The affected columns are not used for referential integrity.

The query in Figure 7-9 updates a row in a heap table so that it no longer fits on the page. In the illustration, the second row on the page is updated to a very long value. The row is deleted from page 1133, and inserted on the last page of the heap, page 1144.

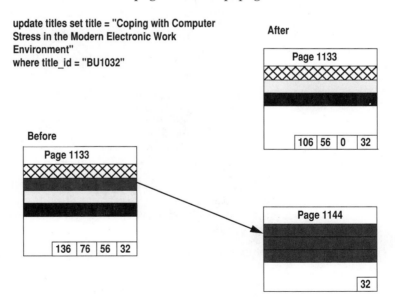

Figure 7-9: Expensive direct update

Expensive direct updates are the slowest type of direct update. The delete is performed on one data page and the insert is performed on a different data page. All index entries must be updated, since the row location changes.

Deferred Updates

SQL Server uses deferred updates when direct update conditions are not met. Deferred updates are the slowest type of update.

The steps involved in deferred updates are:

- Locate the affected data rows, writing the log records for deferred delete and insert of the data pages as rows are located.

- Read the log records for the transaction. Perform the deletes on the data pages and delete any affected index rows.

- At the end of the delete operation, re-read the log, and make all inserts on the data pages and insert any affected index rows.

Deferred updates are always required for:

- Updates that use joins

- Updates to columns used for referential integrity

Some other situations that require deferred updates are:

- The update moves the row to a new page while the table is being accessed via a table scan or clustered index.

- Duplicate rows are not allowed in the table, and there is no unique index to prevent them.

- The index used to find the data row is not unique, and the row moves because the update changes the clustered index key or because the new row does not fit on the page.

Deferred updates incur more overhead than direct updates because they require re-reading the transaction log to make the final changes to the data and indexes. This involves additional traversal of the index trees.

For example, if there is a clustered index on title, this query performs a deferred update:

```
update titles set title = "Portable C Software"
where title = "Designing Portable Software"
```

Deferred Index Insert

SQL Server performs deferred index updates when the update affects the index used in the query or when the update affects columns in a unique index. In this type of update, SQL Server:

- Deletes the index entries in direct mode

- Updates the data page in direct mode, writing the deferred insert records for the index

- Reads the log records for the transaction and inserts the new values in the index in deferred mode

Deferred index insert mode must be used when the update changes the index used to find the row, or when the update affects a unique index. Since any query should update a single qualifying row once and only once, the deferred index update ensures that a row is found only once during the index scan and that the query does not prematurely violate a uniqueness constraint.

The update in the example below only changes the last name, but the index row moves from one page to the next. The steps are:

1. SQL Server reads index page 1133 and deletes the index row for "Greene" from that page and logs a deferred index scan record.

2. SQL Server changes "Green" to "Hubbard" on the data page in direct mode. It then continues the index scan to see if more rows need to be updated.

3. When the scan completes, SQL Server inserts the new index row for "Hubbard" on page 1127.

Figure 7-10 on page 202 shows a table and index before a deferred update, and the steps showing the changes to the data and index pages.

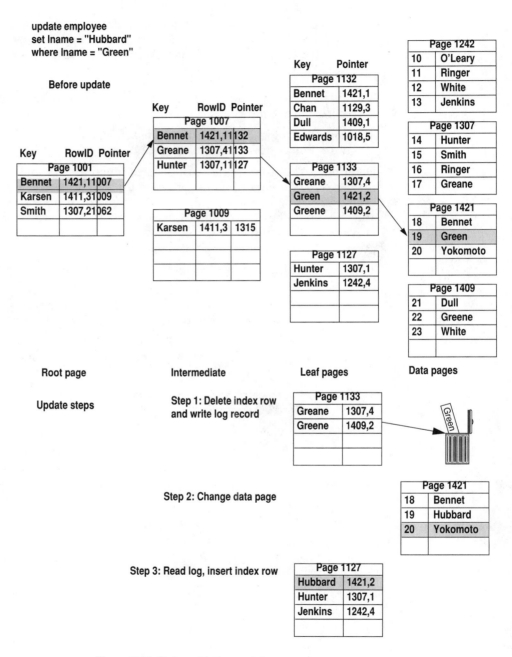

Figure 7-10: Deferred index update

Assume a similar update on the *titles* table:

```
update titles
set title = "Computer Phobic's Manual",
    advance = advance * 2
where title like "Computer Phob%"
```

This query shows a potential problem. If a scan of the nonclustered index on the *title* column found "Computer Phobia Manual," changed the title, and multiplied the advance by 2, and then found the new index row "Computer Phobic's Manual" and multiplied the advance by 2, the author might be quite delighted with the results, but the publishers would not!

Because similar problems arise with updates in joins, where a single row can match the join criteria more than once, join updates are always processed in deferred mode.

A deferred index delete may be faster than an expensive direct update, or it may be substantially slower, depending on the number of log records that need to be scanned and whether the log pages are still in cache.

Optimizing Updates

showplan messages provide information about whether an update will be performed in direct mode or deferred mode. If a direct update is not possible, SQL Server updates the data row in deferred mode. There are times when the optimizer cannot know whether a direct update or a deferred update will be performed, so two **showplan** messages are provided:

- The "deferred_varcol" message shows that the update may change the length of the row because a variable-length column is being updated. If the updated row fits on the page, the update is performed in direct mode; if the update does not fit on the page, the update is performed in deferred mode.

- The "deferred_index" message indicates that the changes to the data pages and the deletes to the index pages are performed in direct mode, but the inserts to the index pages are performed in deferred mode.

The different types of direct updates depend on information that is available only at run time. For example, the page actually has to be fetched and examined in order to determine whether the row fits on the page.

When you design and code your applications, be aware of what differences can cause deferred updates. These guidelines can help avoid deferred updates:

- Create at least one unique index on the table to encourage more direct updates.

- Whenever possible, use non-key columns in the **where** clause when updating a different key.

- If you do not use null values in your columns, declare them as **not null** in your **create table** statement.

Indexing and Update Types

Table 7-4 shows the effects of index type on update mode for 3 different updates: the update of a variable length key column, a variable-length nonkey column, and a fixed-length nonkey column. In all cases, duplicate rows are not allowed. For the indexed cases, the index is on *title_id*. The three update statements are:

```
/*Variable length key update*/
    update titles set title_id = value
        where title_id = "T1234"

/*Fixed length column update*/
    update titles set notes = value
        where title_id = "T1234"

/*Variable length column update*/
    update titles set date = value
        where title_id = "T1234"
```

The following table shows how a unique index can promote a more efficient update mode than a nonunique index on the same key. *Pay particular attention to the differences between direct and deferred in the shaded areas of the table.* For example, with a unique clustered index, all of these updates can be performed in direct mode, but must be performed in deferred mode if the index is not unique.

For tables with clustered indexes that are not unique, a unique index on any other column in the table provides improved update performance. In some cases, you may want to add an identity column to a table in order to include it as a key in an index that would otherwise be non-unique.

Table 7-4: Effects of indexing on update mode

	Update to:		
Indexing	**Variable length Key**	**Fixed length column**	**Variable length column**
No index	N/A	direct	deferred_varcol
Clustered, unique	direct	direct	direct
Clustered, not unique	deferred	deferred	deferred
Clustered, not unique, with a unique index on another column	deferred	direct	deferred_varcol
Nonclustered, unique	deferred_varcol	direct	direct
Nonclustered, not unique	deferred_varcol	direct	deferred_varcol

If the key for a table is fixed length, the only difference in update modes from those shown in the table occurs for nonclustered indexes. For a nonclustered, non-unique index, the update mode is deferred_index for updates to the key. For a nonclustered, unique index, the update mode is direct for updates to the key.

Choosing Fixed-Length Datatypes for Direct Updates

If the actual length of most of the data in *varchar* or *varbinary* columns is close to the maximum length, use *char* or *binary* instead. Each variable-length column adds row overhead, and increases the possibility of deferred updates.

Using *max_rows_per_page* to Increase Direct Updates

Using **max_rows_per_page** to reduce the number of rows allowed on a page increases direct updates, because an update which increases the length of variable-length columns may still fit on the same page. For more information on using **max_rows_per_page**, see "Decreasing the Number of Rows per Page" on page 324.

Using *sp_sysmon* While Tuning Updates

You can use **showplan** to figure out if updates are deferred or direct, but it does not give you more detailed information about which type of deferred or direct update takes place. Output from the system procedure **sp_sysmon** supplies detailed statistics about the type of updates performed during a sample interval.

Run **sp_sysmon** as you tune updates and look for reduced numbers of deferred updates, reduced locking, and reduced I/O.

See "Transaction Profile" on page 485 in Chapter 19, "Monitoring SQL Server Performance with sp_sysmon."

From Observation to Diagnosis and Treatment

This chapter provides the basis for understanding what SQL Server does, and being able to observe its behavior.

The next chapter, "Understanding Query Plans," begins to put you in the driver's seat by providing you access to the SQL Server's optimization costing at the "microeconomic" level. With the help of in-depth, continuous reports from query processing options such as **set showplan** and **set statistics** you can begin to take control of SQL Server's query processing, and plan a strategy for continuous maintenance of desired performance levels.

8

Understanding Query Plans

Diagnostic Tools for Query Optimization

If you suspect your queries need more than a reasonable database design and sound indexing, first get the facts. Rewriting queries for a large application should be undertaken while running diagnostic tools.

The tuning approaches in this chapter entail scrupulous monitoring of performance and selective rewriting of queries. These activities are "fine-tuning", in contrast to the larger-scale actions of manipulating the database design or indexing schemes.

SQL Server provides these diagnostic tools for query optimization:

- **set showplan on** displays the steps performed for each query in a batch. It is often used with **set noexec on**, especially for queries that return large numbers of rows. This chapter explains **showplan** output.

- **set statistics io on** displays the number of logical and physical reads and writes required by the query. This tool is described in Chapter 6, "Indexing for Performance."

- **set statistics subquerycache on** displays the number of cache hits, misses, and the number of rows in the cache for each subquery. See "Subquery Results Caching" on page 194.

- **set statistics time on** displays the time it takes to parse and compile each command and the time it takes to execute each step in the query.

Using *showplan*

The **set showplan on** command is your main tool for understanding how the optimizer executes your queries. The following sections explore query plan output.

In this chapter, the discussion of **showplan** messages is divided into four sections:

- Basic **showplan** messages—those you see when using fairly simple select statements and data modification commands. See Table 8-1 on page 209.

- **showplan** messages for particular clauses, predicates, and so on, such **group by**, aggregates, or **order by**. See Table 8-2 on page 219.

- **showplan** messages describing access methods. See Table 8-3 on page 230.

- **showplan** messages for subqueries. See Table 8-4 on page 243.

Each message is explained in detail under its own heading. The message and related messages are shown in bold type in the **showplan** output.

Combining *showplan* and *noexec*

showplan is often used in conjunction with **set noexec on**, which prevents the SQL statements from being executed. Be sure to issue the **showplan** command, or any other **set** commands, before the **noexec** command. Once you issue **set noexec on**, the only command that SQL Server executes is **set noexec off**.

```
set showplan on
set noexec on
go
select au_lname, au_fname
    from    authors
    where   au_id = "A1374065371"
go
```

If you need to create or drop indexes, remember that **set noexec on** also suppresses execution of these commands for the session that issues them.

showplan, **statistics io**, and other commands produce their output while stored procedures are run. You may want to have hard copies of your table schemas and index information. Or you can use separate windows for running system procedures such as **sp_helpindex** and for creating and dropping indexes.

Echoing Input into Output Files

For longer queries and batches, you may want to save output into files. The "echo input" flag to **isql** echoes the input into the output file, with line numbers included. The syntax is shown on page 168.

Basic *showplan* Messages

This section describes **showplan** messages that are printed for most **select**, **insert**, **update**, and **delete** operations.

Table 8-1:   Basic showplan messages

Message	Explanation	See
Query Plan for Statement N (at line N).	First variable is the statement number within a batch, second variable is the line number within the batch.	page 209
STEP *N*	Each step for each statement is numbered sequentially. Numbers are restarted at 1 on each side of a **union.**	page 210
The type of query is query type.	*query type* is replaced by the type of query: SELECT, UPDATE, INSERT, or any Transact-SQL statement type.	page 210
FROM TABLE	Each occurrence of FROM TABLE indicates a table that will be read. The table name is listed on the next line. *Table 8-3: showplan messages describing access methods* shows the access method messages for each table access.	page 211
TO TABLE	Included when a command creates a worktable and for **insert...select** commands.	page 214
Nested iteration.	Indicates the execution of a data retrieval loop.	page 215
The update mode is direct. The update mode is deferred. The update mode is deferred_varcol. The update mode is deferred_index.	These messages indicate whether an **insert**, **delete** or **update** is performed in direct update mode or deferred update mode. See "Update Mode Messages" on page 215.	page 215

Query Plan Delimiter Message

```
Query Plan for Statement N (at line N)
```

SQL Server prints this line once for each query in a batch. Its main function is to provide a visual cue that separates one clump of **showplan** output from the next clump. Line numbers are provided to help you match query output with your input.

Step Message

```
STEP N
```

showplan output displays "STEP *N*" for every query, where *N* is an integer, beginning with "STEP 1". For some queries, SQL Server cannot effectively retrieve the results in a single step and must break the query plan into several steps. For example, if a query includes a **group by** clause, SQL Server breaks it into at least two steps:

- One step to select the qualifying rows from the table and to group them, placing the results in a worktable
- Another step to return the rows from the worktable

This example demonstrates a single-step query.

```
select au_lname, au_fname
from authors
where city = "Oakland"
QUERY PLAN FOR STATEMENT 1 (at line 1).


    STEP 1
        The type of query is SELECT.

        FROM TABLE
            authors
        Nested iteration.
        Table Scan.
        Ascending scan.
        Positioning at start of table.
        Using I/O Size 2 Kbytes.
        With LRU Buffer Replacement Strategy.
```

Multiple-step queries are demonstrated under the **group by** command on page 220 and in other places in this chapter.

Query Type Message

```
The type of query is query type.
```

This message describes the type of query for each step. For most queries that require tuning, the value for *query type* is SELECT, INSERT, UPDATE, or DELETE. However, the *query type* can include any Transact-SQL commands that you issue while **showplan** is enabled. For example, here is output from a **create index** command:

```
create index ta_idid
        on titleauthor(au_id, title_id)
```

```
QUERY PLAN FOR STATEMENT 1 (at line 1).


    STEP 1
        The type of query is CREATE INDEX.
        TO TABLE
            titleauthor
```

"FROM TABLE" Message

```
FROM TABLE
    tablename
```

This message indicates which table the query is reading from. The "FROM TABLE" message is followed on the next line by the table name. In some cases, it may indicate that it is selecting from a worktable.

When your query joins one or more tables, the order of "FROM TABLE" messages in the output shows you the order in which the query optimizer joins the tables. This order is often different from the order in which the tables are listed in the **from** clause or the **where** clause of the query. The query optimizer examines all the different join orders for the tables involved and picks the join order that requires the least amount of work. This query displays the join order in a three-table join using the indexes shown:

```
create index au_lname_ix on authors(au_lname)

create index au_id_ix on titleauthor(au_id)

create unique clustered index title_id_ix
    on titles(title_id)

select authors.au_id, au_fname, au_lname, title
    from titles, titleauthor, authors
where authors.au_id = titleauthor.au_id
    and titleauthor.title_id = titles.title_id
    and authors.au_lname = "Bloom"

QUERY PLAN FOR STATEMENT 1 (at line 1).


    STEP 1
        The type of query is SELECT.

            FROM TABLE
                authors
            Nested iteration.
            Index : au_lname_ix
```

```
Ascending scan.
Positioning by key.
Keys are:
    au_lname
Using I/O Size 2 Kbytes.
With LRU Buffer Replacement Strategy.

FROM TABLE
    titleauthor
Nested iteration.
Index : au_id_ix
Ascending scan.
Positioning by key.
    Index contains all needed columns. Base
table will not be read.
Keys are:
    au_id
Using I/O Size 2 Kbytes.
With LRU Buffer Replacement Strategy.

FROM TABLE
    titles
Nested iteration.
Using Clustered Index.
Index : title_id_ix
Ascending scan.
Positioning by key.
Keys are:
    title_id
Using I/O Size 2 Kbytes.
With LRU Buffer Replacement Strategy.
```

The sequence of tables in this output shows the order chosen by the SQL Server query optimizer, which is not the order in which they were listed in the **from** clause or **where** clause:

- First, the qualifying rows from the *authors* table are located (using the search clause on *au_lname*).

- Those rows are then joined with the *titleauthor* table (using the join clause on the *au_id* columns).

- Finally, the *titles* table is joined with the *titleauthor* table to retrieve the desired columns (using the join clause on the *title_id* columns).

"FROM TABLE" and Referential Integrity

When you insert or update rows in a table that has a referential integrity constraint, the **showplan** output includes "FROM TABLE" and other **showplan** messages displaying the access methods used to access the referenced table.

This *salesdetail* table definition includes a referential integrity check on the *title_id*:

```
create table salesdetail (
        stor_id                 char(4),
        ord_num                 varchar(20),
        title_id                tid
            references titles(title_id),
        qty                     smallint,
        discount                 float )
```

An insert to *salesdetail*, or an update on the *title_id* column, requires a lookup in the *titles* table to verify that the inserted *title_id* is valid:

```
insert salesdetail values ("S245", "X23A5", "T10",
15, 40.25)

QUERY PLAN FOR STATEMENT 1 (at line 1).


    STEP 1
        The type of query is INSERT.
        The update mode is direct.

        FROM TABLE
            titles
        Using Clustered Index.
        Index : tit_id_ix
        Ascending scan.
        Positioning by key.
        Keys are:
            title_id
        Using I/O Size 2 Kbytes.
        With LRU Buffer Replacement Strategy.
        TO TABLE
            salesdetail
```

The clustered index on *title_id* provided the best access method for looking up the referenced value.

"TO TABLE" Message

```
TO TABLE
    tablename
```

When a command such as **insert, delete, update,** or **select into** modifies or attempts to modify one or more rows of a table, the "TO TABLE" message displays the name of the target table. For operations that require an intermediate step to insert rows into a worktable (discussed later), "TO TABLE" indicates that the results are going to the "Worktable" table rather than a user table. The following examples illustrate the use of the "TO TABLE" statement:

```
insert sales
values ("8042", "QA973", "12/7/95")

QUERY PLAN FOR STATEMENT 1 (at line 1).

    STEP 1
        The type of query is INSERT.
        The update mode is direct.
        TO TABLE
            sales
```

```
update publishers
set city = "Los Angeles"
where pub_id = "1389"

QUERY PLAN FOR STATEMENT 1 (at line 1).


    STEP 1
        The type of query is UPDATE.
        The update mode is direct.

        FROM TABLE
            publishers
        Nested iteration.
            Index : pub_id_ix
        Ascending scan.
        Positioning by key.
        Keys are:
            pub_id
        Using I/O Size 2 Kbytes.
        With LRU Buffer Replacement Strategy.
        TO TABLE
            publishers
```

The second query indicates that the *publishers* table is used as both the "FROM TABLE" and the "TO TABLE." In the case of **update** operations, the optimizer needs to read the table that contains the row(s) to be updated, resulting in the "FROM TABLE" statement, and then needs to modify the row(s), resulting in the "TO TABLE" statement.

Nested Iteration Message

```
Nested Iteration.
```

This message indicates one or more loops through a table to return rows. Even the simplest access to a single table is an iteration.

"Nested iteration" is the default technique used to join tables and/or return rows from a single table. For each iteration, the optimizer is using one or more sets of loops to:

1. Go through a table and retrieve a row

2. Qualify the row based on the search criteria given in the **where** clause

3. Return the row to the front end or insert it into another table (for an **insert...select** or **select into**)

4. Loop again to get the next row, until all rows have been retrieved, based on the scope of the search

The method in which the query accesses the rows (such as using an available index) is discussed in "showplan Messages Describing Access Methods and Caching" on page 230.

The only exception to "Nested iteration" is the "EXISTS TABLE: nested iteration," explained on page 254.

Update Mode Messages

SQL Server uses different modes to perform update operations such as **insert, delete, update,** and **select into**. These methods are called **direct update mode** and **deferred update mode**.

Direct Update Mode

```
The update mode is direct.
```

Whenever possible, SQL Server uses direct update mode, since it is faster and generates fewer log records than deferred update mode.

The direct update mode operates as follows:

1. Pages are read into the data cache.

2. The changes are recorded in the transaction log.

3. The change is made to the data page.

4. The transaction log page is flushed to disk when the transaction commits.

SQL Server uses direct update mode in the following circumstances:

- For all **insert** commands, unless the table into which the rows are being inserted is being read from in the same command (for example, an **insert...select** to a table, from the same table).

- When you create a table and populate it with a **select into** command, SQL Server uses direct update mode to insert the new rows.

- Delete operations are performed in direct update mode unless the **delete** statement includes a join or columns used for referential integrity.

- SQL Server processes **update** commands in direct update mode or deferred update mode, depending on information that is available only at run time. For more information on the different types of direct updates, see the discussion of direct and deferred updates under "Update Operations" on page 195.

For example, SQL Server uses direct update mode for the following **delete** command:

```
delete
from authors
where au_lname = "Willis"
and au_fname = "Max"
QUERY PLAN FOR STATEMENT 1 (at line 1).


    STEP 1
        The type of query is DELETE.
        The update mode is direct.

        FROM TABLE
            authors
        Nested iteration.
```

```
Index : au_names
Ascending scan.
Positioning by key.
Keys are:
     au_lname
     au_fname
Using I/O Size 2 Kbytes.
With LRU Buffer Replacement Strategy.
TO TABLE
     authors
```

Deferred Mode

```
The update mode is deferred.
```

In deferred mode, processing takes place in these steps:

1. For each qualifying data row, SQL Server writes transaction log records for one deferred delete and one deferred insert.

2. SQL Server scans the transaction log to process the deferred inserts, changing the data pages and any affected index pages.

Deferred mode is used:

- For **insert...select** operations from a table into the same table

- For certain updates (see the discussion of direct and deferred updates under "Update Operations" on page 195)

- For delete statements that include a join or columns used for referential integrity

Consider the following **insert...select** operation, where *mytable* is a heap without a clustered index or unique nonclustered index:

```
insert mytable
    select title, price * 2
        from mytable
```

```
QUERY PLAN FOR STATEMENT 1 (at line 1).


    STEP 1
        The type of query is INSERT.
        The update mode is deferred.

        FROM TABLE
            mytable
        Nested iteration.
        Table Scan.
        Ascending scan.
        Positioning at start of table.
        Using I/O Size 2 Kbytes.
        With LRU Buffer Replacement Strategy.
        TO TABLE
            mytable
```

This command copies every row in the table and appends the rows
to the end of the table. The query processor needs to differentiate
between the rows that are currently in the table (prior to the **insert**
command) and the rows being inserted, so that it does not get into a
continuous loop of selecting a row, inserting it at the end of the table,
selecting the row that it just inserted, and re-inserting it again. The
query processor solves this problem by performing the operation in
two steps:

1. It scans the existing table and writes insert records into the
   transaction log for each row that it finds.

2. When all the "old" rows have been read, it scans the log and
   performs the insert operations.

"Deferred Index" and "Deferred Varcol" Messages

```
The update mode is deferred_varcol.
```

```
The update mode is deferred_index.
```

These **showplan** messages indicate that SQL Server may process an
update command as a deferred index update.

SQL Server uses deferred_varcol mode when updating one or more
variable-length columns. This update may be done in deferred or
direct mode, depending on information that is available only at run
time.

SQL Server uses deferred_index mode when the index used to find
to row is unique or may change as part of the update. In this mode,

SQL Server deletes the index entries in direct mode but inserts them in deferred mode.

From more information about how deferred index updates work, refer to "Deferred Index Insert" on page 201.

Using *sp_sysmon* While Tuning Updates

showplan tells you if an update is deferred_varcol, deferred_index, or direct. If you need more information about the type of deferred update, use **sp_sysmon** (or the separate product, SQL Server Monitor).

Run **sp_sysmon** as you tune updates and look for reduced numbers of deferred updates, reduced locking, and reduced I/O.

See "Transaction Profile" on page 485 in Chapter 19, "Monitoring SQL Server Performance with sp_sysmon."

showplan Messages for Query Clauses

Use of certain Transact-SQL clauses, functions, and keywords is reflected in **showplan** output. These include **group by**, aggregates, **distinct**, **order by**, and **select into** clauses.

Table 8-2: Showplan messages for various clauses

Message	Explanation	See
GROUP BY	The query contains a **group by** statement.	page 220
The type of query is SELECT (into WorktableN)	The step creates a worktable to hold intermediate results.	page 220
Evaluate Grouped *type* AGGREGATE or Evaluate Ungrouped *type* AGGREGATE	The query contains an aggregate. "Grouped" indicates that there is a grouping column for the aggregate (vector aggregate); "Ungrouped" indicates there is no grouping column. The variable indicates the type of aggregate.	page 221 page 224
Evaluate Grouped ASSIGNMENT OPERATOR Evaluate Ungrouped ASSIGNMENT OPERATOR	Query includes **compute** (ungrouped) or **compute by** (grouped).	page 223
WorktableN created for DISTINCT.	The query contains a **distinct** keyword in the select list that requires a sort to eliminate duplicates.	page 226

Table 8-2: Showplan messages for various clauses (continued)

Message	Explanation	See
WorktableN created for ORDER BY.	The query contains an **order by** clause that requires ordering rows.	page 228
This step involves sorting.	The query includes on **order by** or **distinct** clause, and results must be sorted.	page 229
Using GETSORTED.	The query created a worktable and sorted it. GETSORTED is a particular technique used to return the rows.	page 229

"GROUP BY" Message

```
GROUP BY
```

This statement appears in the **showplan** output for any query that contains a **group by** clause. Queries that contain a **group by** clause are always executed in at least two steps:

- One step selects the qualifying rows into a worktable and groups them.

- Another step returns the rows from the worktable.

Selecting into a Worktable

```
The type of query is SELECT (into WorktableN).
```

Queries using a **group by** clause first put qualifying results into a worktable. The data is grouped as the table is generated. A second step returns the grouped rows.

The following example returns a list of all cities and indicates the number of authors that live in each city. The query plan shows the two steps: the first step selects the rows into a worktable, and the second step retrieves the grouped rows from the worktable:

```
select city, total_authors = count(*)
    from authors
    group by city
```

```
QUERY PLAN FOR STATEMENT 1 (at line 1).


    STEP 1
                The type of query is SELECT (into
Worktable1).
            GROUP BY
            Evaluate Grouped COUNT AGGREGATE.

            FROM TABLE
                authors
            Nested iteration.
            Table Scan.
            Ascending scan.
            Positioning at start of table.
            Using I/O Size 2 Kbytes.
            With LRU Buffer Replacement Strategy.
            TO TABLE
                Worktable1.

    STEP 2
            The type of query is SELECT.

            FROM TABLE
                Worktable1.
            Nested iteration.
            Table Scan.
            Ascending scan.
            Positioning at start of table.
            Using I/O Size 2 Kbytes.
            With MRU Buffer Replacement Strategy.
```

Grouped Aggregate Message

```
Evaluate Grouped type AGGREGATE
```

This message is printed by queries that contain aggregates and **group by** or **compute by**.

The variable indicates the type of aggregate—COUNT, SUM OR AVERAGE, MINIMUM, or MAXIMUM.

avg reports both COUNT and SUM OR AVERAGE; **sum** reports SUM OR AVERAGE. Two additional types of aggregates (ONCE and ANY) are used internally by SQL Server while processing subqueries. These are discussed on page 250.

Grouped Aggregates and *group by*

When an aggregate function is combined with **group by**, the result is called a grouped aggregate or **vector aggregate**. The query results have one row for each value of the grouping column or columns.

The following example illustrates a grouped aggregate:

```
select type, avg(advance)
from titles
group by type
```

```
QUERY PLAN FOR STATEMENT 1 (at line 1).


    STEP 1
        The type of query is SELECT (into Worktable1).
        GROUP BY
        Evaluate Grouped COUNT AGGREGATE.
        Evaluate Grouped SUM OR AVERAGE AGGREGATE.

        FROM TABLE
            titles
        Nested iteration.
        Table Scan.
        Ascending scan.
        Positioning at start of table.
        Using I/O Size 2 Kbytes.
        With LRU Buffer Replacement Strategy.
        TO TABLE
            Worktable1.

    STEP 2
        The type of query is SELECT.

        FROM TABLE
            Worktable1.
        Nested iteration.
        Table Scan.
        Ascending scan.
        Positioning at start of table.
        Using I/O Size 2 Kbytes.
        With MRU Buffer Replacement Strategy.
```

In the first step, the worktable is created and the aggregates are computed. The second step selects the results from the worktable.

compute by Message

```
Evaluate Grouped ASSIGNMENT OPERATOR
```

Queries using **compute by** display the same aggregate messages as **group by** as well as the "Evaluate Grouped ASSIGNMENT OPERATOR" message. The values are placed in a worktable in one step, and the computation of the aggregates is performed in a second step. This query uses *type* and *advance*, like the **group by** query example above:

```
select type, advance  from titles
having title like "Compu%"
order by type
compute avg(advance) by type
```

In the **showplan** output, the computation of the aggregates takes place in Step 2:

```
QUERY PLAN FOR STATEMENT 1 (at line 1).


    STEP 1
        The type of query is INSERT.
        The update mode is direct.
        Worktable1 created for ORDER BY.

        FROM TABLE
            titles
        Nested iteration.
        Index : title_ix
        Ascending scan.
        Positioning by key.
        Keys are:
            title
        Using I/O Size 2 Kbytes.
        With LRU Buffer Replacement Strategy.
        TO TABLE
            Worktable1.

    STEP 2
        The type of query is SELECT.
        Evaluate Grouped SUM OR AVERAGE AGGREGATE.
        Evaluate Grouped COUNT AGGREGATE.
        Evaluate Grouped ASSIGNMENT OPERATOR.
```

```
This step involves sorting.

FROM TABLE
     Worktable1.
Using GETSORTED
Table Scan.
Ascending scan.
Positioning at start of table.
Using I/O Size 2 Kbytes.
With MRU Buffer Replacement Strategy.
```

Ungrouped Aggregate Message

```
Evaluate Ungrouped type AGGREGATE.
```

This message is reported by:

- Queries that use aggregate functions, but do not use **group by**

- Queries that use **compute**

See "Grouped Aggregate Message" on page 221 for an explanation of *type*.

Ungrouped Aggregates

When an aggregate function is used in a **select** statement that does not include a **group by** clause, it produces a single value. The query can operate on all rows in a table or on a subset of the rows defined by a **where** clause. When an aggregate function produces a single value, the function is called a **scalar aggregate** or ungrouped aggregate. Here is **showplan** output for an ungrouped aggregate:

```
select avg(advance)
from titles
where type = "business"
```
```
QUERY PLAN FOR STATEMENT 1 (at line 1).


STEP 1
     The type of query is SELECT.
     Evaluate Ungrouped COUNT AGGREGATE.
     Evaluate Ungrouped SUM OR AVERAGE AGGREGATE.

     FROM TABLE
          titles
     Nested iteration.
```

```
Index : tp
Ascending scan.
Positioning by key.
Keys are:
    type
Using I/O Size 2 Kbytes.
With LRU Buffer Replacement Strategy.
```

STEP 2
```
The type of query is SELECT.
```

Notice that **showplan** considers this a two-step query, which is similar to the **showplan** from the **group by** query shown earlier. Since the scalar aggregate returns a single value, SQL Server uses an internal variable to compute the result of the aggregate function as the qualifying rows from the table are evaluated. After all rows from the table have been evaluated (Step 1), the final value from the variable is selected (Step 2) to return the scalar aggregate result.

compute Messages

```
Evaluate Ungrouped ASSIGNMENT OPERATOR
```

When a query includes **compute** to compile a scalar aggregate, **showplan** prints the "Evaluate Ungrouped ASSIGNMENT OPERATOR" message. This query computes an average for the entire result set:

```
select type, advance from titles
having title like "Compu%"
order by type
compute avg(advance)
```

The **showplan** output shows that the computation of the aggregate values takes place in the second step:

```
QUERY PLAN FOR STATEMENT 1 (at line 1).


STEP 1
    The type of query is INSERT.
    The update mode is direct.
    Worktable1 created for ORDER BY.

    FROM TABLE
        titles
    Nested iteration.
    Index : titles_ix
    Ascending scan.
    Positioning by key.
```

```
Keys are:
    title
Using I/O Size 2 Kbytes.
With LRU Buffer Replacement Strategy.
TO TABLE
    Worktable1.
```

```
STEP 2
    The type of query is SELECT.
    Evaluate Ungrouped SUM OR AVERAGE AGGREGATE.
    Evaluate Ungrouped COUNT AGGREGATE.
    Evaluate Ungrouped ASSIGNMENT OPERATOR.
    This step involves sorting.
```

```
    FROM TABLE
        Worktable1.
    Using GETSORTED
    Table Scan.
    Ascending scan.
    Positioning at start of table.
    Using I/O Size 2 Kbytes.
    With MRU Buffer Replacement Strategy.
```

Messages for *order by* and *distinct*

Some queries that include **distinct** use a sort step to locate the duplicate values in the result set. **distinct** queries and **order by** queries can avoid the sorting step when the indexes used to locate rows support the **order by** or **distinct** clause.

Here again, proper indexing can help performance by avoiding the overhead of creating worktables.

For those cases where the sort must be performed, the **distinct** keyword in a select list and the **order by** clause share some **showplan** messages:

- Each generates a worktable message

- The message "This step involves sorting."

- The message "Using GETSORTED"

Worktable Message for *distinct*

```
WorktableN created for DISTINCT.
```

A query that includes the **distinct** keyword excludes all duplicate rows from the results so that only unique rows are returned. When there is no useful index, SQL Server performs these steps to process queries that include **distinct**:

1. It creates a worktable to store all of the results of the query, including duplicates.

2. It sorts the rows in the worktable, discarding the duplicate rows. Finally, the rows from the worktable are returned.

The "WorktableN created for DISTINCT" message appears as part of "Step 1" in **showplan** output. "Step 2" for **distinct** queries includes the messages "This step involves sorting" and "Using GETSORTED," which are explained on page 229.

```
select distinct city
from authors

QUERY PLAN FOR STATEMENT 1 (at line 1).


    STEP 1
        The type of query is INSERT.
        The update mode is direct.
        Worktable1 created for DISTINCT.

        FROM TABLE
            authors
        Nested iteration.
        Table Scan.
        Ascending scan.
        Positioning at start of table.
        Using I/O Size 2 Kbytes.
        With LRU Buffer Replacement Strategy.
        TO TABLE
            Worktable1.

    STEP 2
        The type of query is SELECT.
        This step involves sorting.

        FROM TABLE
            Worktable1.
        Using GETSORTED
        Table Scan.
        Ascending scan.
        Positioning at start of table.
        Using I/O Size 2 Kbytes.
        With MRU Buffer Replacement Strategy.
```

Worktable Message for *order by*

```
WorktableN created for ORDER BY.
```

Queries that include an **order by** clause often require the use of a temporary worktable. When the optimizer cannot use an index to order the result rows, it creates a worktable to sort the result rows before returning them. This example shows an **order by** clause that creates a worktable because there is no index on the *city* column:

```
select *
from authors
order by city

QUERY PLAN FOR STATEMENT 1 (at line 1).


    STEP 1
        The type of query is INSERT.
        The update mode is direct.
        Worktable1 created for ORDER BY.

        FROM TABLE
            authors
        Nested iteration.
        Table Scan.
        Ascending scan.
        Positioning at start of table.
        Using I/O Size 2 Kbytes.
        With LRU Buffer Replacement Strategy.
        TO TABLE
            Worktable1.

    STEP 2
        The type of query is SELECT.
        This step involves sorting.

        FROM TABLE
            Worktable1.
        Using GETSORTED
        Table Scan.
        Ascending scan.
        Positioning at start of table.
        Using I/O Size 2 Kbytes.
        With MRU Buffer Replacement Strategy.
```

The messages "This step involves sorting" and "Using GETSORTED" are explained on page 229.

order by Queries and Indexes

Certain queries using **order by** do not require a sorting step, depending on the type of index used to access the data. See "Indexes and Sorts" on page 135 for more information.

Sorting Message

```
This step involves sorting.
```

This **showplan** message indicates that the query must sort the intermediate results before returning them to the user. Queries that use **distinct** or that have an **order by** clause not supported by an index require an intermediate sort. The results are put into a worktable, and the worktable is then sorted. For examples of this message, see "Worktable Message for distinct" on page 226 or "Worktable Message for order by" on page 228.

"GETSORTED" Message

```
Using GETSORTED
```

This statement indicates one of the ways that SQL Server returns result rows from a table. In the case of "Using GETSORTED," the rows are returned in sorted order. However, not all queries that return rows in sorted order include this step. For example, **order by** queries whose rows are retrieved using an index with a matching sort sequence do not require "GETSORTED."

The "Using GETSORTED" method is used when SQL Server must first create a temporary worktable to sort the result rows and then return them in the proper sorted order. The examples for **distinct** on page 226 and for **order by** on page 228 show the "Using GETSORTED" message.

showplan Messages Describing Access Methods and Caching

showplan output provides information about access methods and caching strategies.

Table 8-3:   showplan messages describing access methods

Message	Explanation	
Table Scan.	Indicates that the query performs a table scan.	page 231
Using Clustered Index.	Query uses the clustered index on the table.	page 232
Index : index_name	Query uses an index on the table; the variable shows the index name.	page 233
Ascending scan.	Indicates the direction of the scan. All scans are ascending.	page 233
Positioning at start of table. Positioning by Row IDentifier (RID). Positioning by key. Positioning at index start.	These messages indicate how scans are taking place.	page 233
Scanning only up to the first qualifying row. Scanning only the last page of the table.	These messages indicate **min** and **max** optimization, respectively.	page 234
Index contains all needed columns. Base table will not be read.	Indicates that the nonclustered index covers the query.	page 234
Keys are:	Included when the positioning message indicates "Positioning by key." The next line(s) show the index key(s) used.	page 236
Using *N* Matching Index Scans	Indicates that a query with **in** or **or** is performing multiple index scans, one for each **or** condition or **in** list item.	page 236
Using Dynamic Index.	Reported during some queries using **or** clauses or **in** (*values list*).	page 238

Table 8-3:   showplan messages describing access methods (continued)

Message	Explanation	
WorktableN created for REFORMATTING.	Indicates that an inner table of a join has no useful indexes, and that SQL Server has determined that it is cheaper to build a worktable and an index on the worktable than to perform repeated table scans.	page 239
Log Scan.	Query fired a trigger that uses *inserted* or *deleted* tables.	page 242
Using I/O size N Kbytes.	Variable indicates the I/O size for disk reads and writes.	page 242
With LRU/MRU buffer replacement strategy.	Reports the caching strategy for the table.	page 242

Table Scan Message

```
Table Scan.
```

This message indicates that the query performs a table scan.

When a table scan is performed, the execution begins with the first row in the table. Each row is retrieved, compared to the conditions in the **where** clause, and returned to the user if it meets the query criteria. Every row in the table must be looked at, so for very large tables, a table scan can be very costly in terms of disk I/O. If a table has one or more indexes on it, the query optimizer may still choose to do a table scan instead of using one of the available indexes, if the indexes are too costly or are not useful for the given query. The following query shows a typical table scan:

```
select au_lname, au_fname
from authors
```

```
QUERY PLAN FOR STATEMENT 1 (at line 1).


    STEP 1
        The type of query is SELECT.

        FROM TABLE
            authors
        Nested iteration.
        Table Scan.
        Ascending scan.
        Positioning at start of table.
        Using I/O Size 2 Kbytes.
        With LRU Buffer Replacement Strategy.
```

Clustered Index Message

```
Using Clustered Index.
```

This **showplan** message indicates that the query optimizer chose to use the clustered index on a table to retrieve the rows. The following query shows the clustered index being used to retrieve the rows from the table:

```
select title_id, title
from titles
where title_id like "T9%"
```

```
QUERY PLAN FOR STATEMENT 1 (at line 1).


    STEP 1
        The type of query is SELECT.

        FROM TABLE
            titles
        Nested iteration.
        Using Clustered Index.
        Index : tit_id_ix
        Ascending scan.
        Positioning by key.
        Keys are:
            title_id
        Using I/O Size 2 Kbytes.
        With LRU Buffer Replacement Strategy.
```

Index Name Message

```
Index : indexname
```

This message indicates that the optimizer is using an index to retrieve the rows. The message includes the index name. If the line above this one in the output says "Using Clustered Index," the index type is clustered; otherwise, the index is nonclustered.

The keys used to position the search are reported in the "Keys are..." message described on page 236.

This query illustrates the use of a nonclustered index to find and return rows:

```
select au_id, au_fname, au_lname
from authors
where au_fname = "Susan"
QUERY PLAN FOR STATEMENT 1 (at line 1).


    STEP 1
        The type of query is SELECT.

        FROM TABLE
            authors
        Nested iteration.
        Index : au_name_ix
        Ascending scan.
        Positioning by key.
        Keys are:
            au_fname
        Using I/O Size 2 Kbytes.
        With LRU Buffer Replacement Strategy.
```

Scan Direction Message

```
Ascending scan.
```

This message indicates that the scan direction is ascending. All descending sorts require a worktable and a sort. SQL Server does not currently scan tables or indexes in descending order.

Positioning Messages

```
Positioning at start of table.
Positioning by Row IDentifier (RID).
Positioning by key.
```

```
Positioning at index start.
```

These messages describe how access to a table or to the leaf level of a nonclustered index takes place. The choices are:

- "Positioning at start of table." This message indicates a table scan, starting at the first row of the table.

- "Positioning by Row IDentifier (RID)." This message is printed after the OR strategy has created a dynamic index of row IDs. See "Using Dynamic Index." on page 238 for more information about how row IDs are used.

- "Positioning by key." This messages indicates that the index is used to find the qualifying row or the first qualifying row. It is printed for:

  - Direct access to individual rows in point queries

  - Range queries that perform matching scans of the leaf level of a nonclustered index

  - Range queries that scan the data pages when there is a clustered index

  - Indexed accesses to inner tables in joins

- "Positioning at index start." This message indicates a nonmatching nonclustered index scan, used when the index covers the query. Matching scans are positioned by key.

Scanning Messages

```
Scanning only the last page of the table.
```

This message indicates that a query containing an ungrouped (scalar) **max** aggregate needs to access only the last page of the table. In order to use this special optimization, the aggregate column needs to be the leading column in an index. See "Optimizing Aggregates" on page 188 for more information.

```
Scanning only up to the first qualifying row.
```

This message appears only for queries using an ungrouped (scalar) **min** aggregate. The aggregated column needs to be the leading column in an index.

Index Covering Message

```
Index contains all needed columns. Base table will
not be read.
```

This message indicates that the nonclustered index covers the query. It is printed both for matching index accesses, and for non-matching scans. The difference in **showplan** output for the two types of queries can be seen from two other parts of the **showplan** output for the query:

- A matching scan reports "Positioning by key." A nonmatching scan reports "Positioning at index start," since a nonmatching scan must read the entire leaf level of the nonclustered index.

- If the optimizer uses a matching scan, the "Keys are..." line reports the keys used to position the search. This information is not included for a nonmatching scan, since the keys are not used for positioning, but only for selecting the rows to return.

The next query shows output for a matching scan, using a composite index on *au_lname, au_fname, au_id*:

```
create index au_names_id
    on authors(au_lname, au_fname, au_id)

select au_fname, au_lname, au_id
from authors
where au_lname = "Williams"

QUERY PLAN FOR STATEMENT 1 (at line 1).


    STEP 1
        The type of query is SELECT.

        FROM TABLE
            authors
        Nested iteration.
        Index : au_names_id
        Ascending scan.
        Positioning by key.
            Index contains all needed columns. Base
table will not be read.
        Keys are:
            au_lname
        Using I/O Size 2 Kbytes.
        With LRU Buffer Replacement Strategy.
```

The index is used to find the first occurrence of "Williams" on the nonclustered leaf page. The query scans forward, looking for more occurrences of "Williams" and returning any it finds. Once a value greater than "Williams" is found, the query has found all the matching values, and the query stops. All the values needed in the **where** clauses and select list are included in this index, so no access to the table is required.

With the same composite index on *au_lname*, *au_fname*, *au_id*, this query performs a nonmatching scan, since the leading column of the index is not included in the **where** clause:

```
select au_fname, au_lname, au_id
from authors
where au_id = "A93278"
```

Note that the **showplan** output does not contains a "Keys are..." message, and the positioning message is "Positioning at index start."

```
QUERY PLAN FOR STATEMENT 1 (at line 1).


    STEP 1
        The type of query is SELECT.

        FROM TABLE
            authors
        Nested iteration.
        Index : au_names_id
        Ascending scan.
        Positioning at index start.
            Index contains all needed columns. Base
table will not be read.
        Using I/O Size 2 Kbytes.
        With LRU Buffer Replacement Strategy.
```

This query must scan the entire leaf level of the nonclustered index, since the rows are not ordered and there is no way to know the uniqueness of a particular column in a composite index.

Keys Message

```
Keys are:
    keys_list
```

This message is followed by the key(s) used whenever SQL Server uses a clustered or a matching nonclustered index scan to locate rows. For composite indexes, all keys in the **where** clauses are listed. Examples are included under those messages.

Matching Index Scans Message

```
Using N Matching Index Scans.
```

This **showplan** message indicates that a query using **or** clauses or an **in** list is using multiple index accesses to return the rows directly without using a dynamic index. See "Dynamic Index Message" on page 238 for information on this strategy.

Multiple matching scans can only be used when there is no possibility that the **or** clauses or **in** list items can match duplicate rows—that is, when there is no need to build the worktable and perform the sort to remove the duplicates. This query can use the multiple matching scans strategy, because no rows can match both criteria:

```
select * from titles
where type = "business" or type = "art"
```

This query must create a dynamic index in order to avoid returning duplicate rows, since some rows can match both clauses:

```
select * from titles
where type = "business" or price = $19.95
```

In some cases, different indexes may be used for some of the scans, so the messages that describe the type of index, index positioning, and keys used are printed for each scan.

The following example uses multiple scans to return rows:

```
select title
    from titles
    where title_id in ("T18168","T55370")
QUERY PLAN FOR STATEMENT 1 (at line 1).


    STEP 1
        The type of query is SELECT.

        FROM TABLE
            titles
        Nested iteration.
        Using 2 Matching Index Scans
        Index : title_id_ix
        Ascending scan.
        Positioning by key.
        Keys are:
            title_id
        Index : title_id_ix
        Ascending scan.
        Positioning by key.
        Keys are:
            title_id
        Using I/O Size 2 Kbytes.
        With LRU Buffer Replacement Strategy.
```

Dynamic Index Message

```
Using Dynamic Index.
```

The term "dynamic index" refers to a special table of row IDs that SQL Server creates to process queries that use **or** clauses. When a query contains **or** clauses or an **in (*values list*)** clause, SQL Server can do one of the following:

- Scan the table once, finding all rows that match each of the conditions. You will see a "Table Scan" message, but a dynamic index will not be used.

- Use one or more indexes and access the table once for each **or** clause or item in the **in** list. You will see a "Positioning by key" message and the "Using Dynamic Index" message. This technique is called the OR strategy. For a full explanation, see "Optimization of or clauses and in (values_list)" on page 185.

  When the OR strategy is used, SQL Server builds a list of all of the row IDs that match the query, sorts the list to remove duplicates, and uses the list to retrieve the rows from the table.

Conditions for Using a Dynamic Index

SQL Server does not use the OR strategy for all queries that contain **or** clauses. The following conditions must be met:

- All columns in the **or** clause must belong to the same table.

- If any portion of the **or** clause requires a table scan (due to lack of an appropriate index or poor selectivity of a given index), then a table scan is used for the entire query.

If the query contains **or** clauses on different columns of the same table, and each of those columns has a useful index, SQL Server can use different indexes for each clause.

The OR strategy cannot be used for cursors.

The **showplan** output below includes three "FROM TABLE" sections:

- The first two "FROM TABLE" blocks in the output show the two index accesses, one for "Bill" and one for "William."

- The final "FROM TABLE" block shows the "Using Dynamic Index" output with its companion positioning message, "Positioning by Row IDentifier (RID)." This is the step where the dynamic index is used to locate the table rows to be returned.

```
select au_id, au_fname, au_lname
from authors
where au_fname = "Bill"
    or au_fname = "William"
QUERY PLAN FOR STATEMENT 1 (at line 1).


    STEP 1
        The type of query is SELECT.

        FROM TABLE
            authors
        Nested iteration.
        Index : au_fname_ix
        Ascending scan.
        Positioning by key.
        Keys are:
            au_fname
        Using I/O Size 2 Kbytes.
        With LRU Buffer Replacement Strategy.

        FROM TABLE
            authors
        Nested iteration.
        Index : au_fname_ix
        Ascending scan.
        Positioning by key.
        Keys are:
            au_fname
        Using I/O Size 2 Kbytes.
        With LRU Buffer Replacement Strategy.

        FROM TABLE
            authors
        Nested iteration.
        Using Dynamic Index.
        Ascending scan.
        Positioning by Row IDentifier (RID).
        Using I/O Size 2 Kbytes.
        With LRU Buffer Replacement Strategy.
```

Reformatting Message

```
WorktableN Created for REFORMATTING.
```

When joining two or more tables, SQL Server may choose to use a **reformatting strategy** to join the tables when the tables are large and the tables in the join do not have a useful index. The reformatting strategy:

- Inserts the needed columns from qualifying rows of the smaller of the two tables into a worktable.

- Creates a clustered index on the join column(s) of the worktable. The index is built using the keys that join the worktable to the outer table in the query.

- Uses the clustered index in the join to retrieve the qualifying rows from the table.

See "Saving I/O Using the Reformatting Strategy" on page 179 for more information on reformatting.

➤ **Note**

If your queries frequently employ the reformatting strategy, examine the tables involved in the query. Unless there are other overriding factors, you may want to create an index on the join columns of the table.

The following example illustrates the reformatting strategy. It performs a three-way join on the *titles*, *titleauthor*, and *titles* tables. There are no indexes on the join columns in the tables (*au_id* and *title_id*) in any of the tables, which forces SQL Server to use the reformatting strategy on two of the tables:

```
select au_lname, title
from authors a, titleauthor ta, titles t
where a.au_id = ta.au_id
and t.title_id = ta.title_id
QUERY PLAN FOR STATEMENT 1 (at line 1).


STEP 1
     The type of query is INSERT.
     The update mode is direct.
     Worktable1 created for REFORMATTING.
     FROM TABLE
         titleauthor
     Nested iteration.
     Table Scan.
     Ascending scan.
     Positioning at start of table.
     Using I/O Size 2 Kbytes.
     With LRU Buffer Replacement Strategy.
     TO TABLE
```

Worktable1.

STEP 2
The type of query is INSERT.
The update mode is direct.
Worktable2 created for REFORMATTING.

FROM TABLE
authors
Nested iteration.
Table Scan.
Ascending scan.
Positioning at start of table.
Using I/O Size 2 Kbytes.
With LRU Buffer Replacement Strategy.
TO TABLE
Worktable2.

STEP 3
The type of query is SELECT.

FROM TABLE
titles
Nested iteration.
Table Scan.
Ascending scan.
Positioning at start of table.
Using I/O Size 2 Kbytes.
With LRU Buffer Replacement Strategy.

FROM TABLE
Worktable1.
Nested iteration.
Using Clustered Index.
Ascending scan.
Positioning by key.
Using I/O Size 2 Kbytes.
With LRU Buffer Replacement Strategy.

FROM TABLE
Worktable2.
Nested iteration.
Using Clustered Index.
Ascending scan.
Positioning by key.
Using I/O Size 2 Kbytes.
With LRU Buffer Replacement Strategy.

Trigger "Log Scan" Message

```
Log Scan.
```

When an **insert, update**, or **delete** statement causes a trigger to fire, and the trigger includes access to the *inserted* or *deleted* tables, these tables are built by scanning the transaction log.

I/O Size Message

```
Using I/O size N Kbtyes.
```

This message reports the I/O size used in the query. For tables and indexes, the possible sizes are 2K, 4K, 8K, and 16K. If the table, index, or database used in the query uses a data cache with large I/O sized pools, the SQL Server optimizer can choose to use large I/O for some types of queries.

See Chapter 15, "Memory Use and Performance," for more information on large I/Os and the data cache.

Cache Strategy Message

```
With <LRU/MRU> Buffer Replacement Strategy.
```

Indicates the caching strategy used by the query. See "Overview of Cache Strategies" on page 48 for more information on caching strategies.

showplan Messages for Subqueries

Since subqueries can contain the same clauses that regular queries contain, their **showplan** output can include many of the messages listed in earlier sections.

The **showplan** messages for subqueries, listed in Table 8-4, include special delimiters that allow you to easily spot the beginning and end of a subquery processing block, messages to identify the type of subquery, the place in the outer query where the subquery is executed, or special types of processing performed only in subqueries.

Table 8-4:   showplan messages for subqueries

Message	Explanation	See
Run subquery N (at nesting level N).	This message appears at the point in the query where the subquery actually runs. Subqueries are numbered in order for each side of a union.	page 249
NESTING LEVEL N SUBQUERIES FOR STATEMENT N.	Shows the nesting level of the subquery.	page 249
QUERY PLAN FOR SUBQUERY N (at line N). END OF QUERY PLAN FOR SUBQUERY N.	These lines bracket **showplan** output for each subquery in a statement. Variables show the subquery number, the nesting level, and the input line.	page 249 page 249
Correlated Subquery.	The subquery is correlated.	page 249
Non-correlated Subquery.	The subquery is not correlated.	page 249
Subquery under an IN predicate.	The subquery is introduced by **in**.	page 250
Subquery under an ANY predicate.	The subquery is introduced by **any**.	page 250
Subquery under an ALL predicate.	The subquery is introduced by **all**.	page 250
Subquery under an EXISTS predicate.	The subquery is introduced by **exists**.	page 250
Subquery under an EXPRESSION predicate.	The subquery is introduced by an expression, or the subquery is in the select list.	page 250
Evaluate Grouped <ONCE, ONCE-UNIQUE or ANY> AGGREGATE or Evaluate Ungrouped <ONCE, ONCE-UNIQUE or ANY> AGGREGATE	The subquery uses an internal aggregate.	page 252 page 251
EXISTS TABLE: nested iteration	The query includes an **exists**, **in**, or **any** clause, and the subquery is flattened into a join.	page 254

"Optimizing Subqueries" on page 189 explains how SQL Server optimizes certain types of subqueries by materializing results or flattening the queries to joins. Chapter 5 of the *Transact-SQL User's*

Guide provides basic information on subqueries, subquery types, and the meaning of the subquery predicates.

Output for Flattened or Materialized Subqueries

Certain forms of subqueries can be processed more efficiently when:

- The query is flattened into a join query.
- The subquery result set is materialized as a first step, and the results are used in a second step with the rest of the outer query.

When the optimizer chooses one of these strategies, the query is not processed as a subquery, so you will not see the special subquery message delimiters. The following sections describe **showplan** output for flattened and materialized queries.

Flattened Queries

When subqueries are flattened into existence joins, the output looks like normal **showplan** output for a join, with the possible exception of the message "EXISTS TABLE: nested iteration."

This message indicates that instead of the normal join processing, which looks for every row in the table that matches the join column, SQL Server uses an existence join and returns TRUE as soon as the first qualifying row is located. For more information on subquery flattening, see "Flattening in, any, and exists Subqueries" on page 189.

SQL Server flattens the following subquery into an existence join:

```
select title
from titles
where  title_id in
    (select title_id
        from titleauthor)
and title like "A Tutorial%"
```
QUERY PLAN FOR STATEMENT 1 (at line 1).

    STEP 1
        The type of query is SELECT.

        FROM TABLE
            titles
        Nested iteration.
        Index : title_ix
```
```

```
Ascending scan.
Positioning by key.
Keys are:
    title
Using I/O Size 2 Kbytes.
With LRU Buffer Replacement Strategy.

FROM TABLE
    titleauthor
EXISTS TABLE : nested iteration.
Index : ta_ix
Ascending scan.
Positioning by key.
Index contains all needed columns. Base table will
    not be read.
Keys are:
    title_id
Using I/O Size 2 Kbytes.
With LRU Buffer Replacement Strategy.
```

Materialized Queries

When SQL Server materializes subqueries, the query is reformulated into two steps:

1. The first step stores the results of the subquery in an internal variable or in a worktable

2. The second step uses the internal variable results or the worktable results in the outer query.

This query materializes the subquery into a worktable:

```
select type, title_id
from titles
where total_sales in (select max(total_sales)
            from sales_summary
            group by type)
```

```
QUERY PLAN FOR STATEMENT 1 (at line 1).


    STEP 1
        The type of query is SELECT (into Worktable1).
        GROUP BY
        Evaluate Grouped MAXIMUM AGGREGATE.

        FROM TABLE
            sales_summary
        Nested iteration.
```

```
            Table Scan.
            Ascending scan.
            Positioning at start of table.
            Using I/O Size 2 Kbytes.
            With LRU Buffer Replacement Strategy.
            TO TABLE
                Worktable1.

    STEP 2
            The type of query is SELECT.

            FROM TABLE
                titles
            Nested iteration.
            Table Scan.
            Ascending scan.
            Positioning at start of table.
            Using I/O Size 2 Kbytes.
            With LRU Buffer Replacement Strategy.

            FROM TABLE
                Worktable1.
            EXISTS TABLE : nested iteration.
            Table Scan.
            Ascending scan.
            Positioning at start of table.
            Using I/O Size 2 Kbytes.
            With LRU Buffer Replacement Strategy.
```

The **showplan** message "EXISTS TABLE: nested iteration," near the end of the output, shows that SQL Server has performed an existence join.

Structure of Subquery *showplan* Output

Whenever a query contains subqueries that are not flattened or materialized:

- The **showplan** output for the outer query appears first. It includes the message "Run subquery N (at nesting level N)" indicating the point in the query processing where the subquery executes.

- For each nesting level, the query plans at that nesting level are introduced by the message "NESTING LEVEL N SUBQUERIES FOR STATEMENT N."

- The plan for each subquery is introduced by the message "QUERY PLAN FOR SUBQUERY N (at line N)," and the end of its plan is marked by the message "END OF QUERY PLAN FOR SUBQUERY *N*." This section of the output includes information about:

- The type of query (correlated or uncorrelated)

- The predicate type (IN, ANY, ALL, EXISTS, or EXPRESSION)

The structure is shown in Figure 8-1, using the **showplan** output from this query:

```
select title_id
from titles
where total_sales > all (select total_sales
                         from titles
                         where type = 'business')
```

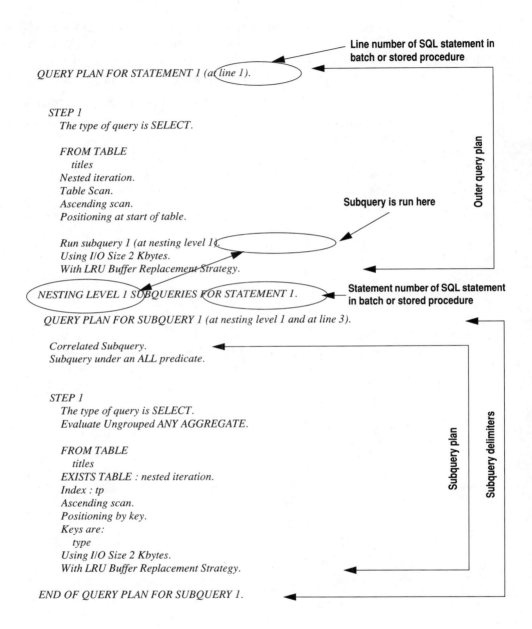

Figure 8-1: Subquery showplan output structure

Subquery Execution Message

```
Run subquery N (at nesting level N).
```

This message shows the place in the execution of the outer query where the subquery execution takes place. SQL Server executes the subquery at the point in the outer query where the optimizer finds it should perform best.

The actual plan output for this subquery appears later under the blocks of output for the subquery's nesting level. The first variable in this message is the subquery number; the second variable is the subquery nesting level.

Nesting Level Delimiter Message

```
NESTING LEVEL N SUBQUERIES FOR STATEMENT N.
```

This message introduces the **showplan** output for all the subqueries at a given nesting level. The maximum nesting level is 16.

Subquery Plan Start Delimiter

```
QUERY PLAN FOR SUBQUERY N (at line N).
```

This statement introduces the **showplan** output for a particular subquery at the nesting level indicated by the previous NESTING LEVEL message.

SQL Server provides line numbers to help you match query output to your input.

Subquery Plan End Delimiter

```
END OF QUERY PLAN FOR SUBQUERY N.
```

This statement marks the end of the query plan for a particular subquery.

Type of Subquery

```
Correlated Subquery.
```
```
Non-correlated Subquery.
```

Every subquery is either correlated or noncorrelated. **showplan** evaluates the type of subquery and, if the subquery is correlated, returns the message "Correlated Subquery." Noncorrelated subqueries are usually materialized, so their **showplan** output does not include the normal subquery **showplan** messages.

A correlated subquery references a column in a table that is listed in the **from** list of the outer query. The subquery's reference to the column is in the **where** clause, the **having** clause or the select list of the subquery. A noncorrelated subquery can be evaluated independently of the outer query.

Subquery Predicates

```
Subquery under an IN predicate.

Subquery under an ANY predicate.

Subquery under an ALL predicate.

Subquery under an EXISTS predicate.

Subquery under an EXPRESSION predicate.
```

Subqueries introduced by **in, any, all,** or **exists** are quantified predicate subqueries. Subqueries introduced by >, >=, <, <=, =, != are expression subqueries.

Internal Subquery Aggregates

Certain types of subqueries require special internal aggregates, as listed in Table 8-5. SQL Server generates these aggregates internally—they are not part of Transact-SQL syntax and cannot be included in user queries.

Table 8-5:   Internal subquery aggregates

Subquery Type	Aggregate	Effect
Quantified Predicate	ANY	Returns 0 or 1 to the outer query.
Expression	ONCE	Returns the result of the subquery. Raises error 512 if the subquery returns more than one value.
Subquery containing **distinct**	ONCE-UNIQUE	Stores the first subquery result internally and compares each subsequent result to the first. Raises error 512 if a subsequent result differs from the first.

Grouped or Ungrouped Messages

The message "Grouped" appears when the subquery includes a **group by** clause and computes the aggregate for a group of rows.

The message "Ungrouped" appears when the subquery does not include a **group by** clause and computes the aggregate for all rows in the table that satisfy the correlation clause.

Quantified Predicate Subqueries and the ANY Aggregate

```
Evaluate Grouped ANY AGGREGATE.
Evaluate Ungrouped ANY AGGREGATE.
```

All quantified predicate subqueries that are not flattened use the internal ANY aggregate. Do not confuse this with the **any** predicate, which is part of SQL syntax.

The subquery returns 1 when a row from the subquery satisfies the conditions of the subquery predicate. It returns 0 to indicate that no row from the subquery matches the conditions.

For example:

```
select type, title_id
from titles
where price > all
      (select price
            from titles
            where advance < 15000)
QUERY PLAN FOR STATEMENT 1 (at line 1).


    STEP 1
        The type of query is SELECT.

        FROM TABLE
            titles
        Nested iteration.
        Table Scan.
        Ascending scan.
        Positioning at start of table.

        Run subquery 1 (at nesting level 1).
        Using I/O Size 2 Kbytes.
        With LRU Buffer Replacement Strategy.

NESTING LEVEL 1 SUBQUERIES FOR STATEMENT 1.
```

```
QUERY PLAN FOR SUBQUERY 1 (at nesting level 1 and at line 4).

    Correlated Subquery.
    Subquery under an ALL predicate.


    STEP 1
        The type of query is SELECT.
        Evaluate Ungrouped ANY AGGREGATE.

        FROM TABLE
            titles
        EXISTS TABLE : nested iteration.
        Table Scan.
        Ascending scan.
        Positioning at start of table.
        Using I/O Size 2 Kbytes.
        With LRU Buffer Replacement Strategy.

END OF QUERY PLAN FOR SUBQUERY 1.
```

Expression Subqueries and the ONCE Aggregate

```
    Evaluate Ungrouped ONCE AGGREGATE.

    Evaluate Grouped ONCE AGGREGATE.
```

Expression subqueries must return only a single value. The internal ONCE aggregate checks for the single result required by an expression subquery.

This query returns one row for each title that matches the **like** condition:

```
    select title_id, (select city + " " + state
                          from publishers
                          where pub_id = t.pub_id)
        from titles t
        where title like "Computer%"
QUERY PLAN FOR STATEMENT 1 (at line 1).


    STEP 1
        The type of query is SELECT.

        FROM TABLE
            titles
        Nested iteration.
        Index : title_ix
```

```
        Ascending scan.
        Positioning by key.
        Keys are:
            title
        Using I/O Size 2 Kbytes.
        With LRU Buffer Replacement Strategy.

        Run subquery 1 (at nesting level 1).

NESTING LEVEL 1 SUBQUERIES FOR STATEMENT 1.

   QUERY PLAN FOR SUBQUERY 1 (at nesting level 1 and at line 1).

        Correlated Subquery.
        Subquery under an EXPRESSION predicate.


        STEP 1
            The type of query is SELECT.
            Evaluate Ungrouped ONCE AGGREGATE.

            FROM TABLE
                publishers
            Nested iteration.
            Table Scan.
            Ascending scan.
            Positioning at start of table.
            Using I/O Size 2 Kbytes.
            With LRU Buffer Replacement Strategy.

    END OF QUERY PLAN FOR SUBQUERY 1.
```

Subqueries with *distinct* and the ONCE-UNIQUE Aggregate

```
        Evaluate Grouped ONCE-UNIQUE AGGREGATE.

        Evaluate Ungrouped ONCE-UNIQUE AGGREGATE.
```

When the subquery includes **distinct**, the ONCE-UNIQUE aggregate
indicates that duplicates are being eliminated:

```
        select pub_name from publishers
        where pub_id =
        (select distinct titles.pub_id from titles
            where publishers.pub_id = titles.pub_id
            and price > $1000)
```

QUERY PLAN FOR STATEMENT 1 (at line 1).

STEP 1
    The type of query is SELECT.

    FROM TABLE
        publishers
    Nested iteration.
    Table Scan.
    Ascending scan.
    Positioning at start of table.
    Using I/O Size 2 Kbytes.
    With LRU Buffer Replacement Strategy.

    Run subquery 1 (at nesting level 1).

NESTING LEVEL 1 SUBQUERIES FOR STATEMENT 1.

QUERY PLAN FOR SUBQUERY 1 (at nesting level 1 and at line 3).

Correlated Subquery.
Subquery under an EXPRESSION predicate.

STEP 1
    The type of query is SELECT.
    Evaluate Ungrouped ONCE-UNIQUE AGGREGATE.

    FROM TABLE
        titles
    Nested iteration.
    Index : comp_i
    Ascending scan.
    Positioning by key.
    Keys are:
        price
    Using I/O Size 2 Kbytes.
    With LRU Buffer Replacement Strategy.

END OF QUERY PLAN FOR SUBQUERY 1.

Existence Join Message

        EXISTS TABLE: nested iteration

    This message indicates a special form of nested iteration. In a regular
    nested iteration, the entire table or its index is searched for qualifying

values. In an existence test, the query can stop the search as soon as it finds the first matching value.

The types of subqueries that can produce this message are:

- Subqueries that are flattened to existence joins
- Subqueries that perform existence tests

Subqueries That Perform Existence Tests

There are several ways an existence test can be written in Transact-SQL, such as **exists, in**, or **=any**. These queries are treated as if they were written with an **exists** clause. The following example demonstrates the **showplan** output with an existence test. This query cannot be flattened because the outer query contains **or**.

```
select au_lname, au_fname
from authors
where exists
    (select *
    from publishers
    where authors.city = publishers.city)
or city = "New York"
```

```
QUERY PLAN FOR STATEMENT 1 (at line 1).


    STEP 1
        The type of query is SELECT.

        FROM TABLE
            authors
        Nested iteration.
        Table Scan.
        Ascending scan.
        Positioning at start of table.

        Run subquery 1 (at nesting level 1).
        Using I/O Size 2 Kbytes.
        With LRU Buffer Replacement Strategy.

NESTING LEVEL 1 SUBQUERIES FOR STATEMENT 1.

  QUERY PLAN FOR SUBQUERY 1 (at nesting level 1 and at line 4).

    Correlated Subquery.
    Subquery under an EXISTS predicate.
```

STEP 1
    The type of query is SELECT.
    Evaluate Ungrouped ANY AGGREGATE.

    FROM TABLE
        publishers
    EXISTS TABLE : nested iteration.
    Table Scan.
    Ascending scan.
    Positioning at start of table.
    Using I/O Size 2 Kbytes.
    With LRU Buffer Replacement Strategy.

END OF QUERY PLAN FOR SUBQUERY 1.

Going Beyond Standard Remedies

Even with the reams of information that SQL Server's query analysis tools provide, some query optimization problems refuse to yield. SQL Server provides a set of techniques that yield more forceful solutions to query optimization problems.

Chapter 9, "Advanced Query Processing Techniques," discusses the techniques you can use when you know what you're doing, and when you've tried everything else.

SQL Server's advanced, cost-based optimizer produces excellent query plans in most situations. But there are times when the optimizer does not choose the proper index for optimal performance or chooses a suboptimal join order, and you need to control the access methods for the query. The options described in Chapter 9 allow you that control.

9

Advanced Optimizing Techniques

What Are Advanced Optimizing Techniques?

This chapter describes query processing options that affect the optimizer's choice of join order, index, I/O size and cache strategy. It also introduces a trace facility that allows you to probe more deeply into the details of the decisions made by the query optimizer.

If you have turned to this chapter without fully understanding the materials presented in earlier chapters of this book, be careful when you use the tools described in this chapter. Some of these tools allow you to override the decisions made by SQL Server's optimizer and can have an extreme negative effect on performance if they are misused. You need to understand their impact on the performance of your individual query, and possible implications for overall performance.

SQL Server provides tools and query clauses that affect query optimization and advanced query analysis tools that let you understand why the optimizer makes the choices that it does.

You can also use these tools while you are tuning, to see the effects of a different join order, I/O size, or cache strategy. Some of these options let you specify query processing or access strategy without costly reconfiguration.

Specifying Optimizer Choices

SQL Server lets you specify these optimization choices:

- The order of tables in a join
- The number of tables evaluated at one time during join optimization
- The index used for a table access
- The I/O size
- The cache strategy

In a few cases, the optimizer fails to choose the best plan. In some of these cases, the plan it chooses is only slightly more expensive than the "best" plan, so you need to weigh the cost of maintaining forced choices over the slightly slower performance of default choices.

The commands to specify join order, index, I/O size, or cache strategy, coupled with the query-reporting commands like **statistics io** and **showplan**, should help you determine why the optimizer makes its choices.

◆ WARNING!

Use these options with caution. The forced plans may be inappropriate in some situations and cause very poor performance. If you include these options in your applications, be sure to check their query plans, I/O statistics, and other performance data regularly.

These options are generally intended for use as tools for tuning and experimentation, not as long-term solutions to optimization problems.

Specifying Table Order in Joins

SQL Server optimizes join orders in order to minimize I/O. In most cases, the order that the optimizer chooses does not match the order of the **from** clauses in your **select** command. To force SQL Server to access tables in the order they are listed, use the command:

```
set forceplan [on|off]
```

The optimizer still chooses the best access method for each table. If you use **forceplan**, specifying a join order, the optimizer may use different indexes on tables than it would with a different table order, or it may not be able to use existing indexes.

You might use this command as a debugging aid if other query analysis tools lead you to suspect that the optimizer is not choosing the best join order. Always verify that the order you are forcing reduces I/O and logical reads by using **set statistics io on** and comparing I/O with and without **forceplan**.

If you use **forceplan**, your routine performance maintenance checks should include verifying that the queries and procedures that use it still require the option to improve performance.

You can include **forceplan** in the text of stored procedures.

forceplan example

This example is executed with these indexes on the tables in *pubtune*:

- Unique nonclustered on *titles(title)*
- Unique clustered on *authors(au_id)*

- Unique nonclustered on *titleauthor(au_id, title_id)*

Without **forceplan**, this query:

```
select title, au_lname
from titles t, authors a, titleauthor ta
where t.title_id = ta.title_id
and a.au_id = ta.au_id
and title like "Computer%"
```

joins the tables with the join order *titles–titleauthor–authors*, the join order that the optimizer has chosen as the least costly.

Here is the **showplan** output for the unforced query:

```
QUERY PLAN FOR STATEMENT 1 (at line 1).


    STEP 1
        The type of query is SELECT.

        FROM TABLE
            titles
        Nested iteration.
        Index : title_ix
        Ascending scan.
        Positioning by key.
        Keys are:
            title
        Using I/O Size 2 Kbytes.
        With LRU Buffer Replacement Strategy.

        FROM TABLE
            titleauthor
        Nested iteration.
        Index : ta_au_tit_ix
        Ascending scan.
        Positioning at index start.
        Index contains all needed columns. Base table will not
be read.
        Using I/O Size 2 Kbytes.
        With LRU Buffer Replacement Strategy.

        FROM TABLE
```

```
        authors
    Nested iteration.
    Using Clustered Index.
    Index : au_id_ix
    Ascending scan.
    Positioning by key.
    Keys are:
        au_id
    Using I/O Size 2 Kbytes.
    With LRU Buffer Replacement Strategy.
```

statistics io for the query shows a total of 154 physical reads and 2431 logical reads:

```
Table: titles   scan count 1,   logical reads: 29,   physical
reads: 27
Table: authors   scan count 34,   logical reads: 102,   physical
reads: 35
Table: titleauthor   scan count 25,   logical reads: 2300,
physical reads: 92

Total writes for this command: 0
```

If you use **forceplan**, the optimizer chooses a reformatting strategy on *titleauthor*, resulting in this **showplan** report:

```
QUERY PLAN FOR STATEMENT 1(at line 1).


    STEP 1
        The type of query is INSERT.
        The update mode is direct.
        Worktable1 created for REFORMATTING.

        FROM TABLE
            titleauthor
        Nested iteration.
        Index : ta_au_tit_ix
        Ascending scan.
        Positioning at index start.
        Index contains all needed columns. Base table will not
be read.
        Using I/O Size 2 Kbytes.
        With LRU Buffer Replacement Strategy.
        TO TABLE
            Worktable1.

    STEP 2
        The type of query is SELECT.
```

```
FROM TABLE
    titles
Nested iteration.
Index : title_ix
Ascending scan.
Positioning by key.
Keys are:
    title
Using I/O Size 2 Kbytes.
With LRU Buffer Replacement Strategy.

FROM TABLE
    authors
Nested iteration.
Table Scan.
Ascending scan.
Positioning at start of table.
Using I/O Size 2 Kbytes.
With LRU Buffer Replacement Strategy.

FROM TABLE
    Worktable1.
Nested iteration.
Using Clustered Index.
Ascending scan.
Positioning by key.
Using I/O Size 2 Kbytes.
With LRU Buffer Replacement Strateg
```

Table: titles scan count 1, logical reads: 29, physical reads: 27
Table: authors scan count 25, logical reads: 5525, physical reads: 221
Table: titleauthor scan count 1, logical reads: 92, physical reads: 60
Table: Worktable1 scan count 125000, logical reads: 389350, physical reads: 27
Total writes for this command: 187

Join Sequence and Scans Required for Each Plan

Figure 9-1 shows the sequence of the joins and the number of scans required for each query plan.

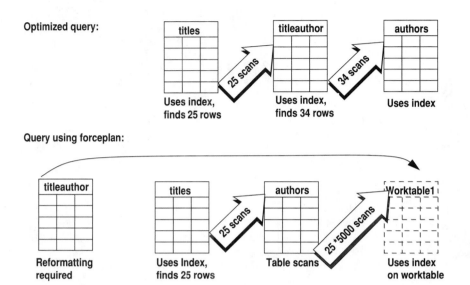

Figure 9-1: Extreme negative effects of using forceplan

Risks of Using *forceplan*

Forcing join order has these risks:

- Misuse can lead to extremely expensive queries.

- It requires maintenance. You must regularly check queries and stored procedures that include **forceplan**. Also, future releases of SQL Server may eliminate the problems which led you to incorporate index forcing, so all queries using forced query plans need to be checked when new releases are installed.

Things to Try Before Using *forceplan*

As the preceding example shows, specifying the join order can be risky. Here are options to try before using **forceplan**:

- Check **showplan** output to determine whether index keys are used as expected.

- Use **dbcc traceon(302)** to look for other optimization problems.

- Be sure that **update statistics** been run on the index recently.

- If the query joins more than four tables, use **set table count** to see if it results in an improved join order. See "Increasing the Number of Tables Considered by the Optimizer" on page 265.

Increasing the Number of Tables Considered by the Optimizer

As described in "Optimizing Joins" on page 175, SQL Server optimizes joins by considering permutations of four tables at a time. If you suspect that an incorrect join order is being chosen for a query that joins more than four tables, you can use the **set table count** option to increase the number of tables that are considered at the same time. The syntax is:

```
set table count int_value
```

The maximum value is 8; the minimum value is 1. As you decrease the value, you reduce the chance that the optimizer will consider all the possible join orders. Increasing the number of tables considered at once during join ordering can greatly increase the time it takes to optimize a query.

With SQL Server's default four-at-a-time optimization, it takes 3,024 permutations to consider all the join possibilities. With eight-table-at-a-time optimization, it takes 40,320 permutations.

Since the time to optimize the query increases with each additional table, this option is most useful when the actual execution savings from improved join order outweighs the extra optimizing time.

Use **statistics time** to check parse and compile time and **statistics io** to verify that the improved join order is reducing physical and logical I/O.

If increasing **table count** produces an improvement in join optimization, but increases CPU time unacceptably, rewrite the **from** clause in the query, specifying the tables in the join order indicated by **showplan** output, and use **forceplan** to run the query. Your routine performance maintenance checks should include verifying that the join order you are forcing still improves performance.

Specifying an Index for a Query

A special clause, (**index *index_name***), for the **select**, **update**, and **delete** statements allows you to specify an index for a particular query. You can also force a query to perform a table scan by specifying the table name. The syntax is:

```
select select_list
   from table_name [table_alias]
      (index {index_name | table_name } )
      [, table_name ...]
   where ...

delete table_name
   from table_name [table_alias]
   (index {index_name | table_name }) ...

update table_name set col_name = value
   from table_name [table_alias]
   (index {index_name | table_name}) ...
```

Here's an example:

```
select pub_name, title
      from publishers p, titles t (index date_type)
      where p.pub_id = t.pub_id
      and type = "business"
      and pubdate > "1/1/93"
```

Specifying an index in a query can be helpful when you suspect that the optimizer is choosing a suboptimal query plan. When you use this option:

- Always check **statistics io** for the query to see whether the index you choose requires less I/O than the optimizer's choice.

- Be sure to test a full range of valid values for the query clauses, especially if you are tuning range queries, since the access methods for these queries are sensitive to the size of the range. In some cases, skew of values in a table or out-of-data statistics may be other causes for apparent failure to use the correct index.

Use this option only after testing to be certain that the query performs better with the specified index option. Once you include this index option in applications, you should check regularly to be sure that the resulting plan is still superior to other choices that the optimizer makes.

➤ **Note**

If you have a nonclustered index with the same name as the table, specifying a table name causes the nonclustered index to be used. You can force a table scan using **select *select_list* from** tableA (0).

Risks of Specifying Indexes in Queries

Specifying indexes has these risks:

- Changes in the distribution of data could make the forced index less efficient than other choices.

- Dropping the index means that all queries and procedures that specify the index print an informational message indicating that the index does not exist. The query is optimized using the best available index or other access method.

- Maintenance costs increase, since all queries using this option need to be checked periodically. Also, future releases of SQL Server may eliminate the problems which led you to incorporate index forcing, so all queries using forced indexes should be checked when new releases are installed.

Things to Try Before Specifying Indexes

Before specifying an index in queries:

- Check **showplan** output for the "Keys are" message to be sure that the index keys are being used as expected.

- Use **dbcc traceon(302)** to look for other optimization problems.

- Be sure that **update statistics** has been run on the index recently.

Specifying I/O Size in a Query

If your SQL Server is configured for large I/Os in the default data cache or in named data caches, the optimizer can decide to use large I/O for:

- Queries that scan entire tables

- Range queries using clustered indexes, such as queries using >, <, **> x** and **< y, between**, and **like "*charstring*%"**

- Queries that use covering nonclustered indexes

In these cases, disk I/O can access up to eight pages simultaneously, if the cache used by the table or index is configured for it.

Each named data cache can have several pools, each with a different I/O size. Specifying the I/O size in a query causes the I/O for that query to take place in the pool that is configured for that size. See Chapter 9, "Configuring Data Caches" in the *System Administration Guide* for information on configuring named data caches.

To specify a different I/O size than the one chosen by the optimizer, add the **prefetch** specification to the **index** clause of a **select, delete,** or **update** statement. The syntax is:

```
select select_list
    from table_name
        (index {index_name | table_name} prefetch size)
        [, table_name ...]
    where ...

delete table_name from table_name
    (index {index_name | table_name } prefetch size) ...

update table_name set col_name = value
    from table_name
    (index {index_name | table_name} prefetch size) ...
```

Valid values for *size* are 2, 4, 8, and 16. If no pool of the specified size exists in the data cache used by the object, the optimizer chooses the best available size.

If there is a clustered index on *au_lname*, this query performs 16K I/O while it scans the data pages:

```
select *
from authors (index au_names prefetch 16)
    where au_lname like "Sm%"
```

If a query normally performs prefetch, and you want to check its I/O statistics with 2K I/O, you can specify a size of 2K:

```
select type, avg(price)
    from titles (index type_price prefetch 2)
    group by type
```

➤ **Note**

If you are experimenting with prefetch sizes and checking **statistics i/o** for physical reads, you may need to clear pages from the cache so that SQL Server will perform physical I/O on the second execution of a query. If the table or index, or its database, is bound to a named data cache, you can unbind and rebind the object. If the query uses the default cache, or if other tables or indexes are bound to the object's cache, you can run queries on other tables that perform enough I/O to push the pages out of the memory pools.

Index Type and Prefetching

To perform prefetching on the data pages, specify either the clustered index name, or the table name. To perform prefetching on the leaf level pages of a nonclustered index (for covered queries, for example), specify the nonclustered index name.

Table 9-1: Index name and prefetching

Index Name Parameter	Prefetching Performed On
Table name	Data pages
Clustered index name	Data pages
Nonclustered index name	Leaf pages of nonclustered index

When *prefetch* Specification Is Not Followed

Normally, when you specify an I/O size in a query, the optimizer incorporates the I/O size into the query's plan. However, the specification cannot be followed:

- If the cache is not configured for I/O of the specified size, the optimizer substitutes the "best" size available.

- If any of the pages included in that I/O request are in cache. If the I/O size specified is eight data pages, but one of the pages is already in the 2K pool, SQL Server performs 2K I/O on the rest of the pages for that I/O request.

- If the page is on the first extent in an allocation unit. This extent holds the allocation page for the allocation unit, and only 7 data pages.

- If there are no buffers available in the pool for that I/O size, SQL Server uses the 2K pool.

- If prefetching has been turned off for the table or index with **sp_cachestrategy**.

The system procedure **sp_sysmon** reports on prefetches requested and denied for each cache. See "Data Cache Management" on page 510.

set prefetch on

By default, SQL Server checks whether prefetching is useful for all queries. To disable prefetching during a session, use the command:

```
set prefetch off
```

To re-enable prefetching, use the command:

```
set prefetch on
```

If prefetching is turned off for an object with **sp_cachestrategy**, this command does not override that setting.

If prefetching is turned off for a session with **set prefetch off**, you cannot override it by specifying a prefetch size in a **select**, **delete**, or **insert** command.

The **set prefetch** command takes effect in the same batch in which it is run, so it can be included in stored procedures to affect the execution of the queries in the procedure.

Specifying the Cache Strategy

For queries that scan a table's data pages or the leaf level of a nonclustered index (covered queries), the SQL Server optimizer chooses one of two cache replacement strategies: the fetch-and-discard (MRU) strategy or the LRU strategy. See "Overview of Cache Strategies" on page 48 for more information about these strategies.

The optimizer may choose fetch-and-discard (MRU) strategy for:

- Any query that table scans
- A range query that uses a clustered index
- A covered query that scans the leaf level of a nonclustered index
- An inner table in a join, if the inner table is larger than the cache
- The outer table of a join, since it needs to be read only once

You can affect the cache strategy for objects:

- By specifying **lru** or **mru** in a **select**, **update**, or **delete** statement
- By using **sp_cachestrategy** to disable or re-enable **mru** strategy

If you specify MRU strategy and a page is already in the data cache, the page is placed at the MRU end of the cache, rather than at the wash marker.

Specifying the cache strategy only affects data pages and the leaf pages of indexes. Root and intermediate pages always use the LRU strategy.

Specifying Cache Strategy in *select*, *delete*, and *update* Statements

You can use **lru** or **mru** (fetch-and-discard) in a **select, delete,** or **update** command to specify the I/O size for the query:

```
select select_list
    from table_name
        (index index_name prefetch size [lru|mru])
        [, table_name ...]
    where ...

delete table_name from table_name (index index_name
                            prefetch size [lru|mru]) ...

update table_name set col_name = value
        from table_name (index index_name
                            prefetch size [lru|mru]) ...
```

This query adds the LRU replacement strategy to the 16K I/O specification:

```
select au_lname, au_fname, phone
    from authors (index au_names prefetch 16 lru)
```

For more discussion of specifying a **prefetch** size, see "Specifying I/O Size in a Query" on page 267.

Controlling Prefetching and Cache Strategies for Database Objects

Status bits in *sysindexes* identify whether a table or index should be considered for prefetching or for MRU replacement strategy. By default, both are enabled. To disable or re-enable these strategies, use the **sp_cachestrategy** system procedure. The syntax is:

```
sp_cachestrategy dbname , [ownername.]tablename
    [, indexname | "text only" | "table only"
    [, { prefetch | mru }, { "on" | "off"}]]
```

This command turns the prefetch strategy off for the *au_name_index* of the *authors* table:

```
sp_cachestrategy pubtune, authors, au_name_index,
prefetch, "off"
```

This command re-enables MRU replacement strategy for the *titles* table:

```
sp_cachestrategy pubtune, titles, "table only", mru,
"on"
```

Only a System Administrator or the object owner can change or view the cache strategy status of an object.

Getting Information on Cache Strategies

To see the cache strategy in effect for a given object, execute **sp_cachestrategy**, including only the database and object name:

```
sp_cachestrategy pubtune, titles
object name        index name         large IO MRU
---------------    ---------------    -------- -------
titles             NULL               ON       ON
```

showplan output shows cache strategy for each object, including worktables.

Tuning with *dbcc traceon 302*

The **dbcc** trace flag **dbcc traceon (302)** can often help you understand why the optimizer makes choices that seem incorrect. It can help you debug queries and help you decide whether to use specific options, like specifying an index or a join order for a particular query. It can also help you choose better indexes for your tables.

showplan tells you the final decisions that the optimizer makes about your queries. **dbcc traceon (302)** helps you understand why the optimizer made the choices that it did. When you turn on this trace facility, you eavesdrop on the optimizer as it examines query clauses.

The output from this trace facility is more cryptic than **showplan** output, but can go further in explaining such questions as why a table scan is done rather than an indexed access, why *index1* is chosen rather than *index2*, or why a reformatting strategy is applied. The trace output provides detailed information on the costs the optimizer has estimated for permutation of the tables, search clause, and join clause as well as how those costs were determined.

Invoking the *dbcc* Trace Facility

Execute the following command from an **isql** batch followed by the query or stored procedure call you want to examine:

```
dbcc traceon(3604, 302)
```

This is what the trace flags mean:

Trace Flag	Explanation
3604	Directs trace output to the client rather than the errorlog
302	Print trace information on index selection

To turn off the output, use:

```
dbcc traceoff(3604, 302)
```

General Tips for Tuning with This Trace Facility

When you trace queries through this facility, run your queries in the same manner as your application, as follows:

- Supply the same parameters and values to your stored procedures or SQL statements.

- If the application uses cursors, use cursors in your tests.

Be very careful to ensure that your trace tests cause the optimizer to make the same decisions as in your application. You must supply the same parameters and values to your stored procedures or **where** clauses.

If you are using stored procedures, make sure that they are actually being optimized during the trial by executing them **with recompile**.

Checking for Join Columns and Search Arguments

In most situations, SQL Server can use only one index per table in a query. This means the optimizer must often choose between indexes when there are multiple **where** clauses supporting both search arguments and join clauses. The optimizer's first step is to match search arguments and join clauses to available indexes.

The most important item that you can verify using the 302 trace facility is that the optimizer is evaluating all possible **where** clauses included in each Transact-SQL statement. If a clause is not included in this output, then the optimizer has determined it is not a valid search argument or join clause. If you believe your query should benefit from the optimizer evaluating this clause, find out why the clause was excluded, and correct it if possible. The most common reasons for "non-optimizable" clauses include:

- Data type mismatches

- Use of functions, arithmetic, or concatenation on the column

- Numerics compared against constants that are larger than the definition of the column

See "Search Arguments and Using Indexes" on page 171 for more information on requirements for search arguments.

Determine How the Optimizer Estimates I/O Costs

Identifying how the optimizer estimates I/O often leads to the root of the problems and to solutions. You will be able to see when the optimizers uses your distribution page statistics and when it uses default values.

Trace Facility Output

Each set of clauses evaluated by the optimizer is printed and delimited within two lines of asterisks. If you issue an unqualified query with no search arguments or join clause, this step is not included in the output, unless the query is covered (that is, a nonclustered index contains all referenced columns).

Output for each qualified clause looks like this:

```
*******************************
Entering q_score_index() for table 'name' (objectid obj_id,
varno = varno).
The table has X rows and Y pages.
Scoring the clause_type CLAUSE
    column_name operator [column_name}

<other query specific info explained later>
*******************************
```

q_score_index() is the name of a routine that SQL Server runs to cost index choices. It finds the best index to use for a given table and set of clauses. The clauses can be either constant search arguments or join clauses.

Identifying the Table

The first line identifies the table name and its associated object ID. The actual output for this line looks like this:

```
Entering q_score_index() for table 'titles' (objectid
208003772), varno = 0
```

The optimizer analyzes all search arguments for all tables in each query, followed by all join clauses for each table in the query.

Therefore, you first see **q_score_index()** called for all tables in which the optimizer has found a search clause. The routine numbers the tables in the order in which they were specified in the **from** clause and displays the numbers as the *varno*. It starts numbering with 0 for the first table.

Any search clause not included in this section should be evaluated to determine whether its absence impacts performance.

Following the search clause analysis, **q_score_index()** is called for all tables where the optimizer has found a join clause. As above, any join clause not included in this section should be evaluated to determine whether its absence is impacting performance.

Estimating Table Size

The next line prints the size of the table in both rows and pages:

```
The table has 5000 rows and 624 pages.
```

These sizes are pulled from the OAM pages where they are periodically maintained. There are some known problems where inaccurate row estimates cause bad query plans, so verify that this is not the cause of your problem.

Identifying the *where* Clause

The next two lines indicate the type of clause and a representation of the clause itself with column names and abbreviations for the operators. It indicates:

- That it is evaluating a search clause, like this:

```
Scoring the SEARCH CLAUSE:
    au_fname EQ
```

- That it is evaluating a join clause, like this:

```
Scoring the JOIN CLAUSE:
    au_id EQ au_id
```

All search clauses for all tables are evaluated before any join clauses are evaluated.

The operator codes are defined in Table 9-2.

Table 9-2: Operators in dbcc traceon(302) output

dbcc output	Comparison
EQ	Equality comparisons (=)
LT	Less than comparisons (<)
LE	Less than or equal to comparisons (<=)
GT	Greater than comparisons (>)

Table 9-2:   Operators in dbcc traceon(302) output

dbcc output	Comparison
GE	Greater than or equal to comparisons (>=)
NE	Not equals (!=)
ISNULL	**is null** comparison
ISNOTNULL	**is not null** comparison

Output for Range Queries

If your queries include a range query or clauses that are treated like range queries, they are evaluated in a single analysis to produce an estimate of the number of rows for the range. For example,

```
Scoring the SEARCH CLAUSE:
    au_lname LT
    au_lname GT
```

Range queries include:

- Queries using the **between** clause
- Interval clauses with **and** on the same column name, such as:

  ```
  datecol1 >= "1/1/94" and datecol1 < "2/1/94"
  ```

- **like** clauses such as:

  ```
  like "k%"
  ```

Specified Indexes

If the query has specified the use of a specific index by including the **index** keyword and the index name in parentheses after the table name in the **from** clause, this is noted in the output:

```
User forces index IndexID.
```

Specifying an index prevents consideration of other alternatives.

If the I/O size and cache strategy are also included in the query, these messages are printed:

```
User forces data prefetch of 8K
User forces LRU buffer replacement strategy
```

Calculating Base Cost

The next line of output displays the cost of a table scan for comparison, provided that there is at least one other qualification or index that can be considered. It reports index ID 0 and should match the table size estimate displayed earlier. The line looks like this:

```
Base cost: indid: IndexID rows: rows pages: pages prefetch: <S|N>
        I/O size: io_size cacheid: cacheID  replace: <LRU | MRU>
```

Here is an example:

```
Base cost: indid: 0 rows: 5000 pages: 624 prefetch: N
        I/O size: 2 cacheid: 0 replace: LRU
```

Table 9-3: Base cost output

Output	Meaning
indid	The index ID from *sysindexes*; 0 for the table itself.
rows	The number of rows in the table.
pages	The number of pages in the table.
prefetch	Whether prefetch would be considered for the table scan.
I/O size	The I/O size to be used.
cacheid	The ID of the data cache to be used.
replace	The cache replacement strategy to be used, either LRU or MRU.

Verify page and row counts for accuracy. Inaccurate counts can cause bad plans. To get a completely accurate count, use the **set statistics io on** command along with a **select * from *tablename*** query. In a VLDB (very large database) or in 24x7 shops (applications that must run 24 hours a day, 7 days a week), where that is not practical, you may need to rely on the reasonable accuracy of the **sp_spaceused** system procedure. **dbcc** allocation-checking commands print the object size and correct the values on which **sp_spaceused** and other object-size estimates are based.

Costing Indexes

Next, the optimizer evaluates each useful index for a given clause to determine its cost. The optimizer first looks for a unique index that is totally qualified—meaning that the query contains **where** clauses on each of the keys in the index. If such an index is available, the optimizer immediately knows that only a single row satisfies the clause, and it prints the following line:

```
Unique index_type index found--return rows 1 pages pages
```

The *index_type* is either clustered or nonclustered. There are three possibilities for the number of pages:

- The unique index is clustered. The logical I/O cost is the height of the index tree. In a clustered index, the data pages are the leaf level of the index, so the data page access is included.

- The unique nonclustered index covers the query. The logical I/O is the height of the index tree. The data page access is not needed, and not counted.

- The unique nonclustered index does not cover the query. An additional logical I/O is necessary to get from the leaf level of the nonclustered index to the data page, so the logical I/O cost is the height of the nonclustered index plus one page.

If the index is not unique, then the optimizer determines the cost, in terms of logical I/Os, for the clause. Before doing so, it prints this line:

```
Relop bits are: integer
```

This information can be ignored. It merely restates the comparison operator (that is, **=, <, >, interval**, and so on) listed in the **q_score_index()** line mentioned earlier as an integer bitmap. This information is only necessary for Sybase Engineering to debug optimizer problems and it has no value for customer-level troubleshooting.

To estimate the I/O cost for each clause, the optimizer has a number of tools available to it, depending on the clause type (search clause or join clause) and the availability of index statistics. For more information, see "Index Statistics" on page 149.

Index Statistics Used in *dbcc 302*

For each index, SQL Server keeps a statistical histogram of the indexed column's data distribution. The distribution table is built automatically when indexes are created and is stored in a with the index. The table is a sampling of the index key values every N rows.

N is dependent on the full size of the key (including overhead) and the number of rows in the table. Each sampling is known as a step. Since the optimizer knows how many rows exist between steps and the density of keys in the index, it can estimate the number of rows satisfying a clause with reasonable accuracy. See "Index Statistics" on page 149 for more information.

Evaluating Statistics for Search Clauses

For search clauses, the optimizer can look up specific values on the distribution page, if these values are known at compile time. In this case, it first prints the distribution page number and the number of steps with the following trace output:

```
Qualifying stat page; pgno: page_number steps: steps
```

For atomic datatypes (datatypes such as *tinyint*, *smallint*, *int*, *char*, *varchar*, *binary*, and *varbinary*, which are not internally implemented as structures), it prints the constant value the search argument supplied to the optimizer. It looks like this:

```
Search value: constant_value
```

If the value is implemented as a structure, the following message is output to indicate that the optimizer does not waste time building the structure's printable representation:

```
    *** CAN'T INTERPRET ***
```

Distribution Page Value Matches

If an exact match is found on the distribution page, the following message is printed:

```
Match found on statistics page
```

This is followed by information pertaining to the number and location of step values found on the distribution page. Since the optimizer knows approximately how many rows exist between step values, it uses this information to estimate how many logical I/Os would be performed for this clause. To indicate this information, one of the following messages is displayed:

```
equal to several rows including 1st or last -use endseveralSC
```

This indicates that several steps matched the constant and that they were found either at the beginning or at the end of the distribution page.

```
equal to a single row (1st or last) -use endsingleSC
```

This indicates that only one step matched the constant and it was found either at the beginning or at the end of the distribution page.

```
equal to several rows in middle of page -use midseveralSC
```

This indicates that several steps matched the constant and that they were found in the middle of the distribution page.

```
equal to single row in middle of page -use midsingleSC
```

This indicates that several steps matched the constant and that they were found in the middle of the distribution page.

Values Between Steps or Out of Range

If an exact match of the search value is not found on the distribution page, the optimizer uses different formulas in its statistical estimate. The computation is based on the relational operator used in the clause, the step number, the number of steps, the number of rows in the table and the density. First, the optimizer needs to find the first step value that is less than the search value. In these cases, you see the following message:

```
No steps for search value -qualpage for LT search value finds
```

Depending on whether the search value is outside the first or last step value or contained within steps, the optimizer will print one of the following messages:

```
value < first step -use outsideSC
value > last step -use outsideSC
```

The first message indicates that the query's search value is smaller than the first entry on the distribution page. The second message indicates that the query's search value is larger than the last entry on the distribution page. If the constant is a valid value in the table, these messages indicate that **update statistics** may need to be run.

```
value between step K, K+1, K=step_number -use betweenSC
```

This message indicates that the query's search value falls between two steps on the distribution page. You can only confirm here that the step number seems reasonable.

For example, if the step value of "K" is 3 and you suspect that the query's search value should fall towards the end of the table, something could be wrong. It would be reasonable then to expect the value of "K" to be larger (that is, towards the end of the distribution page). This may be another indication that **update statistics** needs to be run.

Range Query Messages

For a range query, the trace facility looks up the steps for both the upper and lower bounds of the query. This message appears:

```
Scoring SARG interval, lower bound.
```

After displaying the costing estimates for the lower bound, the net selectivity is calculated and displayed as:

```
Net selectivity of interval: foat_value
```

Search Clauses with Unknown Values

A common problem the optimizer faces is that values for search criteria are not known until run time. Common scenarios that make the optimizer unable to use distribution statistics include:

- **where** clauses based on expressions. For example:

```
select *
    from tableName
    where dateColumn >= getdate()
```

- **where** clauses based on local variables. For example:

```
declare @fKey int
select @fKey=lookUpID
    from mainTable
    where pKey = "999"
select *
    from lookUpTable
    where pKey >= @fKey
```

In cases like these, the optimizer tries to make intelligent guesses based on average values. For example, if a distribution page exists for the index and the query is an equality comparison, the optimizer uses the density of the index (that is, the average number of duplicates) to estimate the number of rows.

Otherwise, the optimizer uses a "magic" number: it assumes that 10 percent of the table will match an equality comparison, 25 percent of the table will match a closed interval comparison, and 33 percent of the table will match for inequality and open interval comparisons. In these cases, the trace facility prints:

```
SARG is a subbed VAR or expr result or local variable (constat =
number) -use magicSC or densitySC
```

Stored procedures and triggers need special attention to ensure efficient query plans. Many procedures are coded with **where** clauses based on input parameters. This behavior can cause some difficulty in troubleshooting. Consider a query whose single **where** clause may be very selective under one parameter and return nearly the entire table under another. These types of stored procedures can be difficult to debug, since the procedure cache could potentially have multiple copies in cache, each with a different plan. Since these plans are already compiled, users may be assigned a plan that may not be appropriate for their input parameter.

Another reason for the optimizer being unable to use an index's distribution table is that the distribution page can be nonexistent. This occurs:

- When an index is created before any data is loaded.

- When **truncate table** is used, and then the data is loaded.

In these cases, the optimizer uses the above mentioned "magic" numbers to estimate I/O cost and you see:

```
No statistics page -use magicSC
```

At this point, the selectivity and cost estimates are displayed.

Cost Estimates and Selectivity

For each qualified clause, the trace facility displays:

- The index ID

- The selectivity as a floating-point value

- The cost estimate in both rows and pages

These values are printed as variables in this message:

```
Estimate: indid indexID, selectivity float_val, rows rows pages
pages
```

If this clause had no qualifications, but the optimizer found a nonclustered index that covered the entire query, it identifies the table, since it would not be listed with a **q_score_index()** section. In this case, you see:

```
Finishing q_score_index() for table table_name (objectid) ID.
```

At this point, the cheapest index is examined and its costs are displayed:

```
Cheapest index is index IndexID, costing pages pages and
generating rows rows per scan using no data prefetch (size 2)
on dcacheid N with [MRU|LRU] replacement
```

This can be somewhat misleading. If there are any nonclustered indexes that match the search arguments in the query, the costs for the cheapest index are printed here, even though a table scan may be used to execute the query. The actual decision on whether to perform a table scan or nonclustered index access is delayed until join order is evaluated (the next step in the optimization process).

This is because the most accurate costing of a nonclustered index depends on the ratio of physical vs. logical I/O and the amount of cache memory available when that table is chosen. Therefore, if the base cost (table scan cost) printed earlier is significantly less than the "cheapest index" shown here, it is more likely that a table scan will be used. Use **showplan** to verify this.

Estimating Selectivity for Search Clauses

The selectivity for search clauses is printed as the fraction of the rows in the table expected to qualify. Therefore, the lower the number, the more selective the search clause and the fewer the rows that are expected to qualify. Search clauses are output as:

```
Search argument selectivity is float_val.
```

Estimating Selectivity for Join Clauses

For joins, the optimizer never looks up specific values on the distribution page. At compile time, the optimizer has no known values for which to search. It needs to make a sophisticated estimate about costing these clauses.

If an index with a distribution page is available, the optimizer uses the density table, which stores the average number of duplicate keys in the index. All leading permutations of the composite key have their density stored, providing accurate information for multi-column joins.

If no distribution page is available for this index, the optimizer estimates the join selectivity to be 1 divided by the number of rows in the smaller table. This gives a rough estimate of the cardinality of a primary key-foreign key relationship with even data distribution. In both of these cases, the trace facility prints the calculated selectivity and cost estimates, as described below.

The selectivity of the clause is printed last. Join clauses are output as:

```
Join selectivity is float_val.
```

The selectivity for join clauses is output as the whole number of the fraction 1 divided by the selectivity. Therefore, the higher the number selectivity, the more selective the join clause, and the fewer the rows are expected to qualify.

At this point, the optimizer has evaluated all indexes for this clause and will proceed to optimize the next clause.

From Analysis to Art

Once you've experimented with the tuning and monitoring techniques described in this chapter, you have probably done most of what is possible at the Transact-SQL level.

In some cases, exhaustive analysis can be usefully supplemented by pulling back a bit and making needed changes based on a query's inherent logic.

Experienced Transact-SQL programmers have learned a few more approaches you can try at the application level. These "handy tips and tricks" are described in Chapter 10.

10 Transact-SQL Performance Tips

Introduction

This chapter presents certain types of SQL queries where simple changes in the query can improve performance. This chapter emphasizes only queries and does not focus on schema design. Many of the tips are not related to the SQL Server query optimizer.

These tips are intended as suggestions and guidelines, not absolute rules. You should use the query analysis tools to test the alternate formulations suggested here. Performance of these queries may change with future releases of SQL Server.

"Greater Than" Queries

This query, with an index on *int_col*:

```
select * from table where int_col > 3
```

uses the index to find the first value where *int_col* equals 3, and then scans forward to find the first value greater than 3. If there are many rows where *int_col* equals 3, the server has to scan many pages to find the first row where *int_col* is greater than 3.

It is probably much more efficient to write this query like this:

```
select * from table where int_col >= 4
```

This optimization is easier with integers, but more difficult with character strings and floating-point data. You need to know your data.

not exists Tests

In subqueries and **if** statements, **exists** and **in** perform faster than **not exists** and **not in** when the values in the **where** clause are not indexed. For **exists** and **in**, SQL Server can return TRUE as soon as a single row matches. For the negated expressions, it must examine all values to determine that there are no matches.

In **if** statements, you can easily avoid **not exists** by rearranging your statement groups between the **if** portion and the **else** portion of the code. This **not exists** test may perform slowly:

```
if not exists (select * from table where...)
    begin
        /* Statement Group 1 */
    end
else
    begin
        /* Statement Group 2 */
    end
```

You can improve the performance of the query by using **exists**, and switching the statement groups:

```
if exists (select * from table where...)
    begin
        /* Statement Group 2 */
    end
else
    begin
        /* Statement Group 1 */
    end
```

You can avoid the **not else** in **if** statements even without an **else** clause. Here is an example:

```
if not exists (select * from table where...)
    begin
        /* Statement Group */
    end
```

This query can be rewritten using **goto** to skip over the statement group:

```
if exists (select * from table where)
    begin
        goto exists_label
    end
/* Statement group */
exists_label:
```

Variables vs. Parameters in *where* Clauses

The optimizer knows the value of a parameter to a stored procedure at compile time, but it cannot predict the value of a declared variable set in the procedure while it executes. Providing the optimizer with the values of search arguments in the **where** clause of a query can help the optimizer make better choices—when the optimizer knows the value of a search clause, it can use the distribution steps to closely predict the number of rows that the query will return. Otherwise, it uses only density statistics or hard-coded values.

Often, the solution to this type of performance problem is to split up stored procedure so that you set the values of variables in the first procedure and c all the second procedure and pass those variables as parameters to it. The second procedure can then be optimized correctly.

For example, the optimizer cannot optimize the final **select** in the following procedure, because it cannot know the value of $@x$ until execution time:

```
create procedure p
as
    declare @x int
    select @x = col
        from tab where ...
    select *
        from tab2
        where indexed_col = @x
```

When SQL Server encounters unknown values, it uses approximations to develop a query plan, based on the operators in the search argument, as shown in Table 10-1.

Table 10-1: Density approximations for unknown search arguments

Operator	Density Approximation
=	Average proportion of duplicates in the column
< or >	33 percent
between	25 percent

The following example shows the procedure split into two procedures. The first procedure calls the second:

```
create procedure base_proc
as
    declare @x int
    select @x = col
        from tab where ...
    exec select_proc @x
create procedure select_proc @x int
as
    select *
        from tab2
        where col2 = @x
```

When the second procedure executes, SQL Server knows the value of
@*x* and can optimize the **select** statement. Of course, if you modify the
value of @*x* in the second procedure before it is used in the **select**
statement, the optimizer may choose the wrong plan because it
optimizes the query based on the value of @*x* at the start of the
procedure. If @x has different values each time the second procedure
is executed, leading to very different query plans, you may want to
use **with recompile**.

Count vs. Exists

Do not use the **count** aggregate in a subquery to do an existence check:

```
select *
    from tab
    where 0 < (select count(*) from tab2 where ...)
```

Instead, use **exists** (or **in**):

```
select *
    from tab
    where exists (select * from tab2 where ...)
```

Using **count** to do an existence check is slower than using **exists**.

When you use **count**, SQL Server does not know that you are doing an
existence check. It counts all matching values, either by doing a table
scan or by scanning the smallest nonclustered index.

When you use **exists**, SQL Server knows you are doing an existence
check. When it finds the first matching value, it returns TRUE and
stops looking. The same applies to using **count** instead of **in** or **any**.

or Clauses vs. Unions in Joins

SQL Server cannot optimize join clauses that are linked with **or** and
may perform Cartesian products to process the query.

> ➤ *Note*

SQL Server does optimize search arguments that are linked with **or, as
described in "The OR Strategy" on page 186**. This description applies only to join
clauses.

SQL Server can optimize selects with joins that are linked with
union.The result of **or** is somewhat like the result of **union**, except for
the treatment of duplicate rows and empty tables:

- **union** removes all duplicate rows (in a sort step); **union all** does not remove any duplicates. The comparable query using **or** might return some duplicates.

- A join with an empty table returns no rows.

For example, when SQL Server processes this query, it must look at every row in one of the tables for each row in the other table:

```
select *
    from tab1, tab2
    where tab1.a = tab2.b
        or tab1.x = tab2.y
```

If you use **union**, each side of the union is optimized separately:

```
    select *
        from tab1, tab2
        where tab1.a = tab2.b
union all
    select *
        from tab1, tab2
        where tab1.x = tab2.y
```

You can use **union** instead of **union all** if you want to eliminate duplicates, but this eliminates all duplicates. It may not be possible to get exactly the same set of duplicates from the rewritten query.

Aggregates

SQL Server uses special optimizations for the **max** and **min** aggregates when there is an index on the aggregated column.

For **min**, it reads the first value on the root page of the index.

For **max**, it goes directly to the end of the index to find the last row.

min and **max** optimizations are not applied if:

- The expression inside the **max** or **min** is anything but a column. Compare **max(*numeric_col**2)** and **max(*numeric_col*)*2**, where *numeric_col* has a nonclustered index. The first performs a scan of the nonclustered index because of the operation performed on the column. The second uses **max** optimization.

- The column inside the **max** or **min** is not the first column of an index. For nonclustered indexes, it can perform a scan on the leaf level of the index; for clustered indexes, it must perform the table scan.

- There is another aggregate in the query.

- There is a **group by** clause.

In addition, the **max** optimization is not applied if there is a **where** clause.

If you have an optimizable **max** or **min** aggregate, you should get much better performance by putting it in a query that is separate from other aggregates.

For example:

```
select max(price), min(price)
    from titles
```

results in a full scan of *titles*, even if there is an index on *colx*.

Try rewriting the query as:

```
select max(price)
    from titles
select min(price)
    from titles
```

SQL Server uses the index once for each of the two queries, rather than scanning the entire table.

Joins and Datatypes

When joining between two columns of different datatypes, one of the columns must be converted to the type of the other. The *SQL Server Reference Manual* shows the hierarchy of types. The column whose type is lower in the hierarchy is the one that is converted.

If you are joining tables with incompatible types, one of them can use an index, but the query optimizer cannot choose an index on the column that it converts. For example:

```
select *
    from small_table, large_table
    where smalltable.float_column =
        large_table.int_column
```

In this case, SQL Server converts the integer column to *float*, because *int* is lower in the hierarchy than *float*. It cannot use an index on *large_table.int_column*, although it can use an index on *smalltable.float_column*.

Null vs. Not Null Character and Binary Columns

Note that *char null* is really stored as *varchar*, and *binary null* is really *varbinary*. Joining *char not null* with *char null* involves a conversion;

the same is true of the binary types. This affects all character and binary types, but does not affect numeric datatypes and datetimes.

It is best to avoid datatype problems in joins by designing the schema accordingly. Frequently joined columns should have the same datatypes, including the acceptance of null values for character and binary types. User-defined datatypes help enforce datatype compatibility.

Forcing the Conversion to the Other Side of the Join

If a join between different datatypes is unavoidable, and it hurts performance, you can force the conversion to the other side of the join.

In the following query, *varchar_column* must be converted to *char*, so no index on *varchar_column* can be used, and *huge_table* must be scanned:

```
select *
from small_table, huge_table
where small_table.char_col =
    huge_table.varchar_col
```

Performance would be improved if the index on *huge_table.varchar_col* could be used. Using the **convert** function on the *varchar* column of the small table allows the index on the large table to be used while the small table is table scanned:

```
select *
from small_table, huge_table
where convert(varchar(50),small_table.char_col) =
    huge_table.varchar_col
```

Be careful with numeric data. This tactic can change the meaning of the query. This query compares integers and floating-point numbers:

```
select *
    from tab1, tab2
    where tab1.int_column = tab2.float_column
```

In this example, *int_column* is converted to *float*, and any index on *int_column* cannot be used. If you insert this conversion to force the index access to *tab1*:

```
select *
from tab1, tab2
where tab1.int_col = convert(int, tab2.float_col)
```

the query will not return the same results as the join without the **convert**. For example, if *int_column* is 4, and *float_column* is 4.2, the original query implicitly converts 4 to 4.0000, which does not match 4.2. The query with the **convert** converts 4.2 to 4, which does match.

It can be salvaged by adding this self-join:

```
and tab2.float_col = convert(int, tab2.float_col)
```

This assumes that all values in *tab2.float_col* can be converted to *int*.

Parameters and Datatypes

The query optimizer can use the values of parameters to stored procedures to help determine costs.

If a parameter is not of the same type as the column in the **where** clause to which it is being compared, SQL Server has to convert the parameter.

The optimizer cannot use the value of a converted parameter.

Make sure that parameters are of the same type as the columns they are compared to.

For example:

```
create proc p @x varchar(30)
as
    select *
        from tab
        where char_column = @x
```

may get a less optimal query plan than:

```
create proc p @x char(30)
as
    select *
        from tab
        where char_column = @x
```

Remember that *char null* is really *varchar* and *binary null* is really *varbinary*.

From Query Processing to Reliability

The preceding three chapters have concerned themselves with query tuning and optimization, concluding with the present chapter's last bits of advice on optimizing certain non-intuitive queries. Creating and tuning queries, however, is by no means the only influence on the overall performance of your application. In a multi-user situation, contention for data resources (when more than one user wants to use the same data at the same time) can significantly affect performance.

SQL Server uses an elaborate scheme for locking data that's being used so that the data will remain consistent. If SQL Server needed only to concern itself with the speed of processing queries, it would be like running a machine without a governor. Accuracy and repeatability of results are, in fact, even more important for a database management system than sheer speed of processing queries.

In a multi-user situation, SQL Server must guarantee that query results are "true," and that repeated actions by many users against the same set of data will produce reliable and repeatable results. When several transactions act on the same set of data, SQL Server sets locks that protect the data from ending up in an inconsistent state. As you might expect, locking some users out of data that is in use by others can have performance implications. The time that a transaction has to wait for its data resources must be added to the time it takes to process the query.

The next chapter, "Locking on SQL Server," delves into SQL Server's locking mechanisms and discusses how you can help the system keep transactions out of each other's way without incurring the overhead of locking.

11 Locking on SQL Server

Introduction

SQL Server protects the tables or data pages currently used by active transactions by locking them. Locking is a concurrency control mechanism: it ensures the consistency of data across transactions. Locking is needed in a multi-user environment, since several users may be working with the same data at the same time.

Locking affects performance when one process holds locks that prevent another process from accessing needed data. The process that is blocked by the lock sleeps until the lock is released.

A more serious locking impact on performance arises from deadlocks. A **deadlock** occurs when two user processes each have a lock on a separate page or table and each wants to acquire a lock on the other process's page or table. The transaction with the least accumulated CPU time is killed and all of its work is rolled back.

Understanding the types of locks in SQL Server can help you reduce lock contention and avoid or minimize deadlocks.

This chapter discusses:

- Consistency issues that arise in multiuser databases
- Locks used in SQL Server
- How different isolation levels affect SQL Server locks
- SQL Server options for enforcing different levels of isolation
- Defining an isolation level using the **set transaction isolation level** command or the **at isolation** clause
- How the **holdlock** and **noholdlock** keywords affect locking
- Cursors and locking
- SQL Server's handling of deadlocks
- Locking and performance issues
- Strategies for reducing lock contention
- System procedures for examining locks and user processes blocked by locks (**sp_lock** and **sp_who**)
- Configuration options that affect locking

Overview of Locking

Consistency of data means that if multiple users repeatedly execute a series of transactions, the results are the same each time. Simultaneous retrievals and modifications of data do not interfere with each other: the results of queries are consistent.

The transactions in Figure 11-1, T1 and T2 are attempting to access data at approximately the same time.

T1	Event Sequence	T2
`begin transaction`	T1 and T2 start	`begin transaction`

`update account`
`set balance = balance - 100`
`where acct_number = 25`
	T1 updates balance for one account by subtracting $100	

	T2 queries the sum balance for several accounts, which is off by $100 at this point in time—should it return results now, or wait until T1 ends?	`select sum(balance)`
		`from account`
		`where acct_number < 50`
		
		`commit transaction`

`update account`
`set balance = balance + 100`
`where acct_number = 45`
 	
`commit transaction`
	T1 updates balance of other account to add the $100	

	T1 ends	

Figure 11-1: Consistency levels in transactions

If transaction T2 runs before T1 starts, or after T1 completes, both executions of T2 return the same value. But if T2 runs in the middle of transaction T1 (after the first **update**), the result for transaction T2 will be different by $100. While such behavior may be acceptable in certain limited situations, most database transactions need to return consistent results.

By default, SQL Server locks the data used in T1 until the transaction finishes. Only then does it allow T2 to complete its query. T2 "sleeps," or pauses in execution, until the lock it needs it is released when T1 completes.

The alternative, returning data from uncommitted transactions, is known as a **dirty read**. If the results of T2 do not need to be exact, it can read the uncommitted changes from T1, and return results immediately, without waiting for the lock to be released.

Locking is handled automatically by SQL Server, with options that can be set at the session and query level by the user. You must know how and when to use transactions to preserve the consistency of your data, while maintaining high performance and throughput. Transactions are described in the *Transact-SQL User's Guide* and in the *SQL Server Reference Manual*.

Granularity of Locks

The granularity of locks in a database refers to how much of the data is locked at one time. In theory, a database server can lock as much as the entire database or as little as one row of data. Such extremes affect the concurrency (number of users that can access the data) and locking overhead (amount of work to process each lock request) in the server.

By increasing the lock size, the amount of work required to obtain a lock becomes smaller, but large locks can degrade performance, by making more users wait until locks are released. Decreasing the lock size makes more of the data accessible to other users. However, small locks can also degrade performance, since more work is necessary to maintain and coordinate the increased number of locks. To achieve optimum performance, a locking scheme must balance the needs of concurrency and overhead.

SQL Server achieves its balance by locking only data and index pages or entire tables. These locking mechanisms are described in the following sections.

Types of Locks in SQL Server

SQL Server has two levels of locking: page locks and table locks. Page locks are generally less restrictive (or smaller) than table locks. A page lock locks all of the rows on data or index page; table locks lock entire tables. SQL Server attempts to use page locks as frequently as possible to reduce the contention for data among users and to improve concurrency.

SQL Server uses table locks to provide more efficient locking when it determines that an entire table, or most of a table's pages, will be accessed by a statement. Locking strategy is directly tied to the query plan, so the query plan can be as important for its locking strategies as for its I/O implications. If an **update** or **delete** statement has no useful index, it does a table scan and acquires a table lock. For example, the following statement generates a table lock:

```
update account set balance = balance * 1.05
```

If the **update** or **delete** statement uses an index, it begins by acquiring page locks, and only attempts to acquire a table lock if a large number of rows are affected.

Whenever possible, SQL Server tries to satisfy requests with page locks. However, once a statement accumulates more page locks than the **lock promotion threshold** allows, SQL Server tries to issue a table lock on that object. If it succeeds, the page locks are no longer necessary and are released.

Table locks also provide a way to avoid lock collisions at the page level. SQL Server automatically uses table locks for some commands.

SQL Server handles all locking decisions. It chooses which type of lock to use after it determines the query plan. The way you write a query or transaction can affect the type of lock the server chooses. You can also force the server to make certain locks more or less restrictive by specifying options for select queries or by changing the transaction's isolation level. These options are described later in this chapter.

Page Locks

The following describes the different types of page locks:

- **Shared locks**

  SQL Server applies **shared lock**s for read operations. If a shared lock has been applied to a data or index page, other transactions can also acquire a shared lock even when the first transaction is not finished. However, no transaction can acquire an exclusive lock on the page until all shared locks on it are released. That is, many transactions can simultaneously read the page, but no transaction can change data or index keys or pointers on the page while the shared lock exists. Transactions that need an exclusive page lock wait or "block" for the release of the shared page locks before continuing.

  By default, SQL Server releases shared page locks after the scan is complete on the page. If SQL Server is scanning several pages, it acquires a shared lock on the first page, completes the scan of that page, acquires the lock on the next page, and drops the lock on the first page. It does not hold shared locks until the statement completes or until the end of its transaction.

- **Exclusive locks**

  SQL Server applies **exclusive lock**s for data modification operations. When a transaction gets an exclusive lock, other transactions cannot acquire a lock of any kind on the page until the exclusive lock is released at the end of its transaction. Those other transactions wait or "block" until the exclusive lock is released, before continuing.

- **Update locks**

  SQL Server applies **update lock**s during the initial portion of an **update, delete**, or **fetch** (for cursors declared **for update**) operation when the pages are being read. The update locks allow shared locks on the page, but do not allow other update or exclusive locks. This is an internal lock to help avoid deadlocks and lock contention. Later, if the pages need to be changed, the update locks are promoted to exclusive locks as soon as no other shared locks exist on the page.

In general, read operations acquire shared locks, and write operations acquire exclusive locks. However, SQL Server can apply page-level exclusive and update locks only if the column used in the search argument is part of an index.

The following examples show what kind of page locks SQL Server uses for the respective statement (with an index on *acct_number*, the search argument used in the queries):

select balance **from account** **where acct_number = 25**	*Shared page lock*
insert account values **(34, 500)**	*Exclusive page lock on data page* *Exclusive page lock on leaf level index page*
delete account **where balance < 0**	*Update page locks* *Exclusive page locks on data pages* *Exclusive page lock on leaf level index pages*
update account **set balance = 0** **where acct_number = 25**	*Update page lock on data page* *Exclusive page lock on data page*

Table Locks

The following describes the types of table locks.

- **Intent lock**

  An **intent lock** indicates that certain types of page-level locks are currently held on pages of a table. SQL Server applies an intent table lock with each shared or exclusive page lock, so an intent lock can be either an intent exclusive lock or an intent shared lock. Setting an intent lock prevents other transactions from subsequently acquiring a shared or exclusive lock on the table that contains that locked page. An intent lock is held as long as the concurrent page locks are in effect.

- **Shared lock**

  This lock is similar to the shared page lock, except that it affects the entire table. For example, SQL Server applies shared table locks with a **select** with **holdlock** that does not use an index, and for the **create nonclustered index** statement.

- **Exclusive lock**

  This lock is similar to the exclusive page lock, except that it affects the entire table. For example, SQL Server applies exclusive table locks during the **create clustered index** command. **update** and **delete** statements generate exclusive table locks if their search arguments do not reference indexed columns of the object (often an indication that you need to examine your indexes or queries.)

The following examples show the respective page and table locks issued for each statement ((with an index on *acct_number*, the search argument used in the queries):

select balance **from account** **where acct_number = 25**	*Intent shared table lock* *Shared page lock*
insert account values **(34, 500)**	*Intent exclusive table lock* *Exclusive page lock on data page* *Exclusive page lock on leaf index pages*
delete account **where balance < 0**	*Intent exclusive table lock* *Update page locks followed by* *exclusive page locks on data pages and* *leaf level index pages*

This next example assumes that there is no index on *acct_number*; otherwise, SQL Server would attempt to issue page locks for the statement:

update account   *Exclusive table lock*
set balance = 0
where acct_number = 25

Exclusive table locks are also applied to temporary tables.

Demand Locks

SQL Server sets a **demand lock** to indicate that a transaction is next in line to lock a table or page. Demand locks prevent any more shared locks from being set. This avoids situations in which read transactions acquire overlapping shared locks, which monopolize a table or page so that a write transaction waits indefinitely for its exclusive lock.

After a write transaction has waited for 3 read transactions, SQL Server gives a demand lock to the write transaction. As soon as the existing read transactions finish, the write transaction acquires its lock and is allowed to proceed. Any new read transactions must then wait for the write transaction to finish, when its exclusive lock is released. Demand locks are internal processes, and are not visible when using **sp_lock**.

Summary of Lock Types

Table 11-1 describes the types of locks SQL Server applies for **insert** and **create index** statements:

Table 11-1: Summary of locks for insert and create index statements

Statement	Table Lock	Data Page Lock
insert	IX	X
create clustered index	X	-
create nonclustered index	S	-
IX = intent exclusive, S = shared, X = exclusive		

Table 11-2 describes the types of locks SQL Server applies for **select**, **delete**, and **update** statements. It divides the **select**, **update**, and **delete** statements into two groups, since the types of locks they use can vary if the statement's search argument references indexed columns on the object.

Table 11-2: Summary of locks for select, update and delete statements

Statement	Indexed		Not Indexed	
	Table Lock	Page Lock	Table Lock	Page Lock
select	IS	S	IS	S
select with holdlock	IS	S	S	-
update	IX	U, X	X	-
delete	IX	U, X	X	-
IS = intent shared, IX = intent exclusive, S = shared, U = update, X = exclusive				

Note that the above tables do not describe situations in which SQL Server initially uses table locks (if a query requires the entire table), or when it promotes to a table lock after reaching the lock promotion threshold.

Lock Compatibility

Table 11-3 summarizes the information about lock compatibility, showing when locks can be acquired immediately.

Table 11-3: Lock compatibility

If one process has a:	Can another process immediately acquire a:		
	Shared Lock	Update Lock	Exclusive Lock
Shared Lock	Yes	Yes	No
Update Lock	Yes	No	No
Exclusive Lock	No	No	No

How Isolation Levels Affect Locking

The SQL standard defines four levels of isolation for SQL transactions. Each **isolation level** specifies the kinds of actions that are not permitted while concurrent transactions execute. Higher levels include the restrictions imposed by the lower levels.

SQL Server supports three different isolation levels for its transactions: 0, 1, and 3. The requirements for isolation level 2 are included with level 3, but SQL Server does not allow you to specifically choose level 2. You can choose which isolation level affects all the transactions executed in your session, or you can choose the isolation level for a specific query in a transaction.

Isolation Level 0

Level 0 prevents other transactions from changing data that has already been modified (using a data modification statement such as **update**) by an uncommitted transaction. The other transactions are blocked from modifying that data until the transaction completes. However, other transactions can still read the uncommitted data (dirty reads). The example in Figure 11-2 shows a "dirty read."

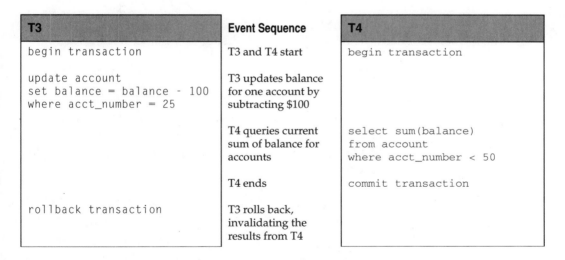

T3	Event Sequence	T4
`begin transaction`	T3 and T4 start	`begin transaction`

`update account`
`set balance = balance - 100`
`where acct_number = 25`
	T3 updates balance for one account by subtracting $100	

	T4 queries current sum of balance for accounts	`select sum(balance)`
		`from account`
		`where acct_number < 50`

	T4 ends	`commit transaction`
`rollback transaction`	T3 rolls back, invalidating the results from T4	

Figure 11-2: Dirty reads in transactions

If transaction T4 queries the table after T3 updates it, but before it rolls back the change, the amount calculated by T4 is off by $100.

At isolation level 0, SQL Server performs dirty reads by:

- Not applying shared locks on pages or tables being searched.

- Allowing reading of pages or tables that have exclusive locks. It still applies exclusive locks on pages or tables being changed, which prevents other transactions from changing the data already modified by the uncommitted transaction.

By default, a unique index is required to perform an isolation level 0 read, unless the database is read only. The index is required to re-start the scan if an update by another process changes the query's result set by modifying the current row or page. You can perform isolation level 0 reads by forcing the query to use a table scan or a nonunique index, but these scans may be aborted if there is significant update activity on the underlying table. For information about forcing indexes or table scans, see "Specifying an Index for a Query" on page 265.

Using the example in *Figure 11-2: Dirty reads in transactions*, the **update** statement in transaction T3 still acquires an exclusive lock on *account*. The difference with isolation level 0 as opposed to level 1 is that transaction T4 does not try to acquire a shared lock before querying *account*, so it is not blocked by T3. The opposite is also true. If T4 begins to query *accounts* at isolation level 0 before T3 starts, T3 could still acquire its exclusive lock on *accounts* while T4's query executes.

Applications that can use dirty reads may see better concurrency and reduced deadlocks when accessing the same data at a higher isolation level. An example may be transaction T4. If it requires only a snapshot of the current sum of account balances, which probably changes frequently in a very active table, T4 should query the table using isolation level 0. Other applications that require data consistency, such as queries of deposits and withdrawals to specific accounts in the table, should avoid using isolation level 0.

Isolation level 0 can improve performance for applications by reducing lock contention, but can impose performance costs in two ways:

- Dirty reads are implemented by making in-cache copies of dirty data that the isolation level 0 application needs to read.

- If a dirty read is active on a row, and the data changes so that the row moves or is deleted, the scan must be restarted, possibly incurring additional logical and physical I/O.

The **sp_sysmon** system procedure reports on both these factors. See "Dirty Read Behavior" on page 516.

Even if you set your isolation level to 0, some utilities still acquire shared locks for their scans. Shared locks are necessary for read operations that must maintain the database integrity by ensuring that the correct data is read before modifying it or verifying its consistency.

Isolation Level 1

Level 1 prevents dirty reads. At isolation level 1, if a transaction has modified a row, and a second transaction needs to read that row, the second transaction waits until the first transaction completes (either commits or rolls back.)

For example, contrast Figure 11-3, showing a transaction executed at isolation level 1 to the dirty read transaction in Figure 11-2.

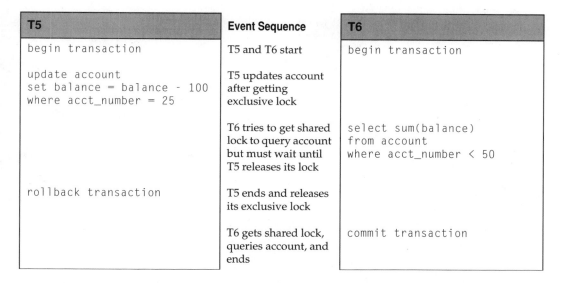

T5	Event Sequence	T6
`begin transaction`	T5 and T6 start	`begin transaction`

`update account`
`set balance = balance - 100`
`where acct_number = 25`
	T5 updates account after getting exclusive lock	

	T6 tries to get shared lock to query account but must wait until T5 releases its lock	`select sum(balance)`
		`from account`
		`where acct_number < 50`

`rollback transaction`	T5 ends and releases its exclusive lock	
	T6 gets shared lock, queries account, and ends	`commit transaction`

Figure 11-3: Transaction isolation level 1 prevents dirty reads

When the **update** statement in transaction T5 executes, SQL Server applies an exclusive lock (a page-level lock if *acct_number* is indexed; otherwise, a table-level lock) on *account*. The query in T6 cannot execute (preventing the dirty read) until the exclusive lock is released, when T5 ends with the **rollback**.

While the query in T6 holds its shared lock, other processes that need shared locks can access the same data, and an update lock can also be granted (an update lock indicates the read operation that precedes the exclusive-lock write operation), but no exclusive locks are allowed until all shared locks have been released.

Isolation Level 2

Level 2 prevents **nonrepeatable reads**. These occur when one transaction reads a row and a second transaction modifies that row. If the second transaction commits its change, subsequent reads by the first transaction yield results that are different from the original read. Figure 11-4 shows a nonrepeatable read.

T7	Event Sequence	T8
begin transaction	T7 and T8 start	begin transaction
select balance from account where acct_number = 25	T7 queries the balance for one account	
	T8 updates the balance for that same account	update account set balance = balance - 100 where acct_number = 25
	T8 ends	commit transaction
select balance from account where acct_number = 25	T7 makes same query as before and gets different results	
commit transaction	T7 ends	

Figure 11-4: Nonrepeatable reads in transactions

If transaction T8 modifies and commits the changes to the *account* table after the first query in T7, but before the second one, the same two queries in T7 produce different results.

Isolation Level 3

Level 3 prevents **phantoms**. These occur when one transaction reads a set of rows that satisfy a search condition, and then a second transaction modifies the data (through an **insert**, **delete**, or **update** statement). If the first transaction repeats the read with the same search conditions, it obtains a different set of rows. An example of phantoms in transactions is shown in Figure 11-5.

T9	Event Sequence	T10
`begin transaction`	T9 and T10 start	`begin transaction`
`select * from account` `where acct_number < 25`	T9 queries a certain set of rows	

	T10 inserts a row that meets the criteria for the query in T9	`insert into account`
		`(acct_number, balance)`
		`values (19, 500)`

	T10 ends	`commit transaction`

`select * from account`
`where acct_number < 25`
 	
`commit transaction`
	T9 makes the same query and gets a new row
	
	T9 ends	

Figure 11-5: Phantoms in transactions

If transaction T10 inserts rows into the table that satisfy T9's search condition after the T9 executes the first **select**, subsequent reads by T9 using the same query result in a different set of rows.

SQL Server also prevents nonrepeatable reads (the restrictions imposed by level 2 are included in level 3) and phantoms by:

- Applying exclusive locks on pages or tables being changed. It holds those locks until the end of the transaction.

- Applying shared locks on pages or tables being searched. It holds those locks until the end of the transaction.

Using and holding the exclusive and shared locks allows SQL Server to maintain the consistency of the results at isolation level 3. However, holding the shared lock until the transaction ends decreases SQL Server's concurrency by preventing other transactions from getting their exclusive locks on the data.

Compare the phantom, shown in Figure 11-5, with the same transaction executed at isolation level 3, as shown in Figure 11-6.

T11	Event Sequence	T12
`begin transaction`	T11 and T12 start	`begin transaction`

`select * from`
`account holdlock`
`where acct_number < 25`
	T11 queries account and holds acquired shared locks	

	T12 tries to insert row but must wait until T11 releases its locks	`insert into account`
		`(acct_number, balance)`
		`values (19, 500)`

`select * from`
`account holdlock`
`where acct_number < 25`
 	
`commit transaction`
	T11 makes same query and gets same results	

	T11 ends and releases its shared locks	`commit transaction`
	T12 gets its exclusive lock, inserts new row, and ends	

Figure 11-6: Avoiding phantoms in transactions

In transaction T11, SQL Server applies shared page locks (if an index exists on the *acct_number* argument) or a shared table lock (if no index exists) and holds those locks until the end of T11. The **insert** in T12 cannot get its exclusive lock until T11 releases those shared locks. If T11 is a long transaction, T12 (and other transactions) may wait for longer periods of time using isolation level 3 instead of the other levels. As a result, you should use level 3 only when required.

SQL Server Default Isolation Level

SQL Server's default isolation level is 1, which prevents dirty reads. SQL Server enforces isolation level 1 by:

- Applying exclusive locks on pages or tables being changed. It holds those locks until the end of the transaction.

- Applying shared locks on pages being searched. It releases those locks after processing the page or table.

Using the exclusive and shared locks allows SQL Server to maintain the consistency of the results at isolation level 1. Releasing the shared lock after the scan moves off a page improves SQL Server's concurrency by allowing other transactions to get their exclusive locks on the data.

Controlling Isolation Levels

SQL Server's default transaction isolation level is 1. You can change the locking behavior for sessions or individual queries to make locks more or less restrictive.

- Using **set transaction isolation level** to set the level for an entire session to level 0, 1 or 3.

- Specifying the isolation level in the **select** and **readtext** commands using the **at isolation level** clause. The choices are: **read uncommitted**, **read committed**, or **serializable**.

- Using the **holdlock**, **noholdlock**, or **shared** options of the **select** command to specify the isolation level for a single query.

When choosing locking levels in your applications, use the minimum locking level consistent with your business model. The combination of setting the session level while providing control over locking behavior at the query level allows concurrent transactions to achieve the results that are required with the least blocking.

Setting Isolation Levels for a Session

The SQL standard specifies a default isolation level of 3. To enforce this level, Transact-SQL provides the **set transaction isolation level** command. For example, you can make level 3 the default isolation level for your session as follows:

```
set transaction isolation level 3
```

If the session has enforced isolation level 3, you can make the query operate at level 1 using **noholdlock**, as described below.

If you are using the default isolation level of 1, or have used the **set transaction isolation level** command to specify level 0, you can enforce level 3 by using the **holdlock** command to hold shared locks until the end of a transaction.

The current isolation level for a session can be determined with the global variable @@*isolation*.

Using *holdlock, noholdlock,* or *shared*

You can override the session's locking level with the **holdlock**, **noholdlock**, or **shared** options of the **select** and **readtext** commands:

Level	Keyword	Effect
1	**noholdlock**	Do not hold locks until the end of the transaction; use from level 3 to enforce level 1
3	**holdlock**	Hold shared locks until the transaction completes; usr from level 1 to enforce level 3
N/A	**shared**	Applies shared rather than update locks in cursors open for update

These keywords affect locking for the transaction: if you use **holdlock**, the locks are held until the end of the transaction.

Using the *at isolation* Clause

You can also change the isolation level for a query by using the **at isolation** clause with the **select** or **readtext** statements. The options in the **at isolation** clause are:

Level	Option	Effect
0	**read uncommitted**	Read uncommitted changes; use from level 1 or 3 to perform dirty reads (level 0)
1	**read committed**	Read only committed changes; wait for locks to be released; use from level 0 to read only committed changes, but without holding locks
3	**serializable**	Hold shared locks until the query completes; use from level 0 enforce level 1

For example, the following statement queries the *titles* table at isolation level 0:

```
select *
from titles
at isolation read uncommitted
```

For more information about the **transaction isolation level** option and the **at isolation** clause, see "Transactions" in the *Transact-SQL User's Guide*.

Making Locks More Restrictive

If isolation level 1 is sufficient for most of your work, but certain queries require higher levels of isolation, you can selectively enforce the highest isolation level using the **holdlock** keyword or **at isolation serializable** in a **select** statement. The **holdlock** keyword makes a shared page or table lock more restrictive. It applies:

- To shared locks
- To the table or view for which it is specified
- For the duration of the statement or transaction containing the statement

The **at isolation serializable** clause applies to all tables in the **from** clause, and is only applied for the duration of the statement. The locks are released when the statement completes, and are not held until the end of the transaction or batch.

In a transaction, **holdlock** instructs SQL Server to hold shared locks until the completion of that transaction instead of releasing the lock as soon as the required table, view, or data page is no longer needed. SQL Server always holds exclusive locks until the end of a transaction.

When you use **holdlock** or **serializable**. locking depending on how the data is accessed:

Table scan	Shared table lock
Clustered index	Intent shared table lock; Shared lock on data pages by the query
Nonclustered index	Intent shared table lock; Shared lock on data pages and on nonclustered leaf level pages used by the query
Covering nonclustered index	Intent shared table lock; Shared lock on nonclustered leaf pages used by the query

The use of **holdlock** in the following example ensures that the two queries return consistent results:

```
begin transaction

select branch, sum(balance)
    from account holdlock
    group by branch

select sum(balance) from account
```

```
commit transaction
```

The first query acquires a shared table lock on *account* so that no other transaction can update the data before the second query runs. This lock is not released until the transaction including the **holdlock** command completes.

Using *read committed*

If your session isolation level is 0, and you need to read only committed changes to the database, you can use the **at isolation level read committed** clause.

Making Locks Less Restrictive

In contrast to **holdlock**, the **noholdlock** keyword prevents SQL Server from holding any shared locks acquired during the execution of the query, regardless of the transaction isolation level currently in effect. **noholdlock** is useful in situations when your transactions require a default isolation level of 3. If any queries in those transactions do not need to hold shared locks until the end of the transaction, you should specify **noholdlock** with those queries to improve the concurrency of your server.

For example, if your transaction isolation level is set to 3, this command does not hold shared locks:

```
select balance from account noholdlock
    where acct_number < 100
```

Using *read uncommitted*

If your session isolation level is 1 or 3, and you wish to perform dirty reads, you can use the **at isolation level read uncommitted** clause.

Using *shared*

The **shared** keyword instructs SQL Server to use a shared lock (instead of an update lock) on a specified table or view in a cursor. See "Using the shared Keyword" on page 316 for more information.

Examples of Locking and Isolation Levels

This section describes the sequence of locks applied by SQL Server for the two transactions in Figure 11-7.

T13	Event Sequence	T14
`begin transaction`	T13 and T14 start	`begin transaction`

`update account`
`set balance = balance - 100`
`where acct_number = 25`
	T13 gets exclusive lock and updates account	

	T14 tries to query account but must wait until T13 ends	`select sum(balance)`
		`from account`
		`where acct_number < 50`

`update account`
`set balance = balance + 100`
`where acct_number = 45`
	T13 keeps updating account and gets more exclusive locks	

`commit transaction`	T13 ends and releases its exclusive locks	`commit transaction`
	T14 gets shared locks, queries account, and ends	

Figure 11-7: Locking example between two transactions

The following sequence of locks assumes an index exists on the *acct_number* column of the *account* table, a default isolation level of 1, and 10 rows per page (50 rows divided by 10 equals 5 data pages):

T13 Locks	T14 Locks
Update lock page 1 Exclusive lock page 1 Intent exclusive table lock on account Update lock page 5 Exclusive lock page 5 Release all locks at commit	Shared lock page 1 denied, wait for release Shared lock page 1 Intent shared table lock on account Shared lock page 2, release lock page 1 Shared lock page 3, release lock page 2 Shared lock page 4, release lock page 3 Shared lock page 5, release lock page 4 Release lock, page 5 Release intent shared table lock

If no index exists for *acct_number*, SQL Server applies exclusive table locks for T13 instead of page locks:

T13 Locks	T14 Locks
Exclusive table lock on account Release exclusive table lock at commit	Shared lock page 1 denied, wait for release Shared lock page 1 Intent shared table lock on account Shared lock page 2, release lock page 1 Shared lock page 3, release lock page 2 Shared lock page 4, release lock page 3 Shared lock page 5, release lock page 4 Release lock page 5 Release intent shared table lock

If you add a **holdlock** or make isolation level 3 the default using the **transaction isolation level** option for transaction T14, the lock sequence is as follows (assuming an index exists for *acct_number*):

T13 Locks	T14 Locks
Update lock page 1 Exclusive lock page 1 Intent exclusive table lock on account Update lock page 5 Exclusive lock page 5 Release all locks at commit	Shared lock page 1 denied, wait for release Shared lock page 1 Intent shared table lock on account Shared lock page 2 Shared lock page 3 Shared lock page 4 Shared lock page 5 Release all locks at commit

If you add **holdlock** or make **transaction isolation level 3** for T14 and no index exists for *acct_number*, SQL Server applies table locks for both transactions instead of page locks:

T13 Locks	T14 Locks
Exclusive table lock on account Release exclusive table lock at commit	Shared table lock denied, wait for release Shared table lock on account Release shared table lock at commit

Cursors and Locking

Cursor locking methods are similar to the other locking methods for SQL Server. For cursors declared as **read only** or declared without the **for update** clause, SQL Server uses shared page locks on the data page that includes the current cursor position. When additional rows for the cursor are fetched, SQL Server acquires a lock on the next page, the cursor position is moved to that page, and the previous page lock is released (unless you are operating at isolation level 3).

For cursors declared with **for update**, SQL Server uses update page locks by default when scanning tables or views referenced with the **for update** clause of the cursor. If the **for update** list is empty, all tables and views referenced in the **from** clause of the *select_statement* receive update locks. Update locks are a special type of read lock, indicating that the reader may modify the data soon. Update locks allow other shared locks on the page, but do not allow other update or exclusive locks.

If a row is updated or deleted through a cursor, the data modification transaction acquires an exclusive lock. Any exclusive locks acquired by updates through a cursor in a transaction are held until the end of that transaction and are not affected by closing the cursor. This also applies to shared or update locks for cursors using the **holdlock** keyword or isolation level 3.

The following describes the locking behavior for cursors at each isolation level:

- At level 0, SQL Server uses no locks on any base table page that contains a row representing a current cursor position. Cursors acquire no read locks for their scans, so they do not block other applications from accessing the same data. However, cursors operating at this isolation level are not updatable, and they require a unique index on the base table to ensure accuracy.

- At level 1, SQL Server uses a shared or update locks on base table or leaf level index pages that contain a row representing a current cursor position. The page remains locked until the current cursor position moves off the page as a result of **fetch** statements.

- At level 3, SQL Server uses a shared or update locks on any base table or leaf level index pages that have been read in a transaction through the cursor. SQL Server holds the locks until the transaction ends; it does not release the locks when the data page is no longer needed or when the cursor is closed.

If you do not set the **close on endtran** option, a cursor remains open past the end of the transaction, and its current page locks remain in effect. It could also continue to acquire locks as it fetches additional rows.

Using the *shared* Keyword

When declaring an updatable cursor using the **for update** clause, you can tell SQL Server to use shared page locks (instead of update page locks) in the cursor's **declare cursor** statement:

```
declare cursor_name cursor
   for select select_list
   from {table_name | view_name} shared
   for update [of column_name_list]
```

This allows other users to obtain an update lock on the table or an underlying table of the view. You can use **shared** only with the **declare cursor** statement.

You can use the **holdlock** keyword in conjunction with **shared** after each table or view name, but **holdlock** must precede **shared** in the **select** statement. For example:

```
declare authors_crsr cursor
for select au_id, au_lname, au_fname
    from authors holdlock shared
    where state != 'CA'
    for update of au_lname, au_fname
```

These are the effects of specifying the **holdlock** or **shared** options (of the **select** statement) when defining an updatable cursor:

- If you don't specify either option, the cursor holds an update lock on the page containing the current row. Other users cannot update, through a cursor or otherwise, a row on this page. Other users can declare a cursor on the same tables you use for your cursor, but they cannot get a a shared or update lock on your current page.

- If you specify the **shared** option, the cursor holds shared locks on the page containing the currently fetched row. Other users cannot update, through a cursor or otherwise, the rows on this page. They can, however, read rows on the page.

- If you specify the **holdlock** option, you hold update locks on all of the pages that have been fetched (if transactions are not being used) or only the pages fetched since the last commit or rollback (if in a transaction). Other users cannot update, through a cursor or otherwise, currently fetched pages. Other users can declare a cursor on the same tables you use for your cursor, but they cannot get an update lock on currently fetched pages.

- If you specify both options, the cursor holds shared locks on all of the pages fetched (if not using transactions) or on the pages fetched since the last commit or rollback. Other users cannot update, through a cursor or otherwise, currently fetched pages.

Deadlocks and Concurrency in SQL Server

Simply stated, a **deadlock** occurs when two user processes each have a lock on a separate data page, index page, or table and each wants to acquire a lock on the other process's page or table. When this happens, the first process is waiting for the second to let go of the lock, but the second process will not let it go until the lock on the first process's object is released.

Figure 11-8 shows a simple deadlock example between two processes (a deadlock often involves more than two processes).

T15	Event Sequence	T16
`begin transaction`	T15 and T16 start	`begin transaction`

`update savings`
`set balance = balance - 250`
`where acct_number = 25`
	T15 gets exclusive lock for savings while T16 gets exclusive lock for checking	`update checking`
		`set balance = balance - 75`
		`where acct_number = 45`

`update checking`
`set balance = balance + 250`
`where acct_number = 45`
 	
`commit transaction`
	T15 waits for T16 to release its lock while T16 waits for T15 to release its lock; deadlock occurs	`update savings`
		`set balance = balance + 75`
		`where acct_number = 25`
		
		`commit transaction`

Figure 11-8: Deadlocks in transactions

If transactions T15 and T16 execute simultaneously, and both transactions acquire exclusive locks with their initial **update** statements, they deadlock waiting for each other to release their locks, which will not happen.

SQL Server checks for deadlocks and chooses the user whose transaction has accumulated the least amount of CPU time as the victim. SQL Server rolls back that user's transaction, notifies the application program of this action with message number 1205, and allows the other user processes to move forward.

In a multiuser situation, each user's application program should check every transaction that modifies data for message 1205 if there is any chance of deadlocking. It indicates that the user transaction was selected as the victim of a deadlock and rolled back. The application program must restart that transaction.

Avoiding Deadlocks

It is possible to encounter deadlocks when many long-running transactions are executed at the same time in the same database. Deadlocks become more common as the lock contention increases between those transactions, which decreases concurrency. Methods for reducing lock contention, such as avoiding table locks and not holding shared locks, are described in "Locking and Performance of SQL Server" on page 320.

Acquire Locks on Objects In the Same Order

Well-designed applications can minimize deadlocks by always acquiring locks in the same order. Updates to multiple tables should always be performed in the same order.

For example, the transactions described in Figure 11-8 could have avoided their deadlock by updating either the *savings* or *checking* table first in both transactions. That way, one transaction gets the exclusive lock first and proceeds while the other transaction waits to receive its exclusive lock on the same table when the first transaction ends.

In applications with large numbers of tables and transactions that update several tables, establish a locking order that can be shared by all application developers.

SQL Server also avoids deadlocks by using the following locks:

- Update page locks permit only one exclusive page lock at a time. Other update or exclusive locks must wait until that exclusive lock is released before accessing the page. However, update locks affect concurrency since the net effect is that all updates on a page happen only one at a time.

- Intent table locks act as a placeholder when shared or exclusive page locks are acquired. They inform other transactions that need a table lock whether or not the lock can be granted without having SQL Server scan the page lock queue. They also help avoid lock collisions between page level locks and table level locks.

Delaying Deadlock Checking

SQL Server performs deadlock checking after a minimum period of time for any process waiting for a lock to be released (sleeping). Previous releases of SQL Server perform this deadlock check at the time the process begins to wait for a lock. This deadlock checking is a time-consuming overhead for applications that wait without a deadlock.

If your applications deadlock very infrequently, SQL Server can delay deadlock checking and reduce the overhead cost. You can specify the minimum amount of time (in milliseconds) a process must wait before it initiates a deadlock check using the **deadlock checking period** configuration parameter. If you set this value to 600, SQL Server initiates a deadlock check for the waiting process after at least 600 milliseconds. For example:

```
sp_configure "deadlock checking period", 600
```

You can specify a number greater than or equal to 0 (zero) for **deadlock checking period**. If you set this value to 0, SQL Server initiates the deadlock checking at the time the process begins to wait for a lock. It is a dynamic configuration value, so any change to it takes immediate effect. SQL Server's default value for **deadlock checking period** is 500.

Configuring **deadlock checking period** to a higher value produces longer delays before deadlocks are detected. However, since SQL Server grants most lock requests before this time elapses, the deadlock checking overhead is avoided for those lock requests. So, if you expect your applications to deadlock very infrequently, you can set **deadlock checking period** to a higher value and avoid the overhead of deadlock checking for most processes. Otherwise, the default value of 500 milliseconds should suffice.

When you set **deadlock checking period** to a value, a process may wait longer than that period before SQL Server checks it for a deadlock. This happens because SQL Server actually performs deadlock checking for all processes at every Nth interval, where N is defined by the **deadlock checking period**. If a specific process waits its designated period of time, during which SQL Server performs a round of deadlock checking, the process must wait until the next interval before SQL Server performs its deadlock checking. This implies that a process may wait anywhere from N to almost twice that value. Information from **sp_sysmon** can help you tune deadlock checking behavior. See "Deadlock Detection" on page 508.

Locking and Performance of SQL Server

Locking affects performance of SQL Server by limiting concurrency. An increase in the number of simultaneous users of a server may increase lock contention, which decreases performance. Locks affect performance when:

- Processes wait for locks to be released

  Anytime a process waits for another process to complete its transaction and release its locks, the overall response time and throughput is affected.

- Transactions result in frequent deadlocks

  As described earlier, any deadlock causes one transaction to be aborted, and the transaction must be restarted by the application. If deadlocks occur often, it severely affects the throughput of applications. Deadlocks cannot be completely avoided. However, redesigning the way transactions access the data can help reduce their frequency.

- Creating indexes locks tables

  Creating a clustered index locks all users out of the table until the index is created. Creating a nonclustered index locks out all updates until it is created. Either way, you should create indexes at a time when there is little activity on your server.

- Turning off delayed deadlock detection causes spinlock contention.

  Setting the deadlock checking period to 0 causes more frequent deadlock checking. The deadlock detection process holds spinlocks on the lock structures in memory while it looks for deadlocks. In a high transaction production environment, do not set this parameter to 0.

Using *sp_sysmon* While Reducing Lock Contention

Many of the following sections suggest changing configuration parameters to reduce lock contention. Use **sp_sysmon** to determine if lock contention is a problem, and then use it to determine how tuning to reduce lock contention affects the system. See "Lock Management" on page 503 for more information about using **sp_sysmon** to view lock contention.

If lock contention is a problem, you can use SQL Server Monitor, a separate Sybase product, to pinpoint where lock problems are.

Reducing Lock Contention

Lock contention can have a large impact on SQL Server's throughput and response time. You need to consider locking during database design, and monitor locking during application design. Redesigning the tables that have the highest lock contention may improve performance.

For example, an **update** or **delete** statement that has no useful index on its search arguments performs a table scan, and holds a table lock for the entire scan time. Table locks generate more lock contention than page locks, since no other process can access the table. Creating a useful index for the query allows the data modification statement to use page locks, improving concurrent access to the table.

If creating an index for a lengthy update or delete transaction is not possible, you can perform the operation in a cursor, with frequent **commit transaction** statements to reduce the number of page locks.

Keeping Transactions Short

Any transaction that acquires locks should be kept as short as possible. In particular, avoid transactions that need to wait for user interaction while holding locks.

begin tran

select balance	*Intent shared table lock*
from account holdlock	*Shared page lock*
where acct_number = 25	
	If user goes to lunch here, no one can update rows on the page that holds this row
update account	*Intent exclusive table lock*
set balance = balance + 50	*Update page lock on data page*
where acct_number = 25	*Exclusive page lock on data page*
	If user goes to lunch here, no one can read rows on the page that holds this row

commit tran

Avoid network traffic as much as possible within transactions. The network is slower than SQL Server. The example below shows a transaction executed from **isql**, sent as two packets:

begin tran	*isql batch sent to SQL Server*
update account	*Locks held waiting for commit*
set balance = balance + 50	
where acct_number = 25	
go	
update account	*isql batch sent to SQL Server*
set balance = balance - 50	*Locks released*
where acct_number = 45	
commit tran	
go	

Keeping transactions short is especially crucial for data modifications that affect nonclustered index keys. Nonclustered indexes are dense: the level above the data level contains one row for each row in the table. All inserts and deletes to the table, and any updates to the key value affect at least one nonclustered index page (and adjoining pages in the page chain, if a page split or page deallocation takes place.) While locking a data page may slow access for a small number of rows, locks on frequently-used index pages can block access to a much larger set of rows. If a table averages 40 data rows per page, a lock on a data page restricts access to those 40 rows. If the leaf-level nonclustered index page that must be updated stores 100 keys and pointers, holding locks on that page restricts access to 4000 rows.

Avoiding "Hot Spots"

Hot spots occur when all updates take place on a certain page, as in a heap table, where all inserts happen on the last page of the page chain. For example, an unindexed history table that is updated by everyone will always have lock contention on the last page. This sample output from **sp_sysmon** shows that 11.9% of the inserts on a heap table need to wait for the lock:

```
Last Page Locks on Heaps
  Granted                     3.0      0.4      185      88.1 %
  Waited                      0.4      0.0       25      11.9 %
```

The best solution to this problem is to partition the history table. Partitioning a heap table creates multiple page chains in the table, and therefore multiple last pages for inserts. Concurrent inserts to the table are less likely to block one another, since multiple last pages are available. Partitioning provides a way to improve concurrency for heap tables without creating separate tables for different groups of users. See "Improving Insert Performance with Partitions" on page 364 for information about partitioning tables.

Another solution for hot spots is to create a clustered index to distribute the updates across the data pages in the table. Like partitioning, this solution creates multiple insertion points for the table. However, it also introduces some overhead for maintaining the physical order of the table's rows.

Decreasing the Number of Rows per Page

Another way to reduce contention is by decreasing the number of rows per page in your tables and indexes. When there is more empty space in the index and leaf pages, the chances of lock contention are reduced. As the keys are spread out over more pages, it becomes more likely that the page you want is not the page someone else needs. To change the number of rows per page, adjust the **fillfactor** or **max_rows_per_page** values of your tables and indexes.

fillfactor (defined by either **sp_configure** or **create index**) determines how full SQL Server makes each data page when it creates a new index on existing data. Since **fillfactor** helps reduce page splits, exclusive locks are also minimized on the index, improving performance. However, the **fillfactor** value is not maintained by subsequent changes to the data. **max_rows_per_page** (defined by **sp_chgattribute**, **create index**, **create table**, or **alter table**) is similar to **fillfactor**, except that SQL Server does maintain the **max_rows_per_page** value as the data changes.

The costs associated with decreasing the **fillfactor** or **max_rows_per_page** values include more memory, more locks, and a higher lock promotion threshold. In addition, a low value for **max_rows_per_page** for a table may increase page splits when data is inserted into the table.

Reducing Lock Contention with max_rows_per_page

The **max_rows_per_page** value specified in a **create table**, **create index**, or **alter table** command restricts the number of rows allowed on a data page, a clustered index leaf page, or a nonclustered index leaf page. This reduces lock contention and improves concurrency for frequently accessed tables.

The **max_rows_per_page** value applies to the data pages of a heap table or the leaf pages of an index. The value of **max_rows_per_page** is stored in the *maxrowsperpage* column of *sysindexes* (this column was named *rowpage* in previous releases of SQL Server; it was renamed when this feature became available in Release 11.0).

Unlike **fillfactor**, which is not maintained after creating a table or index, SQL Server retains the **max_rows_per_page** value when adding or deleting rows.

For example, the following command creates the *sales* table and limits the maximum rows per page to four:

```
create table sales
     (stor_id       char(4)      not null,
      ord_num       varchar(20)  not null,
      date          datetime     not null,)
     with max_rows_per_page = 4
```

If you create a table with a **max_rows_per_page** value, and then create a clustered index on the table without specifying **max_rows_per_page**, the clustered index inherits the **max_rows_per_page** value from the **create table** statement. Creating a clustered index with a **max_rows_per_page** specification changes the value for the table's data pages.

Indexes and max_rows_per_page

The default value for **max_rows_per_page** is 0, which creates clustered indexes with full data pages, creates nonclustered indexes with full leaf pages, and leaves a comfortable amount of space within the index B-tree in both the clustered and nonclustered indexes.

For heap tables and clustered indexes, the range for **max_rows_per_page** is 0–256.

For nonclustered indexes, the maximum value for **max_rows_per_page** is the number of index rows that fit on the leaf page, but the maximum cannot exceed 256. To determine the maximum value, subtract 32 from the page size and divide the difference by the index key size. The following statement calculates the maximum value of **max_rows_per_page** for a nonclustered index:

```
select (@@pagesize - 32)/minlen
    from sysindexes
    where name = "indexname"
```

select into and max_rows_per_page

select into does not carry over the base table's **max_rows_per_page** value, but creates the new table with a **max_rows_per_page** value of 0. Use **sp_chgattribute** to set the **max_rows_per_page** value on the target table.

Applying max_rows_per_page to Existing Data

The **sp_chgattribute** system procedure configures the **max_rows_per_page** of a table or an index. **sp_chgattribute** affects all future operations; it does not change existing pages. For example, to change the **max_rows_per_page** value of the *authors* table to 1, enter:

```
sp_chgattribute authors, "max_rows_per_page", 1
```

There are two ways to apply a **max_rows_per_page** value to existing data:

- If the table has a clustered index, drop and re-create the index with a **max_rows_per_page** value.
- Use the **bcp** utility as follows:
  - Copy out the table data.
  - Truncate the table.
  - Set the **max_rows_per_page** value with **sp_chgattribute**.
  - Copy the data back in.

Additional Locking Guidelines

These locking guidelines can help reduce lock contention and speed performance:

- Use the lowest level of locking required by each application, and use isolation level 3 only when necessary.

  Updates by other transactions may be delayed until a transaction using isolation level 3 releases any of its shared locks at the end of the transaction. Use isolation level 3 only when nonrepeatable reads or phantoms may interfere with your desired results.

  If only a few queries require level 3, use the **holdlock** keyword or **at isolation serializable** clause in those queries instead of using **set transaction isolation level 3** for the entire transaction. If most queries in the transaction require level 3, specify **set transaction isolation level 3**, but use **noholdlock** or **at isolation read committed** in the remaining queries that can execute at isolation level 1.

- If you need to perform mass updates and deletes on active tables, you can reduce blocking by performing the operation inside a stored procedure using a cursor, with frequent commits.

- If your application needs to return a row, provide for user interaction, and then update the row, consider using timestamps and the **tsequal** function rather than **holdlock**.

- If you are using compliant third-party software, check the locking model in applications carefully for concurrency problems.

Also, other tuning efforts can help reduce lock contention. For example, if a process holds locks on a page, and must perform a physical I/O to read an additional page, it holds the lock much longer than it would have if the additional page were already in cache. Better cache utilization or using large I/O can reduce lock contention in this case. Other tuning efforts that can pay off in reduced lock contention are improved indexing and good distribution of physical I/O across disks.

Reporting on Locks and Locking Behavior

The system procedures **sp_who** and **sp_lock** report on locks held by users, and show processes that are blocked by other transactions.

Getting Information About Blocked Processes with *sp_who*

The system procedure **sp_who** reports on system processes. If a user's command is being blocked by locks held by another process:

- The *status* column shows "lock sleep."

- The *blk* column shows the process ID of the process that holds the lock or locks.

If you do not provide a user name, **sp_who** reports on all processes in SQL Server. You can add a user name parameter to get **sp_who** information about a particular SQL Server user.

Viewing Locks with *sp_lock*

To get a report on the locks currently being held on SQL Server, use the system procedure **sp_lock**:

```
sp_lock
```

```
The class column will display the cursor name for locks
associated with a cursor for the current user and the cursor id
for other users.
spid  locktype      table_id     page  dbname  class
----  ----------    ----------   ----  ------  ---------------
1     Ex_intent     1308531695   0     master  Non cursor lock
1     Ex_page       1308531695   761   master  Non cursor lock
5     Ex_intent     144003544    0     userdb  Non cursor lock
5     Ex_page       144003544    509   userdb  Non cursor lock
5     Ex_page       144003544    1419  userdb  Non cursor lock
5     Ex_page       144003544    1420  userdb  Non cursor lock
5     Ex_page       144003544    1440  userdb  Non cursor lock
5     Sh_page       144003544    1440  userdb  Non cursor lock
5     Sh_table      144003544    0     userdb  Non cursor lock
5     Update_page   144003544    1440  userdb  Non cursor lock
4     Ex_table      240003886    0     pubs2   Non cursor lock
4     Sh_intent     112003436    0     pubs2   Non cursor lock
4     Ex_intent-blk 112003436    0     pubs2   Non cursor lock
```

The *locktype* column indicates not only whether the lock is a shared lock ("Sh" prefix), an exclusive lock ("Ex" prefix), or an "update" lock, but also whether it is held on a table ("table" or "intent") or on a "page."

A "blk" suffix indicates that this process is blocking another process that needs to acquire a lock. As soon as the blocking process completes, the other processes move forward. A "demand" suffix indicates that the process will acquire an exclusive lock as soon as all current shared locks are released.

To see lock information about a particular login, give the *spid* for the process:

```
sp_lock 4
```

```
The class column will display the cursor name for locks
associated with a cursor for the current user and the cursor id
for other users.
spid  locktype      table_id     page  dbname  class
----  ----------    ----------   ----  ------  ---------------
4     Ex_table      240003886    0     pubs2   Non cursor lock
4     Sh_intent     112003436    0     pubs2   Non cursor lock
4     Ex_intent-blk 112003436    0     pubs2   Non cursor lock
```

Observing Locks with *sp_sysmon*

Output from the system procedure **sp_sysmon** gives statistics on the page locks, table locks, and deadlocks discussed in this chapter.

Use the statistics to determine whether the SQL Server system is experiencing performance problems due to lock contention. For more information about **sp_sysmon** and lock statistics, see Chapter 11, "Locking on SQL Server" and the topic "Lock Management" on page 503.

SQL Server Monitor, a separate Sybase product, can pinpoint locking problems.

Configuring Locks and Lock Promotion Thresholds

A System Administrator can configure:

- The total number of locks available to processes on SQL Server
- The lock promotion threshold, server-wide, for a database, or for particular tables
- The number of locks available per engine, and the number of locks transferred between the global free lock list and engines

Configuring SQL Server's Lock Limit

Each lock counts toward SQL Server's limit of total number of locks. By default, SQL Server is configured with 5000 locks. A System Administrator can change this limit using the **sp_configure** system procedure. For example:

```
sp_configure "number of locks", 10000
```

You may also need to adjust the **total memory** option of **sp_configure**, since each lock uses 72 bytes of memory.

The number of locks required by a server can vary depending on the number of concurrent processes and the types of actions performed by the transactions. However, a good starting assumption is that each concurrent process uses about 20 locks.

Setting the Lock Promotion Thresholds

The lock promotion thresholds set the number of page locks permitted by a statement before SQL Server attempts to escalate to a table lock on the object. You can set the lock promotion threshold at the server-wide level, for a database and for individual tables. The default values provide good performance for a wide range of table sizes, but you may wish to configure the thresholds higher, especially for very large tables where many queries lock hundreds of data pages.

Table locks are more efficient than page locks when SQL Server suspects an entire table might eventually be needed. At first, SQL Server tries to satisfy most requests with page locks. However, if more page locks than the lock promotion threshold are required on a table during the course of a scan session, SQL Server attempts to escalate to a table lock instead. (A "scan session" is a single scan of a table or index.) A table may be scanned more than once within a single command (in the case of joins, subqueries, **exists** clauses, and so on), and thus more than one scan session per table may be associated with a single command. Since lock escalation occurs on a per-scan session basis, the total number of page locks for a single command can exceed the lock promotion threshold as long as no single scan session acquires more than the lock promotion threshold number of page locks. Locks may persist throughout a transaction, so a transaction that includes multiple commands can accumulate a large number of locks.

Lock promotion from page locks to table locks cannot occur if a page lock owned by another SQL Server process conflicts with the type of table lock that is needed. For instance, if one process holds any exclusive page locks, no other process can promote to a table lock until the exclusive page locks are released. When this happens, a process can accumulate page locks in excess of the lock promotion threshold and exhaust all available locks on SQL Server. You may need to increase the value of the **number of locks** configuration parameter so that SQL Server does not run out of locks.

The three lock promotion thresholds are:

- **lock promotion HWM** (high water mark) sets a maximum of locks on a table. The default values is 200. When the number of locks acquired during a scan session exceeds this number, SQL Server always attempts to acquire a table lock.

  Setting **lock promotion HWM** to a value greater than 200 reduces the chance of any user acquiring a table lock on a particular table. Setting **lock promotion HWM** to a value lower than 200 increases the chances of a particular user acquiring a table lock; generally you want to avoid table locking, although it can be useful in situations where a particular user needs exclusive use of a table for which there is little or no contention.

- **lock promotion LWM** (low water mark) sets a minimum number of locks allowed on a table before SQL Server attempts to acquire a table lock. The default value is 200. SQL Server never attempts to acquire a table lock until the number of locks on a table is equal to the **lock promotion lwm**. The **lock promotion LWM** must be less than or equal to the **lock promotion HWM**.

Setting the **lock promotion LWM** to very high values decreases the chance of a particular user transaction acquiring a table lock, which uses more page locks for the duration of the transaction, potentially exhausting all available locks on SQL Server. If this situation recurs, you may need to increase **number of locks.**

- **lock promotion pct** sets the percentage of locked pages (based on the table size) above which SQL Server attempts to acquire a table lock when the number of locks is between the **lock promotion HWM** and the **lock promotion LWM**. The default value is 100.

Setting **lock promotion PCT** to very low values increases the chance of a particular user transaction acquiring a table lock. If this situation recurs, you may need to increase **number of locks.**

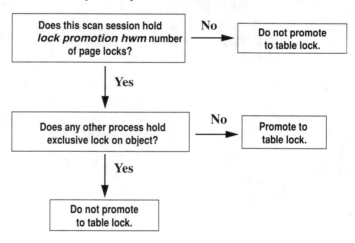

Figure 11-9: Lock promotion logic

Setting Lock Promotion Thresholds Server-Wide

The following command sets the server-wide **lock promotion LWM** to 100, the **lock promotion HWM** to 2000, and the **lock promotion PCT** to 50:

```
sp_setpglockpromote "server", null, 100, 2000, 50
```

In this example, SQL Server does not attempt to issue a table lock unless the number of locks on a table is between 100 and 2000. If a command requires more than 100 but less than 2000 locks, SQL Server compares the number of locks to the percentage of locks on the table. If the number is greater than the percentage, SQL Server attempts to issue a table lock.

SQL Server calculates the percentage as:

```
(PCT * number of rows) / 100
```

The default value for **lock promotion HWM** (200) is likely to be appropriate for most applications. If you have many small tables with clustered indexes, where there is contention for data pages, you may be able to increase concurrency for those tables by tuning **lock promotion HWM** to 80 percent of **number of locks**.

The lock promotion thresholds are intended to maximize the concurrency on heavily used tables. The default server-wide lock promotion threshold setting is 200.

Setting the Lock Promotion Threshold for a Table or Database

To configure lock promotion values for an individual table or database, initialize all three lock promotion thresholds. For example:

```
sp_setpglockpromote "table", titles, 100, 2000, 50
```

After the values are initialized, you can change any individual value. For example, to change the **lock promotion PCT** only, use the following command:

```
sp_setpglockpromote "table", titles, null, null, 70
```

To configure values for a database, use

```
sp_setpglockpromote "database", master, 1000, 1100,
45
```

Precedence of Settings

You can change the lock promotion thresholds for any user database or an individual table. Settings for an individual table override the database or server-wide settings; settings for a database override the server-wide values.

Server-wide values for lock promotion are represented by the **lock promotion HWM**, **lock promotion LWM**, and **lock promotion PCT** configuration parameters. Server-wide values apply to all user tables on the server unless the database or tables have lock promotion values configured for them.

Dropping Database and Table Settings

To remove table or database lock promotion thresholds, use the **sp_dropglockpromote** system procedure. When you drop a database's lock promotion thresholds, tables that do not have lock promotion thresholds configured will use the server-wide values. When you drop a table's lock promotion thresholds, SQL Server uses the database's lock promotion thresholds, if they have been configured, or the server-wide values, if the lock promotion thresholds have not been configured. You cannot drop the server-wide lock promotion thresholds.

Using *sp_sysmon* While Tuning Lock Promotion Thresholds

Use the system procedure **sp_sysmon** to see how many times lock promotions take place and the types of promotions they are. See Chapter 19, "Monitoring SQL Server Performance with sp_sysmon" and the topic "Lock Promotions" on page 509.

If there is a problem, look for signs of lock contention in "Granted" and "Waited" data in the Lock Detail section of the **sp_sysmon** output. (See "Lock Detail" on page 506 for more information.) If lock contention is high and lock promotion is frequent, consider changing the lock promotion thresholds for the tables involved.

Use SQL Server Monitor, a separate Sybase product, to see how changes to the lock promotion threshold affect the system at the object level.

Using Cursors for Row-by-Row Processing

The cursor mechanism provides a pointer to each row affected by a query, for use when your application requires SQL Server to process query results one row at a time. The use of cursors can affect performance when they interact adversely with SQL Server's native set-processing orientation and its page and table-level locking.

Chapter 12, "Cursors and Performance," shows you the best way to use cursors and how to measure their effects on performance. In many cases, developers can achieve the desired processing without the use of cursors.

12 Cursors and Performance

How Cursors Can Affect Performance

Cursors are a mechanism for accessing the results of a SQL **select** statement one row at a time (or several rows, if you use **set cursors rows**). Since cursors use a different model from ordinary set-oriented SQL, the way cursors use memory and hold locks has performance implications for your applications. In particular, cursor performance issues are:

- Locking at the page and at the table level
- Network resources
- Overhead of processing instructions

What Is a Cursor?

A cursor is a symbolic name that is associated with a **select** statement. It enables you to access the results of a **select** statement one row at a time.

Cursor with select * from authors
where state = 'KY'

Result set

➤ A978606525   Marcello   Duncan   KY

➤ A937406538   Carton   Nita   KY

Programming can:
- Examine a row

➤ A1525070956   Porczyk   Howard   KY

- Take an action based on row values

➤ A913907285   Bier   Lane   KY

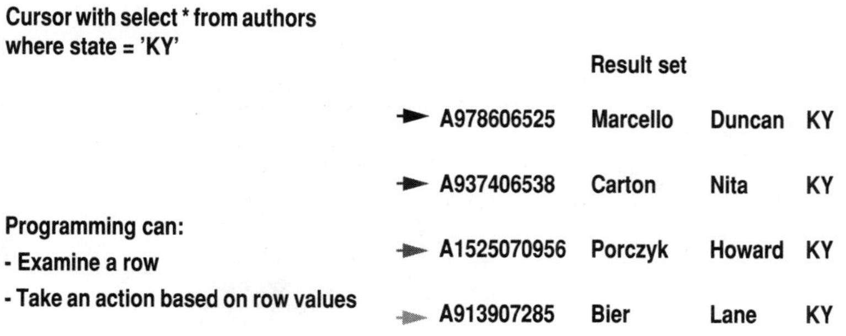

Figure 12-1: Cursor example

You can think of a cursor as a "handle" on the result set of a **select** statement. It enables you to examine and possibly manipulate one row at a time.

Set-Oriented vs. Row-Oriented Programming

SQL was not conceived as a row-oriented language—it is a set-oriented language. SQL Server is extremely efficient when it works in set-oriented mode. Cursors are required by ANSI SQL standards, and when they are needed, they are very powerful. However, they can have a negative effect on performance.

For example, this query performs the identical action to all rows fulfilling conditions:

```
update titles
    set contract = 1
where type = 'business'
```

The SQL Server optimizer finds the most efficient way to perform the update. In contrast, a cursor would examine each row and perform single updates if conditions were met. The application declares a cursor for a **select** statement, opens the cursor, fetches a row, processes it, goes to the next row, and so forth. The application may perform quite different operations based on the values in the current row and may be less efficient than the server's set level operations. However, cursors can provide more flexibility when needed, so when you need the flexibility, use them.

Figure 12-2 shows the steps involved in using cursors. The most important function of cursors is to get to the middle box, where the user or application code examines a row and decides what to do based on its values.

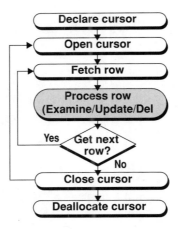

Figure 12-2: Cursor flowchart

Cursors: A Simple Example

Here is a simple example of a cursor with the "Process Rows" part in pseudocode.

```
declare biz_book cursor
    for select * from titles
    where type = 'business'
go
open biz_book
go
fetch biz_book
go
/* Look at each row in turn and perform
** various tasks based on values,
** and repeat fetches, until
** there are no more rows
*/
close biz_book
go
deallocate cursor biz_book
go
```

Depending on the content of the row, the user might delete the current row:

```
delete titles where current of biz_book
```

or update the current row:

```
update titles set title="The Rich
    Executive's Database Guide"
where current of biz_book
```

Resources Required at Each Stage

Cursors use memory and require locks on tables, data pages, and index pages. When you declare a cursor, memory is allocated to the cursor and to store the query plan that is generated. While the cursor is open, SQL Server holds intent table locks and perhaps page locks. When you fetch a row, there is a page lock on the page that stores the row, locking out updates by other processes. If you fetch multiple rows, there is a page lock on each page that contains a fetched row.

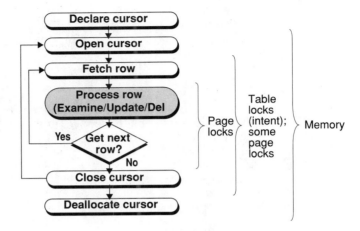

Figure 12-3: Resource use by cursor statement

The memory resource descriptions in Figure 12-3 and Table 12-1 refer to ad hoc cursors sent using **isql** or Client-Library™. For other kinds of cursors, the locks are the same, but the memory allocation and deallocation differ somewhat according to the type of cursor, as described in "Memory Use and Execute Cursors" on page 339.

Table 12-1: Locks and memory use for isql and Client-Library client cursors

Cursor Command	Resource Use
declare cursor	When you declare a cursor, SQL Server allocates memory to the cursor and to store the query plan that is generated. The size of the query plan depends on the **select** statement, but it generally ranges from one to two pages.
open	When you open a cursor, SQL Server starts processing the **select** statement. The server optimizes the query, traverses indexes, and sets up memory variables. The server does not access rows yet unless it needs to build worktables. However, it does set up the required table-level locks (intent locks) and, if there are subqueries or joins, page locks on the outer table(s).
fetch	When you execute a **fetch**, SQL Server acquires a page lock, gets the row or rows required and reads specified values into the cursor variables or sends the row to the client. The page lock is held until a **fetch** moves the cursor off the page or until the cursor is closed. The page lock is either a shared or update page lock, depending on how the cursor is written.
close	When you close a cursor, SQL Server releases the shared locks and some of the memory allocation. You can open the cursor again, if necessary.
deallocate cursor	When you deallocate a cursor, SQL Server releases the rest of the memory resources used by the cursor. To reuse the cursor, you must declare it again.

Memory Use and Execute Cursors

The descriptions of **declare cursor** and **deallocate cursor** in Table 12-1 refer to ad hoc cursors that are sent using **isql** or Client-Library. Other kinds of cursors allocate memory differently:

- For cursors that are declared **on** stored procedures, only a small amount of memory is allocated at **declare cursor** time. Cursors declared on stored procedures are sent using Client-Library or the pre-compiler and are known as "execute cursors."

- For cursors declared **within** a stored procedure, memory is already available for the stored procedure, and the **declare** statement does not require additional memory.

Cursor Modes: Read-Only and Update

There are two cursor modes: read only and update. As the names suggest, read-only cursors can only display data from a **select** statement; update cursors can be used to perform positioned updates and deletes.

Read-only mode uses shared page locks. It is in effect if you specify **for read only** or if the cursor's select statement uses **distinct, group by, union**, or aggregate functions, and in some cases, an **order by** clause.

Update mode uses update page locks. It is in effect if:

- You specify **for update**.

- The **select** statement does not include **distinct, group by, union**, a subquery, aggregate functions, or the **at isolation read uncommitted** clause.

- You specify **shared**.

If *column_name_list* is specified, only those columns are updatable.

Read-Only vs. Update

Specify the cursor mode when you declare the cursor. Note that if the select statement includes certain options, the cursor is not updatable even if you declare it for update.

Index Use and Requirements for Cursors

Any index can be used for read-only cursors. They should produce the same query plan as the **select** statement outside of a cursor. The index requirements for updatable cursors are rather specific, and updatable cursors may produce different query plans.

Update cursors have these indexing requirements:

- If the cursor is not declared for update, a unique index is preferred over a table scan or a nonunique index. But a unique index is not required.

- If the cursor is declared for update without a **for update of** list, a unique index is required. An error is raised if no unique index exists.

- If the cursor is declared for update with a **for update of** list, then only a unique index without any columns from the list can be chosen. An error is raised if no unique index qualifies.

When cursors are involved, an index that contains an IDENTITY column is considered unique, even if the index is not declared unique.

Comparing Performance With and Without Cursors

This section examines the performance of a stored procedure written two different ways:

- Without a cursor – This procedure scans the table three times, changing the price of each book.

- With a cursor – This procedure makes only one pass through the table.

In both examples, there is a unique index on *titles(title_id)*.

Sample Stored Procedure: Without a Cursor

This is an example of programming without cursors.

```
/* Increase the prices of books in the
** titles table as follows:
**
** If current price is <= $30, increase it by 20%
** If current price is > $30 and <= $60, increase
** it by 10%
** If current price is > $60, increase it by 5%
**
** All price changes must take effect, so this is
** done in a single transaction.
*/

create procedure increase_price
as

    /* start the transaction */
    begin transaction
    /* first update prices > $60 */
    update titles
        set price = price * 1.05
        where price > $60

    /* next, prices between $30 and $60 */
    update titles
        set price = price * 1.10
```

```
        where price > $30 and price <= $60

        /* and finally prices <= $30 */
        update titles
        set price = price * 1.20
        where price <= $30

        /* commit the transaction */
        commit transaction


return
```

Sample Stored Procedure With a Cursor

This procedure performs the same changes to the underlying table, but it uses cursors instead of set-oriented programming. As each row is fetched, examined, and updated, a lock is held on the appropriate data page. Also, as the comments indicate, each update commits as it is made since there is no explicit transaction.

```
/* Same as previous example, this time using a
** cursor. Each update commits as it is made.
*/
create procedure increase_price_cursor
as
declare @price money

/* declare a cursor for the select from titles */
declare curs cursor for
    select price
    from titles
    for update of price

/* open the cursor */
open curs

/* fetch the first row */
fetch curs into @price

/* now loop, processing all the rows
** @@sqlstatus = 0 means successful fetch
** @@sqlstatus = 1 means error on previous fetch
** @@sqlstatus = 2 means end of result set reached
*/
while (@@sqlstatus != 2)
begin
    /* check for errors */
```

```
    if (@@sqlstatus = 1)
    begin
        print "Error in increase_price"
        return
    end

    /* next adjust the price according to the
    ** criteria
    */
    if @price > $60
    select @price = @price * 1.05
    else
    if @price > $30 and @price <= $60
    select @price = @price * 1.10
    else
    if @price <= $30
    select @price = @price * 1.20

    /* now, update the row */
    update titles
    set price = @price
    where current of curs

    /* fetch the next row */
    fetch curs into @price
end

/* close the cursor and return */
close curs
return
```

Which procedure do you think will have better performance, one that performs three table scans, or one that performs a single scan via a cursor?

Cursor vs. Non-Cursor Performance Comparison

Table 12-2 shows actual statistics gathered against a 5000-row table. Note that the cursor code takes two and one-half times longer, even though it scans the table only once.

Table 12-2: Sample execution times against a 5000-row table

Procedure	Access Method	Time
increase_price	Uses three table scans	2 minutes
increase_price_cursor	Uses cursor, single table scan	5 minutes

Results from tests like these can vary widely. They are most pronounced on systems with busy networks, larger numbers of active database users, and multiple users accessing the same table.

Cursor vs. Non-Cursor Performance Explanation

In addition to locking, cursors involve much more network activity than set operations and incur the overhead of processing instructions. The application program needs to communicate with SQL Server regarding every result row of the query. This is why the cursor code took much longer to complete than the code that scanned the table three times.

When cursors are absolutely necessary, of course they should be used. But they can adversely affect performance. Cursor performance issues are:

- Locking at the page and table level

- Network resources

- Overhead of processing instructions

Use cursors only if necessary. If there is a set level programming equivalent, it may be preferable, even if it involves multiple table scans.

Locking with Read-Only Cursors

Here is a piece of cursor code you can use to display the locks that are set up at each point in the life of a cursor. Execute the code in Figure 12-4, pausing to execute **sp_lock** each time you type "go":

```
declare curs1 cursor for
select au_id, au_lname, au_fname
    from authors
    where au_id like '15%'
    for read only
go
open curs1
go
fetch curs1
go
fetch curs1
go 100
close curs1
go
deallocate cursor curs1
go
```

Figure 12-4: Read-only cursors and locking experiment input

Table 12-3 shows the results.

Table 12-3: Locks held on data and index pages by cursors

Event	Data Page
After **declare**	No cursor-related locks.
After **open**	Shared intent lock on *authors*.
After first **fetch**	Shared intent lock on *authors*, and shared page lock on a page in *authors*.
After 100 fetches	Shared intent lock on *authors* and shared page lock on a different page in *authors*.
After **close**	No cursor-related locks.

If you issue another **fetch** command after the last row of the result set has been fetched, the locks on the last page are released, so there will be no cursor-related locks.

Locking with Update Cursors

The next example requires two connections to SQL Server.

Open two connections to SQL Server, and execute the commands shown in Figure 12-5.

Connection 1	Connection 2

```
declare curs2 cursor for
select au_id, au_lname
from authors
where au_id like 'A1%'
for update
go
open curs2
go

fetch curs2
go
```

```
                                begin tran
                                go
                                select *
                                from authors
                                    holdlock
                                where au_id = au_id
                                    fetched at left
                                go

                                sp_lock
                                go
```

```
delete from authors
where current of curs2
go
```

```
/* what happens? */             delete
                                from authors
                                where au_id =
                                    same au_id

                                /* what happens? */
```

```
close curs2
go
```

Figure 12-5: Update cursors and locking experiment input

Update Cursors: Experiment Results

Connection 1, which opens a cursor and fetches a row, gets an update lock on that page, which allows shared locks but not exclusive locks or update locks.

When Connection 2 does a **select with holdlock**, that works because it just needs a shared lock.

When Connection 1 (the cursor) tries to delete, it needs an exclusive lock but cannot get it, which means it has to wait. When Connection

2 tries to delete, which requires an exclusive lock, it cannot get it either, and deadlock occurs.

Isolation Levels and Cursors

The query plan for a cursor is compiled and optimized at the time it is declared. You cannot declare a cursor, and then use **set transaction isolation level** and to change the isolation level at which a cursor operates.

Since cursors using isolation level 0 are compiled differently from other isolation levels, you cannot declare a cursor at isolation level 0 and open or fetch from it at level 1 or 3. Similarly, you cannot declare a cursor at level 1 or 3 and then fetch from it at level 0. Attempts to open or fetch from a cursor at an incompatible level result in an error message.

You can include an **at isolation** clause in the cursor to specify an isolation level. The cursor in the example below can be declared at level 1, and fetched from at level 0 because the query plan is compatible with the isolation level:

```
declare cprice cursor for
select title_id, price
    from titles
    where type = "business"
    at isolation read uncommitted
```

If you declare a cursor at level 1, and use set transaction isolation level to change the level to 3, you can still open and fetch from the cursor, but operates at level 1, that is, it does not hold locks on all of the pages that are fetched. The reverse is also true: if you declare the cursor at level 3, and fetch from it at level 1, it continues to hold locks on all of the fetched pages. I

Optimizing Tips for Cursors

There are several optimizing tips specific to cursors:

- Optimize cursor selects using the cursor, not ad hoc queries.
- Use **union** or **union all** instead of **or** clauses or **in** lists.
- Declare the cursor's intent.
- Specify column names in the **for update** clause.
- Use the **shared** keyword for tables.

- Fetch more than one row if you are returning rows to the client.
- Keep cursors open across commits and rollbacks.
- Open multiple cursors on a single connection.

Optimize Using Cursors

A standalone **select** statement may be optimized very differently than the same **select** statement in an implicitly or explicitly updatable cursor. When you are developing applications that use cursors, always check your query plans and I/O statistics using the cursor, not a standalone **select**. In particular, index restrictions of updatable cursors require very different access methods.

Use *union* Instead of *or* Clauses or *in* Lists

Cursors cannot use the dynamic index of row IDs generated by the OR strategy. Queries that use the OR strategy in standalone **select** statements usually table scan using read-only cursors. If they are updatable cursors, they may need to use a unique index and still require access to each data row in sequence in order to evaluate the query clauses. See "The OR Strategy" on page 186 for more information about dynamic indexes and **or** processing.

Read-only cursors using **union** create a worktable when the cursor is declared, and sort it to remove duplicates. Fetches are performed on the worktable. Cursors using **union all** can return duplicates and do not require a worktable.

Declare the Cursor's Intent

Always declare a cursor's intent: read-only or updatable. This gives you greater control over concurrency implications. If you do not specify the intent, SQL Server decides for you, and very often it chooses updatable cursors. Updatable cursors use update locks, thereby preventing other update locks or exclusive locks. If the update changes an indexed column, the optimizer may need to choose a table scan for the query, resulting in potentially difficult concurrency problems. Be sure to examine the query plans carefully for queries using updatable cursors.

Specify Column Names in the *for update* Clause

SQL Server acquires update locks on all tables that have columns listed in the **for update** clause of the cursor **select** statement. If the **for update** clause is not included in the cursor declaration, all tables referenced in the **from** clause acquire update locks.

This query includes the name of the column in the **for update** clause, but acquires update locks only on the *titles* table, since *price* is mentioned in the **for update** clause. The locks on *authors* and *titleauthor* are shared page locks:

```
declare curs3 cursor
for
select au_lname, au_fname, price
    from titles t, authors a,
        titleauthor ta
where advance <= $1000
    and t.title_id = ta.title_id
    and a.au_id = ta.au_id
for update of price
```

Table 12-4 shows the effects of:

- Omitting the **for update** clause entirely—no **shared** clause

- Omitting the column name from the **for update** clause

- Including the name of the column to be updated in the **for update** clause

- Adding **shared** after the name of the *titles* table while using **for update of price**

In the table, the additional locks, or more restrictive locks for the two versions of the **for update** clause are emphasized.

Table 12-4: Effects of for update clause and shared on cursor locking

Clauses	*titles*	*authors*	*titleauthor*
none		sh_page on index	
	sh_page on data	sh_page on data	sh_page on data
for update	**updpage on index**	**updpage on index**	
	updpage on data	**updpage on data**	**updpage on data**
for update of price		sh_page on index	
	updpage on data	sh_page on data	sh_page on data

Table 12-4: Effects of for update clause and shared on cursor locking

Clauses	titles	authors	titleauthor
for update of price + shared	sh_page on data	sh_page index sp_page data	sh_page on data

Declare Shared Locks

If you use the **shared** keyword in the cursor definition of an updatable cursor, SQL Server acquires shared locks rather than update locks, increasing concurrency.

Use *set cursor rows*

The SQL standard specifies a one-row fetch for cursors, wasting network bandwidth. Using the **set cursor rows** query option and Open Client's transparent buffering of fetches you can increase performance:

```
ct_cursor(CT_CURSOR_ROWS)
```

Choose the number of rows returned carefully for frequently executed applications using cursors; tune them to the network. See "Changing Network Packet Sizes" on page 429 for an explanation of this process.

Keep Cursors Open Across Commits and Rollbacks

The ANSI standard specifies that cursors automatically close at the conclusion of each transaction. Transact-SQL provides the **set** option **close on endtran** for applications that must conform to ANSI behavior. By default, however, this option is off. Unless you must meet ANSI requirements, leave this option off in order to maintain concurrency and throughput.

If you must be ANSI compliant, you need to decide how to handle the effects on SQL Server. Should you perform a lot of updates or deletes in a single transaction? Or should you follow the usual advice to keep transactions short?

If you choose to keep transactions short, closing and opening the cursor can affect throughput, since SQL Server needs to rematerialize the result set each time the cursor is opened. If you choose to perform more work in each transaction, this can cause concurrency problems, since the query holds locks.

Open Multiple Cursors on a Single Connection

Some developers simulate cursors by using two or more connections from DB-Library™. One connection performs a select, while the other connection performs updates or deletes on the same tables. This has very high potential to create "application deadlocks":

- Connection A holds a shared lock on a page. As long as there are rows pending from SQL Server, a shared lock is kept on the current page.

- Connection B requests an exclusive lock on the same pages and then waits.

- The application waits for Connection B to succeed before invoking whatever logic is needed to remove the shared lock. But this never happens.

On to Hardware-Related Tuning

Since Connection A never requests a lock that Connection B holds, this is not a server-side deadlock.

Chapter 12 concludes Section B. In Section C, the discussion turns to hardware-related tuning, which is something you'll likely address once your application is up and running. Issues such as how to prevent resource contention by controlling the physical location of database objects, how to analyze the performance of your computer systems and networks, and how best to use the monitoring tool **sp_sysmon**, are all relevant to tuning a fully developed application.

Hardware Tuning Issues and Application Maintenance

The last section of this book covers hardware-related tuning issues such as: placing database objects on specific devices; or detecting performance bottlenecks in the cpu or network.

The very important topics of ongoing maintenance (and the effects on performance of maintenance activities) round out the book. Since it's likely that the system administrator will run the monitoring tool **sp_sysmon** frequently during application tuning and maintenance, **sp_sysmon** is covered in depth as the last chapter of the book.

Chapter 13, "Controlling Physical Data Placement," describes the uses of segments and partitions for controlling the physical placement of data on storage devices.

Chapter 14, "tempdb Performance Issues," stresses the importance of the temporary database, *tempdb*, and provides suggestions for improving its performance.

Chapter 15, "Memory Use and Performance," describes how SQL Server uses memory for the procedure and data caches.

Chapter 16, "Networks and Performance," describes network issues.

Chapter 17, "Using CPU Resources Effectively," provides information for tuning servers with multiple CPUs.

Chapter 18, "Maintenance Activities and Performance," describes the performance impact of maintenance activities.

Chapter 19, "Monitoring SQL Server Performance with sp_sysmon," describes how to use a system procedure that monitors SQL Server performance.

13 Controlling Physical Data Placement

How Object Placement Can Improve Performance

SQL Server allows you to control the placement of databases, tables, and indexes across your physical storage devices. This can improve performance by balancing the workload, equalizing the reads and writes to disk across many devices and controllers.

For example, you can store the database's log on a separate physical device, so that reads and writes to the database's log do not interfere with data access. And, you could segregate a table's nonclustered indexes to a separate device, so that index activity doesn't slow use of the data.

Placing the text or image page chain for a table on a device separate from the table itself can make working with these large data types more efficient. Since the table stores a pointer to the actual data value in the separate database structure, each access to a text or image column requires at least two I/Os. In general, large, heavily used tables should be partitioned across several devices.

Multiuser and Multi-CPU Considerations

In an application environment involving multiple users and multiple devices, the overhead of switching among users and devices must be weighed against the performance benefits of partitioning and isolating database components.

Multiuser systems and multi-CPU systems that perform a great deal of disk I/O need to pay special attention to physical and logical device issues and the distribution of I/O across devices.

The system administrator must plan balanced distribution of objects across logical and physical devices; use enough physical devices, including disk controllers, to ensure physical bandwidth.; and define enough logical devices to minimize contention for internal I/O queues. SQL Server provides support for multi-device environment with features such as the **create database** command's ability to perform parallel I/O on up to six devices at a time, which can significantly speed the process of creating multigigabyte databases.

This chapter discusses:

- General issues with data placement on devices
- Device mirroring and performance issues

- Using segments to improve performance
- Using partitions to increase insert performance on heap tables

Symptoms of Poor Object Placement

The following symptoms may indicate that your system could benefit from attention to object placement:

- Single-user performance is all right, but response time increases significantly when multiple processes are executed.
- Access to a mirrored disk takes twice as long as access to an unmirrored disk.
- Query performance degrades when system table activity increases.
- Maintenance activities seem to take a long time.
- Stored procedures seem to slow down as they create temporary tables.
- Insert performance is poor on heavily used tables.

Underlying Problems

If you are experiencing problems due to disk contention and other problems related to object places, check for these underlying problems:

- Random access (I/O for data and indexes) and serial access (log I/O) processes are using the same disks.
- Database processes and operating system processes are using the same disks.
- Serial disk mirroring is being used because of functional requirements.
- Database maintenance activity (logging or auditing) is taking place on the same disks as data storage.
- *tempdb* activity is on the same disk as heavily used tables.

Using *sp_sysmon* While Changing Data Placement

Use **sp_sysmon** to determine whether data placement across physical devices is causing performance problems.

Use SQL Server Monitor, a separate Sybase product, to pinpoint where the problems are.

Check the entire **sp_sysmon** output during tuning to verify how the changes affect all performance categories.

For more information about using **sp_sysmon** see Chapter 19, "Monitoring SQL Server Performance with sp_sysmon." Pay special attention to the output associated with the discussions in "I/O Device Contention" on page 19-20, "Inserts on Heap Tables" on page 19-25, "Last Page Locks on Heaps" on page 19-43, and "Disk I/O Management" on page 19-66.

Terminology and Concepts

It is important to understand the distinctions between logical or database devices, and physical devices:

The *physical disk* or *physical device* is the actual hardware that stores the data. A *database device* or *logical device* is a portion of a physical disk that has been initialized (with the **disk init** command) for use by SQL Server. A database device can be an operating system file, an entire disk, or a disk partition. See the SQL Server installation and configuration guide for information about specific operating system constraints on disk and file usage.

A *segment* is a named collection of database devices used by a database. The database devices that make up a segment can be located on separate physical devices.

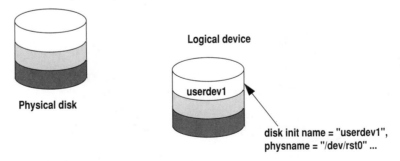

Logical device

userdev1

Physical disk

disk init name = "userdev1",
physname = "/dev/rst0" ...

Figure 13-1: Physical and logical disks

Use the **sp_helpdevice** stored procedure to get information about devices.

Guidelines for Improving I/O Performance

As stated in earlier chapters, overall performance depends in part on how many disk reads occur. Whenever the system administrator can reduce the number of I/Os, performance is likely to improve. Some "golden rules" for improving I/O performance in SQL Server are:

- Spread data across disks to avoid I/O contention.

- Isolate server-wide I/O from database I/O.

- Separate data storage and log storage for frequently updated databases.

- Keep random disk I/O away from sequential disk I/O.

- Mirror devices on separate physical disks.

Each of these guidelines will be discussed in the following sections.

Spreading Data Across Disks to Avoid I/O Contention

Spreading data storage across multiple disks and multiple disk controllers avoids bottlenecks:

- Put databases with critical performance requirements on separate devices. If possible, also use separate controllers from other databases. Use segments as needed for critical tables.

- Put heavily used tables on separate disks.

- Put frequently joined tables on separate disks.

- Use segments to place tables and indexes on their own disks.

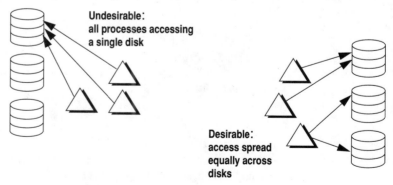

Figure 13-2: Spreading I/O across disks

Isolating Server-Wide I/O from Database I/O

Place system databases with heavy I/O requirements on separate physical disks and controllers from your application databases.

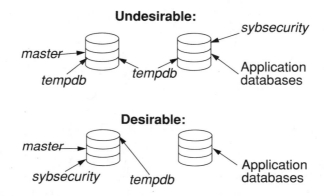

Figure 13-3: Isolating database I/O from server-wide I/O

Where to Place *tempdb*

tempdb is automatically installed on the master device. If more space is needed, *tempdb* can be expanded to other devices. If *tempdb* is expected to be quite active, it should be placed on a disk that is not used for other important database activity. Use the fastest disk available for *tempdb*. It is a heavily used database that affects all processes on the server.

On some UNIX systems, I/O to operating system files is significantly faster than I/O to raw devices. Since *tempdb* is always re-created rather than recovered after a shutdown, you may be able to improve performance by altering *tempdb* onto an operating system file instead of a raw device. You should test this on your own system.

➤ **Note**

Using operating system files for user data devices is not recommended on UNIX systems, since these systems buffer I/O in the operating system. Databases placed on operating system files may not be recoverable after a system crash.

See Chapter 14, "tempdb Performance Issues," for more placement issues and performance tips for *tempdb*.

Where to Place *sybsecurity*

If you use auditing on your SQL Server, the auditing system performs frequent I/O to the *sysaudits* table in the *sybsecurity* database. If your applications perform a significant amount of auditing, place *sybsecurity* on a disk that is not used for tables where fast response time is critical. Placing *sybsecurity* on its own device is optimal.

Also, use the threshold manager to monitor its free space to avoid suspending user transactions if the database fills up.

Keeping Transaction Logs on a Separate Disk

Placing the transaction log on the same device as the data itself is such a common but dangerous reliability problem that both **create database** and **alter database** require the use of the **with override** option if you attempt to put the transaction log on the same device as the data itself. Placing the log on a separate segment:

- Limits log size, which keeps it from competing with other objects for disk space

- Allows use of threshold management techniques to prevent the log from filling up and to automate transaction log dumps

- Improves performance, if the log is placed is on separate physical disk

- Ensures full recovery in the event of hard disk crashes on the data device, if the log is placed on a separate physical disk

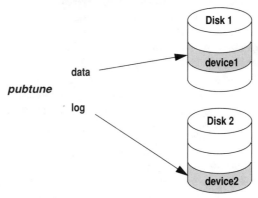

Figure 13-4: Placing log and data on separate physical disks

The log device can perform significant I/O on systems with heavy update activity. SQL Server writes log records to *syslogs* when transactions commit and may need to read log pages into memory for deferred updates or transaction rollbacks.

If your log and data are on the same database devices, the extents allocated to store log pages are not contiguous; log extents and data extents are mixed. When the log is on its own device, the extents tend to be allocated sequentially, reducing disk head travel and seeks, thereby maintaining a higher I/O rate.

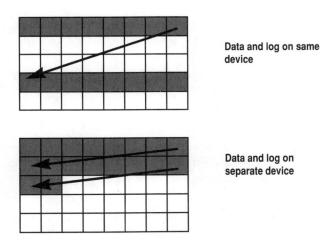

Data and log on same device

Data and log on separate device

Figure 13-5: Disk I/O for the transaction log

If you have created a database without its log on a separate device, see "Moving the Transaction Log to Another Device" in Chapter 14 of the *System Administration Guide* for information about moving the log.

Mirroring a Device on a Separate Disk

If you mirror data, put the mirror on a separate physical disk from the device that it mirrors. Disk hardware failure often results in whole physical disks being lost or unavailable. Do not mirror a database device to another portion of the same physical disk.

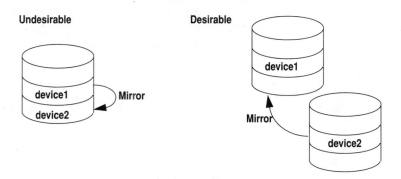

Figure 13-6: Mirroring data to separate physical disks

Mirror on separate disks to minimize performance impact of mirroring.

Device Mirroring Performance Issues

Mirroring is a security and high availability feature that allows SQL Server to duplicate the contents of an entire database device. See Chapter 7, "Mirroring Database Devices," in the *System Administration Guide* for more information on mirroring.

Mirroring is not a performance feature. It can slow the time taken to complete disk writes, since writes go to both disks, either serially or simultaneously. Reads always come from the primary side. Disk mirroring has no effect on the time required to read data.

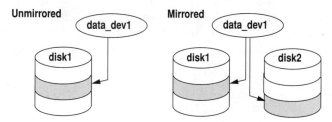

Figure 13-7: Impact of mirroring on write performance

Mirrored devices use one of two modes for disk writes:

- **Noserial** mode can increase the time required to write data. Both writes are started at the same time, and SQL Server waits for both to complete. The time to complete noserial writes is $\max(W_1, W_2)$.

- **Serial** mode increases the time to required write data even more than noserial mode. SQL Server starts the first write, and waits for it to complete before initiating the second write. The time required is W_1+W_2.

Why Use Serial Mode?

Despite its performance impact, serial mode is an important aspect for reliability. In fact, serial mode is the default, because it guards against failures that occur while a write is taking place. Since serial mode waits until the first write is complete before starting the second write, it is impossible for a single failure to affect both disks. Specifying noserial mode improves performance, but you risk losing data if a failure occurs that affects both writes.

◆ *WARNING!*

Unless you are sure that your mirrored database system does not need to be absolutely reliable, do not use noserial mode.

Creating Objects on Segments

Segments are named subsets of the database devices that are available to a given database. A segment is best described as a label that points to one or more database devices. Each database can use up to 32 segments, including the 3 that are created by the system (*system*, *logsegment*, and *default*) when the database is created. Segments label space on one or more logical devices.

Figure 13-8: Segments labeling portions of disks

Tables and indexes are stored on segments. If no segment is named in the **create table** or **create index** statement, then the objects are stored on the default segment for the database. The **sp_placeobject** system procedure can be used to designate the segment to be used for subsequent disk writes. In this way, tables can span multiple segments.

A System Administrator must initialize the device with **disk init**, and the disk must be allocated to the database by the System Administrator or the database owner with **create database** or **alter database**.

Once the devices are available to the database, the database owner or object owners can create segments and place objects on the devices.

If you create a user-defined segment, you can place tables or indexes on that segment with the **create table** and **create index** commands:

```
create table tableA(...) on seg1

create nonclustered index myix on tableB(...)
        on seg2
```

By controlling their location, you can arrange for active tables and indexes to be spread across disks.

Why Use Segments?

Segments can improve throughput by:

- Splitting large tables across disks

- Separating tables and their nonclustered indexes across disks

- Placing the text and image page chain on a separate disk from the table itself where the pointers to the text values are stored

In addition, segments can control space usage:

- A table can never grow larger than its segment allocation; you can use segments to limit table size.

- Tables on other segments cannot impinge on the space allocated to objects on another segment.

- The threshold manager can monitor space usage.

Separating Tables and Indexes

Use segments to isolate tables on one set of disks and nonclustered indexes on another set of disks. By definition, the leaf level of a clustered index is the table data. When you create a clustered index using the **on *segment_name*** clause, the entire table moves to the specified segment, and the clustered index tree is built there. You cannot separate the clustered index from the data pages.

You can achieve performance improvements by placing nonclustered indexes on a separate segment.

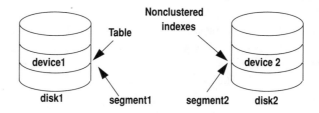

Figure 13-9: Separating a table and its nonclustered indexes

Splitting a Large Table Across Devices

Segments can span multiple devices, so they can be used to spread data across one or more disks. For large, extremely busy tables, this can help balance the I/O load.

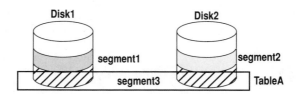

Figure 13-10:Splitting a large table across devices with segments

See "Splitting Tables" in Chapter 16 in the *System Administration Guide* for more information.

Moving Text Storage to a Separate Device

When a table includes a *text* or *image* datatype, the table itself stores a pointer to the text or image value. The actual text or image data is stored on a separate linked list of pages. Writing or reading a text value requires at least two disk accesses, one to read or write the pointer and subsequent reads or writes for the text values. If your application frequently reads or writes these values, you can improve performance by placing the text chain on a separate physical device.

Isolate text and image chains to disks that are not busy with other application-related table or index access.

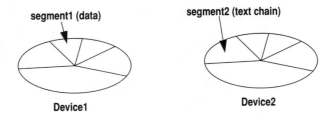

segment1 (data)   segment2 (text chain)

Device1   Device2

Figure 13-11:Placing the text chain on a separate segment

When you create a table with a *text* or *image* column, SQL Server creates a row for the text chain in *sysindexes*. The value in the *name* column is the table name prefixed with a "t"; the *indid* is always 255. Note that if you have multiple *text* or *image* columns in a single table, there is only one text chain. By default, the text chain is placed on the same segment with the table.

You can use **sp_placeobject** to move all future allocations for the text columns to a separate segment. See "Placing Text Pages on a Separate Device" on page 16-13 for more information.

Improving Insert Performance with Partitions

Partitioning a **heap table** creates multiple page chains for the table. This improves the performance of concurrent inserts to the table by reducing contention for the last page of a page chain. Partitioning also makes it possible to distribute a table's I/O over multiple database devices.

You can partition only tables that do not have clustered indexes (heap tables). See "Selecting Tables to Partition" on page 13-16 for additional restrictions.

Page Contention for Inserts

By default, SQL Server stores a table's data in one double-linked set of pages called a **page chain**. If the table does not have a clustered index, SQL Server makes all inserts to the table in the last page of the page chain. When a transaction inserts a row into a table, SQL Server holds an exclusive page lock on the last page while it inserts the row.

If the current last page becomes full, SQL Server allocates and links a new last page.

The single page chain model works well for tables that have modest insert activity. However, as multiple transactions attempt to insert data into the table at the same time, performance problems can occur. Only one transaction at a time can obtain an exclusive lock on the last page, so other concurrent insert transactions block, as shown in Figure 13-12.

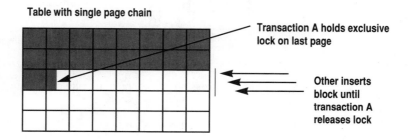

Table with single page chain

Transaction A holds exclusive lock on last page

Other inserts block until transaction A releases lock

Figure 13-12:Page contention during inserts

How Partitions Address Page Contention

A **partition** is another term for a page chain. Partitioning a table creates multiple page chains (partitions) for the table and, therefore, multiple last pages for insert operations. A partitioned table has as many page chains and last pages as it has partitions.

When a transaction inserts data into a partitioned table, SQL Server randomly assigns the transaction to one of the table's partitions (as discussed under "alter table Syntax" on page 13-18). Concurrent inserts are less likely to block, since multiple last pages are available for inserts.

Figure 13-13 shows an example of insert activity in a table with three partitions. Compare this to Figure 13-12, which shows insert activity in a table with a single page chain.

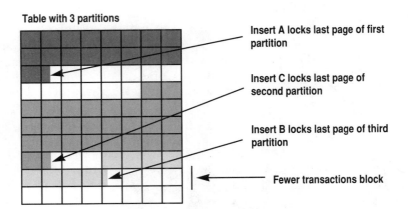

Table with 3 partitions

Insert A locks last page of first partition

Insert C locks last page of second partition

Insert B locks last page of third partition

Fewer transactions block

Figure 13-13:Addressing page contention with partitions

How Partitions Address I/O Contention

Partitioning a table can improve I/O contention when SQL Server writes information in the cache to disk. If a table's segment spans several physical disks, SQL Server distributes the table's partitions across those disks when you create the partitions. When SQL Server flushes pages to disk, I/Os assigned to different physical disks can occur in parallel. See "Speed of Recovery" on page 15-34 for information about when pages are flushed to disk.

To improve I/O performance for partitioned tables, you must ensure that the segment containing the partitioned table is composed of multiple physical devices. Figure 13-14 illustrates the difference between reducing only page contention and reducing both page and I/O contention.

Case 1 reduces page contention, since Table A contains four partitions (and four insertion points). However, I/O performance is not improved, since all I/Os are directed to the same physical disk.

Case 2 reduces I/O contention as well as page contention. Table A and its four partitions reside on a segment that spans two physical disks. Fewer inserts compete for I/O resources, since I/O is distributed over two physical disks.

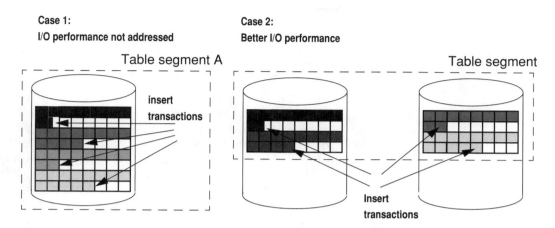

Figure 13-14:Addressing I/O contention with partitions

Read, Update, and Delete Performance

When data in a large table is split over multiple physical devices, it is more likely that small, simultaneous reads, updates, and deletes will take place on separate disks. Because SQL Server distributes a table's partitions over the devices in the table's segment, partitioning large, heavily used tables can improve the overall performance for these statements in those tables. The actual performance benefit depends on many factors, including the number of disk controllers, the hardware platform, and the operating system.

In general, read, update, and delete performance is most improved when a table's data is **evenly** distributed over physical devices. Therefore, if you are partitioning a table to improve the performance of these statements, partition the table before inserting its data. This enables SQL Server to randomly assign inserts to partitions, which helps distribute the data over physical devices in the segment. If you populate a table with data before partitioning it, most of the data remains in the first partition (and the first few physical devices) while other partitions and devices store less data.

Partitioning and Unpartitioning Tables

The following sections explain how to decide which tables to partition and how to use the **partition** and **unpartition** clauses of the **alter table** command.

Selecting Tables to Partition

Heap tables that have large amounts of concurrent insert activity will benefit from partitioning. Partitioning can also reduce I/O contention for certain tables, as discussed under "How Partitions Address I/O Contention" on page 13-15.

If you are unsure whether tables in your database system might benefit from partitioning, use **sp_sysmon** to check for lock contention on the last page of heap tables. It reports contention on both partitioned and unpartitioned heaps. If you discover that the contention is high, one or more tables will likely benefit from partitioning, or from additional partitions.See "Last Page Locks on Heaps" on page 507.

You can partition tables that contain data or tables that are empty. For best performance, partition a table **before** inserting data.

Partitioned tables require slightly more disk space than unpartitioned tables, since SQL Server reserves a dedicated **control page** for each partition. If you create 30 partitions for a table, SQL Server immediately allocates 30 control pages for the table, which cannot be used for storing data.

Restrictions

You cannot partition the following kinds of tables:

- Tables with clustered indexes
- SQL Server system tables
- Tables that are already partitioned

Also, once you have partitioned a table, you cannot use any of the following Transact-SQL commands on the table until you unpartition it:

- **create clustered index**
- **drop table**
- **sp_placeobject**
- **truncate table**
- **alter table** *table_name* **partition** *n*

Restrictions for text and image Datatypes

You can partition tables that use the *text* or *image* datatypes. However, the *text* and *image* columns themselves are not partitioned—they remain on a single page chain. See "text and image Datatypes" in the *SQL Server Reference Manual* for more information about these datatypes.

Cursors and Partitioned Tables

Prior to release 11.0, all of a heap's data was inserted at the end of a single page chain. This meant that a cursor scan of a heap table could read all data up to and including the final insertion made to that table, even if insertions took place after the cursor scan started.

With release 11.0, data can be inserted into one of many page chains of a partitioned table. The physical insertion point may be before or after the current position of a cursor scan. This means that a cursor scan against a partitioned table is **not** guaranteed to scan the final inserts made to that table; the physical location of the insert is unknown.

If your cursor operations require all inserts to be made at the end of a single page chain, **do not** partition the table used in the cursor scan.

Partitioning Tables

The three basic steps for partitioning a table are:

1. Create the segment (with its associated database devices)
2. Create the table on the segment
3. Partition the table using the **alter table** command's **partition** clause

It is important to plan the number of devices for the table's segment if you want to improve I/O performance. For best performance, use dedicated physical disks, rather than portions of disks, as database devices. Also make sure that no other objects share the devices with the partitioned table. See Chapter 16, "Creating and Using Segments," in the *System Administration Guide* for guidelines for creating segments.

After you have created the segment, create the new table on the segment using the **create table...on *segment_name*** command. This creates a table with a single page chain. Once the table exists on the segment, you can create additional page chains using the **alter table** command with the **partition** clause.

alter table Syntax

The syntax for using the **partition** clause to **alter table** is:

```
alter table table_name partition n
```

where *table_name* is the name of the table and *n* is the number of partitions (page chains) to create.

➤ **Note**

You cannot include the **alter table...partition** command in a user-defined transaction.

For example, enter the following command to create 10 partitions in a table named *historytab*:

```
alter table historytab partition 10
```

SQL Server creates the specified number of partitions in the table and automatically distributes those partitions over the database devices in the table's segment. SQL Server assigns partitions to devices so that they are distributed evenly across the segment. Table 13-1 illustrates how SQL Server assigns 5 partitions to 3, 5, and 12 devices, respectively.

Table 13-1: Assigning partitions to segments

Partition ID	Device (D) Assignments for Segment With		
	3 Devices	5 Devices	12 Devices
Partition 1	D1	D1	D1, D6, D11
Partition 2	D2	D2	D2, D7, D12
Partition 3	D3	D3	D3, D8, D11
Partition 4	D1	D4	D4, D9, D12
Partition 5	D2	D5	D5, D10, D11

Any data that was in the table before invoking **alter table** remains in the first partition. Partitioning a table does not move the table's data. If a partition runs out of space on the device to which it is assigned, it will try to allocate space from any device in the table's segment. This behavior is called **page stealing**.

After you partition the table, SQL Server randomly assigns each insert transaction (including internal transactions) to one of the table's partitions. Once a transaction is assigned to a partition, all insert statements within that transaction go to the same partition. You cannot assign transactions to specific partitions.

SQL Server manages partitioned tables transparently to users and applications. Partitioned tables appear to have a single page chain when queried or when viewed with most utilities. The **dbcc checktable** and **dbcc checkdb** commands list the number of data pages in each partition. See Chapter 17, "Checking Database Consistency," in the *System Administration Guide* for information about **dbcc**.

Effects on System Tables

For an unpartitioned table with no clustered index, SQL Server stores a pointer to the last page of the page chain in the *root* column of the *sysindexes* row for that table. (The *indid* value for such a row is 0.)

When you partition a table, the *root* value for that table becomes obsolete. SQL Server inserts a row into the *syspartitions* table for each partition, and allocates a control page and first page for each partition. Each row in *syspartitions* identifies a unique partition, along with the location of its first page, control page, and other status information. A partition's control page functions like the *sysindexes.root* value did for the unpartitioned table—it keeps track of the last page in the page chain.

➤ *Note*

Partitioning or unpartitioning a table does not affect the *sysindexes* rows for that table's nonclustered indexes. (The *indid* values for these rows are greater than 1.) *root* values for the table's nonclustered indexes still point to the root page of each index, since the indexes themselves are not partitioned.

See "sysindexes" and "syspartitions" in the *SQL Server Reference Supplement* for more details about these system tables.

Getting Information About Partitions

To display information about a table's partitions, first use the database in which the table resides. Then enter the **sp_help** or **sp_helpartition** stored procedure with the table's name. The syntax of **sp_helpartition** is:

```
sp_helpartition table_name
```

where *table_name* is the name of the table to examine. For example:

```
    sp_helpartition titles
```

```
partitionid firstpage    controlpage
----------- ------------  -----------
          1          145          146
          2         1025         1026
          3         2049         2050
          4          312          313
          5         1032         1033
          6         2056         2057
          7          376          377
```

sp_helpartition displays the partition number, first page number, and control page number for each partition in the specified table. See "Effects on System Tables" on page 13-20 for information about the control page. **sp_help** displays this same partition information when you specify the table's name with the procedure.

dbcc checktable and dbcc checkdb

The **dbcc checktable** and **dbcc checkdb** commands show the number of data pages in each of a table's partitions. See Chapter 17, "Checking Database Consistency," in the *System Administration Guide* for information about **dbcc**.

Unpartitioning Tables

Unpartitioning a table concatenates the table's multiple partitions into a single partition (page chain). Unpartitioning a table does not move the table's data.

To unpartition a table, use the **alter table** command with the **unpartition** clause. The syntax is:

```
alter table table_name unpartition
```

where *table_name* is the name of the partitioned table.

SQL Server joins the previous and next pointers of the multiple partitions to create a single page chain. It removes all entries for the table from *syspartitions* and deallocates all control pages. The new last page of the single partition is then stored and maintained in the *root* column of *sysindexes*.

For example, to unpartition a table named *historytab*, enter the command:

```
alter table historytab unpartition
```

Changing the Number of Partitions

To change the number of partitions in a table, first unpartition the table using **alter table** with the **unpartition** clause (see "Unpartitioning Tables" on page 13-21). Then re-invoke **alter table** with the **partition** clause to specify the new number of partitions. This does not move the existing data in the table.

You cannot use the **partition** clause with a table that is already partitioned.

For example, if a table named *historytab* contains 10 partitions, and you want the table to have 20 partitions instead, enter the commands:

```
alter table historytab unpartition
alter table historytab partition 20
```

Partition Configuration Parameters

The default SQL Server configuration works well for most servers that use partitioned tables. If you require very large numbers of partitions, you may want to change the default values for the **partition groups** and **partition spinlock ratio** configuration parameters. See Chapter 11, "Setting Configuration Parameters," in the *System Administration Guide* for more information.

Working with tempdb

The current chapter has discussed some of the consequences of improving database partitioning and placement of database objects. The next chapter covers the correct sizing and placement of the temporary database *tempdb*, one of the most active and potentially troublesome objects in a database.

14 *tempdb* Performance Issues

What Is *tempdb*?

tempdb is a database that is used by all users of SQL Server. Anyone can create objects in *tempdb*. Many processes use it silently. It is a server-wide resource that is used primarily for:

- Internal processing of sorts, creating worktables, reformatting, and so on
- Storing temporary tables and indexes created by users

Many applications use stored procedures that purposely create tables in *tempdb* to expedite complex joins or to perform other complex data analysis that is not easily performed in a single step.

How Can *tempdb* Affect Performance?

Good management of *tempdb* is critical to the overall performance of SQL Server. *tempdb* cannot be overlooked or left in a default state. It is the most dynamic database on many servers, and should receive special attention.

If planned for in advance, most problems related to *tempdb* can be avoided. These are the kinds of things that can go wrong if *tempdb* is not sized or placed properly:

- *tempdb* fills up frequently, generating error messages to users who must resubmit their queries when space becomes available.
- Sorting is slow, and users do not understand why their queries have such uneven performance.
- User queries are temporarily locked from creating temporary tables because of locks on system tables.
- Heavy use of *tempdb* objects flushes other pages out of the data cache.

Main Solution Areas for *tempdb* Performance

These main areas can be addressed easily:

- Sizing *tempdb* correctly for all SQL Server activity
- Placing *tempdb* optimally to minimize contention
- Binding *tempdb* to its own data cache

- Minimizing the locking of resources within *tempdb*

Types and Use of Temporary Tables

The use or misuse of user-defined temporary tables can greatly affect the overall performance of SQL Server and your applications.

Temporary tables can be quite useful, often reducing the work the server has to do. However, temporary tables can add to the size requirement of *tempdb*. Some temporary tables are truly temporary, and others are permanent.

tempdb is used for three types of tables:

- Truly temporary tables
- Regular user tables
- Worktables

Truly Temporary Tables

You can create truly temporary tables by using "#" as the first character of the table name:

```
create table #temptable (...)
```

or:

```
select select_list
    into #temptable ...
```

Temporary tables:

- Exist only for the duration of the user session or for the scope of the procedure that creates them
- Cannot be shared between user connections
- Are automatically dropped at the end of the session or procedure (or can be dropped manually)

When you create indexes on temporary tables, the indexes are stored in *tempdb*:

```
create index tempix on #temptable(col1)
```

Regular User Tables

You can create regular user tables in *tempdb* by specifying the database name in the command that creates the table:

```
create table tempdb..temptable
```

or:

```
select select_list
    into tempdb..temptable
```

Regular user tables in *tempdb:*

- Can persist across sessions
- Can be used by bulk copy operations
- Can be shared by granting permissions on them
- Must be explicitly dropped by the owner (else, they are removed when SQL Server is restarted)

You can create indexes in *tempdb* on permanent temporary tables:

```
create index tempix on tempdb..temptable(col1)
```

Worktables

Worktables are automatically created in *tempdb* by SQL Server for sorts and other internal server processes. These tables:

- Are never shared
- Disappear as soon as the command completes

Initial Allocation of *tempdb*

When you install SQL Server, *tempdb* is 2MB, and is located completely on the master device. This is typically the first database that a System Administrator needs to alter, in size and location. The more users on the server, the larger *tempdb* needs to be. It can be altered onto the master device or other devices. Depending on your needs, you may want to stripe *tempdb* across several devices.

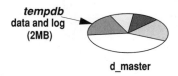

tempdb
data and log
(2MB)

d_master

Figure 14-1: tempdb default allocation

Use **sp_helpdb** to see the size and status of *tempdb*. The following example shows *tempdb* defaults at installation time:

```
1> sp_helpdb tempdb
name        db_size  owner   dbid   created      status
---------   -------  ------  -----  ----------   --------------------
tempdb      2.0 MB   sa      2      May 22, 1995 select into/bulkcopy


device_frag  size     usage          free kbytes
-----------  -------  ------------   ---------
master       2.0 MB   data and log   1248
```

Sizing *tempdb*

tempdb needs to be big enough to handle the following processes for every concurrent SQL Server user:

- Internal sorts
- Other internal worktables that are created for **distinct, group by**, and **order by**, for reformatting and for the OR strategy
- Temporary tables (those created with "#" as the first character of their names)
- Indexes on temporary tables
- Regular user tables in *tempdb*
- Procedures built by dynamic SQL

Some applications may perform better if you use temporary tables to split up multi-table joins. This strategy is often used for:

- Cases where the optimizer does not choose a good query plan for a query that joins more than four tables
- Queries that exceed the 16-table join limit
- Very complex queries
- Applications that need to filter data as an intermediate step

You might also use *tempdb* to:

- Denormalize several tables into a few temporary tables
- Normalize a denormalized table in order to do aggregate processing

Information for Sizing *tempdb*

To estimate the correct size for *tempdb*, you need the following information:

- Maximum number of concurrent user processes (an application may require more than one process)
- Size of sorts, as reported by **set statistics io** writes, for queries with **order by** clauses that are not supported by an index
- Size of worktables, as reported by **set statistics io** writes, for reformatting, **group by**, **distinct**, and the OR strategy (but not for sorts)
- Number of steps in the query plans for reformatting, **group by**, and so on, which indicates the number of temporary tables created
- Number of local and remote stored procedures and/or user sessions that create temporary tables and indexes
- Size of temporary tables and indexes, as reported by **statistics io**
- Number of temporary tables and indexes created per stored procedure

See Chapter 5, "Estimating the Size of Tables and Indexes," for more information about gathering data for sizing *tempdb*.

Sizing Formula

The 25 percent padding in the calculations below covers other undocumented server uses of *tempdb* and covers the errors in our estimates.

1. Compute the size required for usual processing:

Sorts	Users * Sort_size		_____
Other	Users * Worktable_size	+	_____
Subtotal		=	_____
		*	_____ # of query plan steps
Total for usual processing		=	_____

2. Compute the size required for temporary tables and indexes:

Temporary tables	Procs* Table_size * Table_number		_____
Indexes	Procs * Index_size * Index_number	+	_____
Total for temporary objects		=	_____

3. Add the two totals, and add 25 percent for padding:

Processing		_____
Temp tables	+	_____
Estimate	=	_____
	*	1.25
Final estimate	=	_____

Example of *tempdb* Sizing

1. Processing requirements:

Sorts	55 users * 15 pages =	825 pages
Other	55 users * 9 pages =	495 pages
Subtotal	=	1320 pages
	*	3 steps
Total for usual processing		3960 pages or 8.2MB

2. Temporary table/index requirements:

Temporary tables	190 procs * 10 pages * 4 tables =	7600 pages
Indexes	190 procs * 2 pages * 5 indexes =	190 pages
Total for temporary objects		7790 pages, or 16MB

3. Add the two totals, and add 25 percent for padding:

Processing		8.2MB
Temp tables	+	16MB
Estimate	=	24.2MB
	*	*1.25
Final estimate	=	30MB

Placing *tempdb*

Keep *tempdb* on separate physical disks from your critical application databases at all costs. Use the fastest disks available. If your platform supports solid state devices and your *tempdb* use is a bottleneck for your applications, use them.

These are the principles to apply when deciding where to place *tempdb*. Note that the pages in *tempdb* should be as contiguous as possible because of its dynamic nature.

- Expand *tempdb* on the same device as the *master* database. If the original logical device is completely full, you can initialize another database (logical) device on the same physical device, provided there is space. This choice does not help improve performance by spreading I/O across devices.

- Expand *tempdb* on another device, but not one that is used by a critical application. This option can help improve performance.

- Remember that logical devices are mirrored, not databases. If you mirror the master device, you create a mirror of all portions of the databases that reside on the master device. If the mirror uses **serial** writes, this can have a serious performance impact if your *tempdb* database is heavily used.

- Drop the master device from the *default* and *logsegment* segments.

Dropping the *master* Device from *tempdb* Segments

By default, the *system*, *default*, and *logsegment* segments for *tempdb* all include its 2MB allocation on the master device. When you allocate new devices to *tempdb*, they automatically become part of all three segments. Once you allocate a second device to *tempdb*, you can drop the master device from the *default* and *logsegment* segments. This way, you can be sure that the worktables and other temporary tables in *tempdb* are not created wholly or partially on the master device.

To drop the master device from the segments:

1. Alter *tempdb* onto another device, if you have not already done so. The *default* or *logsegment* segment must include at least one database device. For example:

```
alter database tempdb on tune3 = 20
```

2. Issue a **use tempdb** command, and then drop the master device from the segment:

```
sp_dropsegment "default", tempdb, master

sp_dropdegment logsegment, tempdb, master
```

3. If you want to verify that the *default* segment no longer includes the master device, issue the command:

```
select dbid, name, segmap
from sysusages, sysdevices
where sysdevices.low <= sysusages.size + vstart
   and sysdevices.high >= sysusages.size + vstart -1
   and dbid = 2
   and (status = 2 or status = 3)
```

The *segmap* column should report "1" for any allocations on master, indicating that only the *system* segment still uses the device:

```
dbid    name                 segmap
------  ---------------  -----------
     2  master                     1
     2  tune3                      7
```

Spanning Disks Leads to Poor Performance

It is not a good idea to have *tempdb* span disks. If you do, your temporary tables or worktables will span disk media, and this will definitely slow things down. It is better for *tempdb* to have a single, contiguous allocation.

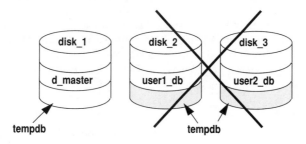

Figure 14-2: tempdb spanning disks

Binding *tempdb* to Its Own Cache

Under normal SQL Server use, *tempdb* makes heavy use of the data cache as temporary tables are created, populated, and then dropped.

Assigning *tempdb* to its own data cache:

- Keeps the activity on temporary objects from flushing other objects out of the default data cache

- Helps spread I/O between multiple caches

Commands for Cache Binding

Use the **sp_cacheconfig** and **sp_poolconfig** commands to create named data caches and to configure pools of a given size for large I/O. Only a System Administrator can configure caches and pools. For instructions on configuring named caches and pools, see "Configuring Data Caches" in Chapter 9 of the *System Administration Guide*. Once the caches have been configured, and the server has been restarted, you can bind *tempdb* to the new cache:

```
sp_bindcache "tempdb_cache", tempdb
```

Temporary Tables and Locking

Locking in *tempdb* can be caused by creating or dropping temporary tables and their indexes.

When users create tables in *tempdb*, information about the tables must be stored in system tables such as *sysobjects*, *syscolumns*, and *sysindexes*. Updates to these tables requires a table lock. If multiple user processes are creating and dropping tables in *tempdb*, heavy contention can occur on the system tables. Worktables created internally do not store information in system tables.

If contention for *tempdb* system tables is a problem with applications that must repeatedly create and drop the same set of temporary tables, try creating the tables at the start of the application. Then use **insert...select** to populate them, and **truncate table** to remove all of the data rows. Although **insert...select** requires logging and is slower than **select into**, it can provide a solution to the locking problem.

Minimizing Logging in *tempdb*

Even though the **trunc log on checkpoint** database option is turned on in *tempdb*, changes to *tempdb* are still written to the transaction log. You can reduce log activity in *tempdb* by:

- Using **select into** instead of **create table** and **insert**
- Selecting only the columns you need into the temporary tables

Minimizing Logging with *select into*

When you create and populate temporary tables in *tempdb*, use the **select into** command, rather than **create table** and **insert...select** whenever possible. The **select into/bulkcopy** database option is turned on by default in *tempdb* to enable this behavior.

select into operations are faster because they are only minimally logged. Only the allocation of data pages is tracked, not the actual changes for each data row. Each data insert in an **insert...select** query is fully logged, resulting in more overhead.

Minimizing Logging via Shorter Rows

If the application creating tables in *tempdb* uses only a few columns of a table, you can minimize the number and size of log records by:

- Selecting just the columns you need for the application, rather than using **select *** in queries that insert data into the tables

- Limiting the rows selected to just the rows that the applications requires

Both of these suggestions also keep the size of the tables themselves smaller.

Optimizing Temporary Tables

Many uses of temporary tables are simple and brief and require little optimization. But if your applications require multiple accesses to tables in *tempdb*, you should examine them for possible optimization strategies. Usually, this involves splitting out the creation and indexing of the table from the access to it by using more than one procedure or batch.

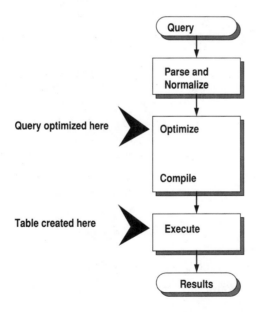

Figure 14-3: Optimizing and creating temporary tables

When you create a table in the same stored procedure or batch where it is used, the query optimizer cannot determine how large the table is, since the work of creating the table has not been performed at the time the query is optimized. This applies to temporary tables and to regular user tables.

The optimizer assumes that any such table has 10 data pages and 100 rows. If the table is really large, this assumption can lead the optimizer to choose a suboptimal query plan.

These two techniques can improve the optimization of temporary tables:

- Creating indexes on temporary tables
- Breaking complex uses of temporary tables into multiple batches or procedures to provide information for the optimizer

Creating Indexes on Temporary Tables

You can define indexes on temporary tables. In many cases, these indexes can improve the performance of queries that use *tempdb*. The optimizer uses these indexes just like indexes on ordinary user tables. The only requirements are:

- The index must exist at the time the query using it is optimized. You cannot create an index and then use it in a query in the same batch or procedure.

- The statistics page must exist. If you create the temporary table and create the index on an empty table, SQL Server does not create a statistics page. If you then insert data rows, the optimizer has no statistics.

- The optimizer may choose a suboptimal plan if rows have been added or deleted since the index was created or since **update statistics** was run.

Especially in complex procedures that create temporary tables and then perform numerous operations on them, providing an index for the optimizer can greatly increase performance.

Breaking *tempdb* Uses into Multiple Procedures

For example, this query causes optimization problems with *#huge_result*:

```
create proc base_proc
as
    select *
        into #huge_result
        from ...
    select *
        from tab,
        #huge_result where ...
```

You can achieve better performance by using two procedures. When the first procedure calls the second one, the optimizer can determine the size of the table:

```
create proc base__proc
as
    select *
        into #huge_result
        from ...
    exec select_proc

create proc select_proc
as
    select *
        from tab, #huge_result where ...
```

If the processing for *#huge_result* requires multiple accesses, joins, or other processes such as looping with **while**, creating an index on *#huge_result* may improve performance. Create the index in *base_proc*, so that it is available when *select_proc* is optimized.

Creating Nested Procedures with Temporary Tables

You need to take an extra step to create the procedures described above. You cannot create *base_proc* until *select_proc* exists, and you cannot create *select_proc* until the temporary table exists. Here are the steps:

1. Create the temporary table outside the procedure. It can be empty; it just needs to exist and to have columns that are compatible with *select_proc*:

```
select * into #huge_result from ... where 1 = 2
```

2. Create procedure *select_proc*, as shown above.

3. Drop *#huge_result*.

4. Create procedure *base_proc*.

Configuring Memory Use

In addition to object placement and sizing, the proper configuration of on-board memory is one of the most important performance factors.

Since SQL Server need not perform a disk read to access pages cached in internal memory, the more often you can assure that frequently-used pages will be found in cache, the better your application's performance will be.

Chapter 15, "Memory Use and Performance," discusses how memory affects performance, cache strategies, and how to determine which queries might benefit from named caches and large I/O configurations Topics covered include:

- How SQL Server uses memory and its cache
- The procedure cache
- The data cache
- User-configured data caches and performance issues
- The audit queue

15 Memory Use and Performance

How Memory Affects Performance

In general, the more memory available, the faster SQL Server's response time will be. Memory conditions that can cause poor performance are:

- Not enough total memory is allocated to SQL Server.
- Other SQL Server configuration options are set too high, resulting in poor allocation of memory.
- Total data cache size is too small.
- Procedure cache size is too small.
- Only the default cache is configured on an SMP system with several active CPUs, leading to contention for the data cache.
- User-configured data cache sizes are not appropriate for specific user applications.
- Configured I/O sizes are not appropriate for specific queries.
- Audit queue size is not appropriate.

Chapter 8, "Configuring Memory" in the *System Administration Guide* describes the process of determining the best memory configuration values for SQL Server, and the memory needs of other server configuration options.

Memory Fundamentals

Having ample memory reduces disk I/O, which improves performance, since memory access is much faster than disk access. When a user issues a query, the data and index pages must be in memory, or read into memory, in order to examine the values on them. If the pages already reside in memory, SQL Server does not need to perform disk I/O.

Adding more memory is cheap and easy, but developing around memory problems is expensive. Give SQL Server as much memory as possible.

How Much Memory to Configure

Memory must not only be available, it must also be properly configured. Memory is the most important configuration option. Setting this parameter incorrectly affects performance dramatically.

To optimize the size of memory for your system, a System Administrator calculates the memory required for the operating system and other uses and subtracts this from the total available physical memory.

If SQL Server requests too little memory:

- SQL Server may not start.
- If it does start, SQL Server may access disk more frequently.

If SQL Server requests too much memory:

- SQL Server may not start.
- If it does start, the operating system page fault rate will rise significantly and the operating system may need to be reconfigured to compensate.

Chapter 8, "Configuring Memory," in the *System Administration Guide* provides a thorough discussion of:

- How to configure the total amount of memory that SQL Server uses
- Other configurable parameters that use memory, affecting the amount of memory left for processing queries

The amount of memory available to SQL Server is set by the configuration parameter **total memory**. When SQL Server starts, it allocates memory for the executable and other static memory needs. What remains after all other memory needs have been met is available for the procedure cache and data cache.

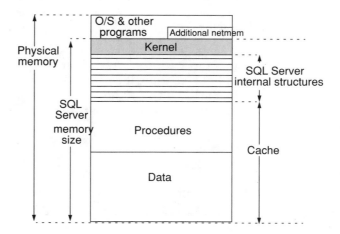

Figure 15-1: How SQL Server uses memory

A System Administrator can change the division of memory available to these two caches by changing **procedure cache percent**. Users can see the amount of memory available by executing **sp_configure**:

```
sp_configure "total memory"
```

See Chapter 8, "Configuring Memory," in the *System Administration Guide* for a full discussion of SQL Server memory configuration.

Caches on SQL Server

The memory that remains after SQL Server allocates all of the memory needs described above is allocated to:

- The **procedure cache** – used for query plans, stored procedures and triggers.
- The **data cache** – used for all data, index, and log pages. The data cache can be divided into separate, named caches, with specific databases or database objects bound to specific caches.

The split between the procedure cache and the data caches is determined by configuration parameters.

Procedure Cache

SQL Server maintains an MRU/LRU chain of stored procedure query plans. As users execute stored procedures, SQL Server looks in the procedure cache for a query plan to use. If a query plan is available, it is placed on the MRU end of the chain and execution begins.

If no plan is in memory, or if all copies are in use, the query tree for the procedure is read from the *sysprocedures* table. It is then optimized, using the parameters provided to the procedure, and put on the MRU end of the chain, and execution begins. Plans at the LRU end of the page chain that are not in use are aged out of the cache.

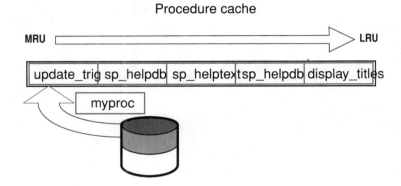

Figure 15-2: The procedure cache

The memory allocated for the procedure cache holds the optimized query plans (and occasionally trees) for all batches, including any triggers.

If more than one user uses a procedure or trigger simultaneously, there will be multiple copies of it in cache. If the procedure cache is too small, users trying to execute stored procedures or queries that fire triggers receive an error message, and have to resubmit the query. Space becomes available when unused plans age out of the cache.

An increase in procedure cache size causes a corresponding decrease in data cache size.

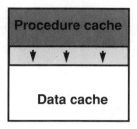

Figure 15-3: Effect of increasing procedure cache size on the data cache

When you first install SQL Server, the default procedure cache size is configured as 20 percent of memory that remains after other memory needs have been met. The optimum value for procedure cache varies from application to application, and it may also vary as usage patterns change throughout the day, week, or month. The configuration parameter to set the size, **procedure cache percent**, is documented in Chapter 11 of the *System Administration Guide*.

Getting Information About the Procedure Cache Size

When SQL Server is started, the error log states how much procedure cache is available.

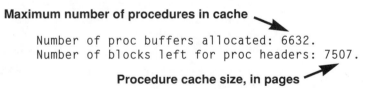

Figure 15-4: Procedure cache size messages in the error log

proc buffers

The number of "proc buffers" represents the maximum number of compiled procedural objects that can reside in the procedure cache at one time. In this example, no more than 6632 compiled objects can reside in the procedure cache simultaneously.

proc headers

This indicates number of 2K pages dedicated to the procedure cache. In this example, 7507 pages are dedicated to the procedure cache. Each object in cache requires at least one page.

Procedure Cache Sizing

How big should the procedure cache be? On a production server, you want to minimize the procedure reads from disk. When users need to execute a procedure, SQL Server should be able to find an unused tree or plan in the procedure cache for the most common procedures. The percentage of times the server finds an available plan in cache is called the **cache hit ratio**. Keeping a high cache hit ratio for procedures in cache improves performance.

The formulas in Figure 15-5 make a good starting point.

$$\text{Procedure cache size} = \frac{\text{(Max \# of concurrent users)} * }{\text{(Size of largest plan)} * 1.25}$$

$$\text{Minimum procedure cache size needed} = \frac{\text{(\# of main procedures)} * }{\text{(Average plan size)}}$$

Figure 15-5: Formulas for sizing the procedure cache

If you have nested stored procedures—procedure A calls procedure B, which calls procedure C—all of them need to be in the cache at the same time. Add the sizes for nested procedures, and use the largest sum in place of "Size of largest plan" in the formula in Figure 15-5.

Remember, when you increase the size of the procedure cache, you decrease the size of the data cache.

The minimum procedure cache size is the smallest amount of memory that allows at least one copy of each frequently used compiled object to reside in cache.

Estimating Stored Procedure Size

To get a rough estimate of the size of a single stored procedure, view, or trigger, use:

```
select(count(*) / 8) +1
    from sysprocedures
where id = object_id("procedure_name")
```

For example, to find the size of the *titleid_proc* in *pubs2*:

```
select(count(*) / 8) +1
    from sysprocedures
where id = object_id("titleid_proc")
- - - - - - - - - - -
           3
```

Monitoring Procedure Cache Performance

sp_sysmon reports on stored procedure executions and the number of times that stored procedures need to be read from disk. For more information, see "Procedure Cache Management" on page 19-61.

Procedure Cache Errors

If there is not enough memory to load another query tree or plan, SQL Server reports Error 701. If the maximum number of compiled objects is already in use, SQL Server also reports an Error 701.

The Data Cache

After other memory demands have been satisfied, all remaining space is available in the data cache. The data cache contains pages from recently accessed objects, typically:

- *sysobjects*, *sysindexes*, and other system tables for each database
- Active log pages for each database
- The higher levels of frequently used indexes and parts of the lower levels
- Parts of frequently accessed tables

Default Cache at Installation Time

When you first install SQL Server, it has a single data cache which is used by all SQL Server processes and objects for data, index, and log pages.

The following pages describe the way this single data cache is used. "Named Data Caches" on page 15-12 describes how to improve performance by dividing the data cache into named caches, and how to bind particular objects to these named caches. Most of the concepts on aging, buffer washing, and caching strategies apply to both the user-defined data caches and the default data cache.

Page Aging in Data Cache

The SQL Server data cache is managed on a most-recently-used/least-recently-used (MRU/LRU) basis. As pages in the cache age, they enter a wash area, where any dirty pages (pages that have been modified while in memory) are written to disk. There are some exceptions to this:

- A special strategy ages out index pages and **OAM pages** more slowly than data pages. These pages are accessed frequently in certain applications, and keeping them in cache can significantly reduce disk reads. See "number of index trips" on page 11-22 and "number of oam trips" on page 11-23 of the *System Administration Guide* for more information.

- For queries that scan heaps or tables with clustered indexes, or perform nonclustered index scans, SQL Server may choose to use a cache replacement strategy that does not flush other pages out of the cache with pages that are used only once for the entire query.

- The checkpoint process tries to ensure that if SQL Server needs to be restarted, the recovery process can be completed in a reasonable period of time. When the checkpoint process estimates that the number of changes to a database will take longer to recover than the configured value of the **recovery interval** parameter, it traverses the cache, writing dirty pages to disk. A housekeeper task also writes dirty pages to disk when idle time is available between user processes.

Effect of Data Cache on Retrievals

Consider a series of random select statements that are executed over a period of time. If the cache is empty initially, the first **select** statement is guaranteed to require disk I/O. As more queries are executed and the cache is being filled, there is an increasing probability that one or more page requests can be satisfied by the cache, thereby reducing the average response time of the set of retrievals. Once the cache is filled, there is a fixed probability of finding a desired page in the cache from that point forward.

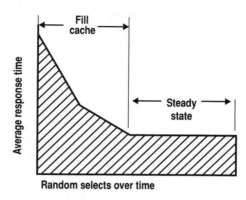

Figure 15-6: Effects of random selects on the data cache

If the cache is smaller than the total number of used pages, there is a chance that a given statement will have to perform disk I/O. A cache does not reduce the maximum possible response time, but it does decrease the likelihood that the maximum delay will be suffered by a particular process.

Effect of Data Modifications on the Cache

The behavior of the cache in the presence of update transactions is more complicated than for retrievals. There is still an initial period during which the cache fills. Then, because cache pages are being modified, there is a point at which the cache must begin writing those pages to disk before it can load other pages. Over time, the amount of writing and reading stabilizes, and subsequent transactions have a given probability of requiring a disk read and another probability of causing a disk write. The steady-state period is interrupted by checkpoints, which cause the cache to write all dirty pages to disk.

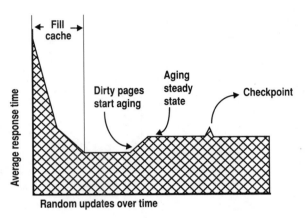

Figure 15-7: Effects of random data modifications on the data cache

Data Cache Performance

Data cache performance can be observed by examining the **cache hit ratio**, the percentage of page requests that are serviced by the cache. One hundred percent is outstanding, but implies that your data cache is as large as the data, or at least large enough to contain all the pages of your frequently used tables and indexes. A low percentage of cache hits indicates that the cache may be too small for the current application load. Very large tables with random page access generally show a low cache hit ratio.

Testing Data Cache Performance

It is important to consider the behavior of the data and procedure caches when you measure the performance of a system. When a test begins, the cache can be in any one of the following states:

- Empty
- Fully randomized
- Partially randomized
- Deterministic

An empty or fully randomized cache yields repeatable test results because the cache is in the same state from one test run to another. A partially randomized or deterministic cache contains pages left by transactions that were just executed. When testing, such pages could be the result of a previous iteration of the test. In such cases, if the next test steps request those pages, then no disk I/O will be needed.

Such a situation can bias the results away from a purely random test and lead to inaccurate performance estimates. The best testing strategy is to start with an empty cache or to make sure that all test steps access random parts of the database. For more precise testing, you need to be sure that the mix of queries executed during the tests accesses the database in patterns that are consistent with the planned mix of user queries on your system.

Cache Hit Ratio for a Single Query

To see the cache hit ratio for a single query, use **set statistics io** to see the number of logical and physical reads, and **set showplan on** to see the I/O size used by the query.

To compute the cache hit ratio, use the formula in Figure 15-8.

$$\text{Cache hit ratio} = \frac{\text{Logical reads - (Physical reads * Pages per IO)}}{\text{Logical reads}}$$

Figure 15-8: Formula for computing the cache hit ratio

With **statistics io**, physical reads are reported in I/O-size units. If a query uses 16K I/O, it reads 8 pages with each I/O operation. If **statistics io** reports 50 physical reads, it has read 400 pages. Use **showplan** to see the I/O size used by a query.

Cache Hit Ratio Information from *sp_sysmon*

The **sp_sysmon** system procedure reports on cache hits and misses for:

- All caches on SQL Server
- The default data cache
- Any user-configured caches

The server-wide report provides the total number of cache searches and the percentage of hits and misses. See "Cache Statistics Summary (All Caches)" on page 19-50.

For each cache, the report contains the search, hit and miss statistics and also reports on the number of times that a needed buffer was found in the wash section. See "Cache Management By Cache" on page 19-54.

Named Data Caches

When you install SQL Server, it has a single default data cache with a 2K memory pool. To improve performance, you can split this cache into multiple named data caches, and bind databases or database objects to them.

Named data caches are not a substitute for careful query optimization and indexing. In fact, splitting the large default cache into smaller caches and restricting I/O to them can lead to worse performance. For example, if you bind a single table to a cache, and it makes poor use of the space there, no other objects on SQL Server can use that memory.

You can also configure 4K, 8K, and 16K memory pools in both user-defined data caches and the default data caches, allowing SQL Server to perform large I/O.

Named Data Caches and Performance

Adding named data caches can improve performance in the following ways:

- When changes are made to a cache by any user process, a **spinlock** denies all other processes access to the cache. Although spinlocks are held for extremely brief durations, they can slow performance in multiprocessor systems with high transaction rates. When you configure multiple caches, each is controlled by a separate spinlock, increasing concurrency on systems with multiple CPUs.

- You can configure caches large enough to hold critical tables and indexes. This keeps other server activity from contending for cache space, and speeds up queries uses these tables since the needed pages are always found in cache.

- You can bind a "hot" table—a table in high demand by user applications—to one cache and indexes on the table to other caches to increase concurrency.

- You can create a cache large enough to hold the "hot pages" of a table where a high percentage of the queries reference only a portion of the table. For example, if a table contains data for a year, but 75% of the queries reference data from the most recent month (about 8 percent of the table), configuring a cache of about 10% of the table size provides room to keep the most frequently used pages in cache, with some space for the less frequently used pages.

- You can assign tables or databases used in decision support (DSS) to specific caches with large I/O configured. This keeps DSS applications from contending for cache space with online transaction processing (OLTP) applications. DSS applications typically access large numbers of sequential pages, and OLTP applications typically access relatively few random pages.

- You can bind *tempdb* to its own cache. All processes that create worktables or temporary tables use *tempdb*, so binding it to its own cache keeps its cache use from contending with other user processes. Proper sizing of *tempdb*'s cache can keep most *tempdb* activity in memory for many applications. If this cache is large enough, *tempdb* activity can avoid performing I/O.

- You can bind a database's log to a cache, again reducing contention for cache space and access to the cache.

Most of these possible uses for named data caches have the greatest impact on multiprocessor systems with high transaction rates or frequent DSS queries and multiple users. Some of them can increase performance on single CPU systems when they lead to improved utilization of memory and reduce I/O.

Large I/Os and Performance

You can configure the default cache and any named caches you create for large I/O by splitting a cache into pools. The default I/O size is 2K, one SQL Server data page. For queries where pages are stored sequentially and accessed sequentially, you can read up to eight data pages in a single I/O. Since the majority of I/O time is spent doing physical positioning and seeking on the disk, large I/O can greatly reduce disk access time.

Large I/O can increase performance for:

- Queries that table scan, both single-table queries and queries that perform joins

- Queries that scan the leaf level of a nonclustered index

- Queries that use text or image data

- Queries that allocate several pages, such as **select into**

- Bulk copy operations on heaps, both copy in and copy out

- The **update statistics** command, **dbcc checktable**, and **dbcc checkdb**

When a cache is configured for 16K I/O and the optimizer chooses 16K I/O for the query plan, SQL Server reads an entire extent, eight

2K data pages, when it needs to access a page that is not in cache. There are some occasions when 16K I/O cannot be performed. See "When prefetch Specification Is Not Followed" on page 9-11.

Types of Queries That Can Benefit From Large I/O

Certain types of SQL Server queries are likely to benefit from large I/Os. Identifying these types of queries can help you determine the correct size for data caches and memory pools.

In the following examples, the database or the specific table, index or text and image page chain must be bound to a named data cache that has large memory pools, or the default data cache must have large I/O pools. Most of the queries shown here use fetch and discard (MRU) replacement strategy. Types of queries that can benefit from large I/O are:

- Queries that scan entire tables, either heap tables or tables with clustered indexes:

```
select title_id, price from titles

select count(*) from authors
    where state = "CA"   /* no index on state */
```

- Range queries on tables with clustered indexes. These include queries like:

```
where indexed_colname < value
where indexed_colname > value
where indexed_colname between value1 and value2
where indexed_colname > value1
    and indexed_colname < value2
where indexed_colname like "string%"
```

- Queries that scan the leaf level of a nonclustered index, both matching and nonmatching scans. If there is a nonclustered index on *type, price*, this query could use large I/O on the leaf level of then index, since all the columns used in the query are contained in the index:

```
select type, sum(price)
    from titles
    group by type
```

- Queries that select *text* or *image* columns:

```
select au_id, copy from blurbs
```

- Join queries where a full scan of the inner table is required:

```
select outer.c1, inner.c3
    from outer, inner
    where outer.c1 = inner.c2
```

If both tables use the same cache, and one of the tables fits completely in cache, that table is chosen as the inner table and loaded into cache with the LRU replacement strategy, using large I/O, if available. The outer table can also benefit from large I/O, but uses fetch and discard (MRU) replacement strategy, so the pages are read into cache just before the wash marker, since the pages for the outer table are needed only once to satisfy the query.

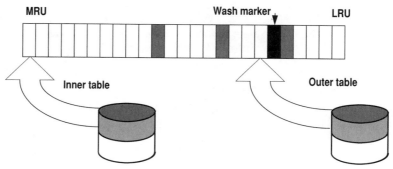

Figure 15-9: Caching strategies joining a large table and a small table

If neither table fits completely in cache, the MRU replacement strategy will be used for both tables, using large I/Os if they are available in the cache.

- Queries that generate Cartesian products, such as:

```
select title, au_lname
    from titles, authors
```

This query needs to scan all of one table, and for each row in that table, it needs to scan the other table. Caching strategies for these queries follows the same principles described for joins.

Choosing the Right Mix of I/O Sizes for a Cache

You can configure up to 4 pools in any data cache, but in most cases, caches for individual objects will perform best with only a 2K pool and a 16K pool. Caches for databases where the log is not bound to a separate cache should also have a 4K pool configured for *syslogs* if 4K log I/O size is configured for the database.

8K pools might sometimes provide better performance in a few cases:

- There may be some applications with extremely heavy logging where an 8K log I/O size would perform better than 4K log I/O, but most performance testing has shown the 4K log I/O size to be optimal.

- In cases where a 16K pool is not being used due to storage fragmentation or because many of the needed pages are already in a 2K pool, an 8K pool might perform better than a 16K pool. For example, if a single page from an extent is in the 2K pool, 7 2K I/Os would be needed to read the rest of the pages from the extent. With an 8K pool, 1 8K I/O (4 pages) and 3 2K I/Os could be used to read the 7 pages. However, if a 16K pool exists, and a large I/O is denied, SQL Server does not subsequently try each successively smaller pool, but immediately performs the 2K I/Os. You would only configure an 8K pool if a 16K pool was not effective in reducing I/O. You can transfer all of the space from the 8K pool to the 16K pool using **sp_poolconfig**.

Cache Replacement Strategies

Pages can be linked into a cache at two locations: at the head of the MRU/LRU chain in the pool, or at the pool's wash marker. The SQL Server optimizer chooses the cache replacement strategy, unless the strategy is specified in the query. The two strategies are:

- "LRU replacement strategy" replaces a least-recently used page, linking the newly read page or pages at the beginning of the page chain in the pool.

- "Fetch-and-discard" strategy or "MRU replacement strategy" links the newly read buffers at the wash marker in the pool.

Cache replacement strategies can affect the cache hit ratio for your query mix:

- Pages that are read into cache with the fetch-and-discard strategy remain in cache a much shorter time than queries read in the MRU end of the cache. If such a page is needed again, for example if the same query is run again very soon, the pages will probably need to be read from disk again.

- Pages that are read into cache with the fetch-and-discard strategy do not displace pages that already reside in cache before the wash mark. This means that pages before wash marker are much more likely to be in cache again when they are needed for a subsequent query.

See Figure 3-9 and Figure 3-10 on page 3-16 for illustrations of these strategies.

The Optimizer and Cache Choices

By the time SQL Server has optimized a query and needs to access data pages, it:

- Has a good estimate of the number of pages it needs to read for each table

- Knows the size of the data cache(s) available to the tables and indexes in the query and the I/O size available for the cache(s), and has used this information to incorporate the I/O size and cache strategy into the query plan

- Has determined whether the data will be accessed via a table scan, clustered index access, nonclustered index, or other optimizer strategy

- Has determined which cache strategy to use for each table and index

The optimizer's knowledge is limited, though, to the single query it is analyzing, and to certain statistics about the table and cache. It does not have information about how many other queries are simultaneously using the same data cache, and it has no statistics on whether table storage is fragmented in such a way that large I/Os would be less effective. This combination of factors can lead to excessive I/O in some cases. For example, users may experience higher I/O and poor performance if many queries with large result sets are using a very small memory pool.

Commands to Configure Named Data Caches

The commands to configure caches and pools are:

Command	Function
sp_cacheconfig	Creates or drops names caches and changes the size or cache type. Reports on sizes of caches and pools.
sp_poolconfig	Creates and drops I/O pools and changes their size.
sp_bindcache	Binds databases or database objects to a cache.

Command	Function
sp_unbindcache	Unbinds specific objects or databases from a cache.
sp_unbindcache_all	Unbinds all objects bound to a specified cache.
sp_helpcache	Reports summary information about data caches and lists the databases and databases objects that are bound to a cache. Also reports on the amount of overhead required by a cache.
sp_sysmon	Reports statistics useful for tuning cache configuration, including cache spinlock contention, cache utilization and disk I/O patterns.

For a full description of the process of configuring named caches and binding objects to caches, see Chapter 9, "Configuring Data Caches," in the *System Administration Guide*. Only a System Administrator can configure named caches and bind database objects to them.

For information on **sp_sysmon**, see Chapter 19, "Monitoring SQL Server Performance with sp_sysmon."

Commands for Tuning Query I/O Strategies and Sizes

You can affect the I/O size and cache strategy for **select**, **delete**, and **update** commands. These options are described in Chapter 9, "Advanced Optimizing Techniques."

- For information about specifying the I/O size, see "Specifying I/O Size in a Query" on page 9-9.

- For information about specifying cache strategy, see "Specifying the Cache Strategy" on page 9-12.

Named Data Cache Recommendations

These cache recommendations can improve performance on single and multiprocessor servers:

- Bind *tempdb* to its own cache, and configure the cache for 16K I/O for use by **select into** queries if these are used in your applications.

- Bind the logs for your high-use databases to a named data cache. Configure pools in this cache to match the log I/O size set with **sp_logiosize**. See "Choosing the I/O Size for the Transaction Log" on page 15-25.

- Bind *sysindexes* and its index (also named *sysindexes*) to a cache. Pages from *sysindexes* are needed almost constantly by SQL Server. *sysindexes* is usually a small table, and may only require a 512K cache. If your applications include frequent adhoc queries rather than stored procedures, you may see improvement by binding *sysobjects*, *syscolumns*, and *sysprotects* to a cache, since these tables are needed to parse and compile adhoc queries.

- If a table or its index is small and constantly in use, configure a cache just for that object, or for a few such objects.

- Keep cache sizes and pool sizes proportional to the cache utilization objects and queries:

  - If 75 percent of the work on your server is performed in one database, it should be allocated approximately 75 percent of the data cache, in a cache created specifically for the database, in caches created for its busiest tables and indexes, or in the default data cache.

  - If approximately 50 percent of the work in your database can use large I/O, configure about 50 percent of the cache in a 16K memory pool.

- It is better to view the cache as a shared resource than to try to micro-manage the caching needs of every table and index. Start cache analysis and testing at the database level, with particular tables and objects with high I/O needs or high application priorities and also with special uses such as *tempdb* and transaction logs.

- On SMP servers, use multiple caches to avoid contention for the cache spinlock:

  - Use a separate cache for the transaction log for busy databases, and separate caches for some of the tables and indexes that are accessed frequently.

  - If spinlock contention is greater than 10 percent on a cache, split it into multiple caches. Use **sp_sysmon** periodically during high-usage periods to check for cache contention. See "Spinlock Contention" on page 19-56.

Sizing Named Caches

Creating named data caches and memory pools and binding databases and database objects to the caches can dramatically hurt or improve SQL Server performance. For example:

- A cache this is poorly used hurts performance. If you allocate 25 percent of your data cache to a database that services a very small percentage of the query activity on your server, I/O increases in other caches.

- A pool that is unused hurts performance. If you add a 16K pool, but none of your queries use it, you have taken space away from the 2K pool. The 2K pool's cache hit ratio will be reduced and I/O will increase.

- A pool that is overused hurts performance. If you configure a small 16K pool and virtually all of your queries use it, I/O rates increase. The 2K cache will be under-used, while pages are rapidly cycled through the 16K pool. The cache hit ratio in the 16K pool will be very poor.

- When you balance your pool utilization within a cache, performance can increase dramatically. Both 16K and 2K queries may experience improved cache hit ratios. The large number of pages often used by queries that perform 16K I/O will not flush 2K pages from disk. Queries using 16K will perform approximately one-eighth the number of I/Os required by 2K I/O.

Cache Configuration Goals

Goals of cache configuration are:

- Reduced contention for spinlocks on multiple engine servers.

- Improved cache hit ratios and/or reduced disk I/O. As a bonus, improving cache hit ratios for queries can reduce lock contention, since queries that do not need to perform physical I/O generally hold locks for shorter periods of time.

- Fewer physical reads due to effective use of large I/O.

- Fewer physical writes, because recently modified pages are not being pushed from cache by other processes.

In addition to the commands such as **showplan** and **statistics io** that help tune on a per-query basis, you need to use a performance monitoring tool such as SQL Server Monitor or **sp_sysmon** to look at the complex picture of how multiple queries and multiple applications share cache space when they run simultaneously.

Development Versus Production Systems

In an ideal world, you would have access to a development system that exactly duplicated the configuration and activity of your production system. You could tune your cache configuration on the development system and reproduce the perfected configuration on your production server. In reality, most development systems can provide only an approximate test-bed for cache configuration, and fine-tuning cache sizes on a development system must be done incrementally in small windows of time when the system can be restarted. Tuning pool sizes and cache bindings is dynamic, and therefore more flexible since a re-start of the server is not required.

In a production environment, the possible consequences of misconfiguring caches and pools are significant enough that you should proceed carefully, and only after thorough analysis of the issues discussed in the following sections. In a test or development environment, you can use **sp_sysmon** or other monitoring tools to run individual queries, particular query mixes, or simulations of your production environment in order to develop an understanding of the interaction these queries have in various cache configurations.

When you transfer what you have learned from a test environment to a production environment, remember that the relative size of objects and caches can be critical to the choice of query plans, especially in the case of join queries using the same cache. If your tests involved tables of a few hundred pages and your production database's tables are much larger, different cache strategies may be chosen using a cache of the same size.

Gather Data, Plan, Then Implement

The first step in developing a plan for cache usage is to provide as much memory as possible for the data cache:

- Configure SQL Server with as much total memory as possible. See Chapter 8, "Configuring Memory" in the *System Administration Guide* for more information.

- Once all other configuration parameters that use SQL Server memory have been configured, check the size of the default data cache with **sp_cacheconfig** to determine how much space is available.

- Use your performance monitoring tools to establish baseline performance, and to establish your tuning goals.

The process of dividing the cache involves looking at existing objects and applications:

- Evaluate cache needs by analyzing I/O patterns and evaluate pool needs by analyzing query plans and I/O statistics.

- Configure the easier choices and biggest wins first:

  - Choose a size for a *tempdb* cache

  - Choose a size for any log caches, and tune the log I/O size

  - Choose a size for specific tables or indexes that you want to keep entirely in cache

  - Add large I/O pools for index or data caches as appropriate

- Once these sizes are determined, examine remaining I/O patterns, cache contention, and query performance. Configure caches proportional to I/O usage for objects and databases.

Keep your performance goals in mind as you configure caches:

- If your major goal in adding caches is to reduce spinlock contention, moving a few high-I/O objects to separate caches may be sufficient to reduce the spinlock contention and improve performance.

- If your major goal is to improve response time by improving cache hit ratios for particular queries or applications, creating caches for the tables and indexes used by those queries should be guided by a thorough understanding of the access methods and I/O requirements.

Evaluating Caching Needs

Generally, your goal is to configure caches in proportion to the number of times that pages in the caches will be accessed by your queries, and to configure pools within caches in proportion to the number of pages used by queries that chooses I/O of that pool's size.

You can use SQL Server Monitor to check physical and logical I/O by object. This provides a good basis for making relative cache-sizing decisions.

If your databases and their logs are on separate logical devices, you can estimate cache proportions using **sp_sysmon** or operating system commands to examine physical I/O by device. See "Disk I/O Management" on page 19-66 for information about the **sp_sysmon** output showing disk I/O.

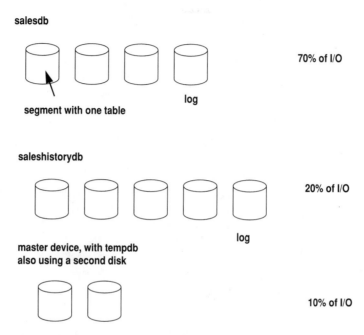

salesdb

70% of I/O

segment with one table

log

saleshistorydb

20% of I/O

**master device, with tempdb
also using a second disk**

log

10% of I/O

Figure 15-10:Checking disk I/O by database

Cache Sizing for Special Objects, *tempdb* and Transaction Logs

Creating caches for *tempdb,* the transaction logs, and for a few tables or indexes that you want to keep completely in cache can reduce cache spinlock contention and improve cache hit ratios.

Determining Cache Sizes for Special Tables or Indexes

You can use **sp_spaceused** to determine the size of tables or indexes that you want to keep entirely in cache. This includes the *sysindexes* table and its index. *sysindexes* is generally smaller than the minimum cache size of 512K, so you might want to have it share a cache with other tables. If you know how fast these tables increase in size, allow some extra cache space for their growth.

Examining *tempdb*'s Cache Needs

Look at your use of *tempdb*:

- Use **statistics io** to determine the size of temporary tables and worktables generated by your queries. Look at the number of pages generated by **select into** queries. These queries can use 16K I/O, so you can use this information to help you size a 16K pool for *tempdb*'s cache.

- Estimate the duration (in wall clock time) of the temporary tables and worktables.

- Estimate how often queries that create temporary tables and worktables are executed. Try to estimate the number of simultaneous users, especially for queries that generate very large result sets in *tempdb*.

With this information, you can a form a rough estimate of the amount of simultaneous I/O activity in *tempdb*. Depending on your other cache needs, you can choose to size *tempdb* so that virtually all *tempdb* activity takes place in cache and few temporary tables are actually written to disk.

In most cases, the first 2MB of *tempdb* are stored on the *master* device, with additional space on another logical device. You can use **sp_sysmon** or SQL Server monitor on those devices to help determine physical I/O rates.

Examining Cache Needs for Transaction Logs

On SMP systems with high transaction rates, binding the transaction log to its own cache can reduce cache spinlock contention.

The current page of the transaction log is written to disk when transactions commit, so your objective in sizing the cache or pool for the transaction log is not avoiding writes. Instead, you should try to size the log to reduce the number of times that processes that need to re-read log pages must go to disk because the pages have been flushed from the cache.

SQL Server processes that need to read log pages are:

- Triggers that use the *inserted* and *deleted* tables, which are built from the transaction log when the trigger queries the tables.

- Deferred updates, deletes and inserts, since these require re-reading the log to apply changes to tables or indexes.

- Transactions that are rolled back, since log pages must be accessed to roll back the changes.

When sizing a cache for a transaction log:

- Examine the duration of processes that need to re-read log pages. Estimate how long the longest triggers and deferred updates last. if some of your long running transactions are rolled back, check the length of time they run.

- Estimate the rate of growth of the log during the this time period. You can check your transaction log size with **sp_spaceused** at regular intervals to estimate how fast the log grows.

Use this estimate of log growth and the time estimate to size the log cache. For example, if the longest deferred update takes 5 minutes, and the transaction log for the database grows at 125 pages per minute, 625 are allocated for the log while this transaction executes. If a few transactions or queries are especially long-running, you may want to size the log for the average length, rather than the maximum length of time.

Choosing the I/O Size for the Transaction Log

When users perform operations that require logging, log records are first stored in a "user log cache" until certain events flush the user's log records to the current transaction log page in cache. Log records are flushed when a transaction ends, when the log page is full, when the transaction changes tables in another database, at certain system events, and when another process needs to write a page referenced in the user log cache.

To economize on disk writes, SQL Server holds partially filled transaction log pages for a very brief span of time so that records of several transactions can be written to disk simultaneously. This process is called "group commit."

In environments with high transaction rates or transactions that create large log records, the 2K transaction log pages fill quickly, and a large proportion of log writes are due to full log pages, rather than group commits. Creating a 4K pool for the transaction log can greatly reduce log writes in these environments.

sp_sysmon reports on the ratio of transaction log writes to transaction log allocations. You should try using 4K log I/O if all of these conditions are true:

- Your database is using 2K log I/O

- The number of log writes per second is high

- The average number of writes per log page is slightly above one

Here is some sample output showing that a larger log I/O size might help performance:

	per sec	per xact	count	% of total
Transaction Log Writes	22.5	458.0	1374	n/a
Transaction Log Alloc	20.8	423.0	1269	n/a
Avg # Writes per Log Page	n/a	n/a	1.08274	n/a

See "Transaction Log Writes" on page 19-32 for more information.

Configuring for Large Log I/O Size

To check the log I/O size for a database, you can check the server's error log. The size of I/O for each database is printed in the error log when SQL Server starts. You can also use the **sp_logiosize** system procedure. To see the size for the current database, execute **sp_logiosize** with no parameters. To see the size for all databases on the server and the cache in use by the log, use:

```
sp_logiosize "all"
```

To set the log I/O size for a database to 4K, the default, you must be using the database. This command sets the size to 4K:

```
sp_logiosize "default"
```

By default, SQL Server sets the log I/O size for user databases to 4K. If no 4K pool is available in the cache that the log uses, 2K I/O is automatically used instead.

If a database is bound to a cache, all objects not explicitly bound to other caches use the database's cache. This includes the *syslogs* table. In order to bind *syslogs* to another cache, you must first put the database in single user mode with **sp_dboption**, and then use the database and execute **sp_bindcache**. Here is an example:

```
sp_bindcache pubs_log, pubtune, syslogs
```

Further Tuning Tips for Log Caches

For further tuning after configuring a cache for the log, check **sp_sysmon** output. Look at output for:

- The cache used by log (the cache it is explicitly bound to, or the cache that its database uses)

- The disk that the log is stored on

- The average number of writes per log page

When looking at the log cache section, check "Cache Hits" and "Cache Misses" to determine whether most of the pages needed for deferred operations, triggers and rollbacks are being found in cache.

In the "Disk Activity Detail" section, look at the number of "Reads" performed.

Basing Data Pool Sizes on Query Plans and I/O

When you choose divide a cache for tables and/or indexes into pools, try to make this division based on the proportion of I/O performed by your queries that use the corresponding I/O sizes. If most of your queries can benefit from 16K I/O, and you configure a very small 16K cache, you may actually see worse performance. Most of the space in the 2K pool will remain unused, and the 16K pool will experience high turnover. The cache hit ratio will be significantly reduced. The problem will be most severe with join queries that have to repeatedly re-read the inner table from disk.

Making a good choice about pool sizes requires:

- A thorough knowledge of the application mix and the I/O size your queries can use

- Careful study and tuning, using monitoring tools to check cache utilization, cache hit rates, and disk I/O

Checking I/O Size for Queries

You can examine query plans and I/O statistics to determine those queries that are likely to perform large I/O and the amount of I/O these queries perform. This information can form the basis for estimating the amount of 16K I/O the queries should perform with a 16K memory pool. For example, a query that table scans and performs 800 physical I/Os using a 2K pool should perform about 100 8K I/Os. See "Types of Queries That Can Benefit From Large I/O" on page 15-14 for a list of types.

To test out your estimates, however, you need to actually configure the pools and run the individual queries and your target mix of queries to determine optimum pool sizes. Choosing a good initial size for your first test using 16K I/O depends on a good sense of the types of queries in your application mix. This estimate is especially important if you are configuring a 16K pool for the first time on an active production server. Make the best possible estimate of simultaneous uses of the cache. Here are some guidelines:

- If you observe that most I/O is occurring in point queries using indexes to access a small number of rows, make the 16K pool relatively small, say about 10 to 20 percent of the cache size.

- If you estimate that a large percentage of the I/Os will be to the 16K pool, configure 50 to 75 percent of the cache for 16K I/O. Queries that use 16K I/O include any query that table scans, those that use the clustered index for range searches and **order by**, and queries that perform matching or nonmatching scans on nonclustered indexes.

- If you are unsure, configure about 20 percent of your cache space in a 16K pool, and use **showplan** and **statistics i/o** while you run your queries. Examine the **showplan** output for the "Using 16K I/O" message. Check **statistics i/o** output to see how much I/O is performed.

- If you feel that your typical application mix uses both 16K I/O and 2K I/O simultaneously, configure 30 to 40 percent of your cache space for 16K I/O. Your optimum may be higher or lower, depending on the actual mix and the I/O sizes chosen by the query. If many tables are accessed by both 2K I/O and 16K I/O, SQL Server cannot use 16K I/O if any page from the extent is in the 2K cache, and performs 2K I/O on the other pages in the extent. This adds to the I/O in the 2K cache.

After configuring for 16K I/O, monitor I/O for the affected devices using **sp_sysmon** or SQL Server Monitor. Also use **showplan** and **statistics io** to observe your queries.

- Look especially for join queries where an inner table would use 16K I/O, and the table is repeatedly scanned using fetch-and-discard (MRU) strategy. This can occur when neither table fits completely in cache. If increasing the size of the 16K pool allows the inner table to fit completely in cache, I/O can be significantly reduced. You might also consider binding the two tables to separate caches.

- Look for excessive 16K I/O, when compared to table size in pages. For example, if you have an 800-page table, and a 16K I/O table scan performs significantly more than 100 I/Os to read this table, you may see improvement by re-creating the clustered index on this table.

Configuring Buffer Wash Size

The wash area for each pool in each cache is configurable. If the wash size is set too high, SQL Server may perform unnecessary writes. If the wash area is too small, SQL Server may not be able to find a clean buffer at the end of the buffer chain and may have to wait for I/O to complete before it can proceed. Generally, wash size defaults are correct, and only need to be adjusted in large pools with very high rates of data modification. See "Changing the Wash Area for a Memory Pool" on page 9-16 of the *System Administration Guide* for more information.

Overhead of Pool Configuration and Binding Objects

Configuring memory pools and binding objects to caches can affect users on a production system, so these activities are best performed during off-hours.

Pool Configuration Overhead

When a pool is created, deleted, or changed, the plans of all stored procedures and triggers that use objects bound to the cache are recompiled the next time they are run. If a database is bound to the cache, this affects all of the objects in a database.

There is a slight amount of overhead involved in moving buffers between pools.

Cache Binding Overhead

When you bind or unbind an object, all of the object's pages that are currently in the cache are flushed to disk (if dirty) or dropped from the cache (if clean) during the binding process. The next time the pages are needed by user queries, they must be read from the disk again, slowing the performance of the queries.

SQL Server acquires an exclusive lock on the table or index while the cache is being cleared, so binding can slow other users of the object. The binding process may have to wait until for transactions to complete in order to acquire the lock.

➤ *Note*

The fact that binding and unbinding objects from caches removes them from memory can be useful when tuning queries during development and testing. If you need to check physical I/O for a particular table, and earlier tuning efforts have brought pages into cache, you can unbind and rebind the object. The next time the table is accessed, all pages used by the query must be read into the cache.

The plans of all stored procedures and triggers using the bound objects are recompiled the next time they are run. If a database is bound to the cache, this affects all the objects in the database.

Maintaining Data Cache Performance for Large I/O

When heap tables, clustered indexes, or nonclustered indexes have just been created, they show optimal performance when large I/O is being used. Over time, the effects of deletes, page splits, and page deallocation and reallocation can increase the cost of I/O.

Ideal performance for an operation that performs large I/O while doing a complete table scan is approximately:

$$\text{I/Os} = \frac{\text{Number of pages in table}}{\text{Number of pages per I/O}}$$

For example, if a table has 624 data pages, and the cache is configured for 16K I/O, SQL Server reads 8 pages per I/O. Dividing 624 by 8 equals 78 I/Os. If a table scan that performs large I/O performs significantly more I/O than the optimum, you should explore the causes.

Causes for High Large I/O Counts

There are several reasons why a query that performs large I/O might require more reads than you anticipate:

- The cache used by the query has a 2K cache and many other processes have brought pages from the table into the 2K cache. If SQL Server is performing 16K I/O and finds that one of the pages it needs to read is already in the 2K cache, it performs 2K I/O on all of the other pages in the extent.

- The first extent on each allocation unit stores the allocation page, so if a query needs to access all 255 pages on the extent, it must perform 2K I/O on the 7 pages that share the extent with the allocation page. The other 31 extents can be read using 16K I/O. So, the minimum number of reads for an entire allocation unit is always 38, not 32.

- In nonclustered indexes, an extent may store both leaf level pages and pages from higher levels of the index. Regular index access, finding pages by starting from the root and following index pointers, always performs 2K I/O, so it is likely that these some of the pages will be in the 2K cache during these index level scans. the rest of the pages in the extent will therefore be read using 2K I/O. Note that this applies only to nonclustered indexes and their leaf pages, and does not apply to clustered index pages and the data pages, which are always on separate extents.

- The table storage is fragmented, due to page-chain pointers that cross extent boundaries and allocation pages. Figure 15-11 shows a table that has become fragmented.

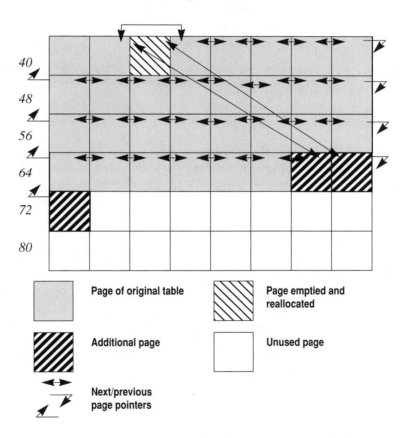

Page of original table		Page emptied and reallocated
Additional page		Unused page
Next/previous page pointers		

Figure 15-11:Fragmentation on a heap table

The steps that lead to the memory use in the preceding figure are as follows:

1. Table is loaded. The gray boxes indicate the original pages of the table.

2. First additional page is allocated for inserts, indicated by the first heavily striped box.

3. Deletes cause page 3 of the table, located in extent 40 to be deallocated.

4. Another page is needed, page 2 is allocated and linked into the page chain, as shown by the lightly striped box.

5. Two more pages are allocated, as shown by the other two heavily striped boxes.

Instead of 5 reads using 16K I/O with the MRU strategy, (because it's occupying 5 extents) the query does 7 I/Os. The query reads the pages following the page pointers, so it:

• Performs a 16K I/O to read the extent 40, and performs logical I/O on pages 1, 2, 4-8, skipping page 3.

• Performs physical I/O the extents, and then logical I/O on the pages on extent 48, 56, and 64, in turn.

• The second-to-last page in extent 64 points to page 3. In this small table, of course, it is extremely likely that extent 40 is still in the 16K pool. It examines page 3, which then points to a page in extent 64.

• The last page in extent 64 points to extent 72.

With a small table, the pages would still be in the data cache, so there would be no extra physical I/O. But when the same kind of fragmentation occurs in large tables, the I/O required rises, especially if a large number of users are performing queries with large I/O that could flush buffers out of the cache. This example sets fillfactor to 80:

```
create unique clustered index title_id_ix
on titles(title_id)
with fillfactor = 80
```

Using *sp_sysmon* to Check Large I/O Performance

The **sp_sysmon** output for each data cache includes information that can help you determine the effectiveness for large I/Os:

• "Large I/O Usage" on page 19-60 reports the number of large I/Os performed and denied, and provides summary statistics.

- "Large I/O Detail" on page 19-61 reports the total number of pages that were read into the cache by a large I/O, and the number of pages that were actually accessed while in the cache.

Re-Creating Indexes to Eliminate Fragmentation

If I/O for heaps, range queries on clustered indexes, or covering nonclustered indexes exceeds your expected values, use one of the following processes:

- For heaps, either create and then drop a clustered index, or bulk copy the data out, truncate the table, and copy it in again.
- For clustered indexes, drop and re-create the clustered index. All nonclustered indexes will be re-created automatically.
- For covering nonclustered indexes, drop and re-create the index.

For clustered indexes and nonclustered indexes on tables that will continue to receive updates, using a fillfactor to spread the data slightly should slow fragmentation. This is described in the next section. Fillfactor does not apply to heap tables.

Using Fillfactor for Data Cache Performance

If your table has a clustered index and queries frequently perform table scans or return large ranges, you should be sure that it uses a cache that allows 16K I/O in order to improve performance.

Tables with clustered indexes can become fragmented by page splits from inserts and expensive direct updates and from the reallocation of pages. Using fillfactor when you create your clustered index can slow down this fragmentation.

When you create a clustered index without specifying a fillfactor, the data pages (the leaf level of the clustered index) are completely filled. If you specify a fillfactor of 80, the pages are 80-percent filled. So, for example, instead of 20 rows on a page, there would be only 16, with room for 4 more rows.

Speed of Recovery

As users modify data in SQL Server, only the transaction log is written to disk immediately, in order to ensure recoverability. The changed or "dirty" data and index pages stay in the data cache until one of these events causes them to be written to disk:

- The checkpoint process wakes up, determines that the changed data and index pages for a particular database need to be written to disk, and writes out all dirty pages in each cache used by the database. The combination of the setting for **recovery interval** and the rate of data modifications on your server determines how often the checkpoint process writes changed pages to disk.

- As pages move down the MRU/LRU chain in the cache, they move into the buffer wash area of the cache, where dirty pages are automatically written to disk.

- SQL Server has spare CPU cycles and disk I/O capacity between user transactions, and the housekeeper task uses this time to write dirty buffers to disk.

- A user issues a **checkpoint** command.

This combination of write strategies has two major benefits:

- Many transactions may change a page in the cache or read the page in the cache, but only one physical write is performed.

- SQL Server performs many physical writes at times when the I/O does not cause contention with user processes.

Tuning the Recovery Interval

The default recovery interval on SQL Server is 5 minutes. Changing the recovery interval can affect performance because it can impact the number of times SQL Server writes pages to disk.

Table 15-1: Effects of recovery interval on performance and recovery time

Setting	Effects on Performance	Effects on Recovery
Lower	May cause unnecessary reads and writes, and may lower throughput. SQL Server will write dirty pages to the disk more often, and may have to read those pages again very soon. Any checkpoint I/O "spikes" will be smaller.	Recovery period will be very short.
Higher	Minimizes unnecessary I/O and improves system throughput. Checkpoint I/O spikes will be higher.	Automatic recovery may take substantial time on start-up. SQL Server may have to re-apply a large number of transaction log records to the data pages.

Housekeeper Task's Effects on Recovery Time

SQL Server's housekeeper task automatically begins cleaning dirty buffers during the server's idle cycles. If the task is able to flush all active buffer pools in all configured caches, it wakes up the checkpoint process. This may result in faster checkpoints and shorter database recovery time.

System Administrators can use the **housekeeper free write percent** configuration parameter to tune or disable the housekeeper task. This parameter specifies the maximum percentage by which the housekeeper task can increase database writes. For information about tuning this parameter, see "Configuring the Housekeeper Task" on page 17-10.

For more information on tuning the housekeeper and the recovery interval, see "Recovery Management" on page 19-63.

Auditing and Performance

Heavy auditing can affect performance:

- Audit records are written to a queue in memory and then to the *sybsecurity* database. If the database shares a disk used by other busy databases, it can slow performance.

- If the in-memory audit queue fills up, user processes that generate audit records sleep.

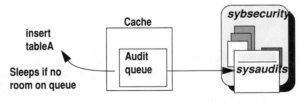

Figure 15-12:The audit process

Sizing the Audit Queue

The size of the audit queue can be set by a System Security Officer. The default configuration is:

- A single audit record requires a minimum of 22 bytes, up to a maximum of 424 bytes. This means that a single data page stores between 4 and 80 records.

- The default size of the audit queue is 100 records, requiring approximately 42K. The minimum size of the queue is 1 record, the maximum size is 65335 records.

There are trade-offs in sizing the audit queue. If the audit queue is large, so that you do not risk having user processes sleep, you run the risk of losing any audit records in memory if there is a system failure. The maximum number of records that can be lost is the size of the audit queue. If security is your chief concern, keep the queue small. If you can risk losing audit records and require high performance, make the queue larger.

Increasing the size of the in-memory audit queue takes memory from the total memory allocated to the data cache.

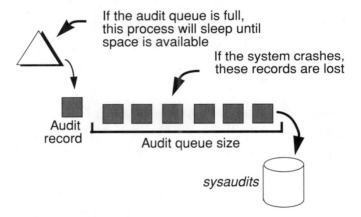

Figure 15-13:Trade-offs in auditing and performance

Auditing Performance Guidelines

- Choose the events that you audit. Heavy auditing slows overall system performance. Audit what you need, and only what you need.

- If possible, place the *sysaudits* database on its own device. If that is not possible, place it on a device that is not used for your most critical applications.

Interconnections among Systems: Analyzing Networks

SQL Server's client/server traffic takes place over one or more networks. In an enterprise application environment, network traffic can significantly affect performance.

Chapter 16, "Networks and Performance," addresses the issues of how SQL Server uses networks and techniques you can employ to minimize network traffic.

16 Networks and Performance

How SQL Server Uses the Network

All client/server communication occurs over a network via packets. Packets contain a header and routing information as well as the data they carry.

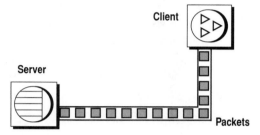

Figure 16-1: Client/server communications model

SQL Server was one of the first database systems to be built on a network-based client/server architecture. Clients initiate a connection to the server. The connection sends client requests and server responses. Applications can have as many connections open concurrently as they need to perform the required task. The protocol used between the client and server is known as the Tabular Data Stream (TDS), which forms the basis of communication for all Sybase products.

Why Study the Network?

You should work with your network administrator to discover potential network problems if:

- Process response times vary significantly for no apparent reason.

- Queries that return a large number of rows take longer than expected.

- Operating system processing slows down during normal SQL Server processing periods.

- SQL Server processing slows down during certain operating system processing periods.

- A particular client process seems to slow all other processes down.

Potential Network-Based Performance Problems

Some of the underlying problems that can be caused by networks are:

- SQL Server uses network services poorly.
- The physical limits of the network have been reached.
- Processes are retrieving unnecessary data values, increasing network traffic unnecessarily.
- Processes are opening and closing connections too often, increasing network load.
- Processes are frequently submitting the same SQL transaction, causing excessive and redundant network traffic.
- SQL Server does not have enough network memory available.
- SQL Server's network packet sizes are not big enough to handle the type of processing needed by certain clients.

Basic Questions About Networks and Performance

Network analysis should begin with gathering data. Here are some areas you'll need to investigate when beginning network analysis:

- Which processes usually retrieve a large amount of data?
- Are a large number of network errors occurring?
- What is the overall performance of the network?
- Which transactions mix SQL and stored procedures?
- Are a large number of processes using the two-phase commit protocol?
- Are replication services being performed on the network?
- How much of the network is being used by the operating system?

Techniques Summary

Once you've gathered the data, you can take advantage of several techniques that should improve network performance. These techniques include:

- Use small packets whenever possible
- Use larger packet sizes for tasks that perform large data transfers
- Use stored procedures to reduce overall traffic

- Filter data to avoid large transfers
- Isolate heavy network users from ordinary users
- Use client control mechanisms for special cases

Using *sp_sysmon* While Changing Network Configuration

Use **sp_sysmon** while making network configuration changes to observe the effects on performance. Use SQL Server Monitor to pinpoint network contention on a particular database object.

For more information about using **sp_sysmon** see Chapter 19, "Monitoring SQL Server Performance with sp_sysmon." Pay special attention to the output in "Network I/O Management" on page 534.

Changing Network Packet Sizes

By default, all connections to SQL Server use a default packet size of 512 bytes. This works well for clients sending short queries and receiving small result sets. However, some applications may benefit from an increased packet size.

OLTP typically sends and receives large numbers of packets that contain very little data. A typical insert statement or update statement may be only 100 or 200 bytes. A data retrieval, even one that joins several tables, may bring back only one or two rows of data, and still not completely fill a packet. Applications using stored procedures and cursors also typically send and receive small packets.

Decision support applications often include large batches of Transact-SQL, and return larger result sets.

In both OLTP and DSS environments, there may be special needs such as batch data loads or text processing that can benefit from larger packets.

Chapter 11, "Setting Configuration Parameters" in the *System Administration Guide* describes how to change these configuration parameters:

- The **default network packet size**, if most of your applications are performing large reads and writes.

- The **max network packet size** and **additional network memory**, which provides additional memory space for large packet connections

Only a System Administrator can change these configuration parameters.

Large Packet Sizes vs. Default-Size User Connections

SQL Server reserves enough space for all configured user connections to log in at the default packet size, Large network packets cannot steal that space. Connections that use the default network packet size always have three buffers reserved to the connection.

Connections that request large packet sizes must acquire the space for their network I/O buffers from the **additional network memory** region. If there is not enough space in this region to allocate three buffers at the large packet size, connections use the default packed size instead.

Number of Packets Is Important

Generally, the number of packets being transferred is more important than the size of the packets. "Network" performance also includes the time needed by the CPU and operating system to process a network packet. This per-packet overhead affects performance the most. Larger packets reduce the overall overhead costs and achieve higher physical throughput, provided you have enough data that needs to be sent.

The following big transfer sources may benefit from large packet sizes:

- Bulk copy
- **readtext** and **writetext** commands
- Large **select** statements

Point of Diminishing Returns

There is always a point at which increasing the packet size will not improve performance, and in fact it may decrease performance, because the packets are not always full. Although there are analytical methods for predicting that point, it is more common to vary the size experimentally and plot the results. If such experiments are conducted over a period of time and conditions, a packet size that works well for a lot of processes can be determined. However, since the packet size can be customized for every connection, specific experiments for specific processes can be beneficial.

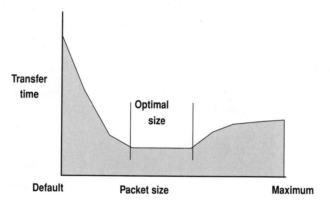

Figure 16-2: Packet sizes and performance

The curve can be significantly different between applications. Bulk copy might fall into one pattern, while large image data retrievals perform better at a different packet size.

Client Commands for Larger Packet Sizes

If testing shows that some specific applications can achieve better performance with larger packet sizes, but that most applications send and receive small packets, clients need to request the larger packet size.

For **isql** and **bcp**, the command line arguments are as follows:

UNIX, Windows NT, and OS/2

```
isql -Asize
bcp -Asize
```

Novell NetWare

```
load isql -Asize
load bcp -Asize
```

VMS

```
isql /tdspacketsize = size
```

```
bcp /tdspacketsize = size
```

For Open Client Client-Library™, use:

```
ct_con_prop(connection, CS_SET, CSPACKETSIZE,
$packetsize (sizeof(packetsize), NULL)
```

Evaluation Tools with SQL Server

The **sp_monitor** procedure reports on packet activity. This report shows only the packet-related output:

```
. . .
packets received packets sent packet err
---------------- ------------ ----------
10866(10580)     19991(19748) 0(0)
. . .
```

You can also use these global variables:

- *@@pack_sent*, number of packets sent by SQL Server
- *@@pack_received*, number of packets received
- *@@packet_errors*, number of errors

These SQL statements show how the counters can be used:

```
select "before" = @@pack_sent

select * from titles

select "after" = @@pack_sent
```

Both **sp_monitor** and the global variables report all packet activity for all users since the last restart of SQL Server.

Evaluation Tools Outside of SQL Server

Operating system commands also provide information about packet transfers. See the documentation for your platform for more information about these commands.

Techniques for Reducing Network Traffic

Server-Based Techniques for Reducing Traffic

Using stored procedures, views, and triggers can reduce network traffic. These Transact-SQL tools can store large chunks of code on the server so that only short commands need to be sent across the network. If your applications send large batches of Transact-SQL to SQL Server, converting them to use stored procedures can reduce network traffic.

Clients should request only the rows and columns they need.

Using Stored Procedures to Reduce Network Traffic

Applications that send large batches of Transact-SQL can place less load on the network if the SQL is converted to stored procedures. Views can also help reduce the amount of network traffic.

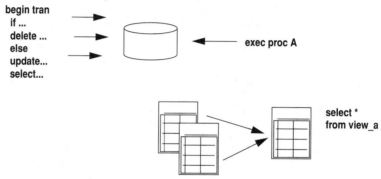

Figure 16-3: Using procedures and views to reduce network traffic

Ask for Only the Information You Need

Applications should request only the rows and columns they need, filtering as much data as possible at the server. In many cases, this can also reduce the disk I/O load.

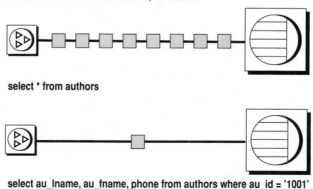

Figure 16-4: Reducing network traffic by filtering data at the server

Fill Up Packets When Using Cursors

Open Client Client-Library Applications that use cursors can request multiple rows for each **fetch** command:

```
ct_cursor(CT_CURSOR_ROWS)
```

To fetch multiple rows in **isql**, use the **set cursor rows** option.

Large Transfers

Large transfers simultaneously decrease overall throughput and increase the average response time. If possible, large transfers should be done during off-hours.

If large transfers are common, consider acquiring network hardware that is suitable for such transfers.

Table 16-1: Network options

Type	Characteristics
Token ring	Token ring hardware responds better than Ethernet hardware during periods of heavy use.
Fiber optic	Fiber-optic hardware provides very high bandwidth, but is usually too expensive to use throughout an entire network.
Separate network	A separate network can be used to handle network traffic between the highest volume workstations and SQL Server.

Network Overload

Overloaded networks are becoming increasingly common as more and more computers, printers, and peripherals are network equipped. Network managers rarely detect a problem before database users start complaining to their System Administrator. Cooperate with your local network managers and be prepared to provide them with your predicted or actual network requirements when they are considering the addition of resources. Also, keep an eye on the network and try to anticipate problems that result from newly added equipment or application requirements. Remember, network problems affect all the database clients.

Impact of Other Server Activities

You need to be aware of the impact of other server activity and maintenance on network activity, especially:

- Two-phase commit protocol
- Replication processing
- Backup processing

These activities involve network communication, especially replication processing and the two-phase commit protocol. Systems that make extensive use of these activities may see network-related problems. Accordingly, these activities should be done only as necessary.

Try to restrict backup activity to times when other network activity is low.

Login Protocol

A connection can be kept open and shared by various modules within an application instead of being repeatedly opened and closed.

Single User vs. Multiple Users

You must take the presence of other users into consideration before trying to solve a database problem, especially if those users are using the same network. Since most networks can transfer only one packet at a time, many users may be delayed while a large transfer is in progress. Such a delay may cause locks to be held longer, which causes even more delays. When response time is "abnormally" high, and normal tests indicate no problem, it could be because of other users on the same network. In such cases, ask the user when the process was being run, if the operating system was generally sluggish, if other users were doing large transfers, and so on. In general, consider multi-user impacts before digging deeper into the database system to solve an abnormal response time problem.

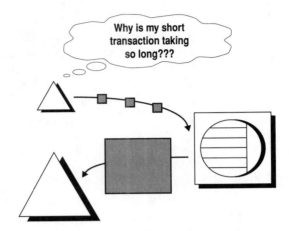

Figure 16-5: Effects of long transactions on other users

Guidelines for Improving Network Performance

Choose the Right Packet Size for the Task

If most applications send and receive small amounts of data, with a few applications performing larger transfers, here are some guidelines:

- Keep **default network packet size** small.

- Configure **max network packet size** and **additional network memory** just for the applications that need it.

**Most applications transfer small amounts of
data, a few applications perform large transfers**

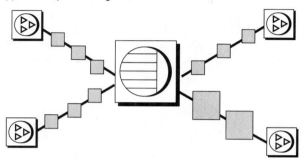

All applications transfer large amounts of data

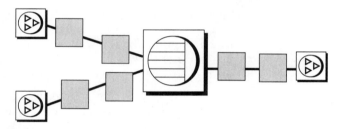

Figure 16-6: Match network packet sizes to application mix

If most of your applications send and receive large amounts of data, increase **default network packet size**. This will result in fewer (but larger) transfers.

Isolate Heavy Network Users

Isolate heavy network users from ordinary network users by placing them on a separate network.

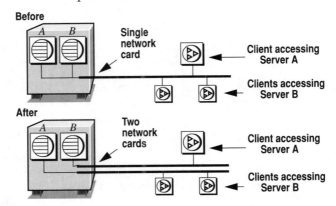

Figure 16-7: Isolating heavy network users

In the "Before" diagram, clients accessing two different SQL Servers use one network card. Clients accessing Servers A and B have to compete over the network and past the network card.

In the "After" diagram, clients accessing Server A use one network card and clients accessing Server B use another.

It would be even better to put your SQL Servers on different machines.

Set *tcp no delay* on TCP Networks

By default, the configuration parameter **tcp no delay** is set to "off," meaning that the network performs packet batching. It briefly delays sending partially full packets over the network. While this improves network performance in terminal-emulation environments, it can slow performance for SQL Server applications that send and receive small batches. To disable packet batching, a System Administrator sets the **tcp no delay** configuration parameter to 1.

Configure Multiple Network Listeners

Use two (or more) ports listening for a single SQL Server. Front-end software may be directed to any configured network ports by setting the DSQUERY environment variable.

Using multiple network ports spreads out the network load and eliminates or reduces network bottlenecks, thus increasing SQL Server throughput.

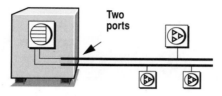

Figure 16-8: Configuring multiple network ports

See your SQL Server installation and configuration guide for information on configuring multiple network listeners.

From Networks to CPUs: Analyzing Processing Efficiency

Your application's processing environment can include one or many CPUs in one or many machines. The relative ease with which a System Administrator can add additional CPUs or engines in a multi-processing system means that any application should be able to obtain enough horsepower to run as fast as it can.

Of course, determining the right load balance among multiple CPUs, engines, and networks is a complex task. You will likely need to supplement fact-finding about SQL Server's CPU usage with specific information about your particular hardware systems and subsystems.

Chapter 17, "Using CPU Resources Effectively," opens with a comprehensive diagram of how SQL Server manages tasks, then covers performance tuning in single- and multi-CPU environments.

17 Using CPU Resources Effectively

CPU Resources and Performance

This chapter discusses how SQL Server handles tasks; how to measure CPU usage; how using the SQL Server "housekeeper" can improve CPU utilization; and how to design applications for multi-CPU machines.

As an introduction and orientation, the following diagram illustrates how SQL Server manages tasks and interacts with CPUs.

Task Management on SQL Server

Figure 17-1 shows the major subsystems of SQL Server and the SQL Server environment:

- Clients
- Disks
- The operating system
- Multiple CPUs
- The shared executable code
- Resources in shared memory:
  - Data caches
  - The procedure cache
  - Queues for network and disk I/O
  - Structures that maintain locks
  - The sleep queue, for processes that are waiting on a resource, or that are idle
  - The run queue, for processes that are ready to execute, or to continue execution

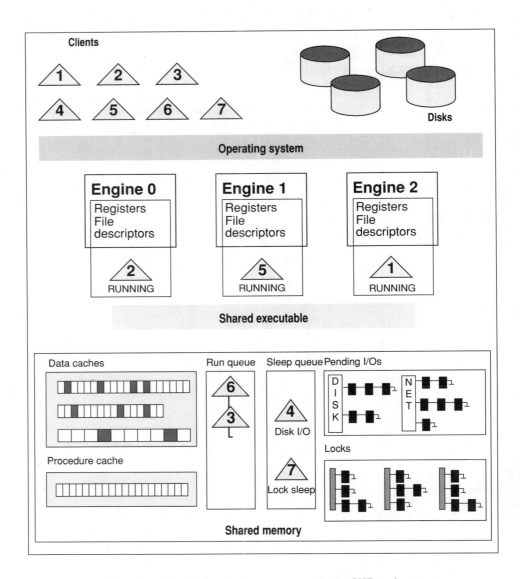

Figure 17-1: SQL Server task management in the SMP environment

The following steps explain how a process is managed on a server with multiple processors. The process is very similar for single CPU systems, except: that the network migration described in the first step and steps 8 and 9 does not take place on single CPU machines. The process of switching tasks, putting them to sleep while the wait for disk or network I/O, and checking queues is handled by the single CPU in same manner.

1. When a new user logs into SQL Server, Engine 0 handles the login to establish packet size, language, character set, and other login settings.

   Once this is complete, Engine 0 determines which engine is currently managing the smallest number of user connections. The connection is migrated to that CPU by passing the file descriptor. For this example, the task is assigned to Engine 1.

   The task is then put to sleep, waiting for the client to send a request.

2. Engine 1 checks the sleep queue once every clock tick looking for incoming tasks.

3. When Engine 1 finds a command for the connection, it wakes up the task and places it on the end of the run queue.

4. When the task reaches the head of the queue, any available engine can begin execution. In this example, Engine 2 executes the task.

5. Engine 2 takes the task, parses, and compiles it and begins execution.

6. If the task needs to perform disk I/O, the I/O request is issued, and the task sleeps again. (There are also other reasons why a task is put to sleep, or yields the engine to other tasks.)

7. Once each clock tick, the pending I/O queue is checked to see if the task's I/O has completed. If so, the task is moved to the run queue, and the next available engine resumes execution.

8. When the task needs to return results to the user, it must perform the network write on Engine 1. So Engine 2 puts the tasks to sleep on a network write.

9. As soon as the task that Engine 1 is executing yields or is put to sleep, Engine 1's scheduler checks to determine if it has any network tasks pending.

10. Engine 1 issues the network writes, removing the data structures from the network I/O queue.

11. When the write completes, the task gets woken up, and placed in the run queue. When it reaches the head of the queue, it is scheduled on the next available engine.

In addition to the reasons for task switching described in the steps above, such a physical and network I/O, tasks are switched off engines for other reasons. The task switch information provided by the **sp_sysmon** system procedure can help you develop a picture of how tasks are using the CPU. See "Task Context Switches Due To" on page 480.

Measuring CPU Usage

This section describes how to measure CPU usage on machines with a single processor and on those with multiple processors.

> ➤ *Note*

Before measuring CPU usage, disable the housekeeper task to eliminate its effect on these measurements.

Single CPU Machines

There is no correspondence between your operating system's reports on CPU usage and SQL Server's internal "CPU busy" information. It is normal for a SQL Server to exhibit very high CPU usage while performing an I/O-bound task.

A multithreaded database engine is not allowed to block on I/O. While the asynchronous disk I/O is being performed, SQL Server services other user tasks that are waiting to be processed. If there are no tasks to perform, it enters a busy-wait loop, waiting for the completion of the asynchronous disk I/O. This low-priority busy-wait loop can result in very high CPU usage but due to its low priority, it is harmless.

Using *sp_monitor* to See CPU Usage

Use **sp_monitor** to see the percentage of time SQL Server uses the CPU during an elapsed time interval:

```
last_run                current_run              seconds
-----------------       -----------------       -------
May 19 1995  4:34PM May 19 1995  4:35PM          20

cpu_busy                io_busy                  idle
-----------------       -----------------       ---------------
658(7)-35%              0(0)-0%                  87986(12)-60%

packets_received        packets_sent             packet_errors
-----------------       -----------------       -------------
9202(4)                 3595(5)                  0(0)

total_read      total_write     total_errors   connections
------------     ------------    -------------  -----------
5639(972)        77647(425)      0(0)             51(0)
```

For more information about **sp_monitor,** see the *SQL Server Reference Manual*.

Using *sp_sysmon*

The "Kernel Utilization" section displays how busy the engine was during the sample period. The percentage in this output is based on the time that CPU was allocated to SQL Server, it is not a percentage of the total sample interval.

The "CPU Yields by Engine" section displays information about how often the engine yielded to the operating system during the interval:

Operating System Commands and CPU Usage

Operating system commands for displaying CPU usage are covered in the SQL Server installation and configuration guide.

If your operating system tools show that CPU usage is above 85 percent most of the time, consider a multi-CPU environment or offloading some work to another SQL Server.

Multiple CPU Machines

Under SQL Server's SMP (symmetric multiprocessing) architecture, any engine can handle any server task and use any CPU. See "SQL Server Task Management for SMP" on page 10-3 of the *System Administration Guide* for a brief description of the process and information about the System Administration tasks and tuning issues for managing SMP configurations.

Determining When to Configure Additional Engines

When determining whether to add additional engines, the major factors to examine are:

- Load on existing engines
- Contention for resources such as locks on tables and pages and cache spinlocks
- Response time

If the load on existing engines is above 80 percent, adding an additional engine should improve response time, unless contention for resources is high, or adding an engine causes contention.

Before configuring more engines, use **sp_sysmon** to establish a baseline. Look particularly at the following lines or sections in the output that may reveal points of contention:

- "Logical Lock Contention" on page 481
- "Address Lock Contention" on page 482
- "ULC Semaphore Requests" on page 494
- "Log Semaphore Requests" on page 495
- "Page Splits" on page 499
- "Deadlock Percentage" on page 506
- "Spinlock Contention" on page 517
- "I/Os Delayed By" on page 531

After increasing the number of engines, run **sp_sysmon** again under similar load conditions, and check "Engine Busy Utilization" and the contention points listed above.

Measuring CPU Usage from the Operating System

When you measure the CPU usage for SQL Server using operating system utilities:

- The percentage of time SQL Server uses CPU during an elapsed time interval is a reflection of a multiple CPU power processing request.
- If CPU usage is at or near 100 percent most of the time, consider adding more CPUs to the hardware configuration.

The *cpu_busy* percentage indicates SQL Server CPU processing during a time interval for the number of engines configured. It is not a direct reflection of CPU usage.

Distributing Network I/O Across All Engines

On SMP systems that support network affinity migration, SQL Server distributes network I/O operations to each engine on a per-connection basis. **Network affinity migration** is the process of moving network I/O from one engine to another. During login, SQL Server selects an engine to handle network I/O for the user connection's tasks. The tasks run network I/O on that engine (network affinity) until the connection is terminated.

Distributing network I/O on more engines than just engine 0 provides these benefits:

- It reduces the performance and throughput bottlenecks that occur due to the increased load on engine 0 (to perform all the network I/O) and due to other engines waiting for engine 0.

- It renders SQL Server more symmetric by allowing any engine to handle user connections.

- It increases the overall number of user connections that SQL Server can handle as you add more engines.

- It distributes the network I/O load among its engines more efficiently by migrating network affinity to the engine with the lightest load.

In general, SQL Server's network performance scales as the number of engines is increased. Because a task's network I/O is assigned to one engine, SQL Server provides better performance results when processing small tasks from many user connections than when processing large tasks from a few connections.

Enabling Engine-to-CPU Affinity

By default, there is no affinity between CPUs and engines on SQL Server. You may see slight performance gains in high-throughput environments by affinitying engines to CPUs.

Not all operating systems support CPU affinity. The command is silently ignored on systems that do not support engine-to-CPU affinity. The **dbcc tune** command must be re-issued each time SQL Server is restarted. Each time CPU affinity is turned on or off, SQL Server prints a message in the errorlog indicating the engine and CPU numbers affected:

```
Engine 1, cpu affinity set to cpu 4.
Engine 1, cpu affinity removed.
```

The syntax is:

```
dbcc tune(cpuaffinity, start_cpu [, on| off] )
```

start_cpu specifies the CPU to bind engine 0 to. Engine 1 gets bound to the CPU numbered (*start_cpu* + 1) and so on. Engine *n* gets bound to ((*start_cpu* + *n*) % number_of_cpus). CPU numbers are in the range 0 through the number of CPUs minus one.

On a 4 CPU machine with CPUs numbered 0 through 3, on a 4 engine SQL Server, this command:

```
dbcc tune(cpuaffinity, 2, "on")
```

causes the following affinity:

Engine	CPU	
0	2	(the *start_cpu* number specified)
1	3	
2	0	
3	1	

On the same machine, with a 3 engine SQL Server, the same command causes the following affinity:

Engine	CPU
0	2
1	3
2	0

In this example, CPU 1 will not be used by SQL Server.

To disable CPU affinity, specify -1 in place of *start_cpu*, and use **off** for the setting:

```
dbcc tune(cpuaffinity, -1, off)
```

You can enable CPU affinity without changing the value of *start_cpu* by using -1 and **on** for the setting:

```
dbcc tune(cpuaffinity, -1, on)
```

The default value for *start_cpu* is 1 if CPU affinity has not been previously set.

To specify a new value of *start_cpu* without changing the **on/off** setting, use:

```
dbcc tune (cpuaffinity, start_cpu)
```

If CPU affinity is currently enabled and the new *start_cpu* is different from its previous value, SQL Server change the affinity for each engine.

If CPU affinity is currently off, SQL Server notes the new *start_cpu* value, and the new affinity takes effect the next time CPU affinity is turned on.

To see the current value and whether affinity is enabled, use:

```
dbcc tune(cpuaffinity, -1)
```

This command only prints current settings to the errorlog, and does not change the affinity or the settings.

You can check the network I/O load across all SQL Server engines using the **sp_sysmon** system procedure. See "Network I/O Management" on page 534.

To determine whether your platform supports network affinity migration, consult your operating system documentation or the SQL Server installation and configuration guide.

How the Housekeeper Task Improves CPU Utilization

When SQL Server has no user tasks to process, a housekeeper task automatically begins writing dirty buffers to disk. Because these writes are done during the server's idle cycles, they are known as free writes. They result in improved CPU utilization and a decreased need for buffer washing during transaction processing. They also reduce the number and duration of checkpoint "spikes," times when the checkpoint process causes a short, sharp rise in disk writes.

➤ **Note**

The housekeeper task does not improve performance for read-only caches or for data that fits entirely within a cache.

Side Effects of the Housekeeper Task

If the housekeeper task can flush all active buffer pools in all configured caches, it wakes up the checkpoint task. The checkpoint task determines whether it can checkpoint the database. The additional checkpoints that occur as a result of the housekeeper process may improve recovery speed for the database.

In applications that repeatedly update the same database page, the housekeeper task may initiate some database writes that are not necessary. Although these writes occur only during the server's idle cycles, they may be unacceptable on systems with overloaded disks.

Configuring the Housekeeper Task

System Administrators can use the **housekeeper free write percent** configuration parameter to control the side effects of the housekeeper task. This parameter specifies the maximum percentage by which the housekeeper task can increase database writes. Valid values range from 0–100.

By default, the **housekeeper free write percent** parameter is set to 1. This allows the housekeeper task to continue to wash buffers as long as the database writes do not increase by more than 1 percent. The work done by the housekeeper task at the default parameter setting results in improved performance and recovery speed on most systems.

Changing the Percentage by Which Writes Can Increase

Use the **sp_configure** system procedure to change the percentage by which database writes can increase as a result of the housekeeper process:

```
sp_configure "housekeeper free write percent",
maximum_increase_in_database_writes
```

For example, issue the following command to stop the housekeeper task from working when the frequency of database writes reaches 5 percent above normal:

```
sp_configure "housekeeper free write percent", 5
```

Disabling the Housekeeper Task

You may want to disable the housekeeper task in order to establish a controlled environment in which only specified user tasks are running. To disable the housekeeper task, set the value of the **housekeeper free write percent** parameter to 0:

```
sp_configure "housekeeper free write percent", 0
```

Allowing the Housekeeper Task to Work Continuously

To allow the housekeeper task to work continuously, regardless of the percentage of additional database writes, set the value of the **housekeeper free write percent** parameter to 100:

```
sp_configure "housekeeper free write percent", 100
```

Checking Housekeeper Effectiveness

The "Recovery Management" section of **sp_sysmon** shows checkpoint information to help you determine the effectiveness of the housekeeper. See "Recovery Management" on page 526.

Multiprocessor Application Design Guidelines

The multiprocessor SQL Server is compatible with uniprocessor SQL Server. Applications that run on uniprocessor servers should run on SMP servers as well. Increased throughput on multiprocessor SQL Servers makes it more likely that multiple processes may try to access a data page simultaneously. It is especially important to adhere to the principles of good database design to avoid contention. Following are some of the application design considerations that are especially important in an SMP environment.

Multiple Indexes

The increased throughput of SMP may result in increased lock contention when tables with multiple indexes are updated. Allow no more than two or three indexes on any table that will be updated often.

For information on index maintenance effects on performance, see "Index Management" on page 496.

Managing Disks

The additional processing power of the SMP product may increase demands on the disks. Therefore, it is best to spread data across multiple devices for heavily used databases. See "Disk I/O Management" on page 529 for information on **sp_sysmon** reports on disk utilization.

Adjusting the *fillfactor* for *create index* Commands

You may need to adjust the **fillfactor** in **create index** commands. Because of the added throughput with multiple processors, setting a lower **fillfactor** may temporarily reduce contention for the data and index pages.

Setting *max_rows_per_page*

The use of **fillfactor** places fewer rows on data and index pages when the index is created, but the **fillfactor** is not maintained. Over time, data modifications can increase the number of rows on a page.

For tables and indexes that experience contention, **max_rows_per_page** provides a permanent means to limit the number of rows on data and index pages.

The **sp_helpindex** system procedure reports the current **max_rows_per_page** setting of indexes. Use the **sp_chgattribute** system procedure to change the **max_rows_per_page** setting.

Setting **max_rows_per_page** to a lower value does not reduce index splitting, and, in most cases, increases the number of index page splits. It can help reduce other lock contention on index pages. If your problem is index page splitting, careful choice of **fillfactor** is a better option.

Transaction Length

Transactions that include many statements or take a long time to run may result in increased lock contention. Keep transactions as short as possible, and avoid holding locks—especially exclusive or update locks—while waiting for user interaction.

Temporary Tables

Temporary tables (tables in *tempdb*) do not cause contention, because they are associated with individual users and are not shared. However, if multiple user processes use *tempdb* for temporary objects, there can be some contention on the system tables in *tempdb*. "Temporary Tables and Locking" on page 384 for information on ways to reduce contention.

Real-World Context: Maintenance Activities and Performance

Much of the discussion in earlier chapters has proceeded as if all the system has to do is continuously process transactions.

In the real world, maintenance activities such as rebuilding indexes, database backup and recovery, or performing database consistency checks are essential to ensuring database integrity and reliability, and for keeping performance from degrading over time.

Chapter 18, "Maintenance Activities and Performance," discusses strategies for scheduling and automating maintenance tasks to minimize their effects on performance.

18 Maintenance Activities and Performance

Maintenance Activities That Affect Performance

No matter how well-designed or finely-tuned, database management applications are seldom static entities. Changes to the universe of data and new features of the application periodically require new databases and indexes.

Application development activities such as creating databases and indexes supplement standard system administration tasks such as creating database backups, checking the consistency of the database, and running update statistics on indexes.

Since maintenance activities that affect the entire database can slow performance for all users of the system, the common-sense approach is to perform maintenance tasks at times when your SQL Server usage is low.

This chapter helps you determine the impact on applications and on overall SQL Server performance of the following activities:

- Creating a database
- Creating indexes
- Dumps and loads
- Bulk copy operations
- Database consistency checks
- Update statistics

Creating or Altering a Database

Creating and altering a database is I/O intensive, and other I/O intensive operations may suffer. When you create a database, SQL Server copies the *model* database to the new database and then initializes all the allocation pages, the first page of each 256-page allocation unit.

The following procedures can help speed database creation or minimize its impact on other processes:

- Use the **for load** option to **create database** if you are restoring a database, that is, if you are getting ready to issue a **load database** command.

When you create a database without **for load**, it copies *model*, and then initializes all of the allocation units. When you use **for load**, it postpones zeroing the allocation units until the load is complete. Then it initializes only the untouched allocation units. If you are loading a very large database dump, this can save a large amount of time.

- Create databases during off-hours if possible.

create database and **alter database** perform concurrent parallel I/O on up to six devices at a time when clearing database pages. If you specify more than six devices, the first six writes take place in parallel, and as the I/O to each device completes, the 16K buffers are used for remaining devices.

The following example names eight separate devices:

```
create database hugedb
        on dev1 = 500,
        dev2 = 600,
        dev3 = 600,
        dev4 = 500,
        dev5 = 500,
        dev6 = 500
log on logdev1 = 500,
        logdev2 = 500
```

➤ *Note*

When create database copies model, it uses 2K I/O.

A single set of six buffers is available for large I/O by **create database**, **alter database, dbcc checkalloc**, and the portion of **load database** that zeros pages. If all six buffers are in use when another process issues one of these commands, the second command performs 2K I/O.

Creating Indexes

Creating indexes affects performance by locking other users out of a table. The type of lock depends on the index type:

- Creating a clustered index requires an exclusive table lock, locking out all table activity. Since rows in a clustered index are arranged in order by the index key, **create clustered index** reorders data pages.

- Creating a nonclustered index requires a shared table lock, locking out update activity.

Configuring SQL Server to Speed Sorting

These configuration parameters can increase the speed of sort operations during **create index** operations:

- **number of extent i/o buffers** configures the number of extents (8 data pages) that can be used for I/O during creating indexes. These buffers are used for intermediate results.

- **number of sort buffers** configures how many buffers can be used in cache to hold pages from the input tables.

- **sort page count** specifies the maximum amount of memory a sort operation can use. These pages store rows in memory during the sort.

Full information on these parameters is available in Chapter 11, "Setting Configuration Parameters," of the *System Administration Guide*.

Extent I/O Buffers

If you do not configure **number of extent i/o buffers**, SQL Server performs 2K I/O while it creates indexes. This parameter allows SQL Server to use 16K buffers for reading and writing intermediate and final results. Each buffer you configure requires 16K of memory.

Configuring **number of extent i/o buffers** has these impacts:

- Increasing this parameter decreases the memory available for the procedure and data caches.

- Only one user at a time can use extent I/O buffers when creating an index. Other users who start **create index** commands are restricted to page I/O.

- Setting **number of extent I/O buffers** to 10 works well with small configurations.

- Settings above 100 yield only marginal benefits.

If you have ample memory and perform frequent index maintenance, configure extent I/O buffers on a permanent basis. In other cases, it makes sense to schedule index maintenance for off-hours. Then, I/O extents can be allocated for optimum performance. When the index maintenance is completed, deallocate the extra I/O extents, and resume normal memory allocations.

➤ *Note*

You need to shut down and restart SQL Server in order to change the number of extents allocated.

Increasing the Number of Sort Buffers and Sort Pages

If you are creating very large indexes at a time when other SQL Server activity is at a minimum, setting **number of sort buffers** and **sort page count** can greatly increase **create index** performance. Both of these configuration parameters are dynamic and use memory from the default data cache for each sort operation.

◆ *WARNING!*

If you use these parameters, be sure to dump the database soon after the index is created to ensure the compatibility of database dumps.

Dumping the Database After Creating an Index

When you create an index, SQL Server writes the **create index** transaction and the page allocations to the transaction log, but does not log the actual changes to the data and index pages. If you need to recover a database, and you have not dumped it since you created the index, the entire **create index** process is executed again while loading transaction log dumps.

If you perform routine index re-creations (for example, to maintain the **fillfactor** in the index), you may want to schedule these operations at a time shortly before a routine database dump.

Creating a Clustered Index on Sorted Data

If your data has already been sorted and is in the desired clustered index order, use the **with sorted_data** option when creating indexes. This saves the time needed for the actual sort phase.

➤ *Note*

The sorted data option still requires space of approximately 120 percent of the table size to copy the data and store the index pages.

Backup and Recovery

All SQL Server backups are performed by a Backup Server. The backup architecture uses a client/server paradigm, with SQL Servers as clients to a Backup Server.

Local Backups

SQL Server sends the local Backup Server instructions, via remote procedure calls, telling the Backup Server which pages to dump or load, which backup devices to use, and other options. Backup Server performs all the disk I/O. SQL Server does not read or send dump and load data, just instructions.

Remote Backups

Backup Server also supports backups to remote machines. For remote dumps and loads, a local Backup Server performs the disk I/O related to the database device and sends the data over the network to the remote Backup Server, which stores it on the dump device.

Online Backups

Backups can be done while a database is active. Clearly, such processing affects other transactions, but do not be afraid to back up critical databases as often as necessary to satisfy the reliability requirements of the system.

See Chapter 18, "Developing a Backup and Recovery Plan," in the *System Administration Guide* for a complete discussion of backup and recovery strategies.

Using Thresholds to Prevent Running Out of Log Space

If your database has limited log space, and you occasionally hit the **last-chance threshold**, install a second threshold that provides ample time to perform a transaction log dump. Running out of log space has severe performance impacts. Users cannot execute any data modification commands until log space has been freed.

Minimizing Recovery Time

You can help minimize recovery time, the time required to reboot SQL Server, by changing the **recovery interval** configuration parameter. The default value of 5 minutes per database works for most installations. Reduce this value only if functional requirements dictate a faster recovery period. It can increase the amount of I/O required. See "Tuning the Recovery Interval" on page 422.

Recovery speed may also be affected by the value of the **housekeeper free write percent** configuration parameter. The default value of this parameter allows the server's housekeeper task to write dirty buffers to disk during the server's idle cycles, as long as disk I/O does not increase by more than 20 percent. See "Configuring the Housekeeper Task" on page 450 for more information on tuning this parameter.

Recovery Order

During recovery, system databases are recovered first. Then, user databases are recovered in order by database ID.

Bulk Copy

Bulk copy into a table on SQL Server runs fastest when there are no indexes or triggers on the table. When you are running fast bulk copy, SQL Server performs reduced logging. It does not log the actual changes to the database, only the allocation of pages. And, since there are no indexes to update, it saves all the time updating indexes for each data insert, and the logging of the changes to the index pages.

To use fast bulk copy, **select into/bulkcopy** option must be set for the database with **sp_dboption.** Remember to turn the option off after the bulk copy operation completes.

During fast bulk copy, rules are not enforced but defaults **are** enforced.

Since changes to the data are not logged, you should perform a **dump database** soon after a fast bulk copy operation. Performing a fast bulk copy in a database blocks the use of **dump transaction**, since the unlogged data changes cannot be recovered from the transaction log dump.

Batches and Bulk Copy

If you specify a batch size during a fast bulk copy, each new batch must start on a new data page, since only the page allocations, and not the data changes, are logged during a fast bulk copy. Copying 1000 rows with a batch size of 1 requires 1000 data pages and 1000 allocation records in the transaction log. If you are using a small batch size to help detect errors in the input file, you may want to choose a batch size that corresponds to the numbers of rows that fit on a data page.

Slow Bulk Copy

If a table has indexes or triggers, a slower version of bulk copy is automatically used. For slow bulk copy:

- The **select into/bulkcopy** option does not have to be set.

- Rules are not enforced and triggers are not fired, but defaults **are** enforced.

- All data changes are logged, as well as the page allocations.

- Indexes are updated as rows are copied in, and index changes are logged.

Improving Bulk Copy Performance

Other ways to increase bulk copy performance are:

- Set the **trunc log on chkpt** option to keep the transaction log from filling up. If your database has a threshold procedure that automatically dumps the log when it fills, you will save the transaction dump time. Remember that each batch is a separate transaction, so if you are not specifying a batch size, setting **trunc log on chkpt** will not help.

- Find the optimal network packet size. See "Client Commands for Larger Packet Sizes" on page 431.

Replacing the Data in a Large Table

If you are replacing all the data in a large table, use the **truncate table** command instead of the **delete** command. **truncate table** performs reduced logging. Only the page deallocations are logged. **delete** is completely logged, that is, all the changes to the data are logged.

The steps are:

1. Truncate the table

2. Drop all indexes on the table

3. Load the data

4. Re-create the indexes

Adding Large Amounts of Data to a Table

When you are adding 10 percent to 20 percent or more to a large table, drop the nonclustered indexes, load the data, and then re-create nonclustered indexes.

For very large tables, leaving the clustered index in place may be necessary due to space constraints. SQL Server must make a copy of the table when it creates a clustered index. In many cases, once tables become very large, the time required to perform a slow bulk copy with the index in place is less than the time to perform a fast bulk copy and re-create the clustered index.

Use Partitions and Multiple Copy Processes

If you are loading data into a table without a clustered index, you can create partitions on the heap table and split the batch of data into multiple batches, one for each partition you create. See "Improving Insert Performance with Partitions" on page 364.

Impacts on Other Users

Bulk copying large tables in or out may affect other users' response time. If possible:

- Schedule bulk copy operations for off-hours.

- Use fast bulk copy, since it does less logging and less I/O.

Database Consistency Checker

It is important to run database consistency checks periodically with **dbcc**. If you back up a corrupt database, the backup is useless. But **dbcc** affects performance, since **dbcc** must acquire locks on the objects it checks.

See "Comparing the dbcc Commands" on page 17-14 of the *System Administration Guide* for information about **dbcc** and locking. Also see "Scheduling Database Maintenance at Your Site" on page 17-15 for more information about how to minimize the effects of **dbcc** on user applications.

Regular Monitoring as a Maintenance Activity

Both initial performance tuning and regular maintenance require constant monitoring of your system's performance. The **sp_sysmon** procedure, which delivers detailed reports from SQL Server's internal counters and registers, is the tool you'll use most often to monitor performance.

Chapter 19, "Monitoring SQL Server Performance with sp_sysmon" covers this invaluable procedure in depth.

19

Monitoring SQL Server Performance with *sp_sysmon*

Introduction

This chapter describes output from **sp_sysmon**, a system procedure that produces SQL Server performance data. When you invoke **sp_sysmon**, it clears all accumulated data from internal counters and enters a **waitfor** loop until the user-specified time interval elapses. During the interval, various SQL Server processes increment the counters. At the end of the interval, the procedure reads the counters, prints out the report, and stops executing. The flow diagram below shows the algorithm.

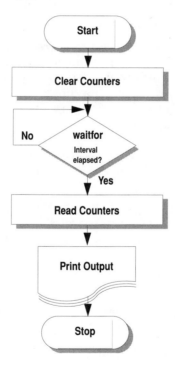

Figure 19-1: sp_sysmon execution algorithm

sp_sysmon reports detailed performance statistics for the following categories of SQL Server system activities:

- Kernel Utilization   19-474

This chapter explains **sp_sysmon** output and gives suggestions for interpreting its output and deducing possible implications. **sp_sysmon** output is most valuable when you use it together with a good understanding of your unique SQL Server environment and its specific mix of applications. The output has little relevance on its own.

➤ *Note*

sp_sysmon will not produce accurate results on pre-11.0 SQL Servers because many of the internal counters **sp_sysmon** uses were added in SQL Server release 11.0. In addition, the uses and meanings of many pre-existing counters have changed.

Invoking *sp_sysmon*

To invoke **sp_sysmon**, execute the following command using **isql**:

```
sp_sysmon interval
```

where *interval* is an integer time in minutes from 1 to 10.

An **sp_sysmon** report contains hundreds of lines of output. Use **isql** input and output redirect flags to save the output to a file. See the SQL Server utility programs manual for more information on **isql**.

Using *sp_sysmon* to View Performance Information

sp_sysmon contributes 5 to 7 percent overhead while it runs on a single CPU server, and more on multiprocessor servers. The amount of overhead increases with the number of CPUs. Only a System Administrator can execute **sp_sysmon**.

➤ *Note*

Because **sp_sysmon** clears the counters it uses when it first starts, and then starts to accumulate results, only one instance should be active at a time. If one session is running **sp_sysmon**, and a second session starts it, the results of the first run of **sp_sysmon** will be inaccurate.

When to Use *sp_sysmon*

You can run **sp_sysmon** both before and after tuning SQL Server configuration parameters to gather data for comparison. This data gives you a basis for performance tuning and lets you observe the results of configuration changes.

Use **sp_sysmon** when the system exhibits the behavior you want to investigate. For example, if you are interested in finding out how the system behaves under typically loaded conditions, run **sp_sysmon** when conditions are normal and typically loaded. In this case, it does not make sense to run **sp_sysmon** for ten minutes starting at 7:00 pm, before the batch jobs begin and after most of the day's OLTP users have left the site. In this example, it would be a good idea to run **sp_sysmon** both during the normal OLTP load and during batch jobs.

In many tests, it is best to start the applications, and then start **sp_sysmon** when caches have had a chance to fill. If you are trying to measure capacity, be sure that the amount of work you give the server to do keeps it busy for the duration of the test. Many of the statistics, especially those that measure data per second, can look extremely low if the server is idle during part of the sample period.

When to Use *sp_sysmon*

In general, **sp_sysmon** produces valuable information for performing the following tuning tasks:

- Before and after changing cache configuration or pool configuration

- Before and after certain **sp_configure** changes
- Before and after adding new queries to your application mix
- Before and after increasing or reducing the number of SQL Server engines
- When adding new disk devices and assigning objects to them
- During peak periods, to look for contention
- During stress tests to evaluate a SQL Server configuration for a maximum expected application load
- When performance seems slow or behaves abnormally

It can also help with micro-level understanding of certain queries or applications during development. Some examples are:

- Working with indexes and updates, you can see if certain updates reported as deferred_varcol are resulting direct vs. deferred updates.
- Checking caching behavior of particular queries or mix of queries.

How to Use the Data

sp_sysmon can give you information about SQL Server system behavior both before and after tuning. It is important to study the entire report to understand the full impact of the changes you make.

There are several reasons for this. Sometimes removing one performance bottleneck reveals another (see Figure 19-2). It is also possible that your tuning efforts might improve performance in one area, while actually causing a performance degradation in another area.

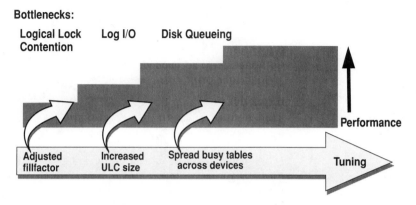

Figure 19-2: Eliminating one bottleneck reveals another

In addition to pointing out areas for tuning work, **sp_sysmon** output is valuable for determining when further tuning will not pay off in additional performance gains. It is just as important to know when to stop tuning SQL Server, or when the problem resides elsewhere, as it is to know what to tune.

Other information can contribute to interpreting **sp_sysmon** output:

- Information on the configuration parameters in use, from **sp_configure** or the configuration file

- Information on the cache configuration and cache bindings, from **sp_cacheconfig** and **sp_helpcache**

- Information on disk devices, segments, and the objects stored on them

Reading *sp_sysmon* Output

sp_sysmon displays performance statistics in a consistent tabular format. For example, in an SMP environment running nine SQL Server engines, the output typically looks like this:

```
Engine Busy Utilization:
      Engine 0                          98.8 %
      Engine 1                          98.8 %
      Engine 2                          97.4 %
      Engine 3                          99.5 %
      Engine 4                          98.7 %
      Engine 5                          98.7 %
      Engine 6                          99.3 %
      Engine 7                          98.3 %
      Engine 8                          97.7 %
      - - - - - - - - -       - - - - - - - - - - - -      - - - - - - - - - - - - - -
      Summary:              Total:   887.2 %          Average:    98.6 %
```

Rows

Most rows represent a specific type of activity or event, such as acquiring a lock or executing a stored procedure. When the data is related to CPUs, the rows show performance information for each SQL Server engine in the SMP environment. The output above shows nine SQL Server engines. Often, when there are groups of related rows, the last row is a summary of totals and an average.

The **sp_sysmon** report indents some rows to show that one category is a subcategory of another. In the following example, "Found in Wash" is a subcategory of "Cache Hits," which is a subcategory of "Cache Searches":

```
Cache Searches
      Cache Hits                  202.1       3.0     12123      100.0 %
            Found in Wash           0.0       0.0         0        0.0 %
      Cache Misses                  0.0       0.0         0        0.0 %
      - - - - - - - - - - - - - - - - - - -   - - - - - - -   - - - - - - - - -
      Total Cache Searches        202.1       3.0     12123
```

Many rows are not printed when the "count" value is 0.

Columns

Unless otherwise stated, the columns represent the following performance statistics:

- "per sec"– average per second during sampling interval

- "per xact" – average per committed transaction during sampling interval

- "count" – total number during the sample interval

- "% of total" – varies depending on context, as explained for each occurrence

Interpreting *sp_sysmon* Data

When tuning SQL Server, the fundamental measures of success appear as increases in throughput and reductions in application response time. Unfortunately, tuning SQL Server cannot be reduced to printing these two values. In most cases, your tuning efforts must take an iterative approach involving a comprehensive overview of SQL Server activity, careful tuning and analysis of queries and applications, and monitoring locking and access on an object-by-object basis.

sp_sysmon is a tool that provides a comprehensive overview of system performance. Use SQL Server Monitor to pinpoint contention on a per-object basis.

Per Second and Per Transaction Data

Weigh the importance of the per second and per transaction data on the environment and the category you are measuring. The per transaction data is generally more meaningful in benchmarks or in test environments where the workload is well defined.

It is likely that you will find per transaction data more meaningful for comparing test data than per second data alone because in a benchmark test environment, there is usually a well-defined number of transactions, making comparison straightforward. Per transaction data is also useful for determining the validity of percentage results.

Percent of Total and Count Data

The meaning of the "% of total" data varies depending on the context of the event and the totals for the category. When interpreting percentages, keep in mind that they are often useful for understanding general trends, but they can be misleading when taken in isolation. For example, 50 percent of 200 events is much more meaningful than 50 percent of 2 events.

The "count" data is the total number of events that occurred during the sample interval. You can use count data to determine the validity of percentage results.

Per Engine Data

In most cases, per engine data for a category will show a fairly even balance of activity across all engines. There are a few exceptions:

- If you have fewer processes than CPUs, some of the engines will show no activity.

- If most processes are doing fairly uniform activity, such as simple inserts and short selects, and one process performs some I/O intensive operation such as a large bulk copy, you will see unbalanced network and disk I/O.

Total or Summary Data

Summary rows provide an overview of SQL Server engine activity by reporting totals and averages.

Be careful when interpreting averages because they can give false impressions of true results when the data are skewed. For example, if you have one SQL Server engine working 98 percent of the time and another that is working 2 percent of the time, a 50 percent average can be misleading.

Sample Interval and Time Reporting

The heading of an **sp_sysmon** report includes the date, the time the sample interval started, "Statistics Cleared at," the time it completed, "Statistics Sampled at," and the duration of the sample interval.

```
===========================================================================
          Sybase SQL Server 11 System Performance Monitor v1.0 Beta
===========================================================================


Run Date                        Dec 20, 1995
Statistics Cleared at               16:05:40
Statistics Sampled at               16:06:40
Sample Interval                 1  min.
```

Kernel Utilization

"Kernel Utilization" reports on SQL Server activities. It tells you how busy SQL Server engines were during the time that the CPU was available to SQL Server, how often the CPU yielded to the operating system, the number of times that the engines checked for network and disk I/O, and the average number of I/Os they found waiting at each check.

Sample Output for Kernel Utilization

The following sample shows **sp_sysmon** output for "Kernel Utilization" in an environment with eight SQL Server engines.

```
Kernel Utilization
------------------

   Engine Busy Utilization:
      Engine 0                98.5 %
      Engine 1                99.3 %
      Engine 2                98.3 %
      Engine 3                97.2 %
      Engine 4                97.8 %
      Engine 5                99.3 %
      Engine 6                98.8 %
      Engine 7                99.7 %
   ----------          ----------------        ----------------
   Summary:            Total:  789.0 %         Average:  98.6 %

   CPU Yields by Engine      per sec    per xact    count   % of total
   ---------------------     --------   ---------   ------  ----------
                              0.0         0.0         0       n/a
   Network Checks
      Non-Blocking          79893.3     1186.1     4793037   100.0 %
      Blocking                  1.1        0.0          67     0.0 %
   ---------------------     --------   ---------   ------
   Total Network I/O Checks 79894.4     1186.1     4793104
   Avg Net I/Os per Check      n/a         n/a      0.00169    n/a


   Disk I/O Checks
      Total Disk I/O Checks  94330.3    1400.4     5659159    n/a
      Checks Returning I/O   92881.0    1378.9     5572210    98.5 %
      Avg Disk I/Os Returned    n/a        n/a      0.00199    n/a
```

In this example, the CPU did not yield to the operating system, so
there are no detail rows.

Engine Busy Utilization

"Engine Busy Utilization" reports the percentage of time the SQL
Server Kernel is busy executing tasks on each SQL Server engine
(rather than time spent idle). The summary row gives the total and
the average active time for all engines combined.

The values reported here may differ from CPU usage values reported
by operating system tools. When SQL Server has no tasks to process,
it enters a loop that regularly checks for network I/O, completed
disk I/Os, and tasks on the run queue. Operating system commands
to check CPU activity may show high usage for a SQL Server engine
because they are measuring the looping activity, while "Engine Busy
Utilization" does not include time spent looping—it is considered
idle time.

One measurement that cannot be made from inside SQL Server is the percentage of time that SQL Server had control of the CPU versus the time the CPU was in use by the operating system. Check your operating system documentation for the correct commands.

See "Engine Busy Utilization" on page 475 for an explanation of why operating system commands report different information on utilization than SQL Server does.

If you want to reduce the time that SQL Server spends checking for I/O while idle, you can lower the **sp_configure** parameter **runnable process search count**. This parameter specifies the number of times a SQL Server engine loops looking for a runnable task before yielding the CPU. For more information, see "runnable process search count" on page 11-88 of the *System Administration Guide*.

"Engine Busy Utilization" measures how busy SQL Server engines were during the CPU time they were given. If the engine is available to SQL Server for 80 percent of a ten-minute sample interval, and "Engine Busy Utilization" was 90 percent, it means that SQL Server was busy for 7 minutes and 12 seconds and idle for 48 seconds as Figure 19-3 shows.

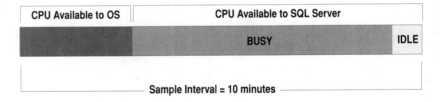

Figure 19-3: How SQL Server spends its available CPU time

This category can help you decide whether there are too many or too few SQL Server engines. SQL Server's high scalability is due to tunable mechanisms that avoid resource contention. By checking **sp_sysmon** output for problems and tuning to alleviate contention, response time can remain high even at "Engine Busy" values in the 80 to 90 percent range. If values are consistently very high (over 90 percent), it is likely that response time and throughput could benefit from an additional engine.

The "Engine Busy" values are averages over the sample interval, so very high averages indicate that engines may be 100 percent busy during part of the interval. When engine utilization is extremely high, the housekeeper process writes few or no pages out to disk (since it runs only during idle CPU cycles.) This means that a checkpoint will find many pages that need to be written to disk, and the checkpoint process, a large batch job, or a database dump is likely to send CPU usage to 100 percent for a period of time, causing a perceptible dip in response time.

If "Engine Busy Utilization" percentages are consistently high, and you want to improve response time and throughput by adding SQL Server engines, carefully check for increased resource contention after adding each engine.

CPU Yields by Engine

"CPU Yields by Engine" reports the number of times each SQL Server engine yielded to the operating system. "% of total" data is the percentage of times a SQL Server engine yielded as a percentage of the combined yields for all SQL Server engines.

"Total CPU Yields" reports the combined data over all SQL Server engines.

If "Engine Busy Utilization" data indicates low engine utilization, use "CPU Yields by Engine" to determine whether "Engine Busy Utilization" data reflects a truly inactive SQL Server engine or one that is frequently starved out of the CPU by the operating system.

When a SQL Server engine is not busy, it yields to the CPU after a period of time related to the **runnable process search count** parameter. A high value for "CPU Yields by Engine" indicates that the SQL Server engine yielded voluntarily.

If you also see that "Engine Busy Utilization" is a low value, then the SQL Server engine really is inactive, as opposed to being starved out. The actual numbers that represents "high" and "low" values depend on the specific operating environment. See "runnable process search count" on page 11-88 of the *System Administration Guide* for more information.

Network Checks

"Network Checks" includes information about blocking and non-blocking network I/O checks, the total number of I/O checks for the interval, and the average number of network I/Os per network check.

SQL Server has two ways to check for network I/O: blocking and non-blocking modes.

Non-Blocking

"Non-Blocking" reports the number of times SQL Server performed non-blocking network checks. With non-blocking network I/O checks, a SQL Server engine checks the network for I/O and continues processing whether or not it found I/O waiting.

Blocking

After a SQL Server engine completes a task, it loops waiting for the network to deliver a runnable task. After a certain number of loops (determined by the **sp_configure** parameter **runnable process search count**), the SQL Server engine goes to sleep after a blocking network I/O.

When a SQL Server engine yields to the operating system because there are no tasks to process, it wakes up once per clock tick to check for incoming network I/O. If there is I/O, the operating system blocks the engine from active processing until the I/O completes.

If a SQL Server engine has yielded and is doing blocking checks, it might continue to sleep for a period of time after a network packet arrives. This period of time is referred to as the latency period.

You can reduce the latency period by increasing the **runnable process search count** parameter so the SQL Server engine loops for longer periods of time. See "runnable process search count" on page 11–88 of the *System Administration Guide* for more information.

Total Network I/O Checks

"Total Network I/O Checks" reports the number of times SQL Server engines poll the sockets for incoming and outgoing packets. This category is helpful when you use it with "CPU Yields by Engine."

When a SQL Server engine is idle, it loops while checking for network packets. If "Network Checks" is low and "CPU Yields by Engine" is high, the engine could be yielding too often and not checking the network sockets frequently enough. If the system can afford the overhead, it might be acceptable to yield less often.

Average Network I/Os per Check

"Avg Net I/Os per Check" reports the average number of network I/Os (both sends and receives) per check for all SQL Server engine checks that took place during the sample interval.

The **sp_configure** parameter **i/o polling process count** specifies the maximum number of processes that SQL Server runs before the scheduler checks for disk and/or network I/O completions. Tuning **i/o polling process count** affects both the response time and throughput of SQL Server. See "i/o polling process count" on page 11-76 of the *System Administration Guide*.

If SQL Server engines check frequently, but retrieves network I/O infrequently, you can try reducing the frequency for network I/O checking.

Disk I/O Checks

This section reports on the total number of disk I/O checks, and the number of checks returning I/O.

Total Disk I/O Checks

"Total Disk I/O Checks" reports the number of times a SQL Server engine checked disk I/O.

When a task needs to perform I/O, the SQL Server engine running that task immediately issues an I/O request and puts the task to sleep waiting for the I/O to complete. The SQL Server engine processes other tasks, if any, but also uses a scheduling loop to check for completed I/Os. When the engine finds completed I/Os, it moves the task from the sleep queue to the run queue.

Checks Returning I/O

"Checks Returning I/O" is the number of times that a requested I/O had completed when a SQL Server engine checked for disk I/O.

For example, if a SQL Server engine checks for expected I/O 100,000 times, this average indicates the percentage of time that there actually was I/O pending. If, of those 100,000 checks, I/O was pending 10,000 times, then 10 percent of the checks were effective, while the other 90 percent were overhead. However, you should also check the average number of I/Os returned per check, and how busy the engines were during the sample period. If the sample includes idle time, or the I/O traffic is bursty, it is possible that during the busy period, a high percentage of the checks were returning I/O.

If the results in this category seem low or high, you can configure **i/o polling process count** so that the SQL Server engine checks less or more frequently. See "i/o polling process count" on page 11–76 in the *System Administration Guide*.

Average Disk I/Os Returned

"Avg Disk I/Os Returned" reports the average number of disk I/Os returned over all SQL Server engine checks combined.

Increasing the amount of time that SQL Server engines wait between checks could result in better throughput because SQL Server engines can spend more time processing if they spend less time checking for I/O. However, you should verify this for your environment. Use the **sp_configure** parameter **i/o polling process count** to increase the length of the checking loop. See "i/o polling process count" on page 11–76 in the *System Administration Guide*.

Task Management

"Task Management" provides information on opened connections, task context switches by engine, and task context switches by cause.

"Task Context Switches Due To" provides an overview of the reasons that tasks were switched off engines. The possible performance problems show in this section can be investigated by checking other **sp_sysmon** output, as indicated below in the sections that describe the causes.

Sample Output for Task Management

The following sample shows **sp_sysmon** output for the "Task Management" categories.

Task Management	per sec	per xact	count	% of total
Connections Opened	0.0	0.0	0	n/a
Task Context Switches by Engine				
Engine 0	94.8	0.8	5730	10.6 %
Engine 1	94.6	0.8	5719	10.6 %
Engine 2	92.8	0.8	5609	10.4 %
Engine 3	105.0	0.9	6349	11.7 %
Engine 4	101.8	0.8	6152	11.4 %
Engine 5	109.1	0.9	6595	12.2 %
Engine 6	102.6	0.9	6201	11.4 %
Engine 7	99.0	0.8	5987	11.1 %
Engine 8	96.4	0.8	5830	10.8 %

```
Total Task Switches:          896.1        7.5    54172

Task Context Switches Due To:
  Voluntary Yields             69.1        0.6     4179     7.7 %
  Cache Search Misses          56.7        0.5     3428     6.3 %
  System Disk Writes            1.0        0.0       62     0.1 %
  I/O Pacing                   11.5        0.1      695     1.3 %
  Logical Lock Contention       3.7        0.0      224     0.4 %
  Address Lock Contention       0.0        0.0        0     0.0 %
  Log Semaphore Contention     51.0        0.4     3084     5.7 %
  Group Commit Sleeps          82.2        0.7     4971     9.2 %
  Last Log Page Writes         69.0        0.6     4172     7.7 %
  Modify Conflicts             83.7        0.7     5058     9.3 %
  I/O Device Contention         6.4        0.1      388     0.7 %
  Network Packet Received     120.0        1.0     7257    13.4 %
  Network Packet Sent         120.1        1.0     7259    13.4 %
  SYSINDEXES Lookup             0.0        0.0        0     0.0 %
  Other Causes                221.6        1.8    13395    24.7 %%
```

Connections Opened

"Connections Opened" reports the number of connections opened to SQL Server. It includes any type of connection, such as client connections and remote procedure calls. It only counts connections that were started during the sample interval. Connections that were established before the interval started are not counted here.

This data is provides a general understanding of the SQL Server environment and the work load during the interval. This data can also be useful for understanding application behavior—it can help determine if applications repeatedly open and close connections or perform multiple transactions per connection.

Task Context Switches by Engine

"Task Context Switches by Engine" reports on the number of times each SQL Server engine switched context from one user task to another. "% of total" is the percentage of SQL Server engine task switches for each SQL Server engine as a percentage of the total number of task switches for all SQL Server engines combined.

"Total Task Switches" summarizes task-switch activity for all engines on SMP servers. You can use "Total Task Switches" to observe the effect of controlled reconfigurations. You might reconfigure a cache or add memory if tasks appear to block on cache search misses and to be switched out often. Then, check the data to see if tasks tend to be switched out more or less often.

Task Context Switches Due To

"Task Context Switches Due To" reports the number of times that SQL Server switched context for a number of common reasons. "% of total" is the percentage of times the context switch was due to each specific cause as a percentage of the total number of task context switches for all SQL Server engines combined.

"Task Context Switches Due To" data can help you identify the problem and give you clues about how to fix it. For example, if most of the task switches are caused by physical I/O, try minimizing physical I/O, by adding more memory or reconfiguring caches.

However, if lock contention causes most of the task switches, check the"Lock Management" on page 506.

Voluntary Yields

"Voluntary Yields" is the number of times a task completed or yielded after running for the configured amount of time. The SQL Server engine switches context from the task that yielded to another task.

The configuration variable **time slice** sets the amount of time that a process can run. A CPU-intensive task that does not switch out due to other causes yields the CPU at certain "yield points" in the code, in order to allow other processes a turn on the CPU. See "time slice" on page 11-94 of the *System Administration Guide* for more information.

A high number of voluntary yields indicates that there is not much contention. If this is consistently the case, consider increasing the **time slice** configuration parameter.

Cache Search Misses

"Cache Search Misses" is the number of times that a task was switched out because a needed page was not in cache and had to be read from disk. For data and index pages, the task is switched out while the physical read is performed.

See "Data Cache Management" on page 512 for more information about the cache-related parts of the **sp_sysmon** output.

System Disk Writes

"Disk Writes" reports the number of times a task was switched out because it needed to perform a disk write or because it needed to access a page that was being written by another process, such as the housekeeper or the checkpoint process.

Most SQL Server writes happen asynchronously, but processes sleep during writes for page splits, recovery, and OAM page writes.

If this number seems high, check "Page Splits" on page 501 to see if the problem is caused by data pages and index page splits. In other cases, you cannot affect this value by tuning.

I/O Pacing

SQL Server paces the number of disk writes that it issues in order to keep from flooding the disk I/O subsystems during certain operations that need to perform large amounts of I/O. Checkpoints and transaction commits that write a large number of log pages are two examples. The task is switched out and sleeps until the batch of writes completes, and then wakes up and issues another batch.

By default, the number of writes per batch is set to 10. You may want to increase the number of writes per batch if:

- You have a high-throughput, high-transaction environment with a large data cache

- Your system is not I/O bound

Valid values are from 1 to 50. This command sets the number of writes per batch to 20:

```
dbcc tune (maxwritedes, 20)
```

Logical Lock Contention

"Logical Lock Contention" reports the number of times a task was switched out because of contention over database locks, such as table and page locks.

Investigate lock contention problems by checking the transaction detail and lock management sections of the report. Refer to "Transaction Detail" on page 490 and "Lock Management" on page 506. Check to see if your queries are doing deferred and direct expensive updates, which can cause additional index locks. Refer to "Updates" on page 492.

For additional help on locks and lock contention, check the following sources:

- "Types of Locks in SQL Server" on page 297 provides information about types of page and table locks.

- "Reducing Lock Contention" on page 321 provides pointers on reducing lock contention.

- Chapter 6, "Indexing for Performance," provides information on indexes and query tuning. In particular, use indexes to ensure that updates and deletes to not lead to table scans and exclusive table locks.

Address Lock Contention

"Address Lock Contention" reports the number of times a task was switched out because of memory address locks. SQL Server acquires address locks on index pages, OAM pages and allocation pages, during updates, and sometimes on data pages when page splits are performed. Address lock contention tends to have more implications in a high throughput environment.

Log Semaphore Contention

"Log Semaphore Contention" is the number of times a task was switched out because it needed to acquire the transaction log semaphore held by another task. This applies to SMP systems only.

High contention for the log semaphore could indicate that the user log cache (ULC) is too small. See "Transaction Management" on page 493. If you decide that the ULC is correctly sized, then think about how to minimize the number of log writes by making application changes.

Another area to check is disk queueing on the disk used by the transaction log. See "Disk I/O Management" on page 532. Also check "Engine Busy Utilization" on page 475. If engine utilization is a low value and response time is within acceptable limits, consider reducing the number of engines. Fewer engines reduces contention by decreasing the number of tasks trying to access the log simultaneously.

Group Commit Sleeps

"Group Commit Sleeps" reports the number of times a task performed a transaction commit and was put to sleep until the log was written to disk. Compare this value to the committed transactions information described in "Committed Transactions" on page 488. If the transaction rate is low, a higher percentage of tasks wait for "Group Commit Sleeps."

If there are a significant number of tasks resulting in "Group Commit Sleeps" and the log I/O size is greater than 2K, a smaller log I/O size can help to reduce commit time by causing more frequent page flushes. Flushing the page wakes up tasks sleeping on the group commit.

In high throughput environments, a large log I/O size is very important to prevent problems in disk queueing on the log device. A high percentage of group commit sleeps should not be regarded as a problem.

Other factors that can affect group commit sleeps are the size of the run queue and the speed of the disk device on which the log resides.

When a task commits, its log records are flushed from its user log cache to the current page of the transaction log in cache. If the page (or pages, if a large log I/O size is configured) is not full, the task is switched out and placed on the end of the run queue. The task wakes up when:

- Another process fills the log page(s), and flushes the log.

- When the task reaches the head of the run queue, and no other process has flushed the log page.

For more information on setting the log I/O size, see "Choosing the I/O Size for the Transaction Log" on page 413.

Last Log Page Writes

"Last Log Page Writes" is the number of times a task was switched out because it was put to sleep while writing the last log page.

The task switched out because it was responsible for writing the last log page as opposed to sleeping while waiting for some other task to write the log page, as described in "Group Commit Sleeps" on page 484.

If this value is high, check "Avg # Writes per Log Page" on page 498 to see if SQL Server is repeatedly rewriting the same last page to the log. If the log I/O size is greater than 2K, reducing the log I/O size might reduce the number of unneeded log writes.

Modify Conflicts

For certain operations, SQL Server uses a special light weight protection mechanism to gain exclusive access to a page without using actual page locks. Access to some system tables and dirty reads on a page are two examples. These processes need exclusive access to the page, even though they do not modify it.

I/O Device Contention

"I/O Device Contention" is the number of times a task was put to sleep while waiting for a semaphore for a particular device.

When a task needs to perform physical I/O, SQL Server fills out the block I/O structure and links it to a per-engine I/O queue. If two SQL Server engines request an I/O structure from the same device at the same time, one of them sleeps while it waits for the semaphore it needs.

If there is significant contention for I/O device semaphores, try reducing it by redistributing the tables across devices or by adding devices and moving tables and indexes to them. See "Spreading Data Across Disks to Avoid I/O Contention" on page 356 for more information.

Network Packet Received

When the cause for task switching is "Network Packet Received," it is due to one of two reasons:

- A task received part of a multi-packet tabular data stream (TDS) batch and was switched out waiting for the client to send the next TDS packet of the batch, or

- A task completely finished processing a command and put into a receive sleep state waiting to receive the next command or packet from the client.

If "Network Packet Received" is the cause for the task switch, see "Network I/O Management" on page 537 for more information about network I/O. Also, you can configure the network packet size for all connections or allow certain connections to log in using larger packet sizes. See "Changing Network Packet Sizes" on page 429 and "default network packet size" on page 11–46 in the *System Administration Guide*.

Network Packet Sent

"Network Packet Sent" reports the number of times a task went into a send sleep state waiting for the network to send each TDS packet.

The TDS model determines that there can be only one outstanding TDS packet per connection at any one point in time. This means that the task sleeps after each packet it sends.

If there is a lot of data to send, and the task is sending many small packets (512 bytes per packet), the task could end up sleeping a number of times. The TDS data packet size is configurable, and different clients can request different packet sizes. For more information, see "Changing Network Packet Sizes" on page 429 and "default network packet size" on page 11-46 in the *System Administration Guide*.

If "Network Packet Sent" is a major cause for task switching, see "Network I/O Management" on page 537 for more information.

SYSINDEXES Lookup

"SYSINDEXES Lookup" shows the number of times a task went to sleep waiting for another task to release control of a page in the *sysindexes* table. This data is meaningful for SMP environments only.

Other Causes

This section reports the number of tasks switched out for any reasons not described above. In a well-tuned server, this value will rise as tunable sources of task switching are reduced.

Transaction Profile

This category reports on transaction-related activities, including the number of data modification transactions, user log cache (ULC) activity, and transaction log activity.

Sample Output for Transaction Profile

The following sample shows **sp_sysmon** output for the "Transaction Profile" section.

```
Transaction Profile
-------------------

Transaction Summary        per sec   per xact    count  % of total
-------------------------  --------- ---------  ------- ----------
  Committed Xacts            120.1       n/a      7261    n/a


Transaction Detail         per sec   per xact    count  % of total
-------------------------  --------- ---------  ------- ----------
  Inserts
    Heap Table               120.1       1.0      7260   100.0 %
    Clustered Table            0.0       0.0         0     0.0 %
-------------------------  --------- ---------  -------
  Total Rows Inserted        120.1       1.0      7260    25.0 %

  Updates
    Deferred                   0.0       0.0         0     0.0 %
    Direct In-place          360.2       3.0     21774   100.0 %
    Direct Cheap               0.0       0.0         0     0.0 %
    Direct Expensive           0.0       0.0         0     0.0 %
-------------------------  --------- ---------  -------
  Total Rows Updated         360.2       3.0     21774    75.0 %

  Deletes
    Deferred                   0.0       0.0         0     0.0 %
    Direct                     0.0       0.0         0     0.0 %
-------------------------  --------- ---------  -------
  Total Rows Deleted           0.0       0.0         0     0.0 %
```

Transaction Summary

"Transaction Summary" reports on committed transactions, rolled back transactions, statistics for all transactions combined, and multidatabase transactions.

Committed Transactions

"Committed Xacts" is the number of transactions committed during the sample interval. "% of total" is the percentage of transactions that committed as a percentage of all transactions that started (both committed and rolled back).

This includes transactions that meet explicit, implicit, and ANSI definitions for "committed," as described here:

- The implicit transaction is composed simply of data modification commands such as **insert, update,** or **delete.** In the implicit model, if you do not specify a **begin transaction** statement, SQL Server interprets every operation as a separate transaction. An explicit **commit transaction** statement is not required. For example:

```
1> insert ...
2> go
1> insert ...
2> go
1> insert ...
2> go
```

is counted as three transactions.

- The explicit transaction encloses data modification commands within **begin transaction** and **commit transaction** statements and counts the number of transactions by the number of commit statements. For example:

```
1> begin transaction
2> insert ...
3> insert ...
4> insert ...
5> commit transaction
6> go
```

is counted as one transaction.

- In the ANSI transaction model, any **select** or data modification command starts a transaction, but a **commit transaction** statement must complete the transaction. **sp_sysmon** counts the number of transactions by the number of **commit transaction** statements. For example:

```
1> insert ...
2> insert ...
3> insert ...
4> commit transaction
5> go
```

is counted as one transaction.

This number reflects a larger number of transactions than the actual number that took place during the sample interval if there were transactions that started before the sample interval began and completed during the interval. If transactions do not complete during the interval, "Total # of Xacts" does not count them. In Figure 19-4, both T1 and T2 are counted, but transaction T3 is not.

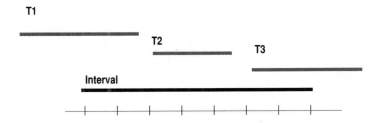

Figure 19-4: How transactions are counted

For more information, see "Transactions" in the SQL Server reference manual.

How to Count Multidatabase Transactions

Multidatabase transactions are also counted. For example, a transaction that modifies 3 databases is counted as 3 transactions.

Multidatabase transactions incur more overhead than single database transactions: they require more log records, more ULC flushes, and involve two-phase commit between the databases.

You can improve performance by reducing the number of multidatabase transaction whenever possible. If you divided a logical database in two because of contention on the log in SQL Server release 10.0, consider putting it back together for System 11.

Transaction Detail

"Transaction Detail" gives statistical detail about data modification operations by type. The work performed by rolled back transactions is included in the output below, although the transaction is not counted in the number of transactions.

See "Update Mode Messages" on page 215 for more information on deferred and direct inserts, updates, and deletes.

Inserts

"Inserts" provides detailed information about the types of inserts taking place on heap tables (including partitioned heap tables), clustered tables, and all inserts with respect to the total number of **insert**, **update**, and **delete** operations.

This figure does not include fast bulk copy inserts, because these are written directly to the data pages and to disk without the normal insert and logging mechanisms.

Inserts on Heap Tables

"Heap Tables" is the number of row inserts that took place on heap tables—all tables that do not have a clustered index. This includes:

- Unpartitioned heap tables
- Partitioned heap tables
- **select into** commands and inserts into work tables
- Slow bulk copy inserts into heap tables

The "% of total" column is the percentage of row inserts into heap tables as a percentage of the total number of inserts.

If there are a large number of inserts to heap tables, determine if these inserts are generating contention. Check the **sp_sysmon** report for data on last page locks on heaps in "Lock Detail" on page 509. If there appears to be a contention problem, SQL Server Monitor can help you figure out which tables are involved.

In many cases, creating a clustered index that randomizes insert activity solves the performance problems for heaps. In other cases, you might need to establish partitions on an unpartitioned table or increase the number of partitions on a partitioned table. For more information, see Chapter 4, "How Indexes Work" and "Improving Insert Performance with Partitions" on page 364.

Inserts on Clustered Tables

"Clustered Table" reports the number of row inserts to tables with clustered indexes. The "% of total" column is the percentage of row inserts to tables with clustered indexes as a percentage of the total number of rows inserted.

Inserts into clustered tables can lead to page splitting. Check "RID Updates from Clustered Split" on page 501 and "Page Splits" on page 501.

Total Rows Inserted

"Total Rows Inserted" reports on all row inserts to heap tables and clustered tables combined. It gives the average number of all inserts per second, the average number of all inserts per transaction, and the total number of inserts. "% of total" shows the percentage of rows inserted compared to the total number of rows affected by data modification operations.

Updates

"Updates" reports the number of deferred and direct row updates. "% of total" is the percentage of each type of update as a percentage of the total number of row updates. **sp_sysmon** reports on the following types of updates:

- Deferred
- Direct In-place
- Direct Cheap
- Direct Expensive

For a description of update types, see "Optimizing Updates" on page 203.

Direct updates incur less overhead than deferred updates and are generally faster because they limit the number of log scans, reduce locking, save traversal of index B-trees (reducing lock contention), and can save I/O because SQL Server does not have to refetch pages to perform modification based on log records.

If there is a high percentage of deferred updates, see "Optimizing Updates" on page 203.

Total Rows Updated

"Total Rows Updated" reports on all deferred and direct updates combined. The "% of total" is the percentage of rows updated, based on all rows modified.

Deletes

"Deletes" reports the number of deferred and direct row deletes. "% of total" is the percentage of each type of delete as a percentage of the total number of deletes. **sp_sysmon** reports on deferred and direct deletes.

Total Rows Deleted

The "Total Rows Deleted" row reports on all deferred and direct deletes combined. "% of total" shows the percentage of deleted rows as a compared to all rows inserted, updated or deleted.

Transaction Management

"Transaction Management" reports on transaction management activities, including user log cache (ULC) flushes to transaction logs, ULC log records, ULC semaphore requests, log semaphore requests, transaction log writes, and transaction log allocations.

Sample Output for Transaction Management

The following sample shows **sp_sysmon** output for the "Transaction Management" categories.

```
Transaction Management
----------------------

  ULC Flushes to Xact Log    per sec   per xact    count   % of total
  -------------------------  --------  ---------  -------  ----------
    by Full ULC                  0.0        0.0        0      0.0 %
    by End Transaction         120.1        1.0     7261     99.7 %
    by Change of Database        0.0        0.0        0      0.0 %
    by System Log Record         0.4        0.0       25      0.3 %
    by Other                     0.0        0.0        0      0.0 %
  -------------------------  --------  ---------  -------
    Total ULC Flushes          120.5        1.0     7286


  ULC Log Records              727.5        6.1    43981      n/a
  Max ULC Size                   n/a        n/a      532      n/a


  ULC Semaphore Requests
    Granted                   1452.3       12.1    87799    100.0 %
    Waited                       0.0        0.0        0      0.0 %
  -------------------------  --------  ---------  -------
    Total ULC Semaphore Req   1452.3       12.1    87799


  Log Semaphore Requests
    Granted                     69.5        0.6     4202     57.7 %
    Waited                      51.0        0.4     3084     42.3 %
  -------------------------  --------  ---------  -------
    Total Log Semaphore Req    120.5        1.0     7286


  Transaction Log Writes        80.5        0.7     4867      n/a
  Transaction Log Alloc         22.9        0.2     1385      n/a
  Avg # Writes per Log Page      n/a        n/a  3.51408      n/a
```

ULC Flushes to Transaction Log

"ULC Flushes to Xact Log" is the total number of times the user log caches (ULCs) were flushed to a transaction log. "% of total" for each category is the percentage of times the type of flush took place as a percentage of the total number of ULC flushes. This category can help you identify areas in the application that cause problems with ULC flushes.

There is one user log cache (ULC) for each configured user connection. SQL Server uses ULCs to buffer transaction log records. On both SMP and uniprocessor systems, this helps reduce transaction log I/O. For SMP systems, it reduces the contention on the current page of the transaction log.

You can configure the size of the ULCs with the **user log cache size** parameter of **sp_configure.** See "user log cache size" on page 11-106 of the *System Administration Guide*.

ULC flushes are caused by the following activities:

- "by Full ULC" – a process's ULC becomes full
- "by End Transaction" – a transaction ended (**rollback** or **commit**, either implicit or explicit)
- "by Change of Database" – a transaction modified an object in a different database (a multidatabase transaction)
- "by System Log Record" – a system transaction (such as an OAM page allocation) occurred within the user transaction
- "by Other" – any other reason, including needing to write to disk
- "Total ULC Flushes" – total number of all ULC flushes that took place during the sample interval

When one of these activities causes a ULC flush, SQL Server copies all log records from the user log cache to the database transaction log.

➤ **Note**

In databases with mixed data and log segments, the user log cache is flushed after each record is added.

By Full ULC

A high value for "by Full ULC" indicates that SQL Server is flushing the ULCs more than once per transaction, negating some performance benefits of user log caches. A good rule of thumb is that if the "% of total" for "by Full ULC" is greater than 20 percent, consider increasing the size of the **user log cache size** parameter.

Increasing the ULC size increases the amount of memory required for each user connection, so you do not want to configure the ULC size to suit a small percentage of large transactions.

By End Transaction

A high value for "by End Transaction" indicates a healthy number of short, simple transactions.

By Change of Database

The ULC is flushed every time there is a database change. If this is the problem, consider decreasing the size of the ULC if it is greater than 2K. If you divided a logical database in two because of contention on the log in SQL Server release 10.0, consider putting it back together for System 11.

By System Log Record and By Other

If these categories are higher than approximately 20 percent, and your ULC size is greater than 2048, consider reducing the ULC size.

The following sections also provide information about transaction log activity:

- "ULC Semaphore Requests" on page 496 reports on contention for semaphore on the user log caches. (SMP only)
- "Log Semaphore Requests" on page 497 reports contention for the log semaphore. (SMP only)
- "Transaction Log Writes" on page 498 reports the number of transaction log writes.

ULC Log Records

This row provides an average number of log records per transaction. It is useful in benchmarking or in controlled development environments to determine the number of log records written to ULCs per transaction.

Many transactions, such as those that affect several indexes or deferred updates or deletes, require several log records for a single data modification. Queries that modify a large number of rows log one or more records for each row.

If this data is unusual, study the data in the next section, "Maximum ULC Size" and look at your application for long-running transactions and for transactions that modify large numbers of rows.

Maximum ULC Size

The value in the "count" column is the maximum number of bytes used in any of the ULCs, across all of the ULCs. This data can help you determine if ULC size is correctly configured.

Since SQL Server flushes the ULC when the transaction completes, any unused memory allocated to the ULCs is wasted. If the value in the "count" column is consistently less than the defined value for the **user log cache size** parameter, reduce **user log cache size** to the value in the "count" column (but no smaller than 2048 bytes).

When "Max ULC Size" equals the user log cache size, check the number of flushes "By Full ULC" on page 494. If the number of times that logs were flushed due to a full ULC is higher than about 20 percent, consider increasing the **user log cache size** using **sp_configure**. See "user log cache size" on page 11–106 in the *System Administration Guide*.

ULC Semaphore Requests

"ULC Semaphore Requests" reports on the number of times a user task was immediately granted a semaphore or had to wait for it. "% of total" shows the percentage of tasks granted semaphores and the percentage of tasks that waited for semaphores as a percentage of the total number of ULC semaphore requests. This is relevant only in SMP environments.

A semaphore is a simple internal locking mechanism that prevents a second task from accessing the data structure currently in use. SQL Server uses semaphores to protect the user log caches since more than one process can access the records of a ULC and force a flush.

This category provides the following information:

- Granted – The number of times a task was granted a ULC semaphore immediately upon request. There was no contention for the ULC.

- Waited – The number of times a task tried to write to ULCs and encountered semaphore contention.

- Total ULC Semaphore Requests – The total number of ULC semaphore requests that took place during the interval. This includes requests that were granted or had to wait.

Log Semaphore Requests

"Log Semaphore Requests" is a measure of contention for the log semaphore that protects the current page of the transaction log in cache. This data is meaningful for SMP environments only.

This category provides the following information:

- Granted – The number of times a task was granted a log semaphore immediately after it requested one. "% of total" is the percentage of immediately granted requests as a percentage of the total number of log semaphore requests.

- Waited – The number of times two tasks tried to flush ULC pages to the log simultaneously and one task had to wait for the log semaphore. "% of total" is the percentage of tasks that had to wait for a log semaphore as a percentage of the total number of log semaphore requests.

- Total Log Semaphore Requests – The total number of times tasks requested a log semaphore including those granted immediately and those for which the task had to wait.

If a high "% of total" for "Waited" shows lot of contention for the log semaphore, some options are:

- Increasing the ULC size, if "By Full ULC" is a frequent source of user log cache flushes. See "ULC Flushes to Transaction Log" on page 494 for more information.

- Reducing log activity through transaction redesign. Aim for more batching with less frequent commits. Be sure to monitor lock contention as part of the transaction redesign.

- Reducing the number of multidatabase transactions, since each change of database context requires a log write.

- Dividing the database into more than one database so that there are multiple logs. If you choose this solution, divide the database in such a way that multidatabase transactions are minimized.

In high throughput environments with a large number of concurrent users committing transactions, a certain amount of contention for the log semaphore is expected. In some tests, very high throughput is still maintained even though log semaphore contention is in the 20 to 30 percent range.

Transaction Log Writes

"Transaction Log Writes" is the total number of times SQL Server wrote a transaction log page to disk. Transaction log pages are written to disk when a transaction commits (after a wait for a group commit sleep) or when the current log page or pages become full.

Transaction Log Allocations

"Transaction Log Alloc" is the number of times additional pages were allocated to the transaction log.

This data is useful for comparing to other data in this section and for tracking the rate of transaction log growth.

Avg # Writes per Log Page

This row uses the previous two values to report the average number of times each log page was written to disk. The value is reported in the "count" column.

In high throughput applications, you want to see this number as close to 1 as possible. With low throughput, the number will be significantly higher. In very low throughput environments, it may be as high as one write per completed transaction.

Index Management

This category reports on index management activity including nonclustered maintenance, page splits, and index shrinks.

Sample Output for Index Management

The following sample shows **sp_sysmon** output for the "Index Management" categories.

```
Index Management
- - - - - - - - - - - - - - - -

Nonclustered Maintenance       per sec    per xact     count   % of total
- - - - - - - - - - - - - - -   - - - - -   - - - - -    - - - - -   - - - - -
  Ins/Upd Requiring Maint        61.0        4.8       37205       n/a
    # of NC Ndx Maint            56.4        4.4       34412       n/a
    Avg NC Ndx Maint / Op        n/a         n/a     0.92493       n/a

  Deletes Requiring Maint         5.2        0.4        3173       n/a
    # of NC Ndx Maint             0.6        0.0         363       n/a
```

Avg NC Ndx Maint / Op	n/a	n/a	0.11440	n/a
RID Upd from Clust Split	0.0	0.0	0	n/a
# of NC Ndx Maint	0.0	0.0	0	n/a
Avg NC Ndx Maint / Op	0.0	0.0	0	n/a
Page Splits	1.3	0.1	788	n/a
Retries	0.2	0.0	135	17.1 %
Deadlocks	0.0	0.0	14	1.8 %
Empty Page Flushes	0.0	0.0	14	1.8 %
Add Index Level	0.0	0.0	0	0.0 %
Page Shrinks	0.0	0.0	0	n/a

Nonclustered Maintenance

This category measures the number of operations that required or potentially required SQL Server to perform maintenance to one or more indexes; that is, it measures the number of operations for which SQL Server had to at least check whether or not it was necessary to update the index. The output also gives the number of indexes that actually were updated and the average number of indexes maintained per operation.

In tables with clustered indexes and one or more nonclustered indexes, all inserts, all deletes, some update operations, and any data page splits, require changes to the nonclustered indexes. High values for index maintenance indicate that you should assess the impact of maintaining indexes on your SQL Server performance. While indexes speed retrieval of data, maintenance to indexes slows data modification. Maintenance requires additional processing, additional I/O, and additional locking of index pages.

Other **sp_sysmon** output that is relevant to assessing this category is:

- The information on total updates, inserts and deletes, as well as data on page splits. See "Transaction Detail" on page 490, and "Page Splits" on page 501.

- Information on lock contention. See "Lock Detail" on page 509.

- Information on address lock contention. See "Address Lock Contention" on page 484 and "Address Locks" on page 509.

For example, you can compare the number of inserts that took place with the number of maintenance operations that resulted. If there is a relatively high number of maintenance operations, page splits, and retries, consider the usefulness of the indexes in your applications. See Chapter 6, "Indexing for Performance" for more information.

Inserts and Updates Requiring Maintenance to Indexes

The data in this section gives information about how insert and update operations affect indexes. For example, an insert to a clustered table with 3 nonclustered indexes requires updates to all three indexes, then the average number of operations that resulted in maintenance to nonclustered indexes is three.

However, an update to the same table may require only one maintenance operation, to the index whose key value was changed.

Inserts and Updates Requiring Maintenance

"Ins/Upd Requiring Maint" is the number of insert and update operations to a table with indexes that potentially required modifications to one or more indexes.

Number of Nonclustered Index Operations Requiring Maintenance

"# of NC Ndx Maint" is the number of nonclustered indexes that actually required maintenance as a result of insert and update operations.

Average Number of Nonclustered Indexes Requiring Maintenance

"Avg NC Ndx Maint/Op" is the average number of nonclustered indexes per insert or update operation that required maintenance.

Deletes Requiring Maintenance

The data in this section gives information about how delete operations affect indexes.

Deletes Requiring Maintenance

"Deletes Requiring Maint" is the number delete operations that potentially required modification to one or more indexes. See "Deletes" on page 492.

Number of Nonclustered Index Operations Requiring Maintenance

"# of NC Ndx Maint" is the number of nonclustered indexes that actually required maintenance as a result of delete operations.

Average Number of Nonclustered Indexes Requiring Maintenance

"Avg NC Ndx Maint/Op" is the average number of nonclustered indexes per delete operation that required maintenance.

RID Updates from Clustered Split

The row ID (RID) entry shows how many times a data page split occurred in a table with a clustered index. These splits require updating the nonclustered indexes for all of the rows that move to the new data page.

Row ID Updates from Clustered Split

"Row ID Updates from Clustered Split" is the total number of nonclustered indexes that required maintenance after a row ID update from clustered split operations.

Number of Nonclustered Index Operations Requiring Maintenance

"# of NC Ndx Maint" is the number of nonclustered indexes that required maintenance as a result of row ID update operations.

Average Number of Nonclustered Indexes Requiring Maintenance

"Avg NC Ndx Maint/Op" is the average number of nonclustered indexes per RID update operation that required maintenance.

Page Splits

"Page Splits" reports on the number of times that SQL Server split a data page, a clustered index page, or non-clustered index page because there was not enough room for a new row.

When a data row is inserted into a table with a clustered index, the row must be placed in physical order according to the key value. Index rows must also be placed in physical order on the pages. If there is not enough room on a page for a new row, SQL Server splits the page, allocates a new page, and moves some rows to the new page. Page splitting incurs overhead because it involves updating the parent index page and the page pointers on the adjoining pages, and adds lock contention. For clustered indexes, page splitting also requires updating all nonclustered indexes that point to the rows on the new page.

See "Choosing Fillfactors for Indexes" on page 158 and "Decreasing the Number of Rows per Page" on page 324 for more information about how to temporarily reduce page splits using **fillfactor** and **max_rows_per_page**. Note that using **max_rows_per_page** almost always increases the rate of splitting.

Reducing Page Splits for Ascending-Key Inserts

If "Page Splits" is high and your application is inserting values into a table with a clustered index, it may be possible to reduce the number of page splits.

The special optimization is designed to reduce page splitting and to result in more completely filled data pages. The most likely scenario involves clustered indexes with compound keys, where the first key is already in use in the table, and the second column is based on an increasing value.

Default Data Page Splitting

The table *sales* has a clustered index on *store_id*, *customer_id*. There are three stores (A,B,C) and each of them adds customer records in ascending numerical order.The table contains rows for the key values A,1; A,2; A,3; B,1; B,2; C,1; C,2 and C,3 and each page holds 4 rows, as shown in Figure 19-5.

Page 1007			Page 1009		
A		1...	B		2...
A		2...	C		1...
A		3...	C		2...
B		1...	C		3...

Figure 19-5: Clustered table before inserts

Using the normal page splitting mechanism, inserting "A,4" results in allocating a new page, and moving one-half of the rows to it, and inserting the new row in place, as shown in Figure 19-6.

Page 1007			Page 1129			Page 1009		
A		1...	A		3...	B		2...
A		2...	A		4...	C		1...
			B		1...	C		2...
						C		3...

Figure 19-6: Insert causes a page split

When "A,5" is inserted, no split is needed, but when "A,6" is inserted, another split takes place, as shown in Figure 19-7.

Page 1007			Page 1129			Page 1134			Page 1009		
A		1...	A		3...	A		5...	B		2...
A		2...	A		4...	A		6...	C		1...
						B		1...	C		2...
									C		3...

Figure 19-7: Another insert causes another page split

Adding "A,7" and "A,8" results in another page split, as shown in Figure 19-8.

Page 1007			Page 1129			Page 1134			Page 1137			Page 1009		
A		1...	A		3...	A		5...	A		7...	B		2...
A		2...	A		4...	A		6...	A		8...	C		1...
									B		1...	C		2...
												C		3...

Figure 19-8: Page splitting continues

Effects of Ascending Inserts

You can set "ascending inserts mode" for a table, so that pages are split at the point of the inserted row, rather than in the middle of the page. Starting from the original table shown in Figure 19-5 on page 502, the insertion of "A,4" results in a split at the insertion point, with a the remaining rows on the page moving to a newly allocated page:

Page 1007			Page 1129			Page 1009		
A		1...	B		1...	B		2...
A		2...				C		1...
A		3...				C		2...
A		4...				C		3...

Figure 19-9: First insert with ascending inserts mode

Inserting "A,5" causes a new page to be allocated, as shown in Figure 19-10.

Page 1007		Page 1134		Page 1129		Page 1009	
A	1...	A	5...	B	1...	B	2...
A	2...					C	1...
A	3...					C	2...
A	4...					C	3...

Figure 19-10:Additional ascending insert causes a page allocation

Adding "A,6", "A,7", and "A,8" fills the new page, as shown in Figure 19-11.

Page 1007		Page 1134		Page 1129		Page 1009	
A	1...	A	5...	B	1...	B	2...
A	2...	A	6...			C	1...
A	3...	A	7...			C	2...
A	4...	A	8...			C	3...

Figure 19-11:Additional inserts fill the new page

Setting Ascending Inserts Mode for a Table

The following commands turns on ascending insert mode for the *sales* table:

```
dbcc tune (ascinserts, 1, "sales")
```

To turn ascending insert mode off, use:

```
dbcc tune (ascinserts, 0, "sales")
```

You must reissue this command each time you restart SQL Server. If tables sometimes experience random inserts and have more ordered inserts during batch jobs, it is better to turn it on explicitly for the batch job.

Retries and Deadlocks

"Deadlocks" is the number of index page splits and shrinks that resulted in deadlocks. SQL Server has a special mechanism that attempts to avoid transaction rollbacks due to index page deadlocks. "Retries" indicates the number of times SQL Server used this mechanism, called deadlock retries.

Deadlocks on index pages take place when two transactions each need to acquire locks held by the other transaction. On data pages, deadlocks result in choosing one process (the one with the least accumulated CPU time) as a deadlock victim, and rolling back the process.

By the time that an index deadlock takes place, however, the transaction has already found and updated the data page, and holds data page locks. Rolling back the transaction causes overhead.

Deadlock retries provide an inexpensive mechanism for allowing both transactions to succeed in a large number of cases. The index locks for one of the processes are released (locks on the data pages are still held), and SQL Server tries the index scan again, traversing the index from the root page of the index. Usually, by the time the scan reaches the page that needs to be split, the other transaction has completed, and no deadlock takes place. By default, any index deadlock is retried up to 5 times before the transaction is considered deadlocked and rolled back. For more information, see "deadlock retries" on page 11-36 of the *System Administration Guide*.

Deadlock retries cause locks on data pages to be held slightly longer and increase locking and overhead, but reduce the number of transactions that are rolled back due to deadlocks. The default value setting provides a reasonable compromise between the overhead of holding date page locks longer, and the overhead of rolling back transactions that have to be re-issued.

A high number of index deadlocks and deadlock retries indicates high contention in a small area of the index B-tree.

If your application encounters a high number of retries, reduce page splits using **fillfactor** when you re-create the index. See "Decreasing the Number of Rows per Page" on page 11-324.

Empty Page Flushes

"Empty Page Flushes" is the number of empty pages resulting from page splits that were flushed to disk.

Add Index Level

"Add Index Level" reports the number of times a new index level was added. This does not happen frequently, so you should expect to see result values of zero most of the time. The count could have a value of 1 or 2 if your sample includes inserts into an empty table or a small table with indexes.

Page Shrinks

"Page Shrinks" is the number of times that deleting index rows caused the index to shrink off a page. Shrinks incur overhead due to locking in the index and the need to update pointers on adjacent pages. Repeated "count" values greater than zero indicate there may be many pages in the index with fairly small numbers of rows per page due to delete and update operations. If there are a high number of shrinks, consider rebuilding indexes.

Lock Management

"Lock Management" reports on locks, deadlocks, lock promotions, and freelock contention.

Sample Output for Lock Management

The following sample shows **sp_sysmon** output for the "Lock Management" categories.

```
Lock Management
---------------
```

Lock Summary	per sec	per xact	count	% of total
Total Lock Requests	2540.8	21.2	153607	n/a
Avg Lock Contention	3.7	0.0	224	0.1 %
Deadlock Percentage	0.0	0.0	0	0.0 %

Lock Detail	per sec	per xact	count	% of total
Exclusive Table				
Granted	403.7	4.0	24376	100.0 %
Waited	0.0	0.0	0	0.0 %
Total EX-Table Requests	0.0	0.0	0	0.0 %
Shared Table				
Granted	325.2	4.0	18202	100.0 %
Waited	0.0	0.0	0	0.0 %
Total SH-Table Requests	0.0	0.0	0	0.0 %
Exclusive Intent				
Granted	480.2	4.0	29028	100.0 %

Waited	0.0	0.0	0	0.0 %
Total EX-Intent Requests	480.2	4.0	29028	18.9 %
Shared Intent				
Granted	120.1	1.0	7261	100.0 %
Waited	0.0	0.0	0	0.0 %
Total SH-Intent Requests	120.1	1.0	7261	4.7 %
Exclusive Page				
Granted	483.4	4.0	29227	100.0 %
Waited	0.0	0.0	0	0.0 %
Total EX-Page Requests	483.4	4.0	29227	19.0 %
Update Page				
Granted	356.5	3.0	21553	99.0 %
Waited	3.7	0.0	224	1.0 %
Total UP-Page Requests	360.2	3.0	21777	14.2 %
Shared Page				
Granted	3.2	0.0	195	100.0 %
Waited	0.0	0.0	0	0.0 %
Total SH-Page Requests	3.2	0.0	195	0.1 %
Exclusive Address				
Granted	134.2	1.1	8111	100.0 %
Waited	0.0	0.0	0	0.0 %
Total EX-Address Requests	134.2	1.1	8111	5.3 %
Shared Address				
Granted	959.5	8.0	58008	100.0 %
Waited	0.0	0.0	0	0.0 %
Total SH-Address Requests	959.5	8.0	58008	37.8 %
Last Page Locks on Heaps				
Granted	120.1	1.0	7258	100.0 %
Waited	0.0	0.0	0	0.0 %
Total Last Pg Locks	120.1	1.0	7258	4.7 %

```
Deadlocks by Lock Type        per sec   per xact    count  % of total
-------------------------    ---------  ---------  -------  ----------
                                  0.0        0.0        0         n/a


Deadlock Detection
  Deadlock Searches               0.1        0.0        4         n/a
  Searches Skipped                0.0        0.0        0         0.0 %
  Avg Deadlocks per Search        n/a        n/a  0.00000         n/a


Lock Promotions
                                  0.0        0.0        0         n/a
```

Note that shared and exclusive table locks, "Deadlocks by Lock Type," and "Lock Promotions" do not contain detail rows because there were no occurrences of them during the sample interval.

Lock Summary

"Lock Summary" provides overview statistics about lock activity that took place during the sample period.

Total Lock Requests

"Total Lock Requests" reports on the total number of lock requests.

Average Lock Contention

"Avg Lock Contention" is the average number of times there was lock contention as a percentage of all of the lock requests combined.

If average lock contention is high, study the lock detail information below and read "Locking and Performance of SQL Server" on page 320.

Deadlock Percentage

"Deadlock Percentage" is the percentage of deadlocks as a percentage of the total number lock requests. If this value is high, see "Deadlocks by Lock Type" on page 510.

Lock Detail

"Lock Detail" provides information that you can use to determine if the application is causing a lock contention or deadlock-related problem.

This output reports on locks by type, displaying the number of times that each lock type was granted immediately, and how many times a task had to wait for a particular type of lock. The "% of total" is the percentage of the specific lock type that was granted or had to wait with respect to the total number of lock requests.

"Lock Detail" reports on the following types of locks:

- Exclusive Table
- Shared Table
- Exclusive Intent
- Shared Intent
- Exclusive Page
- Update Page
- Shared Page
- Exclusive and Shared Address
- Last Page Locks on Heaps

Lock contention can have a large impact on SQL Server performance. Table locks generate more lock contention than page locks because no other tasks can access a table while there is an exclusive table lock on it, and if a task requires an exclusive table lock, it must wait until all shared locks are released.

You can try redesigning the tables that have the highest lock contention or the queries that acquire and hold the locks, to reduce the number of locks they hold and the length of time the locks are held. Table, page, and intent locks are described in "Types of Locks in SQL Server" on page 297.

Address Locks

"Address Locks" reports the number of times there was contention for address locks. Address locks are held on index pages. Address lock contention occurs more often in a higher throughput environment.

Last Page Locks on Heaps

"Last Page Locks on Heaps" is the number of times there was lock contention for the last page of a partitioned or unpartitioned heap table.

This information can indicate if there are tables in the system that would benefit from partitioning or from increasing the number of partitions. If you know that one or more tables is experiencing a problem with last page locks, SQL Server Monitor is a tool that can help.

See "Improving Insert Performance with Partitions" on page 364 for information on how partitions can help solve the problem of last page locking on unpartitioned heap tables.

Deadlocks by Lock Type

"Deadlocks by Lock Type" reports on the number of specific types of deadlocks. "% of total" gives the number of each deadlock type as a percentage of the total number of deadlocks.

Deadlocks may occur when many transactions execute at the same time in the same database. They become more common as the lock contention increases between the transactions.

This category reports data for the following deadlock types:

- Exclusive Table
- Shared Table
- Exclusive Intent
- Shared Intent
- Exclusive Page
- Update Page
- Shared Page
- Address

"Total Deadlocks" summarizes the data for all lock types.

As in the example for this section, if there are no deadlocks, **sp_sysmon** does not display any of the detail information.

To pinpoint exactly where deadlocks occur, try running several applications in a controlled environment with deadlock information printing enabled. See "print deadlock information" on page 11-87 in the *System Administration Guide*.

For more information on lock types, see "Types of Locks in SQL Server" on page 297.

For more information on deadlocks and coping with lock contention, see "Deadlocks and Concurrency in SQL Server" on page 317 and "Locking and Performance of SQL Server" on page 320.

Deadlock Detection

"Deadlock Detection" reports the number of deadlock searches that found deadlocks and deadlock searches that were skipped during the sample interval.

"Deadlocks and Concurrency in SQL Server" on page 317 for a discussion of the background issues related to this topic.

Deadlock Searches

"Deadlock Searches" reports the number of times that SQL Server initiated a deadlock search during the sample interval.

Deadlock checking is time-consuming overhead for applications that experience no deadlocks or very low levels of deadlocking. You can use this data with "Average Deadlocks per Search" to determine if SQL Server is checking for deadlocks too frequently.

Searches Skipped

"Searches Skipped" is the number of times that a task started to perform deadlock checking but found deadlock checking in progress and skipped its check. "% of total" is the percentage of deadlock searches that were skipped as a percentage of the total number of searches.

When a process is blocked by lock contention, it waits for an interval of time set by the **sp_configure** parameter **deadlock checking period**. When this period elapses, it starts deadlock checking. If a search is already in process, the process skips the search.

If you see some number of searches skipped, but some of the searches are finding deadlocks, increase the parameter slightly. If you see a lot of searches skipped, and no deadlocks, or very few, you can increase the counter by a larger amount.

See "deadlock checking period" on page 11–35 in the *System Administration Guide*.

Average Deadlocks per Search

"Avg Deadlocks per Search" reports the average number deadlocks found per search.

This category measures whether SQL Server is checking too frequently. For example, you might decide that finding one deadlock per search indicates excessive checking. If so, you can adjust the frequency with which tasks search for deadlocks by increasing the value configured for the **deadlock checking period** parameter. See "deadlock checking period" on page 11–35 in the *System Administration Guide*.

Lock Promotions

"Lock Promotions" reports on the number of times that the following escalations took place:

- "Ex-Page to Ex-Table" – exclusive page to exclusive table
- "Sh-Page to Sh-Table" – shared page to shared table

The "Total Lock Promotions" row reports the average number of lock promotion types combined per second and per transaction.

If there are no lock promotions, **sp_sysmon** does not display the detail information, as the example for this section shows.

"Lock Promotions" data can:

- Help you detect if lock promotion in your application to is a cause of lock contention and deadlocks.
- Be used before and after tuning lock promotion variables to determine the effectiveness of the values.

Look at the "Granted" and "Waited" data above for signs of contention. If lock contention is high and lock promotion is frequent, consider changing the lock promotion thresholds for the tables involved.

You can configure the lock promotion threshold server-wide, or for individual tables. See "How Isolation Levels Affect Locking" on page 303.

Data Cache Management

sp_sysmon reports summary statistics for all caches, and statistics for statistics for each named cache.

sp_sysmon reports the following activities for the default data cache and each named cache:

- Spinlock contention
- Utilization
- Cache searches including hits and misses
- Pool turnover for all configured pools
- Buffer wash behavior including buffers passed clean, already in I/O, and washed dirty
- Prefetch requests performed and denied
- Dirty read page requests

Figure 19-12 shows how these caching features relate to disk I/O and the data caches.

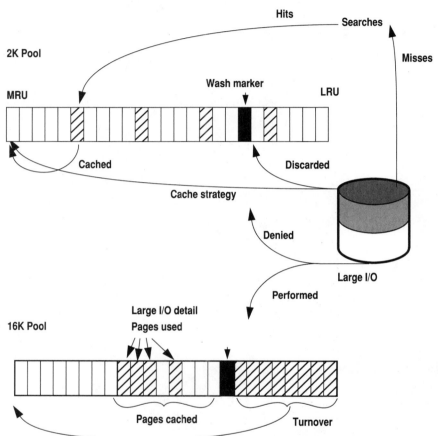

Figure 19-12:Cache management categories

You can use **sp_cacheconfig** and **sp_helpcache** output to help you analyze the data from this category. **sp_cacheconfig** provides information about caches and pools and **sp_helpcache** provides information about objects bound to caches. See Chapter 9, "Configuring Data Caches" in the *System Administration Guide* for more information for information on how to use these procedures. See "Named Data Caches" on page 400 for more information on performance issues and named caches.

Sample Output for Data Cache Management

The following sample shows **sp_sysmon** output for the "Data Cache Management" categories. The first block of data, "Cache Statistics Summary," includes information for all caches. The output also reports a separate block of data for each cache. These blocks are identified by the cache name. The sample output shown here includes only a single user defined cache, although there were more caches configured during the interval.

```
Data Cache Management
---------------------


  Cache Statistics Summary (All Caches)
  -------------------------------------


    Cache Search Summary
      Total Cache Hits         1653.2       13.8      99945       95.8 %
      Total Cache Misses         73.0        0.6       4416        4.2 %
    -------------------------    -------    -------    -------
    Total Cache Searches       1726.2       14.4     104361


    Cache Turnover
      Buffers Grabbed            56.7        0.5       3428        n/a
      Buffers Grabbed Dirty       0.0        0.0          0        0.0 %


    Cache Strategy Summary
      Cached (LRU) Buffers     2155.8       17.9     130333      100.0 %
      Discarded (MRU) Buffers     0.0        0.0          0        0.0 %


    Large I/O Usage
      Large I/Os Performed       20.0        0.2       1211       87.4 %
      Large I/Os Denied           2.9        0.0        174       12.6 %
    -------------------------    -------    -------    -------
    Total Large I/O Requests     22.9        0.2       1385


    Large I/O Effectiveness
      Pages by Lrg I/O Cached     0.0        0.0          0        n/a


    Dirty Read Behavior
      Page Requests               0.0        0.0          0        n/a

  ------------------------------------------------------------------------
  branch_cache
                                per sec   per xact     count   % of total
  -------------------------    ---------  ---------    -------  ----------
```

Spinlock Contention	n/a	n/a	n/a	1.3 %
Utilization	n/a	n/a	n/a	20.9 %
Cache Searches				
Cache Hits	360.3	3.0	21783	100.0 %
Found in Wash	0.0	0.0	0	0.0 %
Cache Misses	0.0	0.0	0	0.0 %
-------------------------	---------	---------	-------	
Total Cache Searches	360.3	3.0	21783	

Pool Turnover				
	0.0	0.0	0	n/a
-------------------------	---------	---------	-------	
Total Cache Turnover	0.0	0.0	0	

Buffer Wash Behavior
  Statistics Not Available - No Buffers Entered Wash Section Yet

Cache Strategy				
Cached (LRU) Buffers	354.9	3.0	21454	100.0 %
Discarded (MRU) Buffers	0.0	0.0	0	0.0 %

Large I/O Usage				
	0.0	0.0	0	n/a

Large I/O Detail
  No Large Pool(s) In This Cache

Dirty Read Behavior				
Page Requests	0.0	0.0	0	n/a

Cache Statistics Summary (All Caches)

This section summarizes behavior for the default data cache and all
named data caches combined. Corresponding information is printed
for each data cache. For a full discussion of these rows, see "Cache
Management By Cache" on page 520.

Cache Search Summary

This section provides summary information about cache hits and
misses. Use this data to get an overview of how effective cache

design is. A high number of cache misses indicates that you should investigate statistics for each cache.

Total Cache Hits

"Total Cache Hits" is the number of times that a needed page was found in any cache. "% of total" is the percentage of cache hits as a percentage of the total number of cache searches.

Total Cache Misses

"Total Cache Misses" reports the number of times that a needed page was not found in a cache and had to be read from disk. "% of total" is the percentage of times that the buffer was not found in the cache as a percentage of all cache searches.

Total Cache Searches

This row reports the total number of cache searches, including hits and misses for all caches combined.

Cache Turnover

This section provides a summary of cache turnover.

Buffers Grabbed

"Buffers Grabbed" is the number of buffers that were replaced in all of the caches. The "count" column represents the number of times that SQL Server fetched a buffer from the LRU end of the cache, replacing a database page. If the server was recently restarted, so that the buffers are empty, reading a page into an empty buffer is not counted here.

Buffers Grabbed Dirty

"Buffers Grabbed Dirty" is the number of times that fetching a buffer found a dirty page at the LRU end of the cache and had to wait while the buffer was written to disk. If this value is non-zero, find out which caches are affected. It represents a serious performance hit.

Cache Strategy Summary

This section provides a summary of the caching strategy used.

Cached (LRU) Buffers

"Cached (LRU) Buffers" is the total number of buffers placed at the head of the MRU/LRU chain in all caches.

Discarded (MRU) Buffers

"Discarded (MRU) Buffers" is the total number of buffers in all caches following the fetch-and-discard strategy – the buffers placed at the wash marker.

Large I/O Usage

This section provides summary information about the large I/O requests in all caches. If "Large I/Os Denied" is high, investigate individual caches to determine the cause.

Large I/Os Performed

"Large I/Os Performed" measures the number of times that the requested large I/O was performed. "% of total" is the percentage of large I/O requests performed as a percentage of the total number of I/O requests made.

Large I/Os Denied

"Large I/Os Denied" reports the number of times that large I/O could not be performed. "% of total" is the percentage of large I/O requests denied as a percentage of the total number of requests made.

Total Large I/O Requests

This row reports the number of all large I/O requests (both granted and denied) for all caches.

Large I/O Effectiveness

"Large I/O Effectiveness" helps determine the performance benefits of large I/O. It compares the number of pages that were brought into cache by a large I/O to the number of pages actually referenced while in the cache. If the percentage for "Pages by Lrg I/O Used" is low, it means that few of the pages brought into cache are being accessed by queries. Investigate the individual caches to determine the source of the problem.

Pages by Lrg I/O Cached

"Pages by Lrg I/O Cached" is the number of pages brought into all caches by all the large I/O operations that took place during the sample interval.

Low percentages could indicate one of the following:

- Allocation fragmentation in the table's storage
- Inappropriate caching strategy

Pages by Lrg I/O Used

"Pages by Lrg I/O Used" is the total number of pages that were actually used after being brought into cache as part of a large I/O. **sp_sysmon** will not print output for this category if there were no "Pages by Lrg I/O Cached."

Dirty Read Behavior

This section provides information to help you analyze how dirty reads affect the system.

Dirty Read Page Requests

"Page Requests" (also known as isolation level 0 page requests) is the average number of pages that were requested at isolation level 0.

The "% of total" output for "Dirty Read Page Requests" shows the percentage of dirty reads with respect to the total number of page reads.

Dirty read page requests incur high overhead if they lead to many dirty read re-starts. Therefore, the dirty page read request data is most valuable when you use it with the data for "Dirty Read Re-Starts".

Dirty Read Re-Starts

"Re-Starts" reports the number of dirty read restarts that took place. This category is only reported for the server as a whole, and not for individual caches. **sp_sysmon** will not print output for this category if there were no "Dirty Read Page Requests."

A dirty read restart occurs when a dirty read is active on a page and another process makes changes to the page that cause the page to be deallocated. The scan for the level 0 must be restarted.

The "% of total" output is the percentage of dirty read re-starts done with isolation level 0 as a percentage of the total number of page reads.

If these values are high, you might take steps to reduce them through application modifications because overhead associated with dirty reads and resulting restarts is very expensive. Most applications should avoid restarts because of the large overhead it incurs.

Cache Management By Cache

There is a section of information on cache utilization for each active cache on the server.

Spinlock Contention

"Spinlock Contention" reports the number of times a SQL Server engine encountered spinlock contention and had to wait, as a percentage of the total spinlock requests for that cache. This is meaningful for SMP environments only.

When a user task makes any changes to a cache, a spinlock denies all other tasks access to the cache while the changes are being made. Although spinlocks are held for extremely brief durations, they can slow performance in multiprocessor systems with high transaction rates.

To improve performance, you can divide the default data cache into named data caches, each controlled by a separate spinlock. This can increase concurrency on multiple CPU systems. See "Named Data Caches" on page 400.

Utilization

"Utilization" reports the percentage of searches that went to the cache in question as a percentage of searches across all caches configured.

You can compare this value for each cache to determine if there are caches that are over- or underutilized. If you decide that a cache is not well utilized, you can:

- Change the cache bindings to balance utilization. See "Caches and Object Bindings" on page 48 and "Binding Objects to Caches" on page 9-11 in the *System Administration Guide* for more information.

- Resize the cache to correspond more appropriately to its utilization. See "Resizing Named Data Caches" on page 9-18 in the *System Administration Guide* for more information.

Cache Search, Hit, and Miss Information

The data on cache searches, hits, and misses is useful for understanding how many searches find the page in cache and how many need to perform physical reads.

Cache hits are roughly comparable to the logical reads values reported by **statistics io**, and cache misses are roughly equivalent to physical reads. **sp_sysmon** will always report higher values than those shown by **statistics io**, since **sp_sysmon** also reports the I/O for system tables, log pages, OAM pages and other system overhead.

Interpreting cache hit data requires understanding of how the application uses each cache. In caches created to hold specific objects such as indexes or look up tables, cache hit ratios may reach 100 percent. In caches used for random point queries on huge tables, cache hit ratios may be quite low but still represent effective cache use.

This data can also help you to determine if adding more memory would improve performance. For example, if "Cache Hits" is high, adding memory probably will not help much.

Cache Hits

"Cache Hits" is the number of times that a needed page was found in the data cache. "% of total" is the percentage of cache hits compared to the total number of cache searches.

Found in Wash

The number of times that the needed page was found in the wash section of the cache. "% of total" is the percentage of times that the buffer was found in the wash area as a percentage of the total number of hits.

If the data indicate a large percentage of cache hits found in the wash section, it may mean the wash is too big. A large wash section might lead to increased physical I/O because SQL Server initiates a write on all dirty pages as they cross the wash marker. If a page in the wash area is re-dirtied, I/O has been wasted.

If queries on tables in the cache use "fetch-and-discard" strategy, the first cache hit for a page in one of these buffers finds it in the wash.

The page is moved to the MRU end of the chain, so a second hit soon after the first finds it still outside the wash area.

See "Specifying the Cache Strategy" on page 270 for information about controlling caching strategy.

If necessary, you can change the wash size. See "Changing the Wash Area for a Memory Pool" on page 9-16 for more information. If you make the wash size smaller, run **sp_sysmon** again under fully loaded conditions and check the output for "Grabbed Dirty" values greater than 0. See "Buffers Grabbed Dirty" on page 517.

Cache Misses

"Cache Misses" reports the number of times that a needed page was not found in the cache and had to be read from disk. "% of total" is the percentage of times that the buffer was not found in the cache as a percentage of the total searches.

Total Cache Searches

This row summarizes cache search activity. Note that the "Found in Wash" data is a subcategory of the "Cache Hits" number and therefore, it is not used in the summary calculation.

Pool Turnover

"Pool Turnover" reports the number of times that a buffer is replaced from each pool in a cache. Each cache can have up to 4 pools, with I/O sizes of 2K, 4K, 8K, and 16K. If there is any "Pool Turnover," **sp_sysmon** prints the "LRU Buffer Grab" and "Grabbed Dirty" information for each pool that is configured and a total turnover figure for the entire cache. If there is no "Pool Turnover," **sp_sysmon** prints only a row of zeros for "Total Cache Turnover," as the example for this section shows.

Here is an example of **sp_sysmon** data that does have pool turnover:

```
Pool Turnover
  2  Kb Pool
     LRU Buffer Grab         1.2           0.3           390       84.2 %
        Grabbed Dirty        0.0           0.0             0        0.0 %

 16 Kb Pool
     LRU Buffer Grab         0.2           0.1            73       15.8 %
        Grabbed Dirty        0.0           0.0             0        0.0 %
 -------------------------   ---------     ------------   ----------
     Total Cache Turnover    1.4           0.3           463
```

This information helps you to determine if the pools and cache are the right size.

LRU Buffer Grab

"LRU Buffer Grab" is only incremented when a page is replaced by another page. If you have recently restarted SQL Server, or you have just unbound and rebound the object or database to the cache, turnover does not count reading pages into empty buffers.

If memory pools are too small for the throughput, you may see high turnover in the pools, reduced cache hit rates, and increased I/O rates. If turnover is high in some pools and low in other pools, you might want to move space from the less active pool to the more active pool, especially if it can improve the cache-hit ratio.

If the pool has a thousand buffers, and SQL Server is replacing a hundred buffers every second, 10 percent of the buffers are getting turned over per second. That might be an indication that buffers do not stay in the cache for an adequate period for that particular object.

Grabbed Dirty

"Grabbed Dirty" gives statistics for the number of dirty buffers that reached the LRU before they could be written to disk. When SQL Server needs to grab a buffer from the LRU end of the cache in order to fetch a page from disk, and finds a dirty buffer instead of a clean one, it must wait for I/O on the dirty buffer to complete. "% of total" is the percentage of buffers grabbed dirty as a percentage of the total number of buffers grabbed.

If "Grabbed Dirty" is non-zero, it indicates that the wash area of the pool is too small for the throughput in the pool. Remedial actions depend on the pool configuration and usage:

- If the pool is very small and has high turnover, consider increasing the size of the pool and the wash area.
- If the pool is large and is used for a large number of data modification operations, increase the size of the wash area.
- If there are several objects using the cache, moving some of them to another cache could help.
- Check query plans and I/O statistics for objects that use the cache for queries that perform a lot of physical I/O in the pool. Tune queries, if possible, by adding indexes.

Check the "per second" values for "Buffers Washed Dirty" on page 525 and "Buffers Already in I/O" on page 525. The wash area should be large enough so that I/O can be completed on dirty buffers before they reach the LRU. This depends on the actual number of physical writes per second that your disk drives achieve.

Also check "Disk I/O Management" on page 532 to see if I/O contention is slowing disk writes.

It might help to increase the **housekeeper free write percent** parameter. See "How the Housekeeper Task Improves CPU Utilization" on page 449 and "housekeeper free write percent" on page 11-72 in the *System Administration Guide*.

Total Cache Turnover

This summary line provides the total number of buffers grabbed in all pools in the cache.

Buffer Wash Behavior

This category reports information about the state of buffers when they reach the pool's wash marker. When a buffer reaches the wash marker it can be in one of three states:

- Clean – the buffer has not been changed while it was in the cache, or it has been changed, and has already been written to disk by the housekeeper or a checkpoint. When the write completes, the page remains in cache and is marked clean.

- Already in I/O – the page was dirtied while in the cache, and the housekeeper or a checkpoint has started I/O on the page, but the I/O has not completed.

- Dirty – the buffer has been changed while in the cache, and has not been written to disk. An asynchronous I/O is started on the page as it passes the wash marker.

If no buffers pass the wash marker during the sample interval, **sp_sysmon** prints:

```
Statistics Not Available - No Buffers Entered Wash
Section Yet!
```

Buffers Passed Clean

"Buffers Passed Clean" is the number of buffers that were clean when they passed the wash marker. "% of total" is the percentage of buffers passed clean as a percentage of the total number of buffers that passed the wash marker.

Buffers Already in I/O

"Buffers Already in I/O" is the number of times that I/O was already active on a buffer when it entered the wash area. "% of total" is the percentage of buffers already in I/O as a percentage of the total number of buffers that entered the wash area.

I/Os active on pages as they cross the wash marker is due to either the housekeeper task or the checkpoint process. See "housekeeper free write percent" on page 11-72 in the *System Administration Guide* for more information about configuring the housekeeper.

Buffers Washed Dirty

"Buffers Washed Dirty" is the number of times that a buffer entered the wash area dirty and not already in I/O. "% of total" is the percentage of buffers washed dirty as a percentage of the total number of buffers that entered the wash area.

Cache Strategy

This section provides statistics on the number of buffers placed in cache following the fetch-and-discard (MRU) or normal (LRU) caching strategies.

Cached (LRU) Buffers

"Cached(LRU) Buffers" is the number of buffers following normal cache strategy and going to the MRU end of the cache. This includes all buffers read directly from disk and going to the MRU end, and all buffers that are found in cache. At the completion of the logical I/O, the buffer is placed at the MRU end of the cache.

Discarded (MRU) Buffers

"Discarded (MRU) Buffers" is the number of buffers following the fetch-and-discard strategy.

If you expect an entire table to be cached, but you are seeing a high value for "Discarded Buffers," use **showplan** to see if the optimizer is generating the fetch-and-discard strategy when it should be using the normal cache strategy. See "Specifying the Cache Strategy" on page 270 for more information.

Large I/O Usage

This section provides data about SQL Server prefetch requests for large I/O. It reports statistics on the numbers of large I/O requests performed and denied.

Large I/Os Performed

"Large I/Os Performed" measures the number of times that a requested large I/O was performed. "% of total" is the percentage of large I/O requests performed as a percentage of the total number of requests made.

Large I/Os Denied

"Large I/Os Denied" reports the number of times that large I/O could not be performed. "% of total" is the percentage of large I/O requests denied as a percentage of the total number of requests made.

SQL Server cannot perform large I/O:

- If any page in a buffer already resides in another pool.
- When there are no buffers available in the requested pool.
- On the first extent of an allocation unit, since it contains the allocation page, which is always read into the 2K pool. This means that on a large table scan, at least one large I/O out of 32 will be denied.

If a high percentage of large I/Os are denied, it indicates that the use of the larger pools might not be as effective as it could be. If a cache contains a large I/O pool, and queries perform both 2K and 16K I/O on the same objects, there will always be some percentage of large I/Os that cannot be performed because pages are in the 2K pool.

If more than half of the large I/Os are denied, and you are using 16K I/O, try moving all of the space from the 16K pool to the 8K pool and rerun the test to see if total I/O is reduced. Note that when a 16K I/O is denied, SQL Server does not check for 8K or 4K pools but simply uses the 2K pool.

You can use information from this category and "Pool Turnover" to help judge the correct size for pools.

Total Large I/O Requests

"Total Large I/O Requests" provides summary statistics for large I/Os performed and denied for all caches combined.

Large I/O Detail

This section provides summary information for each pool individually. It contains a block of information for each 4K, 8K, or 16K pool configured in cache. It prints the pages brought in ("Pages Cached") and pages referenced ("Pages Used") for each I/O size that is configured.

For example, if a query performs a 16K I/O and reads a single data page, "Pages Cached" equals eight, and "Pages Used" equals one.

Pages Cached

"Pages by Lrg I/O Cached" prints the total number of pages read into the cache.

Pages Used

"Pages by Lrg I/O Used" is the number of pages used by a query while in cache.

Dirty Read Behavior

"Page Requests" is the average number of pages that were requested at isolation level 0.

The "% of total" output for "Dirty Read Page Requests" shows the percentage of dirty reads with respect to the total number of page reads.

Procedure Cache Management

"Procedure Cache Management" reports on the number of times stored procedures and triggers were requested, read from disk, and removed.

Sample Output for Procedure Cache Management

The following sample shows **sp_sysmon** output for the "Procedure Cache Management" category.

```
Procedure Cache Management      per sec    per xact    count   % of total
- - - - - - - - - - - - - - - - - - - - -  - - - - - -  - - - - - - -  - - - - - -  - - - - - - -
    Procedure Requests            67.7       1.0       4060      n/a
    Procedure Reads from Disk       0.0       0.0          0      0.0 %
    Procedure Writes to Disk        0.0       0.0          0      0.0 %
    Procedure Removals              0.0       0.0          0      n/a
```

Procedure Requests

"Procedure Requests" reports the number of times that stored procedures were executed.

When a procedure is executed, there are these possibilities:

- There is an idle copy of the query plan in memory, so it is copied and used.

- There is no copy of the procedure in memory, or all copies of the plan in memory are in use, so the procedure must be read from disk.

Procedure Reads from Disk

"Procedure Reads from Disk" reports the number of times that stored procedures were read from disk rather than copied in the procedure cache.

"% of total" is the percentage of procedure reads from disk as a percentage of the total number of procedure requests. If this is a relatively high number, it could indicate that the procedure cache is too small.

Procedure Writes to Disk

"Procedure Writes to Disk" reports the number of procedures created during the interval. This can be significant if application programs generate stored procedures.

Procedure Removals

"Procedure Removals" reports the number of times that a procedure aged out of cache.

Memory Management

Memory management reports on the number of pages allocated and deallocated during the sample interval.

Sample Output for Memory Management

The following sample shows **sp_sysmon** output for the "Memory Management" category.

```
MemMemory Management        per sec   per xact    count  % of total
- - - - - - - - - - - - - - - - - - -   - - - - - - - - -   - - - - - - - - -   - - - - - - -   - - - - - - - - - -
    Pages Allocated            0.0       0.0        0       n/a
    Pages Released             0.0       0.0        0       n/a
```

Pages Allocated

"Pages Allocated" reports the number of times that a new page was allocated in memory.

Pages Released

"Pages Released" reports the number of times that a page was freed.

Recovery Management

This data indicates the number of checkpoints caused by the normal checkpoint process, the number of checkpoints initiated by the housekeeper task, and the average length of time for each type. This information is helpful for setting the recovery and housekeeper parameters correctly.

Sample Output for Recovery Management

The following sample shows **sp_sysmon** output for the "Recovery Management" category.

```
Recovery Management
- - - - - - - - - - - - - - - - - - - -
   Checkpoints              per sec   per xact    count  % of total
- - - - - - - - - - - - - - - - - - - - - - - -   - - - - - - - - -   - - - - - - - - -   - - - - - - -   - - - - - - - - - -
   # of Normal Checkpoints   0.00117   0.00071       1       n/a
   # of Free Checkpoints     0.00351   0.00213       3       n/a
- - - - - - - - - - - - - - - - - - - - - - - -   - - - - - - - - -   - - - - - - - - -   - - - - - - -
   Total Checkpoints         0.00468   0.00284       4

   Avg Time per Normal Chkpt 0.01050 seconds
   Avg Time per Free Chkpt   0.16221 seconds
```

Checkpoints

Checkpoints write all dirty pages (pages that have been modified in memory, but not written to disk) to the database device. SQL Server's automatic (normal) checkpoint mechanism works to maintain a minimum recovery interval. By tracking the number of log records in the transaction log since the last checkpoint was performed, it estimates whether the time required to recover the transactions exceeds the recovery interval. If so, the checkpoint process scans all caches and writes all changed data pages to the database device.

When SQL Server has no user tasks to process, a housekeeper task automatically begins writing dirty buffers to disk. Because these writes are done during the server's idle cycles, they are known as "free writes." They result in improved CPU utilization and a decreased need for buffer washing during transaction processing.

If the housekeeper process finishes writing all dirty pages in all caches to disk, it checks the number of rows in the transaction log since the last checkpoint. If there are more than 100 log records, it issues a checkpoint. This is called a "free checkpoint" because it requires very little overhead. In addition, it reduces future overhead for normal checkpoints.

Number of Normal Checkpoints

"# of Normal Checkpoints" is the number of checkpoints caused by the normal checkpoint process.

If the normal checkpoint is doing most of the work, and especially if the time required is lengthy, it might make sense to increase the number of checkpoints performed by the housekeeper task.

See "recovery interval in minutes" on page 11-18, and "Synchronizing a Database and Its Transaction Log: Checkpoints" on page 18-3 in the *System Administration Guide* for information about changing the number of normal checkpoints.

Number of Free Checkpoints

"# of Free Checkpoints" is the number of checkpoints initiated by the housekeeper task. The housekeeper only performs checkpoints to the log when it has cleared all dirty pages from all configured caches.

If the housekeeper is doing most of the checkpoints, you can probably increase the recovery interval without affecting performance or actual recovery time. Increasing the recovery interval reduces the number of normal checkpoints and the overhead incurred by them.

You can use the **housekeeper free write percent** parameter to configure the maximum percentage by which the housekeeper task can increase database writes. For more information about configuring the housekeeper task, see "How the Housekeeper Task Improves CPU

Utilization" on page 449 and "housekeeper free write percent" on page 11-72 in the *System Administration Guide*.

Total Checkpoints

"Total Checkpoints" is the combined number of normal and free checkpoints that occurred during the interval.

Average Time per Normal Checkpoint

"Avg Time per Normal Chkpt" is the time, on average over the sample interval, that normal checkpoints lasted.

Average Time per Free Checkpoint

"Avg Time per Free Chkpt" is the time, on average over the sample interval, that free (or housekeeper) checkpoints lasted.

Increasing the Housekeeper Batch Limit

The housekeeper process has a built-in batch limit to avoid overloading disk I/O for individual devices. By default, the batch size for housekeeper writes is set to 3. As soon as the housekeeper detects that it has issued 3 I/Os to a single device, it stops processing in the current buffer pool and begins checking for dirty pages in another pool. If the writes from the next pool need to go to the same device, it continues to another pool. Once the housekeeper has checked all of the pools, it waits until the last I/O it has issued has completed, and then begins the cycle again.

The default batch limit of 3 is designed to provide good device I/O characteristics for slow disks. You may get better performance by increasing the batch size for fast disk drives. This value can be set globally for all devices on the server, or to different values for disks with different speeds. This command must be reissued each time SQL Server is restarted.

This command sets the batch size to 10 for a single device, using the virtual device number from *sysdevices*:

```
dbcc tune(deviochar, 8, "10")
```

To see the device number, use **sp_helpdevice**, or this query:

```
select name, low/16777216
from sysdevices
where status&2=2
```

To change the housekeeper's batch size for all devices on the server, use -1 in place of a device number:

```
dbcc tune(deviochar, -1, "5")
```

Legal values for batch size are 1 to 255. For very fast drives, setting the batch size as high as 50 has yielded performance improvements during testing.

You may want to try setting this value higher if:

- The average time for normal checkpoints is high.
- There are no problems with exceeding I/O configuration limits or contention on the semaphores for the devices.

Disk I/O Management

This category is useful when checking for I/O contention.

The first section prints an overview of disk I/O activity: maximum outstanding I/Os, I/Os delayed, total requested I/Os, and completed I/Os. A second section includes output for the master device and for other configured devices, reporting reads, writes, and semaphore contention.

Sample Output for Disk I/O Management

The following sample shows **sp_sysmon** output for the "Disk I/O Management" categories.

```
Disk I/O Management
-------------------

Max Outstanding I/Os          per sec    per xact    count   % of total
-------------------------     ---------  ---------   ------- ----------
    Server                      n/a        n/a         74       n/a
    Engine 0                    n/a        n/a         20       n/a
    Engine 1                    n/a        n/a         21       n/a
    Engine 2                    n/a        n/a         18       n/a
    Engine 3                    n/a        n/a         23       n/a
    Engine 4                    n/a        n/a         18       n/a
    Engine 5                    n/a        n/a         20       n/a
    Engine 6                    n/a        n/a         21       n/a
    Engine 7                    n/a        n/a         17       n/a
    Engine 8                    n/a        n/a         20       n/a


I/Os Delayed by
    Disk I/O Structures         n/a        n/a          0       n/a
    Server Config Limit         n/a        n/a          0       n/a
```

```
      Engine Config Limit              n/a        n/a         0       n/a
      Operating System Limit           n/a        n/a         0       n/a


   Total Requested Disk I/Os          202.8        1.7     12261       n/a

   Completed Disk I/O's
      Engine 0                         25.0        0.2      1512      12.4 %
      Engine 1                         21.1        0.2      1274      10.5 %
      Engine 2                         18.4        0.2      1112       9.1 %
      Engine 3                         23.8        0.2      1440      11.8 %
      Engine 4                         22.7        0.2      1373      11.3 %
      Engine 5                         22.9        0.2      1387      11.4 %
      Engine 6                         24.4        0.2      1477      12.1 %
      Engine 7                         22.0        0.2      1332      10.9 %
      Engine 8                         21.2        0.2      1281      10.5 %
   ----------------------------  ----------  ---------  --------  ----------
   Total Completed I/Os             201.6        1.7     12188


   Device Activity Detail
   ----------------------


   /dev/rdsk/c1t3d0s6
   bench_log                     per sec    per xact     count   % of total
   ----------------------------  ----------  ---------  --------  ----------
      Reads                           0.1        0.0         5       0.1 %
      Writes                         80.6        0.7      4873      99.9 %
   ----------------------------  ----------  ---------  --------  ----------
   Total I/Os                        80.7        0.7      4878      40.0 %

   Device Semaphore Granted          80.7        0.7      4878     100.0 %
   Device Semaphore Waited            0.0        0.0         0       0.0 %


   ------------------------------------------------------------------------


   d_master
   master                        per sec    per xact     count   % of total
   ----------------------------  ----------  ---------  --------  ----------
      Reads                          56.6        0.5      3423      46.9 %
      Writes                         64.2        0.5      3879      53.1 %
   ----------------------------  ----------  ---------  --------  ----------
   Total I/Os                       120.8        1.0      7302      60.0 %

   Device Semaphore Granted         116.7        1.0      7056      94.8 %
   Device Semaphore Waited            6.4        0.1       388       5.2 %
```

Maximum Outstanding I/Os

"Max Outstanding I/Os" reports in the "count" column the maximum number of I/Os pending for SQL Server as a whole (the first line), and for each SQL Server engine at any point during the sample interval.

This information can help configure I/O parameters at the server or operating system level if any of the "I/Os Delayed By" values are non-zero.

I/Os Delayed By

When the system experiences an I/O delay problem, it is likely that I/O is blocked by one or more SQL Server or operating system limits.

In most operating systems there is a kernel parameter that limits the number of asynchronous I/Os that can take place.

Disk I/O Structures

"Disk I/O Structures" is the number of I/Os delayed by reaching the limit on disk I/O structures. When SQL Server exceeds the number of available disk I/O control blocks, I/O is delayed because SQL Server requires that tasks get a disk I/O control block before initiating an I/O request.

If the result is non-zero, try increasing the number of available disk I/O control blocks by increasing the **sp_configure** parameter **disk i/o structures**. See "disk i/o structures" on page 11-27 in the *System Administration Guide*.

Server Configuration Limit

SQL Server can exceed its limit for the number of asynchronous disk I/O requests that can be outstanding for the entire SQL Server at one time. You can raise this limit using **sp_configure** with the **max async i/os per server** parameter. See "max async i/os per server" on page 11-55 in the *System Administration Guide*.

Engine Configuration Limit

A SQL Server engine can exceed its limit for outstanding asynchronous disk I/O requests. This is configurable using **sp_configure** with the **max async i/os per engine** parameter. See "max async i/os per engine" on page 11-54 in the *System Administration Guide*.

Operating System Limit

The operating system kernel has a per process and per system limit on the maximum number of asynchronous I/Os that either a process or the entire system can have pending at any point in time. This value indicates how often the system has exceeded that limit. See "disk i/o structures" on page 11-27 in the *System Administration Guide*, and consult your operating system documentation.

Requested and Completed Disk I/Os

This data shows the total number of disk I/Os requested by SQL Server, and the number and percentage of I/Os completed by each SQL Server engine.

"Total Requested Disk I/Os" and "Total Completed I/Os" should be the same or very close. These values will be very different if requested I/Os are not completing due to saturation.

The value for requested I/Os includes all requests that were initiated during the sample period, and it is possible that some of them completed after the sample period ended. These I/Os will not be included in "Total Completed I/Os," and will cause the percentage to be less than 100, when there are no saturation problems.

The reverse is also true. If I/O requests were made before the sample began and completed during the interval, you would see a "% of Total" for "Total Completed I/Os" value that is more than 100 percent. If you are checking for saturation, make repeated runs, and try to develop your stress tests to perform relatively consistent levels of I/O.

If the data indicates a large number of requested disk I/Os but a smaller number of completed disk I/Os, there could be some bottleneck in the operating system that is delaying I/Os.

Total Requested Disk I/Os

"Total Requested Disk I/Os" reports the number of times that SQL Server requested disk I/Os.

Completed Disk I/Os

"Total Completed Disk I/Os" reports the number of times that each SQL Server engine completed I/O. "% of total" is the percentage of times each SQL Server engine completed I/Os as a percentage of the total number of I/Os completed by all SQL Server engines combined.

You can also use this information to determine if the operating system is able to keep pace with disk I/O requests made by all of the SQL Server engines.

Device Activity Detail

"Device Activity Detail" reports activity on the master device and on each logical device. It is useful for checking that I/O is well balanced across the database devices, and for finding a device that might be delaying I/O. For example, if the "Task Context Switches Due To" data indicates a heavy amount of device contention, you can use "Device Activity Detail" to figure out which device (or devices) is causing the problem.

This section prints the following information about I/O for each data device on the server:

- The logical and physical device names
- The number of reads, writes, and the total number of I/Os
- The number of device semaphores immediately granted on the device and the number of times a process had to wait for a device semaphore

Reads and Writes

"Reads" and "Writes" report the number of times that reads or writes to a device took place. The "% of total" column is the percentage of reads or writes as a percentage of the total number of I/Os to the device.

Total I/Os

"Total I/Os" reports the combined number of reads and writes to a device. The "% of total" column is the percentage of combined reads and writes for each named device as a percentage of the number of reads and writes that went to all devices.

When studying this data, one way to evaluate disk I/O usage is to observe the distribution patterns over the disks. For example, does the data show that some disks are more heavily used than others? If so, consider redistributing data with segments. For example, if you see that a large percentage of all I/O went to a specific named device, you can investigate the tables residing on the device and then determine how to remedy the problem. See "Creating Objects on Segments" on page 361.

Device Semaphore Granted and Waited

The "Device Semaphore Granted" and "Device Semaphore Waited" categories report the number of times that a request for a device semaphore was granted immediately and the number of times the semaphore was busy and the task had to wait for the semaphore to be released. The "% of total" column is the percentage of times the device the semaphore was granted (or the task had to wait) as a percentage of the total number of device semaphores requested. This data is meaningful for SMP environments only.

When SQL Server needs to perform a disk I/O, it gives the task the semaphore for that device in order to acquire a block I/O structure. This is important on SMP systems, because it is possible to have multiple SQL Server engines trying to post I/Os to the same device simultaneously. This creates contention for that semaphore, especially if there are hot devices or if the data is not well distributed across devices.

A large percentage of I/O requests that waited could indicate a semaphore contention issue. One solution might be to redistribute the data on the physical devices.

Network I/O Management

"Network I/O Management" reports on the following network activities for each SQL Server engine:

- Total requested network I/Os

- Network I/Os delayed

- Total TDS packets and bytes received and sent

- Average size of packets received and sent

This data is broken down by SQL Server engine, because each SQL Server engine does its own networking. Imbalances are usually due to one of two causes:

- There are more engines than tasks, so the engines with no work to perform report no I/O.

- Most tasks are sending and receiving short packets, but another tasks is performing tasks with heavy I/O, such as a bulk copy.

Sample Output for Network I/O Management

The following sample shows **sp_sysmon** output for the "Network I/O Management" categories.

```
Network I/O Management
----------------------

  Total Network I/O Requests      240.1        2.0      14514        n/a
  Network I/Os Delayed              0.0        0.0          0        0.0 %
```

Total TDS Packets Received	per sec	per xact	count	% of total
Engine 0	7.9	0.1	479	6.6 %
Engine 1	12.0	0.1	724	10.0 %
Engine 2	15.5	0.1	940	13.0 %
Engine 3	15.7	0.1	950	13.1 %
Engine 4	15.2	0.1	921	12.7 %
Engine 5	17.3	0.1	1046	14.4 %
Engine 6	11.7	0.1	706	9.7 %
Engine 7	12.4	0.1	752	10.4 %
Engine 8	12.2	0.1	739	10.2 %
Total TDS Packets Rec'd	120.0	1.0	7257	

Total Bytes Received	per sec	per xact	count	% of total
Engine 0	562.5	4.7	34009	6.6 %
Engine 1	846.7	7.1	51191	10.0 %
Engine 2	1100.2	9.2	66516	13.0 %
Engine 3	1112.0	9.3	67225	13.1 %
Engine 4	1077.8	9.0	65162	12.7 %
Engine 5	1219.8	10.2	73747	14.4 %
Engine 6	824.3	6.9	49835	9.7 %
Engine 7	879.2	7.3	53152	10.4 %
Engine 8	864.2	7.2	52244	10.2 %
Total Bytes Rec'd	8486.8	70.7	513081	

```
  Avg Bytes Rec'd per Packet       n/a        n/a         70        n/a
```

Total TDS Packets Sent	per sec	per xact	count	% of total
Engine 0	7.9	0.1	479	6.6 %
Engine 1	12.0	0.1	724	10.0 %
Engine 2	15.6	0.1	941	13.0 %
Engine 3	15.7	0.1	950	13.1 %

	per sec	per xact	count	% of total
Engine 4	15.3	0.1	923	12.7 %
Engine 5	17.3	0.1	1047	14.4 %
Engine 6	11.7	0.1	705	9.7 %
Engine 7	12.5	0.1	753	10.4 %
Engine 8	12.2	0.1	740	10.2 %
Total TDS Packets Sent	120.1	1.0	7262	

Total Bytes Sent	per sec	per xact	count	% of total
Engine 0	816.1	6.8	49337	6.6 %
Engine 1	1233.5	10.3	74572	10.0 %
Engine 2	1603.2	13.3	96923	13.0 %
Engine 3	1618.5	13.5	97850	13.1 %
Engine 4	1572.5	13.1	95069	12.7 %
Engine 5	1783.8	14.9	107841	14.4 %
Engine 6	1201.1	10.0	72615	9.7 %
Engine 7	1282.9	10.7	77559	10.4 %
Engine 8	1260.8	10.5	76220	10.2 %
Total Bytes Sent	12372.4	103.0	747986	
Avg Bytes Sent per Packet	n/a	n/a	103	n/a

Total Requested Network I/Os

"Total Requested Network I/Os" represents the total TDS packets received and sent.

If you know the number of packets per second that the network can handle, this data is useful for determining whether the SQL Server system is challenging the network bandwidth.

The issues are the same whether the I/O is inbound or outbound. If SQL Server receives a command that is larger than the TDS packet size, SQL Server will wait to begin processing until it receives the full command. Therefore, commands that require more than one packet are slower to execute and take up more I/O resources.

If the average bytes per packet is near the default packet size configured for your server, you may want to configure larger packet sizes for some connections. You can configure the network packet size for all connections or allow certain connections to log in using larger packet sizes. See "Changing Network Packet Sizes" on page 429 and "default network packet size" on page 11-46 in the *System Administration Guide*.

Network I/Os Delayed

"Network I/Os Delayed" is the number of times I/O was delayed. If this number is consistently non-zero, consult with your network administrator.

Total TDS Packets Received

"Total TDS Packets Rec'd" represents the number of times SQL Server received a packet from a client application.

Total Bytes Received

"Total Bytes Rec'd" is the number of bytes received by each SQL Server engine during the sample interval.

Average Bytes Rec'd per Packet

The average number of bytes received by the SQL Server engine per packet during the sample interval.

Total TDS Packets Sent

"Total TDS Packets Sent" represents the number of times SQL Server sends a packet to a client application.

Total Bytes Sent

"Total Bytes Sent" is the number of bytes sent by each SQL Server engine during the sample interval.

Average Bytes Sent per Packet

The average number of bytes sent by the SQL Server engine per packet during the sample interval.

Reducing Packet Overhead

If your applications use stored procedures, you may see improved throughput by turning off certain TDS messages sent after each select statement that is performed in a stored procedure. This message, called a "done in proc" message, is used in some client products. In some cases, turning of "done in proc" messages also turns off the "rows returned" messages. These messages may be expected in certain Client Library programs, but many clients simply discard these results. Before making a decision to disable this message, test the setting with your client products and Open Client programs to determine whether it affects them.

Turning off these messages can increase throughput slightly in some environments, especially those with slow or overloaded networks, while it has virtually no effect in others. To turn off the messages, issue the command:

```
dbcc tune (doneinproc, 0)
```

To turn them on, use:

```
dbcc tune (doneinproc, 1)
```

This command must be reissued each time SQL Server is restarted.

Glossary

access method

The method used to find the data rows needed to satisfy a query. Access methods include: **table scan**, **nonclustered index** access, **clustered index** access.

affinity

See **process affinity**.

aggregate function

A function that works on a set of cells to produce a single answer or set of answers, one for each subset of cells. The aggregate functions available in Transact-SQL are: average (**avg**), maximum (**max**), minimum (**min**), sum (**sum**), and count of the number of items (**count**).

allocation page

The first page of an allocation unit, which tracks the use of all pages in the allocation unit.

allocation unit

A logical unit of 1/2 megabyte. The **disk init** command initializes a new database file for SQL Server and divides it into 1/2 megabyte pieces called allocation units.

argument

A value supplied to a function or procedure that is required to evaluate the function.

arithmetic expression

An expression that contains only numeric operands and returns a single numeric value. In Transact-SQL, the operands can be of any SQL Server numeric datatype. They can be functions, variables, parameters, or they can be other arithmetic expressions. Synonymous with **numeric expression**.

arithmetic operators

Addition (+), subtraction (-), division (/), and multiplication (*) can be used with numeric columns. Modulo (%) can be used with *int, smallint,* and *tinyint* columns only.

audit trail

Audit records stored in the *sybsecurity* database.

auditing

Recording security-related system activity that can be used to detect penetration of the system and misuse of system resources.

automatic recovery

A process that runs every time SQL Server is stopped and restarted. The process ensures that all transactions that completed before the server went down are brought forward and all incomplete transactions are rolled back.

B-tree

Short for balanced tree, or binary tree. SQL Server uses B-tree indexing. All leaf pages in a B-tree are the same distance from the root page of the index. B-trees provide consistent and predictable performance, good sequential and random record retrieval, and a flat tree structure.

backup

A copy of a database or transaction log, used to recover from a media failure.

batch

One or more Transact-SQL statements terminated by an end-of-batch signal, which submits them to SQL Server for processing.

Boolean expression

An expression that evaluates to TRUE (1), or FALSE (0). Boolean expressions are often used in control of flow statements, such as **if** or **while** conditions.

buffer

A unit of storage in a **memory pool**. A single **data cache** can have pools configured for different I/O sizes, or buffer sizes. All buffers in a pool are the same size. If a pool is configured for 16K I/O, all buffers are 16K, holding eight data pages. Buffers are treated as a unit; all data pages in a buffer are simultaneously read, written, or flushed from cache.

built-in functions

A wide variety of functions that take one or more parameters and return results. The built-in functions include mathematical functions, system functions, string functions, text functions, date functions, and type conversion functions.

bulk copy

The utility for copying data in and out of databases, called **bcp**.

cache hit ratio

For many processes, SQL Server uses an in-memory cache. The cache hit ratio is the percentage of times a needed page or result was found in the cache. For data pages, the cache hit ratio is the percentage of page requests that are serviced by the data cache compared to requests that require disk I/O.

Cartesian product

All the possible combinations of the rows from each of the tables specified in a join. The number of rows in the Cartesian product is equal to the number of rows in the first table times the number of rows in the second table. Once the Cartesian product is formed, the rows that do not satisfy the join conditions are eliminated.

chained transaction mode

Determines whether or not SQL Server automatically starts a new transaction on the next data retrieval or data modification statement. When **set chained** is turned **on** outside a transaction, the next data retrieval or data modification statement begins a new transaction. This mode is ANSI compliant. It ensures that every SQL data retrieval and data modification statement occur inside a transaction. Chained transaction mode may be incompatible with existing Transact-SQL programs. The default value is **off**. Applications which require ANSI SQL (such as the ESQL precompiler) should automatically set the **chained** option **on** at the beginning of each session.

character expression

An expression that returns a single character-type value. It can include literals, concatenation operators, functions, and column identifiers.

cheap direct update

A type of **direct update** operation, performed when the length of the data row changes. The changed data row remains on the same data page, but other rows on the page may move. Contrast to **in-place update** and **expensive direct update**.

check constraint

A **check** constraint limits what values users can insert into a column of a table. A **check** constraint specifies a *search_condition* which any value must pass before it is inserted into the table.

checkpoint

The point at which all data pages that have been changed are guaranteed to have been written to the database device.

clauses

A set of keywords and parameters that tailor a Transact-SQL command to meet a particular need. Also called a **keyword phrase**.

client cursor

A cursor declared through Open Client calls or Embedded-SQL. The Open Client keeps track of the rows returned from SQL Server and buffers them for the application. Updates and deletes to the result set of client cursors can only be done through the Open Client calls.

clustered index

An index in which the physical order and the logical (indexed) order is the same. The leaf level of a clustered index represents the data pages themselves.

column

The logical equivalent of a field. A column contains an individual data item within a row or record.

column-level constraint

Limit the values of a specified column. Place column-level constraints after the column name and datatype in the **create table** statement, before the delimiting comma.

command

An instruction that specifies an operation to be performed by the computer. Each command or SQL statement begins with a keyword, such as **insert**, that names the basic operation performed. Many SQL commands have one or more **keyword phrases**, or **clauses**, that tailor the command to meet a particular need.

comparison operators

Used to compare one value to another in a query. Comparison operators include equal to (=) greater than (>), less than (<), greater than or equal to (>=), less than or equal to (<=), not equal to (!=), not greater than (!>), and not less than (!<).

compatible datatypes

Types that SQL Server automatically converts for implicit or explicit comparison.

composite indexes

Indexes which involve more than one column. Use composite indexes when two or more columns are best searched as a unit because of their logical relationship.

composite key

An index key that includes two or more columns; for example, *authors(au_lname, au_fname)*.

concatenation

Combine expressions to form longer expressions. The expressions can include any combination of binary or character strings, or column names.

constant expression

An expression that returns the same value each time the expression is used. In Transact-SQL syntax statements, constant_expression does not include variables or column identifiers.

control page

A reserved database page that stores information about the last page of a **partition**.

control-of-flow language

Transact-SQL's programming-like constructs (such as **if**, **else**, **while**, and **goto**) that control the flow of execution of Transact-SQL statements.

correlated subquery

A **subquery** that cannot be evaluated independently, but depends on the outer query for its results. Also called a repeating subquery, since the subquery is executed once for each row that might be selected by the outer query. See also **nested query**.

correlation names

Distinguish the different roles a particular table plays in a query, especially a correlated query or **self-join**. Assign correlation names in the **from** clause and specify the correlation name after the table name:

```
select au1.au_fname, au2.au_fname
from authors au1, authors au2
where au1.zip = au2.zip
```

covered query

See **index covering**.

covering

See **index covering**.

cursor

> A symbolic name associated with a Transact-SQL **select** statement through a declaration statement. Cursors consist of two parts: the **cursor result set** and the **cursor position**.

cursor result set

> The set of rows resulting from the execution of the **select** statement associated with the cursor.

data cache

> Also referred to as named cache or cache. A cache is an area of memory within SQL Server that contains the in-memory images of database pages and the data structures required to manage the pages. By default, SQL Server has a single data cache named "default data cache." Additional caches configured by users are also called "user defined caches." Each data cache is given a unique name that is used for configuration purposes.

data definition

> The process of setting up databases and creating database objects such as tables, indexes, rules, defaults, procedures, triggers, and views.

data dictionary

> The system tables that contain descriptions of the **database objects** and how they are structured.

data integrity

> The correctness and completeness of data within a database.

data modification

> Adding, deleting, or changing information in the database with the **insert, delete,** and **update** commands.

data retrieval

> Requesting data from the database and receiving the results. Also called a **query**.

database

> A set of related data tables and other database objects that are organized and presented to serve a specific purpose.

database device

> A device dedicated to the storage of the objects that make up databases. It can be any piece of disk or a file in the file system that is used to store databases and database objects.

database object

> One of the components of a database: table, view, index, procedure, trigger, column, default, or rule.

Database Owner

> The user who creates a database. A Database Owner has control over all the database objects in that database. The login name for the Database Owner is "dbo."

datatype

> Specifies what kind of information each column will hold, and how the data will be stored. Datatypes include *char*, *int*, *money*, and so on. Users can construct their own datatypes based on the SQL Server system datatypes.

datatype conversion function

> A function which is used to convert expressions of one datatype into another datatype, whenever these conversions are not performed automatically by SQL Server.

datatype hierarchy

> The hierarchy that determines the results of computations using values of different datatypes.

dbo

> In a user's own database, SQL Server recognizes the user as "dbo." A database owner logs into SQL Server using his or her assigned login name and password.

deadlock

> A situation which arises when two users, each having a **lock** on one piece of data, attempt to acquire a lock on the other's piece of data. The SQL Server detects deadlocks, and kills one user's process.

default

> The option chosen by the system when no other option is specified.

deferred update

An update operation that takes place in two steps. First, the log records for deleting existing entries and inserting new entries are written to the log, but only the delete changes to the data pages and indexes take place. In the second step, the log pages are rescanned, and the insert operations are performed on the data pages and indexes. Compare to **direct update**.

demand lock

A demand lock prevents any more shared locks from being set on a data resource (table or data page). Any new shared lock request has to wait for the demand lock request to finish.

density

The average fraction of all the rows in an index that have the same key value. Density is 1 if all of the data values are the same and $1/N$ if every data value is unique.

dependent

Data is logically dependent on other data when master data in one table must be kept synchronized with detail data in another table in order to protect the logical consistency of the database.

detail

Data that logically depends on data in another table. For example, in the *pubs2* database, the *salesdetail* table is a detail table. Each order in the *sales* table can have many corresponding entries in salesdetail. Each item in *salesdetail* is meaningless without a corresponding entry in the *sales* table.

device

Any piece of disk (such as a partition) or a file in the file system used to store databases and their objects.

direct update

An update operation that takes place in a single step, that is, the log records are written and the data and index pages are changed. Direct updates can be performed in three ways: **in-place updates**, **on-page updates**, and **delete/insert direct updates**. Compare to **deferred update**.

dirty read

Occurs when one transaction modifies a row, and then a second transaction reads that row before the first transaction commits the change. If the first transaction rolls back the change, the information read by the second transaction becomes invalid.

disk allocation pieces

Disk allocation pieces are the groups of allocation units from which SQL Server constructs a new database file. The minimum size for a disk allocation piece is one **allocation unit**, or 256 2KB pages.

disk initialization

The process of preparing a database device or file for SQL Server use. Once the device is initialized, it can be used for storing databases and database objects. The command used to initialize a database device is **disk init**.

disk mirror

A duplicate of a SQL Server database device. All writes to the device being mirrored are copied to a separate physical device, making the second device an exact copy of the device being mirrored. If one of the devices fails, the other contains an up-to-date copy of all transactions. The command **disk mirror** starts the disk mirroring process.

dump striping

Interleaving of dump data across several dump volumes.

dump volume

A single tape, partition, or file used for a database or transaction dump. A dump can span many volumes, or many dumps can be made to a single tape volume.

dynamic dump

A dump made while the database is active.

dynamic index

A worktable built by SQL Server for the resolution of queries using **or**. As each qualifying row is retrieved, its row ID is stored in the worktable. The worktable is sorted to remove duplicates, and the row IDs are joined back to the table to return the values.

engine

A process running a SQL Server that communicates with other server processes using shared memory. An engine can be thought of as one CPU's worth of processing power. It does not represent a particular CPU on a machine. Also referred to as "server engine." A SQL Server running on a uniprocessor machine will always have one engine, engine 0. A SQL Server running on a multiprocessor machine can have one or more engines. The maximum number of engines running on SQL Server can be reconfigured using the **max online engines** configuration variable.

entity

A database or a database object that can be identified by a unique ID and that is backed by database pages. Examples of entities: the database *pubs2*, the log for database *pubs2*, the clustered index for table *titles* in database *pubs2*, the table *authors* in database *pubs2*.

equijoin

A join based on equality.

error message

A message that SQL Server issues, usually to the user's terminal, when it detects an error condition.

exclusive locks

Locks which prevent any other transaction from acquiring a lock until the original lock is released at the end of a transaction, always applied for update (**insert, update, delete**) operations.

execute cursor

A cursor which is a subset of client cursors whose result set is defined by a stored procedure which has a single **select** statement. The stored procedure can use parameters. The values of the parameters are sent through Open Client calls.

existence join

A type of join performed in place of certain subqueries. Instead of the usual nested iteration through a table that returns all matching values, an existence join returns TRUE when it finds the first value and stops processing. If no matching value is found, it returns FALSE.

expensive direct update

A type of **direct update** operation. The row is deleted from its original location, and inserted at a new location.

expression

A computation, column data, a built-in function, or a subquery that returns values.

extent

Whenever a table or index requires space, SQL Server allocates a block of 8 2K pages, called an extent, to the object.

fetch

A fetch moves the current cursor position down the cursor result set. Also called a cursor fetch.

fetch-and-discard strategy

Reading pages into the data cache at the LRU end of the cache chain, so that the same buffer is available for reuse immediately. This strategy keeps select commands that require large numbers of page reads from flushing other data from the cache.

field

A data value that describes one characteristic of an entity. Also called a **column**.

foreign key

A key column in a table that logically depends on a **primary key** column in another table. Also, a column (or combination of columns) whose values are required to match a primary key in some other table.

fragment

When you allocate only a portion of the space on a device with **create** or **alter database**, that portion is called a fragment.

free-space threshold

A user-specified threshold that specifies the amount of space on a segment, and the action to be taken when the amount of space available on that segment is less than the specified space.

functions

See **built-in functions**.

global variable

System-defined variables that SQL Server updates on an ongoing basis. For example, *@@error* contains the last error number generated by the system.

grouped aggregate

See vector aggregate.

Halloween problem

An anomaly associated with cursor updates, whereby a row seems to appear twice in the result set. This happens when the index key is updated by the client and the updated index row moves farther down in the result set.

heap table

A table where all data is stored in a single page chain. For example, an unpartitioned table that has no clustered index stores all data in a single "heap" of pages.

identifier

A string of characters used to identify a database object, such as a table name or column name.

implicit conversions

Datatype conversions that SQL Server automatically performs to compare datatypes.

in-place update

A type of **direct update** operation. An in-place update does not cause data rows to move on the data page. Compare to **on-page update** and **insert/delete direct update**.

index

A database object that consists of key values from the data tables, and pointers to the pages that contain those values. Indexes speed up access to data rows.

index covering

A data access condition where the leaf-level pages of a nonclustered index contain the data needed to satisfy a query. The index must contain all columns in the select list as well as the columns in the query clauses, if any. The server can satisfy the query using only the **leaf level** of the index. When an index covers a query, the server does not access the data pages.

index selectivity

The ratio of duplicate key values in an index. An index is selective when it lets the optimizer pinpoint a single row, such as a search for a unique key. An index on nonunique entries is less selective. An index on values such as "M" or "F" (for male or female) is extremely nonselective.

initial response time

The time required to return the first result row of a query to a user. For some queries, initial response time can be very brief, even though time to return the full result set can take much longer.

inner query

Another name for a subquery.

int

> A signed 32-bit integer value.

integrity constraints

> Form a model to describe the database integrity in the **create table** statement. Database integrity has two complementary components: **validity**, which guarantees that all false information is excluded from the database, and **completeness**, which guarantees that all true information is included in the database.

intent lock

> Indicates the intention to acquire a share or exclusive lock on a data page.

isolation level

> Specifies the kinds of actions that are not permitted while the current transactions execute; also called "locking level." The ANSI standard defines four levels of isolation for SQL transactions. Level 0 prevents other transactions from changing data already modified by an uncommitted transaction. Level 1 prevents **dirty reads**. Level 2 (not supported by SQL Server) also prevents **non-repeatable reads**. Level 3 prevents both types of reads and **phantoms**; it is equivalent to doing all queries with **holdlock**. The user controls the isolation level with the **set** option **transaction isolation level** or with the **at isolation** clause of **select** or **readtext**. The default is level 1.

join

> A basic operation in a relational system which links the rows in two or more tables by comparing the values in specified columns.

join selectivity

> An estimate of the number of rows from a particular table that will join with a row from another table. If index statistics are available for the join column, SQL Server bases the join selectivity on the **density** of the index (the average number of duplicate rows). If no statistics are available, the selectivity is $1/N$, where N is the number of rows in the smaller table.

kernel

> A module within SQL Server that acts as the interface between SQL Server and the operating system.

key

> A field used to identify a record, often used as the index field for a table.

key value

> Any value that is indexed.

keyword

> A word or phrase that is reserved for exclusive use by Transact-SQL. Also known as a **reserved word**.

keyword phrases

> A set of keywords and parameters that tailor a Transact-SQL command to meet a particular need. Also called a **clause**.

language cursor

> A cursor declared in SQL without using Open Client. As with SQL Server cursors, Open Client is completely unaware of the cursors and the results are sent back to the client in the same format as a normal **select**.

last-chance threshold

> A default threshold in SQL Server that suspends or kills user processes if the transaction log has run out of room. This threshold leaves just enough space for the de-allocation records for the log itself. The last-chance threshold always calls a procedure named **sp_thresholdaction**. This procedure is **not** supplied by Sybase, it must be written by the System Administrator.

leaf level

> The level of an index at which all key values appear in order. For SQL Server clustered indexes, the leaf level and the data level are the same. For nonclustered indexes, the last index level above the data level is the leaf level, since key values for all of the data rows appear there in sorted order.

livelock

> A request for an **exclusive lock** that is repeatedly denied because a series of overlapping **shared locks** keeps interfering. SQL Server detects the situation after four denials, and refuses further shared locks.

local variables

> User-defined variables defined with a **declare** statement.

lock promotion threshold

> The number of page locks allowed in a table before SQL Server attempts to issue a table lock. If the table lock is successful, SQL Server releases the page locks.

locking

The process of restricting access to resources in a multi-user environment to maintain security and prevent concurrent access problems. SQL Server automatically applies locks to tables or pages.

locking level

See **isolation level**.

logical expression

An expression that evaluates to TRUE (1), FALSE (0) or UNKNOWN (NULL). Logical expressions are often used in control of flow statements, such as **if** or **while** conditions.

logical key

The primary, foreign, or common key definitions in a database design that define the relationship between tables in the database. Logical keys are not necessarily the same as the **physical key**s (the keys used to create indexes) on the table.

logical operators

The operators **and, or,** and **not**. All three can be used in **where** clauses. The operator **and** joins two or more conditions and returns results when all of the conditions are true; **or** connects two or more conditions and returns results when any of the conditions is true.

logical read

The process of accessing a data or index page already in memory to satisfy a query. Compare to **physical read**.

login

The name a user uses to log into SQL Server. A login is valid if SQL Server has an entry for that user in the system table *syslogins*.

LRU cache strategy

A caching strategy for replacing the least-recently-used buffers in the data cache. A clean data page is taken from the LRU end of the data cache to store a page read from disk. The new page is placed on the data cache's page chain at the MRU end of the cache, so that it stays in memory.

Master Database

Controls the user databases and the operation of SQL Server as a whole. Known as *master*, it keeps track of such things as user accounts, ongoing processes, and system error messages.

master table

A table that contains data on which data in another table logically depends. For example, in the *pubs2* database, the *sales* table is a master table. The *salesdetail* table holds detail data which depends on the master data in *sales*. The detail table typically has a foreign key that joins to the primary key of the master table.

master-detail relationship

A relationship between sets of data where one set of data logically depends on the other. For example, in the *pubs2* database, the *sales* table and *salesdetail* table have a master-detail relationship. See **detail** and **master table**.

matching index scan

A scan using a nonclustered index when the query has a **where** clause (search argument) on a set of columns, and the columns form a **prefix subset** of keys on the index. The index is used to position the search at the first matching key, and then scanned forward for additional matches on the specified index key columns. The scan stops at the first row that does not match. Matching index scans are quite fast and efficient. Compare to **nonmatching index scan**.

memory pool

An area of memory within a **data cache** that contains a set of buffers linked together on a MRU/LRU (most recently used/least recently used) list.

message number

The number that uniquely identifies an error message.

mirror

See **disk mirror**.

model database

A template for new user databases. The installation process creates *model* when SQL Server is installed. Each time the **create database** command is issued, SQL Server makes a copy of *model* and extends it to the size requested, if necessary.

MRU replacement strategy

A caching strategy for table scans and nonclustered index scans. The optimizer chooses this strategy when it determines that the pages need to be accessed only once for a particular query. Instead of adding all of the pages to the MRU/LRU chain, the pages are immediately flushed as soon as the query finishes examining them, and the next page for the query is read into the buffer.

natural join

A **join** in which the values of the columns being joined are compared on the basis of equality, and all the columns in the tables are included in the results, except that only one of each pair of joined columns is included.

nested queries

select statements that contain one or more subqueries.

nested select statements

See **nested queries**.

nonclustered index

An **index** that stores key values and pointers to data. The **leaf level** points to data pages rather than containing the data itself.

nonmatching index scan

A scan using a nonclustered index when the search arguments do not form a **prefix subset** of the index key columns, although they match some parts of the **composite key**. The scan is performed using the index from the lowest key value to the highest key value, searching for the matches specified in the query. This type of scan is performed on nonclustered indexes when all columns for a table referenced in the query are included in the index. Although cheaper than a table scan, a non-matching index scan is more expensive than a **matching index scan**.

non-repeatable read

Occur when one transaction reads a row and then a second transaction modifies that row. If the second transaction commits its change, subsequent reads by the first transaction yield different results than the original read.

normalization rules

The standard rules of database design in a relational database management system.

not-equal join

A join on the basis of inequality.

null

Having no explicitly assigned value. NULL is not equivalent to zero, or to blank. A value of NULL is not considered to be greater than, less than, or equivalent to any other value, including another value of NULL.

numeric expression

An expression that contains only numeric values and returns a single numeric value. In Transact-SQL, the operands can be of any SQL Server numeric datatype. They can be functions, variables, parameters, or they can be other arithmetic expressions. Synonymous with **arithmetic expression**.

Object Allocation Map (OAM)

Pointers to the allocation pages for each allocation unit.

object permissions

Permissions that regulate the use of certain commands (data modification commands, plus **select, truncate table** and **execute**) to specific tables, views or columns. See also **command permissions**.

objects

See **database objects**.

operating system

A group of programs that translates your commands to the computer, so that you can perform such tasks as creating files, running programs, and printing documents.

operators

Symbols that act on two values to produce a third. See **comparison operators**, **logical operators**, or **arithmetic operators**.

optimizer

SQL Server code that analyzes queries and database objects and selects the appropriate query plan. The SQL Server optimizer is a cost-based optimizer. It estimates the cost of each permutation of table accesses in terms of CPU cost and I/O cost.

OR Strategy

An optimizer strategy for resolving queries using **or** and queries using **in (values list)**. Indexes are used to retrieve and qualify data rows from a table. The row IDs are stored in a worktable. When all rows have been retrieved, the worktable is sorted to remove duplicates, and the row IDs are used to retrieve the data from the table.

outer join

A join in which both matching and nonmatching rows are returned. The operators *= and =* are used to indicate that all the rows in the first or second tables should be returned, regardless of whether or not there is a match on the join column.

outer query

> Another name for the principal query in a statement containing a subquery.

overflow page

> A data page for a table with a nonunique clustered index, which contains only rows that have duplicate keys. The key value is the same as the last key on the previous page in the chain. There is no index page pointing directly to an overflow page.

page chain

> See **partition**.

page split

> Page splits occur when new data or index rows need to be added to a page, and there is not enough room for the new row. Usually, the data on the existing page is split approximately evenly between the newly allocated page and the existing page.

page stealing

> Page stealing occurs when SQL Server allocates a new last page for a partition from a device or extent that was not originally assigned to the partition.

parameter

> An argument to a stored procedure.

partition

> A linked chain of database pages that stores a database object.

performance

> The speed with which SQL Server processes queries and returns results. Performance is affected by several factors, including indexes on tables, use of raw partitions compared to files, and segments.

phantoms

> Occur when one transaction reads a set of rows that satisfy a search condition, and then a second transaction modifies the data (through an **insert, delete, update,** and so on). If the first transaction repeats the read with the same search conditions, it obtains a different set of rows.

physical key

> A column name, or set of column names, used in a **create index** statement to define an index on a table. Physical keys on a table are not necessarily the same as the **logical key**s.

physical read

> A disk I/O to access a data, index, or log page. SQL Server estimates physical reads and logical reads when optimizing queries. See **logical read**.

point query

> A query that restricts results to a single specific value, usually using the form "where *column_value = search_argument*".

precision

> The maximum number of decimal digits that can be stored by *numeric* and *decimal* datatypes. The precision includes **all** digits, both to the right and to the left of the decimal point.

prefetch

> The process of performing multipage I/O's on a table, nonclustered index, or the transaction log. For logs, the server can fetch up to 256 pages, for nonlog tables and indexes, the server can fetch up to 8 pages.

prefix subset

> Used to refer to keys in a composite index. Search values form a prefix subset when leading columns of the index are specified. For an index on columns A, B, and C, these are prefix subsets: A, AB, ABC. These are not: AC, B, BC, C. See **matching index scan** and **non-matching index scan** for more information.

primary key

> The column or columns whose values uniquely identify a row in a table.

primary key constraint

> A primary key constraint is a **unique** constraint which does not permit null values for the component key columns. There can only be one primary key constraint per table. The primary key constraint creates a unique index on the specified columns to enforce this data integrity.

process

> An execution environment scheduled onto physical CPUs by the operating system.

process affinity

Describes a process in which a certain SQL Server task runs only on a certain engine, or that a certain engine runs only on a certain CPU.

projection

One of the basic query operations in a relational system. A projection is a subset of the columns in a table.

qualified

The name of a database object can be qualified, or preceded by, the name of the database and the object owner.

query

1. A request for the retrieval of data with a **select** statement.

2. Any SQL statement that manipulates data.

query plan

The ordered set of steps required to carry out a query, complete with the access methods chosen for each table.

query tree

An internal tree structure to represent the user's query. A large portion of query processing and compilation is built around the shape and structure of this internal data structure. For stored procedures, views, triggers, rules and defaults these tree structures are stored in the *sysprocedures* table on disk, and read back from disk when the procedure or view is executed.

range query

A query that requests data within a specific range of values. These include greater than/less than queries, queries using **between**, and some queries using **like**.

recovery

The process of rebuilding one or more databases from database dumps and log dumps. See also **automatic recovery**.

referential integrity

The rules governing data consistency, specifically the relationships among the primary keys and foreign keys of different tables. SQL Server addresses referential integrity with user-defined triggers.

referential integrity constraint

Referential integrity constraints require that data inserted into a "referencing" table which defines the constraint must have matching values in a "referenced" table. You cannot delete rows or update column values from a referenced table that match values in a referencing table. Also, you cannot drop the referenced table until the referencing table is dropped or the referential integrity constraint is removed.

reformatting strategy

A strategy used by SQL Server to resolve join queries on large tables that have no useful index. SQL Server builds a temporary clustered index on the join columns of the inner table, and uses this index to retrieve the rows. SQL Server estimates the cost of this strategy and the cost of the alternative—a table scan—and chooses the cheapest method.

relational expression

A type of Boolean or logical expression of the form:

```
arith_expression
relational_operator arith_expression
```

In Transact-SQL, a relational expression can return TRUE, FALSE, or UNKNOWN. The results can evaluate to UNKNOWN if one or both of the expressions evaluates to NULL.

relational operator

An operator that compares two operands and yields a truth value, such as "5 <7" (TRUE), "ABC" = "ABCD" (FALSE) or "@value > NULL" (UNKNOWN).

remote procedure calls

A **stored procedure** executed on a different SQL Server from the server the user is logged into.

response time

The time it takes for a single task, such as a Transact-SQL query sent to SQL Server, to complete. Contrast to **initial response time**, the time required to return the first row of a query to a user.

restriction

A subset of the rows in a table. Also called a **selection**, it is one of the basic query operations in a relational system.

return status

> A value that indicates that the procedure completed successfully or indicates the reason for failure.

RID

> See **row ID**.

roles

> Provide individual accountability for users performing system administration and security-related tasks in SQL Server. The System Administrator, System Security Officer, and Operator roles can be granted to individual server login accounts.

rollback transaction

> A Transact-SQL statement used with a user-defined transaction (before a **commit transaction** has been received) that cancels the transaction and undoes any changes that were made to the database.

row

> A set of related **columns** that describes a specific entity. Also called **record**.

row aggregate function

> Functions (**sum**, **avg**, **min**, **max**, and **count**) that generate a new row for summary data when used with **compute** in a **select** statement.

row ID

> A unique, internal identifier for a data row. The row ID, or RID, is a combination of the data page number and the row number on the page.

rule

> A specification that controls what data may be entered in a particular column, or in a column of a particular user-defined datatype.

run values

> Values of the configuration variables currently in use.

sa

> The login name for the Sybase **System Administrator**.

scalar aggregate

An aggregate function that produces a single value from a **select** statement that does not include a **group by** clause. This is true whether the aggregate function is operating on all the rows in a table or on a subset of rows defined by a **where** clause. (See also **vector aggregate**.)

scale

The maximum number of digits that can be stored to the right of the decimal point by a *numeric* or *decimal* datatype. The scale must be less than or equal to the **precision**.

search argument

A predicate in a query's **where** clause that can be used to locate rows via an index.

segment

A named subset of database devices available to a particular database. It is a label that points to one or more database devices. Segments can be used to control the placement of tables and indexes on specific database devices.

select list

The columns specified in the main clause of a **select** statement. In a dependent view, the target list must be maintained in all underlying views if the dependent view is to remain valid.

selection

A subset of the rows in a table. Also called a restriction, it is one of the basic query operations in a relational system.

selectivity

See **index selectivity, join selectivity**.

self-join

A join used for comparing values within a column of a table. Since this operation involves a join of a table with itself, you must give the table two temporary names, or **correlation names**, which are then used to qualify the column names in the rest of the query.

server cursor

A cursor declared inside a stored procedure. The client executing the stored procedure is not aware of the presence of these cursors. Results returned to the client for a **fetch** appear exactly the same as the results from a normal **select**.

server engine

See **engine**.

server user ID

The ID number by which a user is known to SQL Server.

severity level number

The severity of an error condition.

shared lock

A **lock** created by nonupdate ("read") operations. Other users may read the data concurrently, but no transaction can acquire an **exclusive** lock on the data until all the shared locks have been released.

sort order

Used by SQL Server to determine the order in which to sort character data. Also called **collating sequence**.

spinlock

A special type of lock or semaphore that protects critical code fragments that must be executed in a single-threaded fashion. Spinlocks exist for extremely short durations and protect internal server data structures such as a data cache.

SQL Server

The server in Sybase's client-server architecture. SQL Server manages multiple databases and multiple users, keeps track of the actual location of data on disks, maintains mapping of logical data description to physical data storage, and maintains data and procedure caches in memory.

statement

Begins with a **keyword** that names the basic operation or command to be performed.

statement block

A series of Transact-SQL statements enclosed between the keywords **begin** and **end** so that they are treated as a unit.

stored procedure

A collection of SQL statements and optional control-of-flow statements stored under a name. SQL Server-supplied stored procedures are called **system procedures**.

subquery

A **select** statement that is nested inside another **select, insert, update** or **delete** statement, or inside another subquery.

System Administrator

A user authorized to handle SQL Server system administration, including creating user accounts, assigning permissions, and creating new databases.

system databases

The databases on a newly installed SQL Server: *master*, which controls user databases and the operation of the SQL Server; *tempdb*, used for temporary tables; *model*, used as a template to create new user databases; and *sybsystemprocs*, which stores the system procedures.

system function

A function that returns special information from the database, particularly from the system tables.

system procedures

Stored procedures that SQL Server supplies for use in system administration. These procedures are provided as shortcuts for retrieving information from the system tables, or mechanisms for accomplishing database administration and other tasks that involve updating system tables.

system table

One of the data dictionary tables. The system tables keep track of information about the SQL Server as a whole and about each user database. The *master* database contains some system tables that are not in user databases.

table

A collection of rows (records) that have associated columns (fields). The logical equivalent of a database file.

table scan

A method of accessing a table by reading every row in the table. Table scans are used when there are no conditions (**where** clauses) on a query, when no index exists on the clauses named in the query, or when the SQL Server optimizer determines that an index should not be used because it is more expensive than a table scan.

table-level constraint

Limits values on more than one column of a table. Enter table-level constraints as separate comma-delimited clauses in the **create** statement. You must declare constraints that operate on more than one column as table-level constraints.

task

An execution environment within the SQL Server scheduled onto engines by the SQL Server.

temporary database

The temporary database in SQL Server, *tempdb*, that provides a storage area for temporary tables and other temporary working storage needs (for example, intermediate results of **group by** and **order by**).

text chain

A special data structure used to store text and image values for a table. Data rows store pointers to the location of the text or image value in the text chain.

theta join

Joins which use the comparison operators as the join condition. Comparison operators include equal (=), not equal (!=), greater than (>), less than (<), greater than or equal to (>=), and less than or equal to (<=).

threshold

The estimate of the number of log pages required to back up the transaction log, and the action to be taken when the amount of space falls below that value.

throughput

The volume of work completed in a given time period. It is usually measured in transactions per second (TPS).

transaction

A mechanism for ensuring that a set of actions is treated as a single unit of work. See also **user-defined transaction**.

transaction log

A system table (*syslogs*) in which all changes to the database are recorded.

trigger

A special form of **stored procedure** that goes into effect when a user gives a change command such as **insert**, **delete**, or **update** to a specified table or column. Triggers are often used to enforce referential integrity.

trigger test tables

When a data modification affects a key column, triggers compare the new column values to related keys by using temporary work tables called trigger test tables.

ungrouped aggregate

See scalar aggregate.

unique constraint

A constraint requiring that all non-null values in the specified columns must be unique. No two rows in the table are allowed to have the same value in the specified column. The **unique** constraint creates a unique index on the specified columns to enforce this data integrity.

unique indexes

Indexes which do not permit any two rows in the specified columns to have the same value. SQL Server checks for duplicate values when you create the index (if data already exists) and each time data is added.

update

An addition, deletion, or change to data, involving the **insert, delete, truncate table**, or **update** statements.

update in place

See **in-place update**.

update locks

Locks which ensure that only one operation can change data on a page. Other transactions are allowed to read the data through shared locks. SQL Server applies update locks when an **update** or **delete** operation begins.

variable

An entity that is assigned a value. SQL Server has two kinds of variables, called **local variables** and **global variables**.

vector aggregate

A value that results from using an aggregate function with a **group by** clause. See also **scalar aggregate**.

view

An alternative way of looking at the data in one or more tables. Usually created as a subset of columns from one or more tables.

view resolution

In queries that involve a view, the process of verifying the validity of database objects in the query, and combining the query and the stored definition of the view.

wash area

An area of a buffer pool near the LRU end of the MRU/LRU page chain. Once pages enter the wash area, SQL Server initiates an asynchronous write on the pages. The purpose of the wash area is to provide clean buffers at the LRU for any query that needs to perform a disk I/O.

wildcard

Special character used with the Transact-SQL **like** keyword that can stand for one (the underscore, _) or any number of (the percent sign, %) characters in pattern-matching.

write-ahead log

A log, such as the transaction log, that SQL Server automatically writes to when a user issues a statement that would modify the database. After all changes for the statement have been recorded in the log, they are written to an in-cache copy of the data page.

Bibliography

The following books should provide valuable additional information and insights into Sybase SQL Server and performance tuning. These books can be ordered from your local bookstore, or through an Internet bookstore such as Compubooks (www.compubooks.com) or Computer Literacy Bookstore (www.clbooks.com).

Performance Tuning

Gillette, Rob, Dean Muench, and Jean Tabaka. *Physical Database Design for Sybase SQL Server.* Prentice Hall, 1994.

Phillips, Ronald A., Bonnie O'Neil, and Marshall Brain. *Sybase System XI: Performance Tuning Strategies.* Prentice Hall, 1996.

Roy, Shaibal, and Marc Sugiyama. *Sybase Performance Tuning.* Prentice Hall, 1996.

Shasha, Dennis E. *Database Tuning: A Principled Approach.* Prentice Hall, 1992.

Client/Server

Anderson, George. *Client/Server Database Design with Sybase.* McGraw-Hill, 1996.

Berman, Alex and George Anderson. *Sybase and Client/Server Computing.* McGraw-Hill, 1995; 2nd Edition, 1997.

Sybase Transact-SQL

Rozenshtein, David, et al. *Optimizing Transact-SQL: Advanced Progamming Techniques.*SQL Forum Press, 1996.

SQL Server 11.0

Garbus, Jeff et al. *Sybase SQL Server 11 DBA Survival Guide.*, 2nd Edition. SAMS, 1996.

Hogoboom, Karen. *Sybase Systems Management.* Prentice Hall, 1997.

Kirkwood, John. *Sybase SQL Server 11: An Administrator's Guide.* International Thomson Computer Press, 1996.

Kotta, Sri, Gopinath Chandra and Tanya Knoop. *Understanding Sybase SQL Server 11*. International Thomson Computer Press, 1996.

Panttaja, Jim and Mary, and Judy Bowman. *The Sybase SQL Server Survival Guide*. Wiley, 1996.

Rankins, Ray, et al. *Sybase SQL Server 11 Unleashed*. Macmillan, 1996.

Index

The index is divided into three sections:

- Symbols

  Indexes each of the symbols used in Sybase SQL Server documentation.

- Numerics

  Indexes entries that begin numerically.

- Subjects

  Indexes subjects alphabetically.

C

Cache hit ratio
  data cache *400*
  procedure cache *396*
  sp_sysmon report on *517, 521*
Cache, procedure
  cache hit ratio *396*
  errors *397*
  query plans in *393*
  size report *395*
  sizing *396*
  sp_sysmon report on *527*
  task switching and *482*
Cached (LRU) buffers *518, 525*
Caches, data *397*
  aging in *48*
  binding objects to *48*
  cache hit ratio *400*
  data modification and *50, 399*
  deletes on heaps and *51*
  fillfactor and *423*
  guidelines for named *408*
  hits found in wash *521*
  hot spots bound to *402*
  I/O configuration *47, 405* to *406*
  I/O statistics for *125*
  inserts to heaps and *51*
  joins and *49*
  large I/O and *403*
  misses *522*
  MRU replacement strategy *49*
  named *402*
  page aging in *398*
  pools in *47, 405* to *406*
  spinlocks on *402*
  strategies chosen by optimizer *406, 525*
  subquery results *194*
  table scans and *128*
  task switching and *482*
  tempdb bound to own *385, 403*
  total searches *522*
  transaction log bound to own *403*
  updates to heaps and *51*

  utilization *520*
  wash marker *48*
  writes and statistics *127*
Chain of buffers (data cache) *48*
Chains of pages
  calculating size of *text* and *image* 110
  data and index *37*
  index pages *60*
  overflow pages and *66*
  partitions *367*
  unpartitioning *374*
Changing
  configuration parameters *469*
char datatype
  null becomes *varchar* 290
Cheap direct updates *197*
checkalloc option, **dbcc**
  object size report *88*
Checkpoint process *398, 529*
  average time *531*
  housekeeper task and *451*
  I/O statistics and *127*
  sp_sysmon and *529*
  total *531*
Client
  packet size specification *433*
Client/server architecture *429*
close command
  memory and *339*
close on endtran option, **set** 350
Clustered indexes **58**
  computing number of pages *96, 97*
  computing size of rows *96*
  dbcc and size of *89*
  delete operations *66*
  estimating size of *95* to *106*
  fillfactor effect on *107*
  guidelines for choosing *139*
  insert operations and *63*
  not allowed on partitioned tables *370*
  order of key values *60*
  overflow pages and *66*
  overhead *52*
  page reads *62*

SyBooks Installation Guide

At the end of this book, you will find a copy of the SyBooks CD-ROM. This CD contains complete sets of the Sybase documentation for SQL Server 11. These collections are fully text searchable. The CD contains five separate collections:

- Sybase SQL Server manuals

- Replication Server manuals

- SQL Server Monitor and SQL Server Manager manuals

- Open Client/Server manuals

- Open Client/Server supplements

You can find all of the manuals referenced throughout *Upgrading and Migrating to Sybase SQL Server 11* in the first collection of the CD-ROM (Sybase SQL Server manuals).

You can view SyBooks on most Microsoft Windows systems (Windows 3.1, Windows NT, and Windows 95) and most popular UNIX systems.

To install SyBooks on a Microsoft Windows-based system, simply go to the \pc\install directory on the CD, select the setup.exe file, and follow the onscreen instructions. To run SyBooks, click on the SyBooks icon.

To install SyBooks on a UNIX system, go to the unix subdirectory on the CD and execute the install.me program. Before you can run SyBooks, you must create a /sybooks/annot directory in your home directory and set two environmental variables. (Note that all users must complete these steps.) The SYBROOT variable points to the SyBooks installation directory, and the EBTRC variable points to the *.ebtrc* configuration file. The *.ebtrc* file is automatically created when you install SyBooks; you find this file in a subdirectory of the SyBooks installation directory. This subdirectory is named after your UNIX platform. To run SyBooks, simply type *sybooks*.

For more information about SyBooks, visit Sybase's web site:

http://www.sybase.com/Products/Sybooks/

SYBASE, INC. LICENSE AGREEMENT (THIS IS A LICENSE AND NOT A SALE)

SYBASE'S ACCEPTANCE OF YOUR ORDER AND DELIVERY OF THIS SOFTWARE
ARE EXPRESSLY CONDITIONED ON YOUR AGREEING TO THE FOLLOWING LICENSE AGREEMENT.
BY OPENING THIS PACKAGE, YOU INDICATE YOUR AGREEMENT WITH THE FOLLOWING.

1. **LICENSE.** You may use those enclosed software programs (and accompanying documentation) which were ordered by you ("Programs") solely for your internal business purposes. No more than the number of Users for which the license was ordered are authorized to access such Program at any one time. A User is a person (or identifiable unique accessor of information used in place of human interaction) who is authorized by you to access the Program or use a foreground or background process to access a Program.

2. **COPYRIGHT AND OWNERSHIP.** The Programs are owned by Sybase and are protected by United States and Canadian copyright laws and international treaty provisions. You acquire only the right to use the Programs and do not acquire any rights of ownership in the Programs or the media on which they are provided.

3. **COPY RESTRICTIONS AND OTHER RESTRICTIONS.** You may not copy the Programs except to make up to one (1) copy for each User and one (1) copy for backup or archival purposes. You may not copy the written materials and manuals accompanying the Programs assigned, or otherwise conveyed (whether by operation of law or otherwise) to another party without Sybase's prior written consent. You may not use the Programs for timesharing, rental or service bureau purposes. You shall not remove any product identification, copyright notices or other notices or proprietary restrictions from the Programs. Upon reasonable notice to you, Sybase may audit the number of Users using the Programs and the number of copies of the Programs in use by you.

4. **U.S. GOVERNMENT RESTRICTED RIGHTS.** If this license is acquired under a U.S. Government contract, use, duplication or disclosure by the U.S. Government is subject to restrictions as set forth in DFARS 252.227–7013(c)(ii) for Department of Defense contracts and as set forth in FAR 52.227–19(a)–(d) for civilian agency contracts. Sybase reserves all unpublished rights under the United States copyright laws.

5. **TERMINATION.** Either party may terminate this Agreement if the other party breaches any of its obligations hereunder and such breach is not cured within sixty (60) days after written notice. Sybase may terminate this Agreement if you fail to make any payment when due to Sybase and such failure is not cured within fifteen (15) days after written notice. Upon termination, you shall cease using the Programs and shall return to Sybase all copies of the Programs and Documentation in any form.

6. **LIMITED WARRANTY AND LIABILITY.** Sybase warrants that the Programs when properly used, will operate in all material respects in conformity with Sybase published specifications for the applicable version, and the Program media shall be free of defects, for one (1) year from the date of shipment of such version to you. In the event of a failure to meet the foregoing limited warranty, your sole remedy in the event of nonconformity of a Program, at Sybase's option, shall be replacement of the defective materials or a refund of the license fees paid for the affected Program. This limited warranty gives you specific legal rights. **SYBASE DISCLAIMS ALL OTHER WARRANTIES AND CONDITIONS, EXPRESS OR IMPLIED, INCLUDING WITHOUT LIMITATION THE IMPLIED WARRANTIES OR CONDITIONS OF MERCHANTABLE QUALITY AND FITNESS FOR A PARTICULAR PURPOSE, AND WHETHER ARISING BY STATUTE OR IN LAW OR AS A RESULT OF A COURSE OF DEALING OR USAGE OF TRADE, WITH RESPECT TO THE PROGRAMS OR THE DOCUMENTATION. NO WARRANTY IS MADE REGARDING THE RESULTS OF ANY PROGRAM OR INFORMATION CONTAINED THEREIN, THAT ALL ERRORS IN THE PROGRAMS WILL BE CORRECTED, OR THAT THE PROGRAMS' FUNCTIONALITY WILL MEET YOUR REQUIREMENTS. IN NO EVENT WILL SYBASE OR ITS SUPPLIERS BE LIABLE FOR ANY LOSS OR INACCURACY OF DATA, LOSS OF PROFITS OR INDIRECT, SPECIAL, INCIDENTAL OR CONSEQUENTIAL DAMAGES, EVEN IF SYBASE HAS BEEN ADVISED OF THE POSSIBILITY OF SUCH DAMAGES. SYBASE'S TOTAL LIABILITY, IF ANY, ARISING OUT OF OR RELATING TO THIS AGREEMENT SHALL NOT EXCEED THE LICENSE FEES PAID BY YOU FOR THE PROGRAMS. THE FOREGOING RESTRICTIONS, DISCLAIMERS AND LIMITATIONS SHALL APPLY AND REMAIN IN FORCE EVEN IN THE EVENT OF A BREACH BY SYBASE HEREUNDER OF A CONDITION OR FUNDAMENTAL TERM HEREUNDER, OR IN THE EVENT OF A BREACH WHICH CONSTITUTES A FUNDAMENTAL BREACH.**

7. **GOVERNING LAW; COMPLETE AGREEMENT.** THIS AGREEMENT IS GOVERNED BY THE LAWS OF THE STATE OF CALIFORNIA IF THE USER IS LOCATED IN THE UNITED STATES, AND BY THE LAWS OF THE PROVINCE OF ONTARIO IF THE USER IS LOCATED IN CANADA, AND CONSTITUTES THE COMPLETE AGREEMENT BETWEEN THE PARTIES WITH RESPECT TO THE PROGRAMS. The terms of this Agreement supersede the terms of any purchase order, order letter or other document issued or signed by you to authorize its license of the Programs. If any provision of this Agreement is held to be unenforceable, such provision shall be limited, modified or severed as necessary to eliminate its unenforceability, and all other provisions shall remain unaffected.

8. **WAIVERS.** The failure or delay of either party to exercise any of its rights shall not be deemed a waiver thereof and no waiver by either party of any breach of this Agreement shall constitute a waiver of any other subsequent breach.

9. **TRANSLATION.** The parties have requested that this Agreement and all documents contemplated hereby be drawn up in English. Les parties aux presentes ont exigé que cerre entente et tous nutree documents envisagés par les présentes soíent rédigés en anglais.